UNIVERSITY (

I

NORTH CAROLINA STUDIES
IN THE ROMANCE LANGUAGES AND LITERATURES

Founder: URBAN TIGNER HOLMES

Editor: JUAN CARLOS GONZÁLEZ ESPITIA

Distributed by:

UNIVERSITY OF NORTH CAROLINA PRESS

CHAPEL HILL
North Carolina 27515-2288
U.S.A.

NORTH CAROLINA STUDIES IN THE
ROMANCE LANGUAGES AND LITERATURES
Number 320

WORD *MINGAS*

Oralitegraphies and Mirrored Visions on Oralitures and Indigenous Contemporary Literatures

WORD *MINGAS*

ORALITEGRAPHIES AND MIRRORED VISIONS ON ORALITURES AND INDIGENOUS CONTEMPORARY LITERATURES

MIGUEL ROCHA VIVAS
2016 Casa de las Américas de Cuba Prize

TRANSLATED BY
PAUL M. WORLEY AND MELISSA BIRKHOFER

CHAPEL HILL

NORTH CAROLINA STUDIES IN THE ROMANCE
LANGUAGES AND LITERATURES
U.N.C. DEPARTMENT OF ROMANCE STUDIES
2021

Library of Congress Cataloging-in-Publication Data

Names: Rocha Vivas, Miguel, author. | Worley, Paul M., 1976- translator. |
  Birkhofer, Melissa, translator.
Title: Word mingas : oralitegraphies and mirrored visions on oralitures and
  indigenous contemporary literatures / Miguel Rocha Vivas ; translated by
  Paul M. Worley and Melissa Birkhofer.
Other titles: Mingas de la palabra. English | North Carolina Studies in
  the Romance languages and literatures ; no. 320.
Description: Chapel Hill : U.N.C. Department of Romance Studies, 2021. |
  Series: North Carolina Studies in the Romance languages and literatures ;
  number 320 | Translation of: Mingas de la palabra : textualidades
  oralitegráficas y visiones de cabeza en las oralituras y literaturas
  indígenas contemporáneas / Miguel Rocha Vivas. Bogotá, D. C.,
  Colombia : Universidad de los Andes, Ediciones Uniandes : Editorial
  Pontificia Universidad Javeriana, 2018. | Includes bibliographical
  references.
Identifiers: LCCN 2021024158 | ISBN 9781469667348 (paperback)
Subjects: LCSH: Colombian literature--Indian authors--History and
  criticism. | Oral tradition in literature.
Classification: LCC PQ8162 .R6313 2021 | DDC 860.9/89809861--dc23
LC record available at https://lccn.loc.gov/2021024158

Cover design: Ana Cristina Juan Gómez

Cover image: Human hands in black and white by Salah Ait Mokhtar via
  Unsplash. Woven palm by Miguel Rocha Vivas.

ISBN 978-1-4696-6734-8

Layout and copyediting by CJV Publicidad y Edición de Libros
claudialibros3@gmail.com, Cel.: (57) 3045698330 (Colombia)

For Alelí.

In homage to the Hispanic and Indigenous migrants in North Carolina.

In memory of Steven Heller, Architect of friendships between worlds.

CONTENTS

ACKNOWLEDGMENTS

GIVEN THAT this book was originally written as my doctoral dissertation, I would first like to thank the Department of Romance Studies at the University of North Carolina at Chapel Hill for their support. There are, of course, innumerable people whom I should thank for supporting me in the completion of the present work. Above all, I would like to thank the Indigenous writers with whom I have dialogued, walked, and collaborated for over a decade and a half. I appreciate each and every one of the meetings and conversations we have had across different communities, cities, and countries.

I would also like to express my sincere thanks to Emilio del Valle Escalante/Emil' Keme, as well as to the other members of my doctoral committee: Arturo Escobar, Gloria Chacón, Monica Rector, and especially to Juan Carlos González Espitia, my editor. Their close reading and stimulating advice have guided me throughout this project. Special thanks to my friends and colleagues Paul Worley and Melissa Birkhofer for this wonderful translation.

Special thanks are also due to the Casa de las Américas in Cuba for awarding my work the Casa de las Américas Prize, as well as to Caridad Tamayo and Jaime Triana for their support in publishing the book's first edition. Thanks to the Universidad Javeriana and the Universidad de los Andes in Colombia for the book's second edition in Spanish.

Additional thanks go out to Miguel Rojas, Beatriz Riefkohl, Teresa Chapa, Juan Duchesne, Fernando Urbina, Jorge Tapia, Carlos Abreu, Anka Koczkas, Noah Myers, Hosun Kim, Dayuma Albán,

Zully Amaya, Andrew Stewart, Christopher Teuton, Glynis Cowell, Oswaldo Estrada, Carlos Miguel Gómez, Juan Carlos Caicedo, the Kryder family, students from the Programa de Interacciones Inter-culturales in Bogotá, the Institute for the Study of the Americas, and to my friends from Cineminga and the Abya Yala Working Group at UNC-Duke. Finally, I would like to thank my wife, Alejandra, whose readings of the manuscript and tremendous affection have been cru-cial for me, as well as my parents, Carmenza and Álvaro, for their ongoing, unconditional support.

The North Carolina Studies in the Romance Languages and Lit-eratures gives special thanks to the College of Arts and Sciences and the Institute for the Study of the Americas at the University of North Carolina at Chapel Hill for their generous support of this project.

INTRODUCTION

THE *MINGAS* are traditional Indigenous meetings in which community members can come together to support each other in any kind of labor. In Colombia's Andean Southeast the mingas or *minkas*, a word that comes from quechua-aymara languages, are a prominent activity in projects that imply exchange, discussion of ideas, solidarity, and alliances. Mingas stand for processes of inter- and intra-cultural communication and cooperation. For the Pastos, a binational native community along the border of Colombia and Ecuador, what we commonly refer to as literature forms part of the collectively named and celebrated *word mingas* and *thought mingas*. This book partakes in this tradition of conversational exchanges and intercultural creative proposals.[1]

Word Mingas [Mingas de la palabra] focuses on oralitures and written literatures by self-identified Indigenous Colombian authors from the early nineties to the present, interweaving and comparing two threads of literary critique which I refer to as "oralitegraphies" and "mirrored visions," respectively. As a point of departure, the earliest publications dealt with herein intersect with two of the most important events in Colombia's history: the 1991 Constitution in which Colombia declares itself a multiethnic and pluricultural country; and the protests surrounding the five-hundreth anniversary (1492–1992) of Europeans' colonization of the so-called Americas. Indeed, 1992 marks the

---

[1] This introduction contextualizes and lays down the theoretical foundation of the book. Nevertheless, the reader can go directy to "Part I. Reading Oralitegraphies", where the ideas discussed here are first applied.

precise moment when Colombia's first generation of Indigenous writers, specifically Berichá (U'wa), Abadio Green (Gunadule), Vito Apüshana (Wayuu), and Fredy Chikangana (Yanakuna), rose to prominence in the country's literary scene. Nonetheless, this wave of writers and their works is only circumstantially related to the new Constitution and the Quincentennial. In fact, the emergence of these writers and their works is also the product of longstanding personal and communal processes of self-inquiry and self-representation, and the surge in the formation of Indigenous organizations in the seventies and eighties.[2]

Within this context, the book focuses on the following works: *Tengo los pies en la cabeza* [I Have the Feet on My Head] (1992) by Berichá, an U'wa writer from the Sierra Nevada of Cocuy in the eastern Andes, *Contrabandeo sueños con aríjunas cercanos* [Smuggling Dreams with *Arijunas* Nearby] (1992) and *Shiinalu'uirua shiirua ataal/En las hondonadas maternas de la piel* [In the Skin's Maternal Folds] (2010),[3] two poetry collections by the Wayuu writer Miguelángel López, who publishes under the pseudonym Vito Apüshana; the story "Esa horrible costumbre de alejarme de ti" [This awful habit of leaving you] (1995) and the open letter to the President of Colombia by another Wayuu writer from the Guajira Peninsula, Vicenta Siosi Pino (2012); the poetry collection *Samay pisccok pponccopi mushcoypa/Espíritu de pájaro en pozos del ensueño* [A Bird's Spirit within the Depths of a Daydream] (2010) by Fredy Chikangana/Wiñay Mallki, a Yanakuna oralitor from Huila and Cauca in the central Andes; ten poems from the partially unedited *Versos de sal* [Verses of Salt,] one of whose authors is the Andoke-Uitoto writer from the Amazon Basin Yenny Muruy Andoque (Yiche); *Bínÿbe oboyejuayëng/Danzantes del viento* [Wind Dancers] (2005 and 2010) a work of oraliture by the Camëntsá writer from the Amazonian-Andean piedmont, Hugo Jamioy Juajibioy; the stories "Manifiesta no saber firmar. Nacido: 31 de diciembre" [Declares Not to Know How To Sign. Born on December 31] (2006) and "Daño emergente, lucro cesante" [Consequential Damage, Profit Loss] by the Afro-Wayuu writer Estercilia Simanca Pushaina; and *Anmal gaya burba: isbeyobi daglege nana nabgwana bendaggegala/Significados de vida: espejo*

---

[2] Take, for example, the formation of the *Consejo Regional de la Cauca* [Regional Council of the Cauca] (CRIC) in 1971, and the *Organización Nacional Indígena de Colombia* [Colombian National Indigenous Organization] (ONIC) in 1982.

[3] Many of the works examined here have a bilingual titles in the Spanish and the author's maternal language. As such, the slash punctuation mark "/" indicates that the two titles are the same work.

de nuestra memoria en defense de la madre tierra [Meanings of Life: A Reflection of our Collective Memory in the Defense of Mother Earth] (2011), a compilation of narratives and the doctoral work of Abadio Green/Manibinigdiginya, a Gunadule writer and researcher born in Panamá now residing in Colombia.[4]

In addition, I analyze a map designed by the Camëntsá artist Juan Carlos Jamioy that was the central image on the poster for the 2010 Minga Nacional de Educación Superior de Pueblos Indígenas [National Minga of Indigenous Peoples' Higher Education], and that represents a cartographic reimagining of the Colombian nation.

As I explain in detail later on, each of the aforementioned works is a milestone in the emergence of Indigenous literatures and oralitures, in terms of their national and international recognition, support for community projects, and the creation of new educational projects.[5] Throughout this book, I refer to works by the Wayuu writers Antonio Joaquín López Epieyú, Miguel Ángel Jusayú, Juan Pushaina, and Nemesio Montiel, as well as allude to works of Indigenous revindication that were written by earlier authors, such Manuel Quintín Lame Chantre, a Nasa leader from Cauca, Alberto Juajibioy Chindoy, a Camëntsa writer from the Putumayo, and Don Diego de Torres y Moyachoque, a colonial-era Muisca cacique from Turmequé who wrote a number of letters and to whom many attribute the authorship of two sixteenth-century maps of the provinces of Tunja and Santa Fe. Of particular note is the case of the Okaina-Uitoto writer and singer, Anastasia Candre Yamakuri whose unexpected passing in 2014 meant canceling a trip that we had planned to take together and made it impossible for me to learn more about her work. Because of this, I've left the work of constructing an in-depth critique of her fascinating oralitegraphic work for another time.

Given that these authors explore multiple genres, a comparative study like this one cannot be limited to the analysis of a single con-

---

4   Depending on the stage of their career or the genre in which they are publishing, some authors use two different names while others only use one. Throughout this book, I will cite both names when speaking of an author in general—Fredy Chikangana/Wiñay Mallki and Abadio Green/Manibinigdiginya, for example—and only one when emphasizing the particular name under which a text was published: as in Yiche, Vito Apüshana or Miguel Ángel López.

5   This particular focus does not imply that these authors' other works, or the works of other authors are any less important. Rather, given my limited space and the vast number of texts that one could draw upon, I hope the present work will promote critical interest in these works, and stimulate additional proposals for the construction of respectful, dialogic, and collaborative relationships between Indigenous and non-Indigenous peoples.

ventional literary genre (poetry, short story, essay, novel). Moreover, many of these authors write in genres that originate from within their own cultures' verbal arts, drawing on genres such as the *botamán biyá* (the beautiful word of the Camëntsa), the *rafue* (the strong word of the Murui/Uitoto), and the *haylli* (a collective, elegiac composition among the Quechua). Although this book focuses on Colombia, its analyses can be applied to other regions, nations, and projects given that the literary works it examines are not "national literatures" insofar as they do not articulate a national (Colombian) or regional (Latin American) identity. On the contrary, they are written and articulated within complex relationships that transcend national borders, as seen in the case of the binational literatures of the Wayuu (Colombia-Venezuela), the Gunadule (Panamá-Colombia), the plurinational literatures of the Quechua (Colombia-Ecuador-Perú-Bolivia-Argentina), and continental aesthetic projects like oraliture. Take, for example, Manibinigdiginya/Abadio Green, who was born in the Guna Yala region of the Panamá's San Blas archipelago, but whose academic and literary work has been essential for the Gunadule (Tule) on the Colombian side of the border, as well as for the organizations he has directed, the *Organización Nacional Indígena de Colombia* [National Indigenous Organization of Colombia] (ONIC) and the *Organización Indígena de Antioquia* [Indigenous Organization of Antioquia] (OIA). In much the same way, Simanca, Apüshana, Siosi, and many other Wayuu writers describe how the national border between Colombia and Venezuela divides their community and its territory, as well as the fact that community members can obtain dual Colombian-Venezuelan citizenship. A precursor to contemporary literary movements, the Wayuu writer Miguel Ángel Jusayú, is an example of this binationalism insofar as he lived and wrote from the Venezuelan side of the border despite having been born on the Colombian side. Similarly, I should mention the oralitor Fredy Chikangana, who learned Quechua as a literary language while in the Central Andes. His work thus revindicates both a Yanakuna Mitmak and a Pan-Andean identity, a literary project which in turn aligns him with other poets who wrote and sang in Quechua, such as the Peruvian José María Arguedas (1911–1969).

Brief Historical Context

Colonization marks Colombia down to its very name. In a country that once believed itself to be monolingual and Hispanic, the constitutional recognition of the nation's multiethnic and pluricultural reality are necessary steps in the visibilization of Indigenous oralitures and Indigenous literatures. Although many Indigenous Colombian artists such as Rómulo Rozo and Luis Alberto Acuña helped initiate discussions about Indigenous representations and Indigenous issues, Indigenous artists as a group were not visible in such discussions until the last decade of twentieth century, when representatives from several Indigenous nations, such as Lorenzo Muelas (Misak-Guambiano), Francisco Rojas Birry (Embera), and other political and student leaders, were active participants in debates surrounding the 1991 Constitution. For the first time in Colombian history, the Constitution was translated into seven different native languages: Wayuunaiki, Nasa Yuwe, Namuy Wam, Arhuaco- Iku, Inga, Camëntsá, and Cubeo. To a certain extent, this act of plurilingual translation did indeed generate a good deal of public recognition for speakers of the country's sixty-five Indigenous languages (Landaburu). This said, Spanish remained the language of production and publication for Indigenous writers throughout the nineties, with notable exceptions being pedagogical materials aimed at Indigenous communities and the literary-linguistic work of this movement's precursors, among them the works by Alberto Juajibioy in the Putumayo, and by Miguel Ángel Jusayú in Venezuela.[6] Writers' preference for monolingual publication in Spanish at this point in time is due in part to the impact of centuries of colonization and evangelization in Castilian or Spanish, the dominant language spoken by the country's majority population. Nonetheless, in the first decade of the twentyfirst century, authors such as Hugo Jamioy and Fredy Chikangana self-consciously began upending this situation by translating and/or writing directly in their respective languages, Camëntsá and Quechua.

During the late eighties and early nineties in Colombia, there were ongoing debates about how to best reimagine the country and move beyond its tremendous social inequalities, racial prejudices inherited from centuries of colonialism, and wounds inflicted by an internal war against narcos, M-19, and many other armed groups,

---

[6] Among these authors' key works are *Relatos ancestrales del folclor camëntsá* [Ancestral Tales from Camëntsá Folklore], published in 1989 by Juajibioy, and the story *Ni era vaca ni era caballo* [Neither Cow nor Horse], published by Jusayú for the first time in 1975, and later on in 1984 and in 2004 in an illustrated edition by Ekaré in Caracas, Venezuela.

with the 1991 Constitution representing these hopes for a new social contract. At the same time, continental commemorations of the
Quincentenary of the so-called "discovery" of the Americas simultaneously generated new questions about identity, diversity, and the
presence of the country's Indigenous populations.[7]

1992, in particular, saw the publication of numerous Indige-
nous-language texts.[8] From Colombia's Andean Northeast, Berichá, a
young U'wa who was educated by Catholic missionaries and worked
as an informant for several anthropologists, decided to act upon the
advice of her uncle, a *uejea* (*uerjayá* or traditional religious guide)
living in the region of Aguablanca, who "wanted the people from the
government and the priests to know how the U'wa had come to be
and why we are different from white people" [quería que la gente del
gobierno y los curas conocieran cómo había aparecido U'wa y por
qué somos distintos a los blancos] (Berichá en Rocha Vivas, *Pütchi*
1: 86). With her uncle's encouragemet and drawing upon the stories
of her mother, a traditional wise woman, Berichá wrote the almost
unclassifiable autoethnographic, autobiographic work *Tengo los pies
en la cabeza* from 1988 to 1992.

In Colombia's warm, arid northeast, the University of La Guajira
began publishing a basic Wayuu newsletter in conjunction with the
state government and the Secretary of Indigenous Affairs in 1992.

---

[7] It should also be mentioned that the winds of change were circulating on a
global scale after the fall of the Berlin Wall in 1989, the beginning of the end of
Chile's dictatorship in 1990, and the dissolution of the Soviet Union in 1991. The
short and bloody twentieth century, which began in 1914 with the First World
War, even seemed to end prematurely with the social transformations of the early
nineties and the symbolic coincidence of the year 1992, which many Indigenous nations hoped would herald a new beginning, a spatio-temporal reversal (*pachakuti* in
Quechua-Aymara), that could be understood as the moment when things that had
been oppressed during "the long, 500-year night" would be restored to their rightful
place. Along these lines, the demands of the Mexican Revolution were reborn with
1994's Zapatista uprising in Chiapas, a year after the United Nations ratified the first
International Decade of the World's Indigenous People.

[8] As anticipated by the International Labor Organization's 1989 Convention
Concerning Tribal and Indigenous Peoples in Independent Countries, the 1990s
were an important decade for Indigenous peoples the world over. In 1992 Pope
John Paul II asked Indigenous peoples forgiveness for the Church's abuses, and
Rigoberta Menchú, the K'iche' writer and activist from Guatemala, won the Nobel
Prize. Moreover, discussions that would eventually result in the 2007 United Nations
Declaration on the Rights of Indigenous Peoples were well underway. As such, the
nineties ended up being a decade of transition between both centuries and millennia,
with the hopes and expectations that these activities represent generating one of the
best possible scenarios for reopening and reconsidering artistic and literary canons
at a continental level.

Vito Apüshana—pen name of Miguelángel López—appears among its pages, contributing poems that would later be published in *Contrabandeo sueños con aríjunas cercanos*.[9] The Gunadule leader Abadio Green became the first Indigenous Poet invited to Medellín's International Poetry Festival, where he read from his pedagogical texts.[10]

Meanwhile, Fredy Romeiro Campo Chikangana,[11] who was born in the Andes Mountains in Colombia's Southeast, was writing and reflecting on his experience as an urban immigrant. Writing in monolingual Spanish in the 1992 poem "En verbo ajeno" [In Another's Words], the Yanakuna writer declares, "I'm speaking about what is mine with words that aren't mine; I'm speaking with another's words" [Hablo de lo propio con lo que no es mío; hablo con verbo ajeno] (Rocha Vivas, *Pütchi* 1: 59) Five years later Chikangana published his article "La oralitura" [On Oraliture] in Bogotá's *El Espectador* newspaper, the same year he had attended the South America Workshop for Writers in Indigenous Languages in Temuco and Purén, in the Mapuche territory of Wallmapu in Chile, where he met the writer Elicura Chihuailaf, the Mapuche promoter of the oraliture project. Chikangana's article gave notice to readers in the capital and in the rest of Colombia that a continental movement of writers in Indigenous languages, a movement of which he was part, was imminent.[12]

Other Indigenous Colombian writers rose to national and regional prominence as the decade wore on. Wayuu author Vicenta Siosi,

---

[9] In Wayuunaiki "l" is pronounced like the letter "r." Alijuna is thus read "aríjuna," as Vito Apüshana himself pronounces it. For consistency, in this book I will use the written form "arijuna."

[10] He would also become known as Manibinigdiginya. Living in Medellín, he would lead the University of Antioquia's Pedagogical Program in La Madre Tierra, as well as several other community-based academic projects. Two decades on, *Anmal gaya burba/Significados de vida* [The Meanings of Life] (2011), the culmination of his doctoral work, would deal with traditional Gunadule narratives, education, and land, among others. In sum, Green was a pedagogue and an intellectual coming out of the Gunadule tradition long before he became the author of poetic texts.

[11] To avoid the use of his Castilian last names, he would become known as simply Fredy Chikangana, and later on as Wiñay Mallki in order to reinforce his Quechua identity.

[12] The epicenters of these simultaneously emerging literatures in the 1990s were Riohacha in La Guajira department, Leticia in the Amazonas department, Medellín in Antioquia department, and Bogotá, the nation's capital situated in the eastern Andean plateau. People in these cities organized calls for participation, offered economic incentives, and published through university and local presses. The University of La Guajira and several campuses of the Universidad Nacional played important regional roles in supporting and/or visibilizing authors such as Vicenta Siosi and Vito Apüshana in Riohacha, Fredy Chikangana in Bogotá, and later on, Anastasia Candre in Leticia.

published one of the most important stories for young readers from La Guajira, "Esa horrible costumbre de alejarme de ti" [This awful habit of leaving you], in 1995. Here Siosi tells the story of a young Wayuu girl whose mother gives her to an arijuna, or non-Wayuu family in the city, so that she can grow up in supposedly "better" conditions. In 1998 Siosi's story "El dulce corazón de los piel cobriza" [The Sweet Heart of the Copper Skin People] won an honorable mention from the Enka-Premio Andino y Panamá de Literatura Infantil (Enka-Andean and Panamanian Prize in Juvenile Literature). That same year, Yenny Muruy Andoque's collection *Versos de sal* won the Amazonia Department Poetry Prize from that state's Ministry of Culture. In addition, Benjamín Jacanamioy Tisoy, an Inga researcher from Putumayo who had been awarded a grant from the Ministry of Culture, presented the results of his grant entitled, *El chumbe Inga, una forma artística de percepción del mundo* [The Inga Chumbe: An Artistic Way of Understanding the World]. Importantly, in his report, Jacanamijoy refers to the chumbe, a woven belt with picto-ideographic designs, as a form of artisanal writing. Similarly, Hugo Jamioy treats the chumbe as a graphic complement to the poetic text in his first book, *Mi fuego y mi humo, mi tierra y mi sol* [My Fire and My Smoke, My Land and My Sun], published in 1999.

Towards the end of the decade, the armed conflict between guerrilla groups and the Colombia state—which would become even worse with US economic support when Plan Colombia took effect in the year 2000—, and the economic-military empowerment of paramilitary groups darkened the hopes and possibilities for social change. Further, the war exacerbated the problems of Colombia's Indigenous nations, who at the time were simply recognized as "groups" or ethnic "minorities," despite the fact that they were not themselves participants in the conflict.[13] As will be seen in the following chapters, video has been the most prominent platform for Indigenous denouncements of and reflections upon the war. Video's prominence is due in part to the efforts of groups such as the Asociación de Cabildos Indígenas del Norte del Cauca [Association of Indigenous Organizations from the North Cauca] (ACN) and the Gonawindua Tayrona Organization's Colectivo Zhigoneshi. While

---

[13] Indigenous displacement from Colombia's countryside to its cities reached a critical level at the outset of the twenty-first century's second decade, with official statistics stating that Colombia had the second-largest internally displaced population in the world, after Sudan.

Indigenous writers seldom comment upon the armed conflict in their work, these same authors frequently comment upon it in interviews, video-documentaries, and public readings.

The first decade of the twenty-first century opened with Malohe (the abbreviated name of Miguelángel López Hernández) winning Cuba's Casa de las Américas Prize for his book *Encuentros en los senderos de Abya Yala* [Meeting along the Roads of Abya Yala] on January 15, 2000. The award was the highest literary honor bestowed upon a Colombian Indigenous writer at that time, and it generated renewed interest in the country's Indigenous literatures. Compared to collections published under his pen name Vito Apüshana, López's *Encuentros* only partially focuses on Wayuu culture. Instead, the book articulates poetic encounters between "the universes of Indigenous Latin America," with each of these being one of Abya Yala' unique continental paths. The Wayuu, the Kogui, the pre-Hispanic poet Acomiztli Nezahualcóytl, and contemporary Indigenous writers such as Mapuche Lionel Lienlaf and Kichwa Ariruma Kowii, all play major roles in the volume's verses.

By the year 2000 Colombia found itself in a state of rapid transformation. Of primary concern to this book are the significant changes that were taking place in government-sponsored education programs for Indigenous peoples, programs that had previously been turned over to US-based protestant missionaries associated with the Summer Institute of Linguistics (SIL) in 1962. While work related to these projects continued until 2002, the agreement between the government and these missionary groups officially ended on May 31, 2000. The agreement's ending thus marked a break with the missionaries' linguistic vision, a vision in which Indigenous verbal art was baptized as "folklore" beginning in the 1970s.

The new millennium witnessed the emergence of Estercilia Simanca Pushaina, a writer whose hometown on the Caribbean coast, Barranquilla, has been an epicenter of the Wayuu literary movement since the nineties. She first rose to prominence when her book *Caminemos juntos por las sombras de la sabana* [Let's Walk Together through the Shadows of the Savannah] took second place in 2002's Third National Poetry Competition. In 2003 Simanca's story "El encierro de una pequeña doncella" [The Confinement of a Young Virgin], was a finalist for the National Children's Literature Competition. In April of the following year, she published the story for which she is best known, "Manifiesta no saber firmar. Nacido: 31 de diciembre" [Declares Not to Know How To Sign. Born on December

31], and garnered the only honorable mention awarded in the National Metropolitan Story Competition organized by the Metropolitan University of Barranquilla. Simanca later reissued "Manifiesta no saber firmar" as an illustrated limited edition complete with ID cards that showed the disrespectful treatment granted to the communities by civil servants, unveiling it at Bogotá's 2005 International Book Fair. While uncovering the activities of the politicians and functionaries who gave the Wayuu citizens IDs with ridiculous names in order to win elections in La Guajira, in this story Simanca uses irony and wit to gain the reader's sympathies for a female protagonist who finds herself caught between wanting to reject and being attracted to the arijuna, the narrative's "civilized people." Consciously or not, through these characters Simanca explores one of the "originary sins" in the Americas, the colonization of names, which began in the Caribbean in 1492 with the figure of Columbus himself.

In 2005 Hugo Jamioy published *Bínÿbe oboyejuayëng/Danzantes del viento*, the first book by a Colombian Indigenous author that was written as a work of oraliture. The Camëntsá oralitor won a national research grant from the Ministry of Culture for his project *Oralitura Indígena de Colombia* [Indigenous Oraliture from Colombia] the following year, and in 2007 worked to promote the Ministry's first national oraliture grant competition.[14]

In 2009, a multicultural team of Afro-descended and Indigenous researchers from the Ministry of Culture under the leadership of the Basque-French linguist Jon Landaburu drafted the Ley de Lenguas Nativas [Law on Indigenous Languages]. Colombia's Congress then ratified Law 1381 on Indigenous Languages (Romani, Afro, and Indigenous) in January 2010 ("Ley 1381"). The promulgation of these laws coincided with state-sponsored projects to publish the works of Indigenous authors, projects which culminated in the August

---

[14] Despite the fact that the competition's call does not explicitly define oraliture, it nonetheless had a broad impact on how Colombia's Afro and Indigenous communities see their processes of writing, given that they frequently understand these processes as tied to oral tradition. At this point, Jamioy had gone further than either Chihuailaf or Chikangana in articulating himself as an oralitor. By gaining national funding to carry out his project, Jamioy generated a new stimulus for Afro-Indigenous literatures in Colombia. Public acknowledgment of oraliture as a collaborative project shared between Jamioy, Chikangana, and Chihuailaf, was made in the year 2007, when Chihuailaf was invited to read at Bogotá's International Book Fair. While there, the author of *Sueños azules y contrasueños* said that he was in the company of his "brothers, the oralitors of Colombia," these being Fredy Chikangana and Hugo Jamioy.

2010 publication of the Biblioteca Básica de los Pueblos Indígenas [Indigenous Peoples' Basic Library]. The Biblioteca de Literatura Afrocolombiana del Ministerio de Cultura de Colombia [Colombia's Ministry of Culture Library of Afrocolombian Literature] was released at the same time. Focused primarily on Indigenous oraliture and literature from Colombia, the Biblioteca Indígena contained three new volumes of poetry by Chikangana, Apüshana, and Jamioy, respectively, and was distributed free of charge in both digital and print editions. Additionally, part of the print run was distributed in Indigenous Communities, and the ONIC received a significant number of complete collections for further dissemination. As a project, the Library constituted not only an exercise of Indigenous peoples' constitutional rights but also of their historic rights insofar as texts that had been collected by many researchers throughout the twentieth century were made available to both Indigenous and non-Indigenous publics.[15]

THEORETICAL FRAMEWORK: NOTIONS

I develop two theoretical notions for the interpretation of contemporary Indigenous writing, notions that I refer to as oraliteographies and mirrored visions. Given ongoing cultural debates and sociopolitical tensions that surround topics such as (self)representation, "authenticity," and various definitions of identity, I seek to articulate these notions in both theory and practice. In turn, I hope that other authors and, above all, collectivities, will create from and build upon them. In doing so, I do not intend to arrive at any definitive conclusions or craft a terminology that, as the word terminology itself suggests, would indicate that I have the final word in an argument or discussion.

For me, a notion designates something that exists but remains unclear and loosely defined. As such, the concept of a "notion" is a useful way to signal, suggest, or mention. By contrast, a "term" goes beyond these connotations in that, beyond naming or suggesting, a

---

[15] A broader perspective on the historical context in which this project took shape can be found in my article: "Oralituras y literaturas indígenas en Colombia: de la Constitución del 1991 a la Ley de Lenguas del 2010" [Oralitures and Indigenous Literatures in Colombia: From the 1991 Constitution to the Language Law of 2010], which can be found in the journal *A Contracorriente.*

"term" can be used to determine and/or classify a particular kind of knowledge. Likewise, and as a concept, a "term" is generally a definition that functions within the logic of a theoretical argument. Within the context of the present work, I use "notion" to identify before categorizing, to discuss before classifying, and to propose before ordering. I feel that even within the frame of a theoretical argument the suggestive nature of the notion can be a useful way to outline perspectives, stimulate connections, and signal the presence of certain possibilities and processes without being categorical or overly determined, particularly within the current intercultural dynamics of dialogue and interpellation that implicate the authors of these works, their readers, and the public at large. In this context, the notions I elaborate here, oralitegraphies and mirrored visions, become critical reflections that broaden our possibilities for reception and reading. They forward larger collective and interpersonal processes that are constantly being sharpened and reconsidered.

Oralitegraphies and Oralitegraphic Textualities

Throughout this book, I understand a text to be the concrete manifestation of a particular interweaving and interaction among specific textualities. That is, I see a text as a doing, a joining, and a weaving of something within a larger network (Arnold and Yapita 14). In turn, I argue that textualities are networks formed across fields of symbolic interaction that are themselves pluricommunicative. At the same time, these fields can be expressed within physical spaces or through formats where they manifest any one of their multiple textualities. For example, we can think of the book as a field in which phonetic codes are predominant. By comparison, the *chumbe* (a woven belt) would be a field in which ideographic codes predominate, and the mola (a blouse embroidered with layered textiles), a field in which Gunadule weavers employ primarily pictographic signs. In fact, books written in phonetic script are not the exclusive domain of the fields and media through which semasiographs are transmitted, textualities are combined, and texts expressed. Further, and as will be demonstrated in the following chapters, "books" and other forms of communication are not even necessarily mutually exclusive, but rather interrelated.

When I refer to oralitegraphies and oralitegraphic textualities, then, I am describing a polysynthetic notion that expresses relations

of meaning and textual linkages among oral genres, phonetic literatures, and ideographic symbols. In short, oralitegraphies are textual
intersections among diverse systems of oral, literary, and graphic-visual communication. In some works these intersections happen between visual languages—such as those in the graphic systems found
in textiles, pottery, and even audio-visual communication—, bilingual works that use the alphabet—as in versions of Spanish and English that incorporate a number of loan words from different Indigenous Languages—, and in experiments, continuities with, and/or the
recuperation of oral verbal arts, such as the *haylli* (Quechua elegaic
hymn) or the *botamán biyá* (the "beautiful word" of the Camëntsá).

The notion of oralitegraphies can also be understood as under-
scoring how these different communicative systems exist in a state
of exchange and conflict. Within this context, alphabetic writing is
a medium that can be adapted for Indigenous literary production
to the extent that it meets Indigenous creators' diverse linguistic,
ideological, and visual needs and intentions. Through their creative
synthesis of multiple forms of expression, the producers and authors
of these communicative modalities propose new intersectional fields
or textualities.

While these textualities can certainly be found in non-Indigenous contexts, as in the multimedia work of the Chilean artist Vio-
leta Parra, the textualities dealt with here are analyzed within the
context of their relationship to specific Indigenous cultures' codes
and traditional ways of writing. Authors' own recognition of what we
could refer to as "autochthonous forms" of non-alphabetic writing,
visual languages, or semasiographic systems of communication, give
these works a more intimate inflection. For example, one thinks of
how Anastasia Candre (Murui/Okaina) connects painting on cloth
(*yanchama*), oral songs, and poetic writing in her work, or the case of
Hugo Jamioy, in which the author signals a plurality of graphic modalities through his self-identification with multiple forms of visual
communication, such as the Camëntsá *chumbe* and the Ikʉ/Arhuaca
tutu (woven bag).

In order to simplify the notion of oralitegraphic textualities,
throughout the rest of the work I will use the term oralitegraphic to
refer to a specific kind of text where diverse oral, literary, and graphic
systems of communication intersect. In this sense, oralitegraphies are
the material expression of these textualities or intersectional fields.
Whether we are discussing a book, a weaving, or a stone, oralitegraphies are neither isolated from nor reduced to being an adjunct to

any one of these. As such, the ideograms on a vase (as on a painted Wayuu ceramic), or picto-ideograms painted on a body (as in the body painting practiced by the Embera of the Pacific region, which is known as *kipará*), are not in-and-of-themselves oralitegraphies. In the first place, oralitegraphies—as opposed to a traditional ideogram or pictogram—do not exclusively depend on a single system of communication. Moreover, neither oralitegraphic textualities nor their manifestation as oralitegraphies are completely independent of phonetic language, as on being expressed they are interwoven and resound with texts that authors have written in Latin script. As I will discuss in Chapter 2, through the notion of oralitegraphies we can develop any number of other ideas, such as the *poegraph*, the easiest way of talking about a poem that has been in graphic form, or a textilegraph, a specific way of referring to a poegraph based upon a textile design.

In short, in this book I argue that contemporary Indigenous authors do not simply write "literature," but instead create across multiple and complex textualities.[16] This position implies that these authors create bridges of communication, images for self-reflection and interpellation between cultures, and—as in Indigenous movements themselves—even new ways of transmitting knowledge within their respective communities. Given this orientation one better understands the roles that these writers frequently play in educational processes within their communities, as well as my decision to begin the following chapter with oralitegraphic readings of the map from the Intercultural Minga of Indigenous Peoples.

MIRRORED VISIONS

Similarly, here I use the notion of mirrored visions to describe a polivalent notion of reading that enables us to gain a deeper understanding of how many works of contemporary Indigenous literature articulate projects of (self) representation. Mirrored visions represent a particular kind of ideosymbolic production that tends to or as-

---

[16] This observation does not contradict the fact that many of these authors' works are aimed at a "non-Indigenous" public. That said, the complexity involved in the elaboration of oralitegraphies buttresses the argument that these works cannot be read as though their authors had simply appropriated and begun writing "literature" in the Western sense of the word.

pires to subvert and expose conventional, stereotyped, dominant, or hegemonic perspectives and readings on or about Indigenous peoples. Mirrored visions can thus be images, a series of images, and/or narratives produced by self-identified Indigenous artists about people, institutions, cultural practices, worlds, and representations that are derived from or are associated with people who are non-Indigenous. As a mode of self-representation, these images and perspectives are simultaneously about Indigenous communities and a way of contrasting differences and similarities between what these authors consider to be "Indigenous" and "non-Indigenous." That is, mirrored visions are a type of symbolic production that tends to take shape at the crossroads of unequal exchange between distinct ways of viewing the world. These works are usually generated through complex processes of self-recognition and social re-articulation, occur at moments where such processes would seem to be impossible, or express the extremes of opposing worldviews with irony and humor. In Spanish I have been using "Visiones de cabeza" to express the same notion. A literal English translation would be "head-down" or "upside-down" or "turned on its head" visions. Such translations, however, are imprecise because this notion does not seek to represent the kind of inverted, hierarchical new order that they would imply. In this sense, through "mirrored visions," a translation suggested by professor Paul Worley, we are avoiding intercultural misunderstandings while sacrificing the symbolic connotations that the head has throughout the Andes. With both "Visiones de cabeza" and "Mirrored Visions," I understand, on the one hand, a reflective mode of representing images of the non-Indigenous world, and on the other, a symbolic way of "recuperating one's head," of thinking collectively and for oneself about processes of self-representation and communal rearticulation. Following this argument and metaphor, I also propose the concept of symbolic decapitation as a way to refer to colonial processes that have entailed the fragmentation and disarticulation of Indigenous peoples, as well as the image of reattaching one's head to understand the projects undertaken by the generation of Indigenous writers who have risen to prominence in Colombia and throughout the Continent since the 1990s. In short, the mirrored visions studied here not only tend to emphasize disenchantment with modernity, but also images of contrast that appropriate modernity itself.

Created as part of the Minga de Educación, the map in Figure 1 offers an example of a mirrored vision that both contests and dia-

logues with conventional images of Colombia. To some extent, all of
the texts analyzed here address topics such as experiences of urban
life, how urban life is perceived by people living in cities, the appearance of outsiders in Indigenous communities, the impact of government policies, and multinational corporations' recent increase in
resource extraction. Another common theme is the use of alphabetic
writing and above all the exigencies created by the bureaucratiza-
tion of literacy itself, which in many mirrored visions makes an appearance as a kind of reverse (il)literacy. For example, Hugo Jamioy
(Camëntsá) creates images like that of a "non-indigenous" reader
who is illiterate with regard to "Indigenous peoples," and Estercilia
Simanca (Wayuu) articulates protagonists who are victims of a kind
of alphabetized violence.

The notion of mirrored visions thus enables us to better understand how these texts interrogate both dominant society and projects
that seek to achieve the multicultural aims of many Latin American
Constitutions, such as Colombia's. As a theoretical intervention, it
also helps us approach the production of images and narratives about
the contemporary world from the perspectives found in texts written by Indigenous authors.[17] In this sense, we can say that mirrored
visions are literary gestures or communicative strategies that help to
overturn things or generate new perspectives in situations of intercultural contact. As a notion, mirrored visions is equally useful as a
tool to dialogue with Indigenous perspectives and demands, such
that the amplification of Indigenous voices and Indigenous movements for educational and territorial rearticulation. Mirrored visions
express the dynamics of subversion found in many images and texts,
as well as constitute enunciations from multiple linguistic and cultural borders. As a first step, they re-symbolize the current order
from a change in perspective: what was above is now below, "upside
down." Even so, it cannot be simply reduced to the concept of "upside down" in English. Moreover, it cannot be thoroughly explained
through the Quechua-Aymara concept of *pachakuti* (the upending of
space-time), insofar as *pachakuti* is usually thought of as being a symbolic, political, and cultural movement upwards from below. What's
interesting about *pachakuti* is not this sense of inversion in-itself, but

---

[17] Although here I am focused on literary texts, mirrored visions frequently occur in audiovisual texts, as well as in community oral traditions, where numerous
representations of mestizos, colonizers, or other actors are elaborated with humor,
irony, and mythic complexity.

rather the possibility of turning something over (Gutiérrez Aguilar 51), as in the case of a knot that is tied and untied, offering different perspectives as it exposes and re-exposes the textures of the threads that comprise the warp and woof of intercultural contact. Similarly, mirrored visions are not simply about inverting the present hierarchical, binary order, and replacing the current dominant term with another or a better one, nor do they justify a mere revolutionary response to the larger macropolitical climate. Rather, mirrored visions seek to simultaneously privilege multiple centers from which one can examine, understand, and build. Moreover, I should emphasize that numerous mirrored visions are based on images that originate from the experiences and practices of particular cultures (like Wayuu smuggling in Apüshana) and/or from the perspectives of traditional oral narratives (for example, how in the story of the Wayuu dreamer the train that runs through Cerrejón becomes a gigantic serpent). In other works these authors build upon recurrent and self-referential images—like writing with your feet in your head (Jamioy) or having your feet in your head (Berichá)—to express a deeper need to think for oneself; for communities to represent themselves from within their own spaces; and for Indigenous peoples to revitalize their connections with their ancestral lands with their heads/thoughts well-grounded and on straight.

THEORETICAL CONTEXTS

There are numerous authors and projects who have helped me shape, rethink and consolidate this project's theoretical structure, and in this section, I outline some of the main thoughts and ideas with which I have been in dialogue. The order in which I present them here in no way implies that some are more or less important than others.

First, I would like to address a collection of theoretical works that share an emphasis on diverse forms of graphic communication, and that emerge from communal reflections written for the most part by indigenous intellectuals in South America. Writing on the context of Bolivia's central Andes, in *El rincón de las cabezas* [The Heads' Nook], Denise Arnold and Juan de Dios Yapita propose multiple readings of "textual, numeric, and literary practices" (67). Their ideas about what constitutes "text" align with what I argue here insofar as, and as I have laid out, for me a text evokes the idea of doing and weaving within a network. In short, my notion of interrelated textual fields can be related to their exercise in interweaving texts and different textual practices, including literary ones.

Along these lines, we also have the important theoretical contributions of Benjamín Jacanamijoy and Manibinigdiginya/Abadio Green in *Chumbe: arte inga* [Chumbe: Inga Art] (1993) and in *Anmal gaya burba/Significados de vida* (2011), respectively. In these works, Jacanamijoy and Manibinigdiginya examine the narratives of their respective communities (Inga and Gunadule). Based upon these narratives, they then develop readings of their communities' non-alphabetic texts, the chumbe textile in the case of Jacanamijoy and the mola textile in that of Manibinigdiginya. Jacanamijoy argues that the chumbe, or woven belt, is a form of intergenerational visual communication that in its own way constitutes a kind of book or mnemonic device. He also offers a model for reading textiles based on the design of a diamond or womb: the *uigsa*. For his part, Manibinigdiginya interweaves an analysis of traditional stories and scripts (molas and their visual language) with a linguistic analysis of gunadule etymologies or "the meanings of life." These then become the structural basis of his pedagogical proposals for the recovery of ancestral memory and the broader rearticulation of the Gunadule community. When I think about other forms of graphic communication, their work, specifically the chumbe as a book and Gunadule etymologies as "the meanings of life," has helped me conceive of other ways of thinking of the book, and underscores the importance of proposing the notion of oralitegraphies as a way of approaching the works of Indigenous and non-Indigenous authors.

Second, I should mention the Native American literary critics who have articulated important theoretical perspectives in the United States. Although they are written in the context of North America, theoretical works by Cherokee scholars such as *That the People Might Live* (1997) by Jace Weaver and *Deep Waters* (2010) by Christopher Teuton have helped me to think from the different context of Colombia, Abya Yala, and Turtle Island, in order to better understand how textualities like oralitegraphies and oralitures function. Weaver affirms that Native literature is "communitism," that is, an ongoing relationship between activism and connection to communities. This neologism provides a useful framework for understanding the close ties between literary production, different public activities, and communities, as represented in the works of many contemporary Indigenous writers. Teuton develops the concept of textual continuum between graphic and oral discourses (*Deep Waters* xviii). In doing so, he analyzes three kinds of impulses: the oral impulse, which emphasizes a relational and experiential mode connected to the world via cultural knowledge; the graphic impulse, which emphasizes the formalized, permanent fixity of knowledge; and the critical impulse, which seeks to generate a dynamic balance between oral and graphic discourses. These three impulses have shaped my understanding of oralitegraphic textualities, whose intersectional fields are related to Teuton's idea of the *textual continuum.*

Third, I would like to mention a number of key works on colonization and decolonization that come from regions of the world such as India and Aoteara/New Zealand, as well as studies that address the ongoing debates surrounding writing, diverse ways of reading texts, and the multiple political positions of contemporary literature. Linda Tuhiwai Smith's *Decolonizing Methodologies* (1999) and Meenakshi Sharma's *Postcolonial Indian Writing* (2003) have guided my approach to disarticulation and rearticulation in postcolonial writing. In her book, Tuhiwai Smith identifies twenty-five decolonial Indigenous projects. Two are of particular relevance to my analysis here, specifically the importance of writing about experiences of colonialism and imperialism, and of projects of self-representation, reenvisioning, and reconnecting. In short, for Tuhiwai Smith, the idea of creating and sharing is key to establishing new alliances (160), and something that one finds in the tours, workshops, and declarations, that are the collective efforts of Indigenous authors in Colombia, and from throughout the continent. Written within the context of India, Sharma's work helped lay the foundation for the notion of mirrored visions, which in her case would be the equivalent of representations of British people and of British influence in Indian literary works.

Regarding debates on other forms of writing, Paul Worley and Rita Palacios's *Unwriting Maya Literatures* (2019) and Elizabeth Hill Boone's *Stories in Red and Black* (2000) provide valuable insights on how thought can be communicated visually. In the case of the former, Worley and Palacios depart from the Maya category of *ts'íib* instead of writing in order to understand better how contemporary Maya literatures dialogue with a number of different ways of recording human knowledge and interaction, from ceramics and textiles to the Maya corn garden. Hill Boone's work is an important, convincing exploration of how semasiografic systems can convey ideas independently from speech ("Writing and Recording (Introduction)" 10), as in the cases of diagrams, maps, and other visual languages.

Similarly, Walter Mignolo's reflections on the advent of print which, in his formulation, facilitated the subordination of graphic languages (illustrations, drawings) to alphabetic writing conceived of as the inscription of oral speech ("Writing and Recording (Afterword)" 293), have also had a profound impact on my research.

Chadwick Allen's work has been illuminating all these same lines, particularly his contention that we should read and evaluate Indigenous literatures in relation to multiple semiotic systems and communitarian aesthetics. In short, Allen proposes a trans-Indigenous methodology, and his critical work juxtaposes literary and aesthetic forms from regions as distinct as the United States and Aotearoa/New Zealand. More broadly, the joint reflection by Arturo Arias, Luis Cárcamo-Huechante, and Emilio del Valle Escalante/Emil' Keme, on the works and processes of what they refer to as the literatures of Abya Yala, has also influenced this book, especially as they understand Abya Yala as a locus of enunciation, "from which Indigenous subjects articulate their languages and politics" [desde el cual el sujeto indígena articula sus lenguajes y sus políticas] (9). As these theorists state, Spanish is provincialized by the eruption and political positioning of the numerous Indigenous languages in which these literatures are written. Following Dipesh Chakrabarty's formulation, Europe is provincialized the moment it ceases to be indispensable, central, and dominant in the stories we tell (39).

Fourth, this book's theoretical framework has also been influenced by works of contemporary literary criticism from Colombia that focus on Indigenous Literary production, interculturality, and education in the region. Betty Osorio and Hugo Niño in particular, have played a leading role in researching contemporary Indigenous writing in Colombia.[18] Osorio's work on the Nasa leader Quintín Lame helps us better grasp how Indigenous intellectuals respond to a plurality of private and public spaces, and in the specific case of the Lame, to *letrado*, Christian, and legal ones (95). In developing the concept of the ethnotext, Hugo Niño lays the foundation for a textual approach that has been useful in understanding projects like oraliture. For Niño the ethnotext is usually connected to a commu-

---

[18] That said, I should also mention the latest generation of Colombian scholars and critics who are articulating their own lines of inquiry, and who have also made important contributions to the field: Ana María Ferreira, Selnich Vivas, Angie Puentes, Adriana Campos, Dania Gómez, Camilo Vargas, Jerónimo Salazar, Andrea Echeverría, and Juan Guillermo Sánchez, among others.

nity's orality, and composed in languages not associated with works of "universal literature" that have remained by definition outside of accepted cultural canons. His research, however, goes beyond the oral, the ethnic, and the linguistic, and his observations on an eth-notext's extraverbal interventions (40) have impacted how I think about "oralitegraphic textualities."

Catherine Walsh and Joanne Rappaport—US intellectuals who have been in continual contact with Indigenous movements in Ecua-dor and Colombia, respectively—have also put forth important ideas concerning the ongoing debates on contemporary interculturality. For Walsh, interculturality is, "a concept and a practice, process and project" [concepto y práctica, proceso y proyecto] (41). In other words, interculturality is dynamic and arises from the need to gen-erate "interactions that recognize and confront social, cultural, po-litical, economic, and institutional asymmetries" [interacciones que reconozcan y enfrenten las asimetrías sociales, culturales, políticas, económicas e institucionales] (Walsh 233). Her thoughts on intercul-tural contact arise from an Ecuadorian context that emphasizes Afro and Indigenous projects and movements, and yet she also states that these, "should not be simply thought in terms of ethnicity but rather from permanent states of relatedness, communication, and learning among distinct persons, groups, knowledges, values, traditions, log-ics, and rationalities" [no deben ser pensados simplemente en térmi-nos étnicos sino a partir de la relación, comunicación y aprendizaje permanentes entre personas, grupos, conocimientos, valores, tradi-ciones, lógicas y racionalidades distintas] (41).

Rappaport, who has been immersed since the 1970s in the ac-tivities of Indigenous intellectuals from the Cauca region in Co-lombia, and specifically in those of the CRIC, elaborates in *Inter-cultural Utopias* a slightly different notion of interculturality. First, methodologically speaking, interculturalism for her is a "method of appropriating external ideas, connecting the diverse network of ac-tivists, collaborators, and occasional supporters of the indigenous movement into a common sphere or orientation" (7). Second, po-litically-philosophically, interculturalism is "a utopian political phi-losophy aimed at achieving interethnic dialogue based on relations of equivalence and at constructing a particular mode of indigenous citizenship in a plural nation" (7). Third, ethnographically, "it poses a challenge to traditional forms of ethnographic research, replacing classic thick description with engaged conversation and collabora-tion" (7).

Rappaport's work partially connects with Walsh's proposed idea of interculturality insofar as her definition also describes the ongoing, dynamic relationships and interactions that exist among cultures in contact. Rappaport's position is thus similar to the way many writers interpellate dominant society from within the context of their respective communities, pointing out or fomenting debate about different ways of seeing the world. My work similarly intersects with Walsh's affirmation of an interculturality that "intends to break with hegemonic history which supports a dominant culture and subordinates others" [intenta romper con la historia hegemónica de una cultura dominante y otras subordinadas] (41), the kind of ruptures that one finds in projects like the map from the Minga as well as in numerous texts of oraliture that reelaborate Indigenous memories and histories. These projects do not necessarily invalidate others' memories and histories. Rather, they defy dominant society's subordination of them through concepts like literacy, which privileges phonetic writing over and above other forms of communication and textuality.

Since I am not looking to develop an ethnographic perspective or report on ethnographic fieldwork, I diverge from Rappaport's ideas about an interculturality that reenvisions ethnography in the context of collaborative research. Instead, my project homes in on Indigenous authors' representations of themselves and their communities in literary texts. Through the very act of writing these authors cease to be potential ethnographic collaborators. Moreover, my project is not aligned with an interculturalism based on the kind of utopian political philosophy that Rappaport describes when she writes that "the CRIC and other indigenous organizations are in the business of formulating utopias" (8). She goes on to say that these utopias are not impossible dreams, but part of intercultural designs whose ultimate objective is for Indigenous people "to live as indigenous people in a plural society that recognizes them as equal actors who have something to contribute to the nation" (8). By comparison, and within the specific context of mirrored visions, interculturalities imply processes of rethinking and recreating via self-representations that are not necessarily utopian. However, Rappaport's concept of interculturality hits the mark insofar as she understands interculturality as a way of mutual appropriation, connection, and support that can be found in many of the spaces in which Indigenous and non-Indigenous peoples collaborate.

Indeed, the map from the 2010 Educational Minga (see fig. 1) can be thought of as a communally owned intercultural compass. We

can also understand it as an intersectional and textual oralitegraphic field, a topic I will return to in Chapter 1. In sum, I argue that
some Indigenous and student movements that came together in the
Minga created and self-identified with this map-symbol because it
interweaves different forms of cultural knowledge and graphic communication in ways that neither exclude dominant Colombian society nor are subordinated to it. By proposing its own image of the
country, the map creates relationships among Colombia's peoples
that originate from a number of different epistemological, political,
and pluri-scriptural perspectives. However, while the map from the
Minga is an intercultural proposal with roots in the country's diverse
Indigenous communities, it is not only for these communities, nor is
it an exclusionary vision of Colombianess, given that, as seen in the
example of the *wiphala* (see fig. 10) or Pan-Andean rainbow flag, its
various ideograms transcend national frontiers. In addition, its role
in the Intercultural Educational Minga generates new pedagogical
social processes. In particular, it brings together aspects of diverse
textualities and visions of the world as a kind of tool for dialogue
with those who, for lack of a better way to put it, are referred to as
non-Indigenous.

I would also like to be clear that here I am using the term interculturality in ways that should not be confused with the tolerant
multiculturalism promised by Colombia's 1991 Constitution. I agree
with the Colombian philosopher Carlos Miguel Gómez Rincón's as-
sessment that intercultural dialogue, "has to be constructed and re-
constructed each time for particular contexts and problems" (173).
In the specific context of oralitegraphies, interculturality takes shape
in the specific interactions among and between texts. Intertextualities
are expressions of fields of interaction between textual forms of communication. In this sense, the literary analyses I construct in the book's
first section understand the concept of interculturality as also constituting processes of intertextuality, that is, points of contact between
textual projects. People from different cultural origins, including
those who self-identity as Indigenous and those who do not, are usually joint participants in the creation and reception of these projects.

Identifying the different kinds of relationships that exist among
intercultural texts has been indispensable in constructing these comparative readings. Moreover, my analysis here is not simply centered
on literary texts themselves, but also the relationships they have with
other texts and projects. Altogether, these intersecting fields connect
at least three dimensions:

Collaborative projects that are shared among authors. For example, one can think of oralitors or, how writers elaborate characters impacted by colonialism in similar ways, as in the case of Wayuu writers like Simanca and Siosi.

Multiple oralitegraphic textual proposals (the Educational Minga's map, multilingual texts, and even audiovisual recordings in which multiple forms of communication are present).

Themes derived from the creation of mirrored visions, like illiteracy and the impact of multinational corporations.

Rounding out these theoretical reflections, it is evident that one of the inherent methodological limitations of my project is the fact that I, like many scholars, critics, and readers of Indigenous texts, do not know all of the languages (Wayuunaiki, Chibcha U'wa, Chibcha Gunadule, Camëntsá) into and from which some of the texts I analyze here have been translated. However, it should also be noted that most of the texts I work with here were originally composed in Spanish and then translated into the languages of the writers' respective communities. In many cases, then, but certainly not in all, there exist two original versions of the same text, with the first version actually being composed in Spanish. Vicenta Siosi and Estercilia Simanca, for example, both write in Spanish. Miguelángel López writes mostly in Spanish and the translations or revisions of his works—at least until 2010—were done by a third party. Berichá originally published *Tengo los pies en la cabeza* in Spanish, and in 2010 I asked her to translate a few passages from her work into Chibcha U'wa language for publication in the anthology *Pütchi biya uai*. The Yanakuna Mitmak nation, the people to which Fredy Chikangana belongs, is Spanish speaking, as are a number of other communities and indigenous nations throughout Colombia (Pasto, Kankuamo, Pijao). Chikangana himself only began to write in Quechua during the first decade of the 2000s, with his work prior to that being published in Spanish. All of this said, my basic knowledge of Quechua has nonetheless shaped my approach to certain texts written by Chikangana and Arguedas. When possible, I have also incorporated the authors' own reflections that were written in their native languages and make use of oral genres such as Botamán Biyá, Haylli, Nvtram, and Rafue. As pointed out by the Colombian critic Juan Carlos González Espitia, the book's analytical framework and some of its theoretical constructs—reverse illiteracy, word mingas, mirrored visions, among others—have arisen from or been the result of conversations with indigenous writers, critics, and storytellers themselves. This orientation, in turn, implies new challenges for accepted academic traditions. In a sense, I hope this work's more dialogic, conversational tone and approach becomes one of its foremost contributions.

CHAPTER OUTLINE

Word Mingas is divided into two, three-chapter sections. The first section constructs readings based on the notion of oralitegraphies, while the second section takes up the notion of mirrored visions. That said, I deal with both of these throughout the book. The first chapter and the book's second section establish broad thematic relationships between Elicura Chihuailaf's *Recado confidencial a los chilenos* (1999), Fredy Chikangana/Wiñay Mallki's *Samay pisccok pponccopi mushcoypa/Espíritu de pájaro en pozos del ensueño* (2010) and Hugo Jamioy's *Bínÿbe oboyejuayëng/Danzantes del viento* (2005). As already seen in our brief explications of oralitegraphies (the Minga map, the oraliture project) and mirrored visions (extractivism, illiteracy), from a methodological perspective this approach emphasizes the fields of interaction among these projects.[19]

Chapter one lays out an oralitegraphic reading of the map from the 2010 Educational Minga that was organized by Colombian students and Indigenous organizations. I argue that the map can be understood as a mirrored vision of the country's hegemonic cartographic image of itself. While based upon an outline of Colombia's national borders, the map's cartography uses ideo- and pictograms drawn from multiple Indigenous communities's systems of graphic communication to propose a new representation of Colombian national space. Given that these visual languages are also found and evoked in works of Colombian oraliture and Indigenous literature by authors such as Anastasia Candre, Hugo Jamioy, Vito Apüshana, and Fredy Chikangana, my analysis draws upon a number of connections between the oral, (carto)graphic, and literary dimensions, of the map and other texts. The map can thus be understood as a poli-communicative *minga*, a project whose cartographic proposal arises from the confluence of multiple systems of Indigenous visual communication.

---

[19] Over the past several years I have had the opportunity to speak with most of the Indigenous writers and several of the literary theorists whose work is dealt with here. As such, throughout this work, I cite from our personal communication as opposed to formal interviews.

Drawing on the concept of oraliture and related threads of literary criticism such as Hugo Niño's ethnotext (2008), Jace Weaver's
communitism (1997), storytelling, and oral literature, Chapter 2 addresses the underlying theoretical principles of the continental Indigenous oraliture project. I perform close readings to demonstrate
how oraliture functions and is expressed through specific works, as
well as in Indigenous verbal genres that oralitors revindicate as their
own unique kinds of verbal art, such as the *nvtram* (conversation),
the *taki* (song), and the *haylli* (elegiac hymn). The chapter begins
by examining the origins of the oraliture project and its eventual
elaboration in *Recado confidencial a los chilenos* (1999) by Elicura
Chihuailaf, a Mapuche writer from the Wallmapu in Chile. From
there the chapter moves into the work of a Yanakuna writer from
Colombia's southwest, Fredy Chikangana, who, upon meeting his
Mapuche counterpart in the 1990s, contributed to the expansion of
the oraliture project through the publication of his article "Indigenous Oraliture as a Voyage to Memory" [Oralitura indígena como
un viaje a la memoria] (2014). In order to better grasp Chikangana's
approach, I take up several texts from the collection *Samay pisccok
pponccopi mushcoypa* [A Bird's Spirit within the Depths of a Day-
dream] (2010), which he published under his Quechua pen name,
Wiñay Mallki. In addition to the sense of orality that it has in common with works by other oralitors, Chikangana's text stands out for
its cultivation of a graphic language through its placement of text on
the page. As such, I use the notion of oralitegraphies to connect it to
the literary visual readings that I present earlier.

The third chapter continues the work of the previous chapter
insofar as it explores the oralitor project's expansion in the work of
the Camëntsá oralitor Hugo Jamioy Juajibioy. Given that Jamioy's
oralitegraphic project takes shape in connection with Andean graphic forms of communication that he refers to as "beautiful writing,"
my analysis of *Bínÿbe oboyejuayëng*, a collection that Jamioy originally published in 2005 and then edited for re-release in 2010, offers
a deeper understanding of why we must read this work in dialogue
with an oralitegraphic perspective. I examine the literary work's textualities throughout the chapter, noting that these are expressed as
much in the work's roots in orality as in the ideographic language of
the chumbe (woven belt), and the sculptural and corporal language
of masks carved in wood, among other technologies and fields of
visual and communal communication. Opening the book's second
section, Chapter four deepens our understandings of the symbolism

found in mirrored visions. The chapter begins by looking at reflections on and narratives about education and communal rearticulation written by Manibinigdiginya/Abadio Green. These narratives come from his doctoral dissertation *Anmal gaya burba* [Meanings of Life] (2011), which he wrote in the context of the Gunadule binational project, Nangalaburba Oduloged Igala (Returning to Revive our Mother's bones). I use the idea of symbolic decapitation to refer to colonial processes that have fragmented and disarticulated Indigenous communities, and the idea of "reattaching one's head" to understand the proposals of Indigenous writers who have risen to prominence in Colombia since the 1990s. Further, I include reflections on the work of Berichá, the first female U'wa writer whose work first appeared in 1992. The title of her book *Tengo los pies en la cabeza* underscores the ideas of thinking for oneself and of self-representation.

In Chapter five I compare three themes that recur as mirrored visions (illiteracy, the city, and returning) in literary works by contemporary Indigenous authors. In the first section, I explore mirrored visions surrounding so-called (il)literacy, a social prejudice that many members of Indigenous communities consider a form of discrimination that they suffer at the hands of dominant society. In this chapter, I look at Estercilia Simanca's "Manifiesta no saber firmar. Nacido: 31 de diciembre" (2006), which contests the alphabetized pressures exerted by government bureaucracies, as well as the idea of *post mortem* illiteracy in a Gunadule story by Manibinigdiginya. I also draw on Hugo Jamioy's idea about the reverse illiteracy of those who do not understand Indigenous peoples' symbols and graphic scriptural languages such as those found in chumbes, masks, wood sculptures, woven beads, and bags. In the second section, I explore mirrored visions in works about life in the city, a place that, in addition to shaping many contemporary Indigenous movements, has also been where many works of oraliture and literature are written. In fact, in the poetic imagery of oralitors like Jamioy and Chikangana, the city is not only a space of loneliness and crisis but also a place of reflection and creation. Finally, in the third section, I focus on poetic images of the return to the communal homeland, whether this be symbolic or physical, temporary or permanent. The texts analyzed in this section are notable for how their authors elaborate mirrored visions that juxtapose life in communal lands with life in the city, homing in on *Versos de sal*, whose coauthor, Yíche/Yenny Muruy Andoque, is an Andoke-Uitoto/Murui writer from the Amazon rainforest.

Chapter 6 continues with comparative readings of other themes frequently encountered in mirrored visions: time and/or Indigenous rhythms, borders and ethnic tourism in Indigenous communities, and the impact of political projects that were promoted by a government in league with extractivist corporations and businesses. I read several poems by Jamioy and Apüshana, as well as Wayuu narratives by Siosi, Jusayú, and Simanca, showing how certain images and stories interpellate dominant society as they construct forms of self-representation that are capable of forwarding processes of social transformation. Examples of these kinds of texts would be the fight against abuses of multinationals and expansionist extractivism in the story "Lucro cesante, daño emergente" by Estercilia Simanca, and the literary letter written by Vicenta Siosi to the former President of Colombia, which played a key role in momentarily delaying the diversion of the Ranchería/Calancala River.

By way of conclusion, the final section includes a story that contextualizes oralitegraphies and mirrored visions in interpersonal, dialogic settings with these oralitors and writers themselves. I also recap what I feel are the book's main contributions to the field, and suggest future avenues for further exploration and/or expanding upon the notions I propose here.

PART I

READING ORALITEGRAPHIES

1
MIRRORED VISIONS AND ORALITEGRAPHIES IN A "NEW" READING OF COLOMBIA'S CARTOGRAPHY

IN 2010, the Indigenous Peoples' National Commission for Labor and Collective Action on Education (CONTCEPI) convened the National Minga on Higher Education and Indigenous Peoples in Colombia. In order to promote the Minga's [collective work] call for participation, they designed and printed a poster in which Colombia was represented from multiple Indigenous perspectives through a map created from Indigenous ideograms, some of which are centuries old (see fig. 1).

Figure 1: Map from the National Minga on Higher Education and Indigenous Peoples. Juan Carlos Jamioy. *Mapa Minga Nacional de Educación Superior de los Pueblos Indígenas.*

According to statistics cited by the historian Ilse Gröll, it is es-
timated that there were "more than 300 languages [in Colombia]
prior to the Spanish Conquest" [se calcula que antes de la conquista
española existían más de 300 lenguas] (21), and "from six to ten
million people in what is today Colombia's national territory" [seis
a 10 millones de personas en el actual territorio colombiano] (42).
As published by Colombia's National Administration for Statistics,
in Colombia's 2018 National Census 4.4% of the country's population, some 1,900,000 people, self-identified as Indigenous. In the
2005 National Census more than 500,000 of these people reported
not speaking an Indigenous language ("Censo"). Overall, Colombia
recognizes 115 Indigenous nationalities and 65 Indigenous languages, the latter being grouped into twenty-one branches composed of
eight discrete languages and thirteen linguistic families (Landaburu
4). Despite the existence of numerous linguistic/cultural maps that
locate and represent these Indigenous languages and populations,
the perspective found in the Educational Minga's map questions and
destabilizes the self-authorized, official power to cartographically
represent the country's Indigenous Peoples, Peoples who were la-
beled "infidels" or "naturales" during the colonial period, and frequently referred to as "minorities" or ethnic "groups" at present.

Through a surprising aesthetic comprised of polychromatic icons
and figures drawn from multiple Indigenous systems of visual communication, systems popularly conceived of as artisanal or folklor-
ic, the map in the center of the poster re-signifies arbitrary borders
found in conventional cartography. That is, the image I will refer to
here as "the Minga's map" is a multigraphic proposal from the field
of intercultural education that is rooted in contemporary Indigenous
movements' aspirations for a multi-ethnic and pluri-lingual country,
aspirations which can also be observed in the 1991 Constitution. In
this sense, here I argue that we can expand our reception of contemporary Indigenous literary texts by understanding these within the
context of and as resonating with different textualities, graphic representations, and/or visual ideosymbolic expressions. It is thus prob-
lematic that these modes of communication are typically constructed
as extraliterary or preliterate by the phono-centric criteria that cur-
rently dominates literary studies, a field in which literature is limited
to works written and published in alphabetic script. Given the map's
self-representational character, I will also show how we can use it
as a valid and important point of reference—although certainly not
the only point of reference, nor necessarily the most representative

one—when talking about a number of the verbal, visual, and literary proposals articulated by Colombia's Indigenous writers.

CONSIDERATIONS FOR CONSTRUCTING ORALITEGRAPHIC READINGS BASED UPON THE EDUCATIONAL MINGA'S MAP

Led by the National Indigenous Organization of Colombia (ONIC) and a group of Indigenous university students, the Indigenous movement commissioned the Camëntsá audiovisual creator Juan Carlos Jamioy to design a map for the Educational Minga. A relative of the Camëntsá poet Hugo Jamioy, the artist says that as he designed the map he researched Indigenous writing systems and consulted with members of different Indigenous nations, in particular with a Kankuamo friend of his from the Sierra Nevada de Santa Marta.[1] The map was then created by using the iconography of a number of different Indigenous nations, as in his mind an image is, as they say, worth a thousand words. Given the impossibility of creating a map containing graphic representations from each of the country's Indigenous nations, Jamioy carefully selected figures from specific visual systems and placed them on the map in relation to their respective territories. As such, he feels that the "textures" or "forms" that he selected for inclusion in the map express graphic elements that encourage different Indigenous peoples self-identify with the map. He has also said that by using Colombia's outline as a framework to produce the Educational Minga's map, the map responds to the need for dialogue among the country's Indigenous and non-Indigenous peoples.

A detailed reading of the map reveals the presence of what I am referring to as oralitegraphies insofar as it represents the creative intersections of literary, oral, and graphic texts. The makers and Indigenous authors who work in these communicative modalities thus create intersectional fields or textualities through their syntheses of literary, oral, and graphic expressions.

In my theoretical discussion of the Minga map, oralitegraphies function as multiple textualities in which diverse systems of picto-ideographic writing intersect with literary texts that, as in the case

---

[1] These and the following comments are drawn from my personal communication with Juan Carlos Jamioy.

of proposals arising from oraliture, privilege voices based in orality (testimonies, verbal genres, the transcription or evocation of myths). Within my reading, *textualities*, in the plural, unites oral, graphic, and alphabetic-literary expressions that, at present, are given different values in contemporary textual production. These textualities can be expressed as texts but, given that oralitegraphies are part of broader webs of interaction among diverse systems of communication that authors are capable of interweaving, cannot be reduced to them. Alternatively, a text can capture a particular interaction or interweaving of textualities, being, in essence, a concrete manifestation of these, as in the case of a poem or a story. As mentioned in the introduction, my way of thinking here coincides with how Denise Arnold and Juan de Dios Yapita understand the use of the word 'text' (from the Latin *textus*) in its sense of 'doing' and, more specifically, of 'weaving.' Here it is relevant to stress the word's dynamism of 'joining,' interweaving or 'intertwining,' things such as the voice and writing; 'text' evokes the idea of something woven or constructed like a net (14).

We can also think of the Educational Minga's map map as a "mirrored vision," the notion I will use to construct literary analyses of texts in the second part of this work. By "mirrored vision" I am referring to images or series of images produced by self-identified Indigenous authors that are about people, institutions, cultural practices, worlds and paradigms from or associated with the people who are (or consider themselves to be) non-Indigenous. Specifically, "mirrored visions" represent a particular kind of ideosymbolic production that tends or aspires to subvert conventional, stereotyped, dominant, or hegemonic readings and views about the Indigenous world.

Given that oralitegraphies and mirrored visions are developed in or interconnected with spaces of confluence, collision, and/or collaboration between different worldviews, languages, and situations of contact, I feel that both notions are tools that we can use to generate, revise, or explain processes of intercultural dialogue, in the sense alluded to by Catherine Walsh, as they offer us a perspective that exists between cultures (15). Further, they are of particular relevance here insofar as this book focuses on the graphic and scriptural projects of Indigenous authors who publish for themselves, their communities, and beyond, who routinely participate in local, national, and international politics, and whose locus of enunciation derives its authority from their cultural identities without necessarily making them a spokesperson for or representative of their communities.

On one level, when I allude to mirrored visions, the dynamics of subversion in images or texts, or utterances that come from the multiple linguistic and cultural borders, we understand that things here are re-signified via a change in position: what was once on top is now below; things as they were are now upside down. This idea clearly relates to the Central Andean concept of Quechua-Aymara *pachakuti*, whose most basic image of overturning or transforming the world is derived from *chaquitaclla*, the foot plow, that the Andean farmer uses to dig in the earth, bringing buried dirt to the surface in order to begin a new planting cycle. However, I agree with Gutiérrez Aguilar that, "conceptualizing the transformation of the 'inside to outside' does not suggest an inversion produced by a symmetrical 'rotation' of top to bottom and vice versa. Instead, it is a 'turning around'" (51). In short, mirrored visions invert things in order to observe, relate to, and construct from multiple centers that are in a constant process of being turned over, and not simply an inversion of a hierarchical order from binary categories that replaces what is privileged with something similar or better, nor is it about a mere revolutionary response in the macropolitical field.[2]

For example, at the 2008 edition of Chile's International Book Fair, Hugo Jamioy put forward the idea that non-Indigenous people can be illiterate regarding Indigenous Peoples, or what I will refer to here as reverse illiteracy. From the perspective of this kind of illiteracy, Indigenous Peoples, the country's rural population, and those at the fringes of its urban centers more generally, peoples who are typically stigmatized as illiterate and needing literacy due to their limited access to Greco-Roman phonetic writing, can reverse this stigmatization. In his view, those who are unfamiliar with Indigenous writing systems can also be, in a sense, "illiterate."

Diverse Indigenous scriptural systems are characterized by the visual communication of ideas as opposed to speech, as well as by their use of a wide variety of media to transmit messages within their

---

[2] Silvia Rivera Cusicanqui draws a distinction between the macropolitics of the nation-state and the micropolitics, the realm in which one can affect actual change for the majority of people. For her, *pachakuti* is "the time of renovation/revolution" (11), and as such pertains to a cyclical and reversible conception of time, which tends and will tend to overturn the present "mundo al revés" [world upside-down] or state of colonial domination mentioned and denounced by the Andean *cronista* Guamán Poma de Ayala in his early-sixteenth century *Nueva Corónica y buen gobierno*. Writing in the context of a Bolivia that has undergone significant changes since Rivera Cusicanqui's first published this idea, for the sociologist Raquel Gutiérrez Aguilar *pachakuti* implies the desire and search for a new social contract (51).

ancestral territories and beyond. These media include weavings (baskets, bags, hammocks, girdles, bands, pins, beaded necklaces), ceramics (painted or sculpted), sculpture (in stone, wood, bone), painting (on the body, on canvas, on rocks, on fabric such as the *yanchama*), and even extend to more recent technological audiovisual developments and interactive virtual media like blogs, book objects, and web pages. Following Jamioy, ignorance of these media, their intracultural connotations, codes, and possible intercultural readings, is what makes non-Indigenous peoples "illiterate." It's worth noting that Jamioy himself makes use of multiple media, writing both in alphabetic script and in the ideographic signs of weaving *chaquira* (small round beads of plastic or glass). As such, Jamioy is conscious of the fact that alphabetic writing is a colonial imposition on Indigenous scriptural media, saying that "when I think back now on the beautiful way of writing they made me forget when I learned to write in Spanish, back then not being illiterate was more important" [pienso ahora en aquella bonita escritura, que me hicieron olvidar cuando aprendí a escribir en español, era más importante por entonces no ser analfabeta] ("Pensando" 150). In effect, and as Arnold and Yapita affirm in the context of the Bolivian Andes, "the conquest initiates a textual struggle arising from the forced contact between different 'texts' and 'writings,' between different textual, numeric, and literary practices" [con la conquista, comienza una lucha textual resultado del forzoso contacto entre diferentes "textos" y "escrituras", diferentes prácticas textuales, numéricas y literarias] (67).

Within the framework of the Educational Minga's map, the readings in the following section are interwoven with images produced by the following authors: Hugo Jamioy (Camëntsá), Anastasia Candre (Okaina-Uitoto/Murui), Yenny Muruy (Andoke-Uitoto/Murui), Fredy Chikangana (Yanakuna Quechua), Miguelángel López (Wayuu), and Berichá (U'wa). Owing to their relatively recent authorship and the intercultural projects they seek to communicate, certain visual expressions that arise from Indigenous movements, like the map from the Minga and its vision of a pluri-scriptural Colombia, can broaden our understanding of works of oraliture and Indigenous literature. However, as I think/feel within the context of intersecting fields, I am not necessarily proposing that we understand these texts as being determined by the aims of social movements, nor that we generate a number of different critical perspectives, even on those movements themselves. What I am referring to here is the possibility, not yet fully explored, of understanding certain educational and intercultural projects in concert with visual, literary, and verbal texts that they dialogue with. From this perspective, the philosophical conception and artistic realization of the so-called Minga map can be seen as a mirrored vision whose reception can be expanded if we look at it through the notion of oralitegraphic textualities. These textualities themselves can also be understood as alternative practices for producing, accumulating, and communicating knowledge from a semiotic perspective. As such, the present chapter broadens our critical perspective by examining the confluence of cartography with the phonetic-literary, and then upon the oral, verbal dimension that Indigenous authors evoke and capture in many of their texts.

Following Elizabeth Hill Boone, the production, accumulation, and communication of knowledge through the use of diagrams and maps can be a way of "envisioning information" ("Writing" 10). All of these, of course, are characteristics of the Minga map and its oralitegraphies. As an ethno-historian of Pre-columbian art and a specialist in iconography, for Hill Boone written language is not always the optimal medium through which to express thought, which is why in some cases graphic or visual registers are even preferable to alphabetic ones (10).

According to Hill Boone, glotographic systems of representing speech, also referred to as phonetic or phonographic systems, are commonly seen as a "complete" writing ("Writing" 15). Meanwhile, semasiographic (the expression of ideas independent from language) systems of writing, Indigenous modes of writing that employ pictograms (communication through partially "realist" images) or ideograms (communication through images that symbolize or convey ideas), are not seen as conventional writing. Even so, in the context of Hill Boone's studies, oralitegraphies can be partially understood as semasiographic systems or "containers of meaning" (*semasia* in Greek), in which "marks convey meaning directly and within the structure of their own system" (15). However, the readings I present here do not adopt a specifically semasiographic focus given that ideas in oralitegraphies are not completely independent from phonetic language, but rather interwoven with alphabetic texts. Indeed, it may be better to refer to oralitegraphies as multimedia systems of representation, as these codes of communication do not necessarily imply a dependence upon the structure of a "closed" graphic system. In the case of oraliture projects analyzed, Chihuailaf, Chikangana, and Jamioy cooperate within an interconnected web despite their cultural differences—upon which I will elaborate in the following chapters—, while at the same time arguing for a convergent kind of writing in which orality thrives alongside the will to write graphically. In this sense, we can assert that oralitegraphies imply a continuous intertextual expansion and contraction, as well as the fact that they are not examples of visual systems that subordinate phonetic systems but, on the contrary, that enable visual and phonetic systems to be placed in a kind of non-dualistic (orality versus written) complementarity that may appear utopian from the prejudices of abstract phonetic writing, given that it is considered one of the ultimate and most "civilized" achievements in the history of human communication.

To gain a deeper understanding of oralitegraphies' creative possibilities and intercultural projects that they can express, we need to understand them within the context of writing in so-called "colonial" or "post-colonial" situations. Analyzing the Eurocentric context of the letter in which most paradigms of writing literary culture continue to orbit, the Argentinian academic Walter Mignolo suggests that, "while, in medieval illuminated books, connections were made between the forms of letters and expressions of the human body and manual labor, the printing press detached the hand from drawing and writing and contributed to the subordination of drawings and illustrations to alphabetic writing and to the conception of alphabetic writing as the inscription of speech" ("Writing and Recorded Knowledge" 293).

Here, however, the graphic literacies found in the literary works of Indigenous authors are not understood as by-products of secondary editorial processes, nor do they revindicate illustrated editions of gift-books that were common in the early twentieth century or the illuminated manuscripts of medieval Europe. Indeed, the visual creations found in the literary works analyzed here have clear relationships to community graphies, as well as to iconographic proposals of Indigenous and Political student movements, such as in the case of the Educational Minga's map. Further, through these oralitegraphic readings, I propose interpretations that seek to operate within the dynamics of potential complementarity and co-creation, not simply between writing and orality, but more precisely in the continuities and expanded understandings—or the de-subordinations to borrow from Mignolo—that arise from recognizing textual continuums among the critical, graphic, and oral impulses. Following Christopher Teuton, a US-based Cherokee academic and expert in Indigenous systems of signification, the oral impulse emphasizes a relational and experiential mode of connection with the world insofar as "oral discourses are living forms of cultural knowledge" (*Deep Waters* xvi). By comparison, the graphic impulse "expresses a desire for the permanent recording of cultural knowledge in formats that will allow for recollection and study" (xvii). According to Teuton, these impulses are complementary even as they generate imbalances between themselves, as is the case when the discourses of one impulse intervene within the discourses of the other. In this sense, Teuton characterizes the critical impulse as the constant need to generate a "dynamic balance between oral and graphic discourses on the textual continuum ... disrupted by Euro-American colonialism and the privileging of alphabetic writing" (xviii). As is true of Teuton's work, my work here "is not strictly an individualistic affair, but is also a socially located and socially constructed process on the textual continuum" (xxii). That is, despite the fact that the readings found here are influenced and framed by a temporal academic experience in North America, they are nonetheless also situated historically within the frame of intercultural pedagogical movements that originated in Colombia and the Andes at the beginning of the millennium, such as the mingas and other practices. Essentially, in Colombia's Andean Southeast the mingas or minkas, a word that comes from quechua-aymara, tend to be a prominent activity in projects that imply exchange, ideas, solidarity, and alliances. In short, they stand for processes of inter- and intra-cultural communication and cooperation. For the Pastos, a binational community along the border of Colombia and Ecuador, what we commonly refer to as literature forms part of the collectively named and celebrated mingas of the word and mingas of thought. According to local ethnoeducators, these mingas are meetings where community members can come together to support each other in any kind of labor and share in stories told by elders, or sung in any number of popular musical genres like te Spanish *coplas* by younger adults.[3] In fact, some of the collective pedagogical books from the Colimba Reservation can be interpreted as oralitegraphic textualities. For example, Ruano's educational text, *Kury pugyu*, employs images as a visual supplement for oral memory, while alphabetic writing in Quechua and Spanish is reduced to only a few words to guide the reader along (see fig. 2). Any interpretation of *Kury pugyu* depends on the wise-person and/ or ethnoeducator, making use of images and keywords drawn from

---

[3] I discussed this particular idea about the mingas with Aldemar Ruano in 2013.

oral storytelling and communal knowledge. In the case of the Pasto, the people who interpret such a text would increasingly privilege Quechua, as well as the re-incorporation of pre-Hispanic symbols derived from the picto-ideographs of rock art and Nariño ceramics.

Figure 2. Key words and images from regional Pre-Hispanic pottery. Aldemar Ruano. *Kury pugyu, coloreando y pintando la cultura pasto, Nariño*, pp. 28–29.

We can interpret the Minga map as a kind of oralitegraphic textuality and a mirrored vision given that, as we shall see, it forms part of a broader textual *continuum* that serves as a symbolic framework, web of images, and historical starting point for the appreciation of certain literary works. The map is a public document that invites multiple personal and collective readings that in the near future will likely shape another kind of minga or web of readers of its cartographic and ideosymbolic text—my proposal here is but a single reading that seeks to generate further readings and responses.

I would also like to emphasize that the Educational Minga's map offers us a new and decolonizing vision of Colombia as it transforms the country's hegemonic and conventional forms of representation (lines, dots, colors, names in phonetic script). In effect, the map's cartographic configuration can be understood as a mirrored vision, a concept better understood when one thinks of the famous version of a cartographic mirrored vision: the map of the world upside-down, with the south on top. This upside-down configuration or cartographic perspective questions the supposed superiority of the globe's northern imperial powers (West Europe, Russia, Japan, China, and the United States, among other countries). It also exposes the fact that the North's being positioned on top, as well as its large scale and

the supposed centrality of North America and Europe, are techni-
cally arbitrary and better reflect political as opposed to geographic
positioning. Made public in 1979 by Australian Stuart McArthur, the
Universal Corrective Map was one of the first modern-world maps
to be published with the South appearing on top (see fig. 3). Included with this cartographic representation is an alphabetic gloss that
categorically concludes: "No longer will the South wallow in a pit
of insignificance, carrying the North on its shoulders for little or no
recognition of her efforts. Finally, South emerges on top" (Wood,
Kaiser, and Abramms 50).

That said, the Uruguayan artist Joaquín Torres-García had already painted an inverted map of Latin America some four decades
earlier, and he had his own ideas about this kind of map and its
representations of the North and the South (see fig. 4): "I have said
School of the South; because in reality, *our North is the South*. There
should be no North for us, except in opposition to our South ... That
is why we now turn the map upside down, and now we know what
our true position is, and it is not the way the rest of the world would
like to have it. From now on, the elongated tip of South America will
point insistently at the South, our North" (Torres-García 53).

As Pedro Orgambide affirms, "as a counter reading of European
aesthetic models, this upside-down map can be read from different
points of view across Latin America, whether by Di Cavalcanti's mulatas in the impoverished, undulating hills of Brazil, or Antonio Berni's dispossessed in Argentina. Within this map Picasso's language
can cohabitate with the Yoruba rites of the Cuban artist Wifredo
Lam, himself the son of a Chinese man and a mulata" [Ese mapa
dado vuelta, contralectura de los modelos estéticos europeos, puede
leerse desde diferentes puntos de vista en América Latina: desde los
morros de la pobreza con las ondulantes mulatas de Di Cavalcanti en
Brasil, hasta los desocupados de Antonio Berni en la Argentina. En
ese mapa puede coincidir el lenguaje piccasiano con los ritos yorubas
del artista cubano Wifredo Lam, hijo de un chino y una mulata] (48).

In other words, Torres-García's upside-down map lets us question not only the hegemonic vision of global politics, but also the
severe systems of race and class within our own countries, as well as
our hyper-dependence on artistic and educational models from the
supposedly more "developed" North. Through the mirrored visions
of these upside-down maps, Torres-García, McArthur, and other intellectuals from the South provoke their viewers to question whether
or not the North is necessarily on top, with the South subordinated

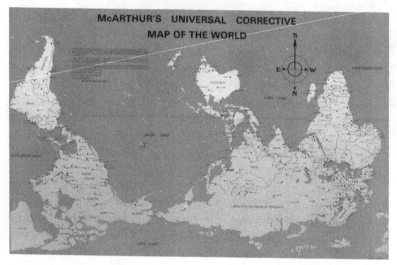

Figure 3. McArthur's universal map. Denis Wood, Ward L. Kaiser and Bob Abramms. *Seeing Through Maps: Many Ways to See the World,* p. 50.

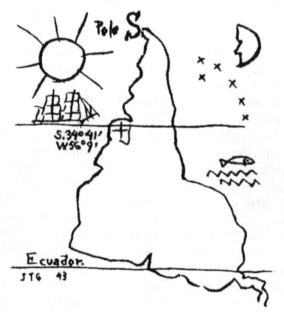

Figure 4. Torres-García's inverted map. Joaquín Torres-García. *El Taller Torres-García. The School of the South and Its Legacy,* p. 53.

under it? Similarly, the Educational Minga's map provokes a number of related questions concerning colonial de-insubordination: is the map of Colombia itself the product of a hegemonic narrative, a homogenizing model, a dominant regime of representation? What roles could this kind of symbolic cartography play in present and future re-imaginings of the country? My oralitegraphic analysis of the map echoes the kinds of readings undertaken in Native American Studies by Chadwick Allen, a critic who correlates Native American literatures from the United States with Maori literatures and semiotic systems from Aotearoa New Zealand. Allen explores, "the possibility of engaging distinct and specific Indigenous aesthetic systems in the appreciation and interpretation of diverse works of Indigenous art, including written literature" (106). From a similar perspective, my readings of the ideograms that comprise the map and other literary images, also depart from my observing the possible connections that exist among different textual systems from dissimilar cultures. With regard to the former, other researchers have argued for the existence of different continuums as a way to understand the diversity of Indigenous artistic and literary projects. In the case of the Maori, Robert Jahnke identifies the presence of aesthetic continuities among traditional and non-traditional art (qtd. in Allen, 153–54). As previously stated, Teuton develops the idea of a textual *continuum* between the graphic, oral, and critical impulses. By comparison, the readings here reference particular kinds of textual *continuums* that emphasize contemporary intersections among different forms of oral, alphabetic-literary, and graphic communication.

Given that they come out of the intercultural pedagogical context of the mingas, my readings of the Educational Minga's map does not come from a political or indigenist epistemic position, but from dialogues and exchanges among young people and elders from diverse Indigenous nations during the last few years. These readings can also be understood as the critical continuity of personal conversations I have had with several writers whose works are the central axis of these pages. My participation in and co-organization of multiple meetings and events during the last two decades has meant, for example, that in 2010 I was part of the network of collaborators that informally disseminated the map under discussion here. My supporting of the map's diffusion came out of my participation in the National Minga on Higher Education for Indigenous Peoples with a group of students from different Indigenous nationalities with whom I was working in intercultural education. All-in-all, my aim here is not to retell these collective and personal experiences, but rather to give them critical and reflexive continuity.

The following oralitegraphic readings arise from these dialogues surrounding the Educational Minga's map. In brief, here I analyze a series of images that are close-ups of various figures from the map. My oralitegraphic approach to the map will be constructed through intertextual readings among these figures, other visual projects, and a number of different literary texts.

PETROGLYPHS, *MOLAS*, *CHUMBES*, AND SKETCHES OF HUMANITY

In the southeast of the Educational Minga's map (see fig. 1), petroglyphs (images carved in stone) are used to represent the Putumayo and Caquetá Rivers (see fig. 5). These graphic symbols are connected to mythic narratives on the origins of humanity.

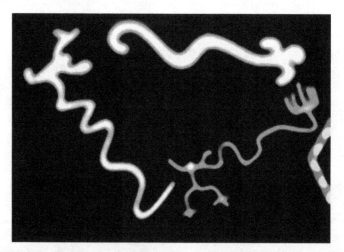

Figure 5. Petroglyphs. Detail. Juan Carlos Jamioy. *Mapa Minga Nacional de Educación Superior de los Pueblos Indígenas.*

One of the precursors of the study of Amazonian rock art in Colombia, the poet-philosopher Fernando Urbina Rangel, found this particular series of anthropomorphic and serpentine glyphs along the bank of the Caquetá River in February of 1978. In his "Mito, rito y arte rupestre en la amazonia" [Myth, Ritual, and Rock Art of the Amazon], the researcher from Norte de Santander explains that these glyphs are associated with the Panamazonian myth of the an-

cestral anaconda whose different segments gave birth to humanity.[4]
For Urbina, the art found along the rocky banks of the Caquetá represents a kind of continuity with contemporary oral narratives found
in the area's Amazonian communities, and with those of the Uitoto/
Murui and the Muinane in particular.[5] Regarding the glyphs' antiq-
uity, he cites the archeologist Elizabeth Reichel, who, "calculates that
the petroglyphs found along the Caquetá River are more than two
centuries old" [calcula que los petroglifos del río Caquetá datan de
más de dos siglos] (qtd. in Urbina, "Mito, rito" 5).

The pairs of rectangular icons in the middle of the map, are motifs derived from textile designs (see fig. 6a). Similar to the letter "E,"
these can evoke abstract, seated anthropomorphic figures. In fact,
such abstractions of human figures and men and women seated in a
pensive position frequently occur in sculpture, metalsmithing, and
ceramics from pre-Hispanic times (among the Tumaco, Quimbaya,

---

[4] "The Amazonian myth about the unity of the human race explains how human
beings came from the womb of the Canoe-Snake. This snake was the Canoe Ana-
conda-Ancestor who followed the rivers upstream going from east to west. When
it arrived in a new place (for example, the place from which the tribe of the person
telling the story at that moment originated), the serpent's segmentation would give
birth to the great ancestors of different human groups. In some of the mytheme's versions, the snake gives birth not just to the different Indigenous nations around them,
but to all the world's peoples" [El mito amazónico que habla de la unidad del género
humano narra cómo los seres humanos venían en el vientre de la Canoa-culebra. Era
la Canoa Anaconda-Ancestral que remontaba los ríos desde oriente. Una vez que
llega al lugar (el hábitat de la tribu a la que pertenece el relator de la variante mítica
que se narra en ese momento), la segmentación de la serpiente da origen a los grandes
ancestros de los diferentes grupos humanos, incluyendo, en algunas de las múltiples
versiones del mitema, no solo las naciones indias vecinas del clan al que pertenece el
relator, sino también a todas las gentes del mundo] (Urbina, "Mito, rito" 6).
[5] "Members of an Indigenous nation in the Colombian-Peruvian Amazon are
known as the Huitotos. At present they are very dispersed. Their main settlements
can be found near the Igara Paraná and Cara Paraná Rivers, halfway up the Caquetá,
and several places in Perú. Smaller groups are mostly found in Leticia, Puerto Leguízamo, Florencia, and even in Bogotá" [se conoce con el nombre de huitotos a los
integrantes de una nación amerindia que habita en la Amazonia colombo-peruana.
En la actualidad, su dispersión es muy amplia. Los principales asentamientos se ubi-
can en los ríos Igaraparaná, Caraparaná, el curso medio del Caquetá y en algunas
localidades peruanas. Grupos más reducidos se encuentran principalmente en Leticia, Puerto Leguízamo, Florencia e incluso en Bogotá] (Urbina, *Las palabras* 9). In
Las palabras del origen [Words of the Origin], Urbina also says that, "the Muinanes
are as old a cultural group as the Huitotos, whom they have lived next to since time
immemorial. Their language is in the same family as Bora (the name of another Amazonian nation), which is why linguists refer to it as the 'Muinane-Bora' family" [los
muinanes constituyen una cultura de tan arcaica data como la de los uitotos, y sus
hábitats tradicionales fueron vecinos desde tiempo inmemorial. Poseen una lengua
emparentada con el bora (que también denomina otra nación amazónica), razón por
la cual los lingüistas la denominan "muinane-bora"] (*Las palabras* 9).

Calima, Muisca, among others) down to the present (the Emberá and Gunadule, for example).

The molas of the Gunadule or Kuna people are polichromatic, embroidered, layered textiles that are placed on women's blouses, and comprise a kind of feminine writing that is manifested on the body of the wearer. As Eduardo Galeano states, molas are a "splendid art of painting that employs a needle and thread instead of a brush" [espléndido arte de una pintura que usa hilo y aguja en lugar de pincel] (*Los hijos* 73). In essence, as part of their extensive ideo-geometric repertoire, the women who weave molas have a design in which a double "E" can be seen from the front, and not the back, as in Figure 6a, in which a labyrinthine composition with a cruciform structure in the middle is created (Duque Duque 526). Gunadule molas are a picto-ideographic writing done by women that would appear to be a contemporary, woven manifestation of a much longer tradition of visual communication through ancestral designs that were painted on the body, and which have been transformed and moved from painting to textiles through contact with European colonizers around Urabá and Darién. As laid out by French anthropologist Michel Perrin, one of the world's foremost specialists in this particular pictorial textile language, the "the art of molas is therefore recent. It appeared in the second half of the nineteenth century when the Kuna migrated to the islands and expanded their relationships with non-Kuna peoples. It is an art of reaction, a hybrid art stemming from contact and conflict with whites. Until white men arrived, women went around bare-breasted and painted their bodies" (*Magnificent Molas* 25).

Figure 6a. Textile patterns. Detail. Juan Carlos Jamioy. *Mapa Minga Nacional de Educación Superior de los Pueblos Indígenas.*

The four-sided ideograms with designs inside of them are known as *uigsas* or wombs among the Inga from the Sibundoy Valley, in the Putumayo region. As suggested by the location of these dualistic designs in the map's representation of the area where the Andes and the Amazon meet, this part of the Amazonian Piedmont is a zone of exchange with the jungle below it and the mountains that surround it. The ideograms of radiant diamonds are often present in the Sibundoy Valley's textile writing found on multicolor belts that the Inga call *chumbes* and the Camëntsá *tsombiach* (see fig. 6b).

Figure 6b. *Uigsas.* Detail. Juan Carlos Jamioy. *Mapa Minga Nacional de Educación Superior de los Pueblos Indígenas.*

Chumbes—as they are called throughout most of the Andes—are also woven and worn by women from other communities in the Colombian Southwest, such as the Nasa and the Misak-Guambiana. In other parts of the Andes, as, for example, among the Quechua who live around Lake Titiqaqa in Perú, the icons on these woven belts are an expression of the traditional agricultural calendar (Granadino). Following Benjamín Jacanamijoy, the Inga-Quechua researcher from the Sibundoy Valley, chumbes are actually books several meters long that one can read either vertically or wear horizontally. In his work *Chumbe: arte inga*, he also states that the chumbe "creates a history told through signs-symbols" [supone una historia contada mediante diseños-símbolos], and functions as protection for the origin of life, the womb of a female wearer.

The radiant rhombus icons on the map are called *indi* [sun] or *indi-llajtu* [sun-feathers] in the Quechua language of the Inga, and *shinÿe* [sun] in the language of the Camëntsá (see fig. 6b). These designs can symbolize the authority exercised by elders, the awareness or dawn that the sunlight brings with it, solar cycles, or time itself, among other things.

Indi or *shinÿe*, an ideogram associated with heat-color and life, can also be connected with the profound significance of the *tulpa* or domestic hearth under which people bury a newborn's placenta, and from which things are unwound, where people share wise words as well as food and plants associated with knowledge and wisdom like coca leaves. The ideogram's duplication in Figure 6b can suggest a feminine sun (mama) and a masculine sun (taita), a pair of mythological twins, and even the double affirmation of the sun's light and pregnancy. As I will explain in detail further down, a kind of fetal spiral surges precisely from the uigsa-womb-uterus on the left.

Although similar to 6b, the figure of the taita *shinÿe* is masculine (see fig. 7). It is also the figure that presides over one section of Hugo Jamioy's *Bínÿbe oboyejuaÿeng*, as well as the ideogram from which the poetry collection as a whole takes its name.

Figure 7. Ideogram of Shinÿ or Shinÿe. Hugo Jamioy Juajibioy. *Bínÿbe oboyejuayëng/Danzantes del viento* (2005), p. 43.

The possibility of there being a female sun remains restricted to the map's symbolic possibilities. In a starry idyl that the oralitor calls "eclipse" or "*shinÿ* and *juashcón*," Jamioy describes the sun as masculine and the moon as feminine, and the two celestial bodies become united. (*Bínÿbe* [2010] 94–5). Specifically, the sun or *shinÿ* is a boy and the moon or *juashcón* a girl: "Chë shinÿ basetem tonjebtotëjajo/Juashcón jishacham entsebos" [The young sun runs / To catch the moon] ([2010] 94–5).

A number of graphic arts compliment Hugo Jamioy's oralitegraphic texts. Pastora Juajibioy, the bilingual oralitor's mother and a designer of textile ideograms, says that weaving the chumbe is a form of writing. For her, the writing used on the chumbe is the writing of the ancestors.[6] With regard to the ideograms founds on her *tsombiach*, mamá Pastora says, "I have invented a few new things. New designs" [yo me he inventado unas cosas nuevas. Dibujos nuevos]. Explaining how her weavings hold little stories, she explains, "people also use these designs in beadwork. Everything has its meaning" [en la chaquira también se plasman los dibujos. Todo tiene su significado]. However, she worries about the transmission of these ideograms and writing with threads and beads in general given that young people are now unable to recognize the significance behind them.

These explanations of contemporary Camëntsá visual language—the "symbols of life" or "beautiful writing" as Hugo Jamioy likes to call it—enable us to craft a nuanced oralitegraphic reading of "Achbe bichtaja matobopormá" [Dress Yourself with Your Language]. I have added numbers to the verses below in order to facilitate my analysis of the poem within the context of the oralitegraphic textual *continuum*:

[1] Every viajiy celebration	[1] En cada fiesta del viajiy
[2] the elders come, arriving,	[2] los taitas van llegando,
[3] they come whispering their song.	[3] vienen susurrando su canto.
[4] Dress yourself with your language.	[4] Vístete con tu lengua.
[5] Otherwise as they pass	[5] Pueda que a su paso
[6] they might not recognize you…	[6] no te reconozcan…
	(Jamioy, *Bínÿbe* [2010] 101)

Here, in both my conversation with mamá Pastora and in Jamioy's text (line 6) the word "recognize" alludes to reading or interpreting in the broadest sense, as well as identifying others intra- and interculturally through dress, writing, and language. This brief poem also gives the reader advice. Lines 1, 2, and 3 are located within a recurring ritual time, "every viajiy celebration." Viajiy is a medicinal drink (yajé or ayawasca), and its celebration is as much about viajiy's ritual consumption as it is a large annual gathering of coming together and abundance among the Camëntsá.[7] Lines 2 and 3 emphasize

---

[6] These comments by Pastora Juajibioy (mamá Pastora), as well as those that follow, come from a conversation we had at the Expoartesanías event in Bogotá, in December of 2013.
[7] The *bëtscanaté, clestrinye*, or carnival of forgiveness is an annual Camëntsá celebration in which migrants, locals, families, and authorities all come together. It is recognized as carnival within the Catholic calendar and precedes Lent, though on a deeper level it is also an annual agricultural festival that celebrates the harvest and promotes abundance, among other things. The neighboring Inga people simultaneously celebrate what they refer to in Quechua language as *hatunpuncha* [the great day].

a perspective that originates from the present tense of ritual, myth, and oral communication: "the elders come, arriving, / they come whispering their song."

Jamioy evokes orality in line 3, although the reader does not receive any information concerning the song being whispered. Even so, this detail underscores the fact that those arriving are the elders or taitas. The taitas are the principal authorities and/or doctors who work with the medicinal plant yagé (viajiy), and in a wider sense they are community members who personify the ancestors through their transmission of knowledge down through the generations (celebration of the viajiy, song). The authoritative voice in lines 4, 5, and 6, gives a command ("Dress yourself with your language") and advice (Otherwise as they pass / they might not recognize you…"). Line 4 articulates a Camëntsá metaphor insofar as both the chumbe and beadwork are forms of writing that one wears. That is, in cases like these one "wears" one's language. In addition to being a traditional girdle or belt cinched around the waist that women wear every day, during celebrations like the Viajiy chumbes can be worn as small ribbons that hang from one's headpiece. By comparison, beadwork appears in a wider variety of formats: on chest plates, on bracelets, or earrings. The drawings or designs found in beadwork and textiles are a kind of writing on the body that expresses ideas through symbols. These symbols not only have names in Camëntsá, but above all they can also be narrated, forming part of a web of interrelated narratives. Interwoven with the ideograms, these stories deal with nature and the human world, as evidenced by the names of many of the ideograms themselves: bear, heart, sun, mountains, community. Weavers do not always agree about how to interpret individual designs and, as explained by mamá Pastora, in some cases innovate on old designs or invent new ones as they weave.

Wearing one's language and, in a broader sense, wearing ideas and histories, is a very Andean and a very Camëntsá metaphor. Writing on one's clothing is an ancestral form of identification. It is for this reason that when mamá Pastora states that these designs are no longer being recognized, she is not only alerting us to the "illiteracy" of young people "unable" to read the drawings, but also to the fact that the ancestors or elders, the taitas in the poem, are likely unable to recognize these younger generations (Otherwise as they pass / they may not recognize you…"). Coming right after the command to "dress in your language," the speaker's pointing this out not only implies that the young "do not dress themselves with their language," but also that they do not know how to read the writing of their ancestors. That is, because of their ignorance and the fact that they have forgotten "the ancient writing," the taita-ancestors cannot be read by and cannot read younger generations.

At this point, we can better understand how the command and the warning contained in the poem's final three lines give voice to anxieties about the loss of identity and the intergenerational transmission of a language that one wears, that is, a language that one writes or communicates through its own dynamics and media. Here, recognition of this identity depends on the survival of a textual *continuum* formed by generational oral communication (songs, language, the viajiy celebration), embodied graphic communication (wearing one's language), and, of course, the oraliterary text itself, which is codified via alphabetic writing. In this way, then, the oral, the graphic, and the literary flow together in an intersectional field (textuality) of a bilingual poetic text, that has been edited to include page numbers and, in its first edition, ideograms that appear on chumbes (see fig. 8).

The oralitor Hugo Jamioy, the narrator-weaver mamá Pastora Juajibioy, and the graphic designer Juan Carlos Jamioy (co-creator of the Minga's map) are cognizant of the importance of rescuing and giving new life to different kinds of writing like that expressed

Acbe bichtajac matobopormá

Chë biajiyec joboyejuam or
Taitang mochantsachjajuan
mondabó chëngbe bersiayánac,
acbe bichtajac matobopormá
nderad chamojachnëngo or
ndoñ cmatjotëmba...

Vístete con tu lengua

En cada fiesta del Viajiy
los taitas van llegando vienen
susurrando su canto; vístete
con tu lengua
pueda que a su paso
no te reconozcan...

Figure 8. A bilingual oralitegraphic proposal. Hugo Jamioy Juajibioy. *Bínÿbe oboyejuayëng/Danzantes del viento* (2005), pp. 112–13.

through the ideograms on chumbes, beadwork, and even carved masks. As will be shown later on in Chapter 3, all of these elements complement *Bínÿe oboyejuagyëng*'s graphic project. For Hugo Jamioy and other writers whose texts will be interwoven into the following pages, alphabetic writing simply becomes a tool for evoking and/or recuperating "the beautiful writing" ("Pensando, hilando" 150) that has been supplanted by abstract phoneticism.

Finally, we should also emphasize the other visual sympathies that connect the Andes and the Amazon, sites of the cultural and physical intersection of the Inga and Camëntsá. These links become apparent when we compare the elongated, serpentine forms of traditional chumbes from the Sibundoy's Valley in Figure 9 with the stylized, serpentine forms of the three anthropomorphic icons in Figure 5.[8]

Figure 9. A comparison of elongated serpentiform designs on chumbes.
Top and Bottom: Author's personal collection. Left: "Chumbe inga."
Instituto Colombiano de Antropología e Historia. Right: Detail.
Juan Carlos Jamioy. *Mapa Minga Nacional de Educación Superior de los Pueblos Indígenas.*

In sum, the beaded, embroidered, or painted radiant rhombi, the quadrangular ideograms on textiles, the female attire of the mola or the chumbe, the rock designs along Amazonian Rivers, and the works of oraliture cited here, generate both a textual *continuum* and an intercultural web of oralitures and epistemic connotations related to the ancestors, the roads, the paths, the snakes, the womb, the sun, the moon, whispered/suggested orality, the origins of humanity,

---

[8] Top and bottom, the serpentine fragments of a chumbe designed and woven by mamá Pastora Juajibioy (personal collection). Top left, note the radiant rhomboidal design, which appears in Figures 6a and 6b on the map, as well as the icon *shinÿ* (sun) found in Hugo Jamioy's book in Figure 7. In the middle and on the left: an Inga chumbe from the Sibundoy Valley. In the middle and on the right, Figure 5 from the map provides a direct comparison with these anthropomorphic icons.

transformations of identity and the intergenerational transmission of language and knowledge, among other epistemological dimensions, that serve as a complement to the critical impulse.

Tawantinsuyu and Abya Yala

One of the most popular Indigenous symbols in the Andes today is called the *wiphala*, also known as the Andean flag or the rainbow flag (see fig. 10). This ideogram identifies individuals from the Andes and from Andean communities that see themselves as being the inheritors of Tawantinsuyu (Inca Empire: 1400–1532 approximately) and/or any of the cultures that preceded it (Chavín, Tiwanaku, Moche, Wari, among others).

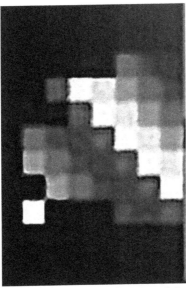

Figure 10. Wiphala (traditional Andean flag): Detail. Juan Carlos Jamioy. *Mapa Minga Nacional de Educación Superior de los Pueblos Indígenas*

The wiphala's location in the map's southwest quadrant alludes to the continuity of an Andean multicultural legacy that originally encompassed the entire mountain range, including the lands of what are now Chile, Argentina, Colombia, and Venezuela. Indeed, one of the so-called "Andean World"'s notable characteristics is the vitality of the region's pluricultural Quechua/Kichwa/Quichua inheritance.

Although he happens to be from a Spanish-speaking community, Fredy Chikangana/Wiñay Mallki recuperates Quechua or Runa Shimi as a ritual and literary language in order to reclaim this inheritance and its roots. In one of his poems he states that "Quechua sonccoycaimi" [My heart is Quechua] (*Samay* 97):

Quechua is the heart	[Quechua es el corazón
that is stirred by flutes and drums	que se agita entre flautas y tambores
in the neighing of ancient time	en el relincho del tiempo milenario
smelling of *kiñiwa* [quinoa] and toasted corn,	con olor a *kiñiwa* y maíz tostado,
where we still say: our hands	donde aún decimos: nuestras manos,
our bodies, our voice,	nuestros cuerpos, nuestra voz,
our music, our resistance	nuestra música, nuestra resistencia.]
	(97)

As can be found in Chikangana's Quechua-language poetic work, in these lines Yanakuna Mitmakuna (or Yanakuna) culture does not seem to be a predetermined ethnic identity, but something that expands into an intercultural Quechua dimension of shared feeling ("stirred by flutes and drums"); collective voice ("our voice, our music"); food sovereignty ("smelling of *kiñiwa* and toasted corn"); survival ("we still say"); ancestral identity ("our hands, our bodies"); and continuity and vitality ("in the neighing of ancient time"). The poet suggests further connections between his Yanakuna Mitmak poetics and the rainbow *wiphala* when he proclaims, "Taki nuqapi k'uichimanta / chachayri patatatatamanta urkumanta" [My songs are rainbows / that come from the mountain's heartbeat] (*Samay* 89).

Only partially translated into English as rainbow, *k'uichi* is called *cueche* among the Inga and the Yanakuna. *K'uichi* have a number of different colors and are associated with illnesses and cures. In the Inga myth, the *cuichi*-serpent or rainbow-serpent, assumes the form of a traditional healer who has a large, multi-color crown of feathers. The Inga story says that after assuming the guise of an elder Kuichi Rainbow saves the *yaya* or person in charge of Hatun Puncha [The Great Day or The Carnaval of Forgiveness], who was being persecuted by monstrous men with tails and paws, an image likely associated with the colonizers.

The Yanakuna conceive of crossroads as dark places where ghosts, the ancestors, and the *cueche* [rainbow] intermittently appear. These visions and beliefs let us grasp how the Quechuas in Peru, and the Inga and the Yanakuna in Colombia, associate images of the *k'uichi* rainbow with ancestral memory and other beliefs. For example, according to many Yanakuna people like Chikangana, the *wiphala* rainbow is a *k'uichi wiphala* (see fig. 10). In other words, the *k'uichi wiphala* is simultaneously representative of both their own identity and Pan-Quechua identity. Chikangana's poem "Yuyay yakuk" [Memory of Water] suggests this very kind of relationship:

I sing
so that the flowers and paths,
the hills and the lakes, sing;
so the moon knows that I am Yanakuna
a man of the water and the rainbow

[*Ima yaraví*
ñampi ttica maythu quinquinam yaraví
waikus pas urkus cay
yanakuna quilla yachina
inti k'uchi waiku runa.]
(*Samay* 83)

"Yuyay yakuk" is thus a poetic ritual in which Yanakuna memory is expressed via images drawn from a specific place on earth (water/ waiku/lake), and regional knowledge of the heavens (inti k'uichi/sun rainbow). Through this imagining, Chikangana appears to suggest a fullness of identity, or at least the fullness of his personal identity, which arises from the complementary relationship that exists in this particular place between the Yanakuna Mitmak—his immediate community—, and the region itself—Quechua Pan-Andeanism—, in short: the k'uichi wiphala. Finally, it is important to point out that the wiphala ideogram is more than an allusion to a PanAndean, PanIncan, or PanQuechua project. Through its multiple colors, in the context of the Educational Minga's map, the wiphala symbolizes the enormous diversity of people, forms of life, and languages that interact in the northwestern part of the continent that today we call Colombia.

The divergent spiral which appears to originate in or extend from the radiant yellow textile design in the lower right part of Figure 11, visibly expands through the Colombian Pacific—along the map's top left border—and beside where the wiphala's colors express this confluence of Andean cultures.

An extremely rainy area of the country with a number of rivers, the Pacific region runs from the collective territories of both Afro-descended people and the Indigenous Wounán and Eperara Siapidara in the South, to those of the Emberá Katío and Gunadule in the North. This part of the map stands out for the numerous superimpositions it contains, signifying the multiple positions and perspectives on the world that coexist within Colombia. Figure 11 has an enormous icon in the shape of a honeycomb that is comprised of several diamonds, which is superimposed upon an elongated spiral that is located precisely in the place where its central line begins to blur. This multi-diamond design is similar to the *molokonoutaya*, a *kanasü* or ideogram in Wayuu textile arts from the Guajira, that refe-

Figure 11. Spirals and diamonds. Detail. Juan Carlos Jamioy. *Mapa Minga Nacional de Educación Superior de los Pueblos Indígenas.*

rences the shell of the morrocoy, a turtle native to the area. Sikuani iconography from the Orinoco contains a similar ideogram that also refers to the turtle (Duque Duque 525). Another similar design is also found in the iconographic beadwork of the Emberá Eyabidá, although in this case it does not allude to turtles.

From a geometric perspective, the honeycomb design expresses variation and multiplication within a repeating structure: the diamonds repeat, in several different colors, and new figures come into view when you focus on different structural details. X's, squared crosses, L's, T's, Y's, squares, and diamond shapes are revealed as the reader follows the colored lines. The image suggests a number of potential relationships and ideas. For example, figure 11 could connote the complex coexistence of diverse civilizations and perspectives on the world, and we should keep in mind that the space on that map that this figure represents is a region that has been one of the major zones of contact and confrontation between Colombia's Afro-descended population after their liberation from slavery and the rest of the country. It is also a zone of contact between foreign explorers, colonists from the country's interior, and Indigenous communities. The double geo-positioning of the bi-colored spiral, a symbol of origin/pregnancy, and the multicolored diamonds, symbols of multiplicity and diversity, could also form an ideogram that represents the intercultural idea of Abya Yala, an expression that comes from the region's Gunadule people, and more specifically those Gunadule who live along the Atrato River.

One of the contemporary political meanings of the Chibcha expression *Abya Yala* is "land in a state of full maturity." Abya Yala thus symbolically differs from colonizing images of the "New World," whether these be as the *terra nullius* found on many European maps, or the popular and cinematic image of a red cross blazoned across the white sails of Colombus's ships. Following the political interpretation proposed by the Aymara activist Takir Mamani in the 1980s, "land in a state of full maturity" is an image of the earth itself, if not also one that also refers to plants and even agriculture, and in this sense can be expressed via a fully developed spiral like the one in Figure 11. This is even more true when the divergent spiral finds itself united with the diamond image of the honeycomb.

Within this ordering of things, the word *Yala*—earth, mountain, territory, region, continent (Orán and Wagua 100)—has visual sympathies with the graph of the earthen spiral, while the word *abe* or *ablis* [blood] (19) can refer to the multiple multicolored diamonds that are similar to the cell structures of honeycombs or even whole beehives. In effect, other potential relationships between the word yala and the spiral on the map are derived from the word's etmology in Chibcha or Dulegaya, insofar as the earth is a support (bone), the place of origin (mother), and protection (sustenance).

The Kichwa researcher Armando Muyolema defines Abya Yala as "an alternative civilizing referent that is radically other" [referente civilizatorio alternativo, radicalmente otro] (348), and he proposes using the term to construct a critical reading of Latinamericanism and of mestizaje. Following Muyolema, Abya is the mother and Yala woman (346). In his polemical reading, he argues that the mestizo is a being who, by denying who he is, has distanced himself from his Indigenous mother while embracing his European father, acts that ultimately make him an unviable political subject. According to Muyolema, the political positioning of Abya Yala reaffirms the Indigenous mother and the emergence of a continental civilizing project that have been erased by the very idea of Latin America.

Following a different line of argument, Gunadule linguist Manibinigdiginya/Abadio Green states that Yala, "references the ancestral territories of the Gunadule and comes from the words 'protect,' 'care,' 'carry'; g(ala) that means 'bone'; gu(e) which is the verb 'to be' and (a)li which refers to a 'beginning,' 'origin,' 'start'" [hace referencia al territorio originario de los gunadule y viene de las palabras "proteger", "cuidar", "llevar"; g(ala) que indica "hueso"; gu(e) que es el verbo "ser" y (a)li que hace referencia a "comienzo", "origen", "inicio"] (*Anmal gaya burba* 139). According to Manibinigdiginya, Abya Yala also refers to childbirth, the blood-bone of the earth, and at the same time the gathering of blood that has spilled in battles caused by the European invasion all throughout the continent.[9] Following the etymologies that Manibinigdiginya provides, we can build an argument that to inhabit this continent is to live on bloody land, land that bleeds, land that gives birth, land that has given birth. In short, as a result of the encounter and conflict between diverse peoples and civilizations, we are living within a wound and a constant (re)creation. Manibinigdiginya proposes that we speak of "Abya Yala's mestizo culture" [la cultura mestiza de Abya Yala] (*Anmal gaya burba* 51) while at the same time recognizing that

> the decolonization of knowledge is necessary because colonialism has done a lot of damage to us, not only to Indigenous people but also to the sons and daughters of the colonizers themselves, the mestizos and mestizas of this continent, who have been denied their Indigenous mother, their African mother, their European mother, and their Arab grandmother; we live in a society built and developed on the patriarchal, machista, Catholic, and individualist model of the Spanish.

> [hay que seguir descolonizando el saber, porque la colonia nos hizo mucho daño, no solamente a los pueblos indígenas sino a sus propios hijos e hijas, los mestizos y las mestizas de este continente, a quienes les negaron a su "madre india", a su "madre negra", a su "madre europea" y a su "abuela árabe"; una sociedad construida y edificada desde el modelo patriarcal, machista, católico e individualista de los castellanos.] (46)

As explained by the Maya K'iche' intellectual from Guatemala Emilio del Valle Escalante/Emil' Keme, as a civilizational project Abya Yala, "is not exclusive to Indigenous Peoples" [no es exclusivo de los Pueblos Originarios] (14). He goes on to add, "it's worth emphasizing that those of us who agree with this project do so as a way to transcend the oppressive politics established by colonialism.

---

[9] Manibinigdiginya shared this idea with me in a conversation in February 2013.

It's about forging a Hemispheric and transcontinental Indigeneity …
In this sense Abya Yala as a project implies global conversations and
exchange" [vale subrayar que quienes nos adherimos a este proyecto lo hacemos como una forma de trascender políticas opresivas es-
tablecidas por el colonialismo. Se trata de forjar una indigeneidad
hemisférica y transcontinental … En este sentido el proyecto de
Abya Yala implica una conversación de intercambio global] (14).

The Gunadule poet, linguist, and researcher Aiban Wagua says
that "Abiayala" is the fourth name of mother earth, there being three
previous epochs that have renewed the planet through cataclysmic
events (*En defensa* 347). Gwalagunyala ended with cyclones. Dagar-
gunyala ended in darkness. Dinguayala ended with fire. Abiayala
would have ended with tsunamis and floods, but its land was saved.
Within this context, Orán and Wagua's Gunadule-Spanish dictionary goes beyond simply defining the term by providing a synthesis
of the different meanings and events that are associated with Abya
Yala as a word-symbol: "a rescued land, land of blood, mature land,
the American continent" [territorio salvado, tierra de sangre, tierra
madura, continente americano] (20).

Owing in part to the Indigenous peoples' struggle for survival
and continuance on the continent, this association of the land with
blood is expressed in one of Wagua's poems, "River of Verses:"

Rivers of verses	[Torrentes de versos
creak, armed in the mountains of Abia Yala.	crujen armados por las sierras de Abia Yala.
The Indian closes his fist to dance to life	El indio cierra el puño para danzar a la vida
Death is almost his sister	La muerte es casi su hermana
because she's the only one	porque es la única
who does not abandon	que no le abandona,
or betray him.	ni le traiciona.]
	(*Kaaubi* 131)

In this sense, the intertextual connection between the multicolored diamonds and the bicolored spiral in Figure 11 suggests the
idea of earthy/civilizatory maturity that is associated with Abya Yala's ideological positions. This connection also suggests the kinds
of intercultural practices that this positioning demands in order to
avoid becoming a new kind of exclusive radicalism. In sum, Figure
11's polyvalence, its graphic symbols of pregnant spirals and webbed
cells-honeycombs that symbolize diversity, conversation, and coexistence from multiple origins, bloodlines, bones, and races, suggests
these aspects of a mature land, capable of symbolizing the whole
continent.

SITUATING THE HEAD

Figure 12 corresponds to the Atlantic or Caribbean Region. A radiant, red design, its triangular shape suggests the country's tallest mountains in the Sierra Nevada de Santa Marta, or Gonawindua in Iku.

Figure 12. Triangle and stepped crosses. Detail. Juan Carlos Jamioy. *Mapa Minga Nacional de Educación Superior de los Pueblos Indígenas.*

The icon's interior contains a different kind of diamond than those seen in Figures 6b and 7, the basic design of which would seem to function as a way to give a 3D effect to the mountains mentioned above. Beneath this triangle you can see four stepped crosses diagonally descending from a white rhombus, each one composed of little diamonds that symbolize the mountains or, as their inhabitants prefer to call them, the heart of the world. Given their quadripartite sense of space, the stepped crosses—a design that recurs in Nariño metalwork and in pre-Hispanic ceramics, as well as in contemporary Cubeo basketry in the Amazon—are appropriate symbols for how the contemporary Chibcha see the mountains of the Sierra Nevada as a "table" whose legs are the four Indigenous groups that live there: the Kankuamo, the Iku (Arhuaco), the Wiwa, and the Kogui. In addition, the ideogram of stepped triangles, known as *chinuzatu*, can be found in the textile writing of Iku woven bags. According to Luz Helena Ballestas Rincón, a professor who specializes in textile iconography, this representation "recalls the movement of a rattlesnake" [recuerda el movimiento de la culebra cascabel] (26).

That said, this proliferation of diamonds can also suggest the number of different Chibcha peoples whose territory extends beyond the "classic" ethnicized land of the Sierra. As such, these designs may equally evoke the Ette in the Ariguani and the Barí in Perijá. Devastated from putting up armed resistance to the Spanish into the seventeenth century, the Tairona are the region's best-known pre-Hispanic group. Their architectonic legacy is present in a number of their former population centers in the form of stepped platforms, terraces, and stone stairs that extend for hundreds of miles throughout the Sierra Nevada's lower and middle-elevations. Teyuna, the world-famous Lost City of the Tairona, is found in the Sierra's northern slope.

The visual recurrence of stepped designs in this section of the map is highly suggestive if we consider that a number of the region's Indigenous Peoples continue to engage in agricultural, religious, and commercial exchanges throughout the Sierra's various elevations (see fig. 12). Likewise, in the upper-right of Figure 12 we can observe the lower part of an orange textile motif that forms part of a larger icon, similar in shape to the letter Z, that becomes the lower part of the Guajira Peninsula at its terminus. This fragment coincides with the northernmost point of Spanish colonization, while at the same time signaling a zone of cultural confluence between different Chibcha groups, as well as between the cultures and languages of the Wayuu (from the Arawak language family) and the Yukpa (who pertain to the Caribe language family). In this sense we can assert that Figure 12 is one of the Map's most symbolically dense areas.

Figure 13 is a tricolor icon that appears to be "incomplete" or asymmetric on its right side and has a good deal in common with one of the anthropomorphic ideograms that is commonly found of the woven bags of the Iku (Arhuaco) (see fig. 13).

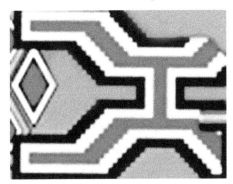

Figure 13. Anthropomorphic ideogram. Detail. Juan Carlos Jamioy. *Mapa Minga Nacional de Educación Superior de los Pueblos Indígenas.*

An abstract human figure with its hands and feet extended to form an "X," some weavers say that this ideogram is Serankua, one of the most important spiritual fathers in Ikụ cosmovision. The iconographic appendix of *Lenguaje creativo de las etnias indígenas de Colombia* [Creative Language of Colombia's Indigenous Peoples] identifies a similar design framed between two square grids as the ideogram for female thought (Duque Duque 527). As with the polyvalent nature of a number of picto-ideographic systems the world over, in the processes of abstraction and graphic elaboration weavers will frequently omit one or several of a given ideogram's most recognizable aspects.

As one finds in contemporary Ikụ woven bags, perhaps Figure 13 simply omits the figure's head. Armando Aroca Araújo, a Colombian mathematician, has studied this particular ideogram, and he identifies it as Kaku Serankwa or the Father-Creator of the Sierra Nevada (70). A similar design appears in the following picture of Ikụ woven bags, on the bottom row, second picture from the left (see fig. 14).

Rotating the ideogram in Figure 13 brings a very suggestive interpretation, as this change of positioning may indicate a complementary design for a head, or even an eye, through the red and white diamond at the top (see fig. 15). Rotating Figure 13 means overturning the design, elevating the side to the top, such that Figure 15 literally represents an eye or a mirrored vision. Thus, our reading of the anthropomorphic ideogram acquires new meanings when we turn it upside down, something that reminds us of the need to approach both the map's cartographic proposal and textualities themselves through multiple perspectives.

The complex designs that stand out on the center-right of the map evoke the artistic basketry of the eastern grasslands in the macro-region of Orinoquia. These intricate designs tend to be found on the *guapa* of the Sikuani, and are better known as *balay* among communities from the Amazonian region (see fig. 16).[10] A similar type

---

10 Among the Cubeo in Vaupés, the *balay* is, "a round and concave weaving that varies in size, and is used to serve cazabe (cake of bitter yuca). The balay requires specialized knowledge regarding how to dye the fibre with natural pigments, how to weave, how to add figures to the textile, as well as how to explain the name and significance of each figure" [tejido redondo y cóncavo de diferentes tamaños, utilizado para servir el cazabe (la torta de yuca brava), tejidos a partir de conocimientos especializados sobre cómo teñir la fibra con pigmentos naturales, cómo es la trama del tejido, cómo plasmar figuras en él, y cuál es el nombre y significado de cada figura] (qtd. in Duque Duque 79).

Garwa: Padre de los caminos	Kunsumana Cheirua: Pensamiento del hombre	Kambiru: Cola de alacrán	Chinuzatu: Las cuatro esquinas del mundo
Zikamu: Gusano ciempiés	Kunsumana A'mia: Pensamiento de la mujer	Kanzachu: Hoja de árbol	Sariwuwu: meses del embarazo
Urúmu: Caracol	Háku: La serpiente de cascabel	Gwirkunu: Cerros y lagunas	Makuru: Gallinazo
Gamako: Rana	Kaku Seránkwa: Padre Creador de la Sierra	Phundwas: Picos Nevados de la Sierra	Kutía: Costillas

Figure 14. A table comparing ideographs on mochilas or *tutu* of the Iku People. Armando Aroca Araujo. "Una propuesta metodológica en etnomatemáticas," p. 70.

Figure 15. Ideogram with a diamond. Detail. Juan Carlos Jamioy. *Mapa Minga Nacional de Educación Superior de los Pueblos Indígenas.*

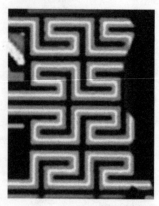

Figure 16a. Basketry designs. Detail. Juan Carlos Jamioy. *Mapa Minga Nacional de Educación Superior de los Pueblos Indígenas.*

of labyrinthine ideogram is associated with designs with the Curri-paca snake in basketry by the Tukano of Vaupés (Ballestas Rincón 63). Here the phosphorescent color scheme also evokes the *fosfenos* or geometric figures associated with the drawings or symbolic vi-sions produced through the ingestion of medicinal drinks such as yajé (ayawasca; *Banisteriopsis caapi*), the ritual consumption is both a purgative, and a way to acquire knowledge of value to the communi-ty. As articulated by the anthropologist Gerardo Reichel-Dolmatoff, those who have consumed yajé have visions that tend to take place in public spaces like common houses (malocas), as well as on *balayes*, and even on people's skin in the case of communities from the Tu-kano linguistic family.

A poem by the Amazonian poet and singer Anastasia Candre (Okaina-uitoto/murui) interweaves these relationships (plant, ser-pent, painting on the skin) as the spirit of yajé speaks intimately with the person who has consumed it:

I, I am yajé, you can't tell me who you are	[Yo, soy el yagé, no puede decirme quién eres
I am, your grandfather	Soy, tu abuelo
Boa, that's how I manifest myself	Boa, así me presento
My presence is frightening	Mi presencia es miedosa
I, I am yajé	Yo, soy el yagé
I am like the jaguar, I sit, with my painted skin	Soy como el jaguar, que me siento, con mi piel pintada
Don't be scared of me, embrace me!	No te asustes de mi presencia, ¡abrázame!]
	("Unao" 215)

Drinking yajé and the ritual consumption of plants like tobacco and coca are epistemic practices that imply an awakening, a situating of one's thoughts that tends to be expressed through advice or ritual warnings that are associated with the plant. In this sense the poetic voice identifies with yajé insofar as it says "my presence is frightening." Even though yajé is not a traditional medicinal plant among the Okaina and the Uitoto (Murui Muina), in both Candre's poem and in the poet's journey, the ritual consumption of yajé is associated with related concepts like the intergenerational transmission of knowledge ("I am, your grandfather"), the strong word (*rafue*) of healing ("I, I am yajé / I am like the jaguar"), and pedagogical words of advice (*yetarafue*) that one internalizes in the same fashion as one fills a basket with knowledge (kɨrɨgaɨ), that is, one incorporates them into one's own body and consciousness ("Don't be scared of me, embrace me!"). According to the text, knowing implies giving oneself over to a force that envelopes like the boa, or that devours like the jaguar.

When we rotate Figure 16a, the design acquires a different kind of dynamic (see fig. 16b). Carefully observing the multiple configurations of this new situation, we find two swastikas traced by green lines with a phosphorescent yellow border on both sides.

Figure 16b. Swastikas. Detail. Juan Carlos Jamioy. *Mapa Minga Nacional de Educación Superior de los Pueblos Indígenas.*

The composition's center consists of a figure similar to the letter "E" (see fig. 6a), only now it is upside down outlined by red lines with a yellow border, becoming a kind of static, abstract, headless anthropomorph with its extremities outstretched. The swastikas give the design a tremendous amount of dynamism. In effect, if we look closely, the two figures along the sides that are formed by the swastikas suggest two more anthropomorphic figures moving their hands and feet.

The visual relationships that exist between these sets of anthropomorphic figures who are raising and/or moving their extremities can be better understood by comparing different pictographic (those that appear to be more "realistic") and ideographic representations (those that are geometric or more figurative in appearance, whose ideas are usually recognizable through by a piece of the figure or its full representation) found on the Minga's map (see fig. 17) .

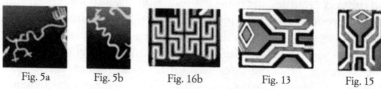

Fig. 5a   Fig. 5b   Fig. 16b   Fig. 13   Fig. 15

Figure 17. A composed comparison of details of anthropomorphic figures with their extremities extended. Juan Carlos Jamioy. *Mapa Minga Nacional de Educación Superior de los Pueblos Indígenas.*

Having what appear to be three toes on its feet, and a large arm whose hand evokes the hands found in rock art from the southern part of the continent, Figure 5a has metahuman characteristics.[11] Figure 5b elevates its "arms" and extends its serpentine-shaped appendage-foot to represent part of the Putumayo River on the Map. Figure 16b is three anthropomorphic figures, one standing still in the center, and two moving beside it. Their extremities are raised as in 5a and 5b, but as in Figure 13, their heads are not represented. As seen here, when we turn Figure 13 over it seems to recover its head, because when we rotate it to the left it overlaps with the red diamond design that becomes a kind of eye-head (see fig. 15). In short, the configuration of this series of diamonds stepped crossed and "mirrored" visions, shows that, despite the apparent scriptural (rock art, basketry, textiles) and cultural differences among Indigenous nations represented on the Educational Minga's map, many of these images suggest related concepts and what we can understand as visual affinities among them (Allen 153). The symbolic frameworks that generate these kinds of visual expressions are not only contemporaneous with oraliture and literary proposals of Indigenous authors in Colombia and throughout the continent, but also participate in similar projects that seek to exercise representational sovereignty through

---

[11] For example, in places where ancient pictographs have been recorded like in Colombia's Guaviare' Chiribiquete mountain range or the cave of the hands in Argentina. These kinds of hands can be considered proto-signatures, usually collective in nature, on the walls of different rocky shelters, as well as an affirmation of the communicative creativity that arises from them, like a gesture or an ideographic outline.

the representation of Indigenous perspectives about themselves and the rest of the world. In this sense these readings are connected with "the possibility for [an] appreciation and interpretation of Indigenous Literatures [that is] informed by multiple, distinct systems of Indigenous aesthetics across tribal, national, geographic, and cultural borders" (Allen 106).

As I will discuss in greater detail in the following chapters, oraliterary proposals like those of Hugo Jamioy and Fredy Chikangana/Wiñay Mallki can also be understood through their evocation and incorporation of visual aesthetics derived from their communities' textile arts, even as they are also oralitegraphies that transcend national and cultural borders. For example, these authors have creative and intercultural relationships with the concept-practice of oraliture first formulated in Senegal, Africa, by Yoro Fall, and later theorized in the Wallmapu Mapuche (Chile) by Elicura Chihuailaf. As explained by Emilio del Valle Escalante/Emil' Keme, however, we should also recognize that, as compared to oralitegraphic proposals, diverse systems of ideo-pictographic communication, operate in different spheres. These may even be more effective within those spheres than alphabetic writing, insofar as they are expressed to members of the community whose ability to read and interpret them comes from their experiences as members of those communities, as opposed to from books.[12] Following these observations, the Educational Minga's map is above all else an intercultural proposal, or as I am referring to them here, a mirrored vision, given that it questions conventional images of the nation, and nothing less than the image of the nation itself, through its multimedia representation of Colombia. In this sense, although the map respects the frame of the country's borders, it also proposes the series of different textures and meanings that we have emphasized here through these oralitegraphic readings.

The Educational Minga's map can be read as a concrete proposal that comes out of Colombia's Indigenous movement. In 2010 it had the more immediate function of advertising the country's national pedagogical minga. As a poster that was both printed and distributed via the internet, the map was interpreted through diverse personal and community experiences, generating a common symbol—not "a single symbol"—or more precisely a shared horizon. Interculturally the map seeks to affirm the kind of peoplehood described by Ruth

----

[12] Keme articulated this in a personal communication in 2014.

Moya. Writing about the intercultural challenges of revising our understandings of the continent, the Ecuadorian pedagogue writes that "for Indigenous peoples the concept of unity has more to do with the concept of their unity as 'peoples' and as 'nations'" [para los indios el concepto de unidad más bien tiene que ver con el concepto de unidad como "pueblos" y como "naciones"] (Moya and Moya 70).

The Pluriscriptural Minga Map

The Minga map's symbolic intentions are thrown into further relief when we analyze the two zigzag figures that correspond to Colombia's two geographic extremes: the Guajira Peninsula (see fig. 18) and the Amazon (see fig. 19). While they recur in a number of different textile arts, through their carto-ideographic location these zigzag figures evoke the *kanasü* or ideograms from Wayuu textiles. These zigzagging *kanasü* or *wayuu kanas* can frequently be found in their multicolored *süi* "chinchorros" or hammocks and *susu* "handwoven bags."

These kinds of ideograms hold multiple meanings and tend to change from weaver-to-weaver. This simple zigzag design can symbolize hooks in the domestic space where one hangs different objects or cooking utensils in the kitchen, and one commonly sees the handwoven bags on which these designs appear hanging from hooks in Wayuu homes (see fig. 18). They appear as an intracultural image in a poem by Vito Apüshana that taken out of context is almost incomprehensible. Directing itself to the *arijuna* "non-wayuu" the poetic voice says, "you will bring nothing back with you if you don't hang your fears in the family's woven bags" [nada se llevarán sino cuelgan sus miedos en el interior de las mochilas familiares] (*Shiinalu'uirua* 64).

Figure 18. Zigzag representing the Guajira Peninsula. Detail. Juan Carlos Jamioy. *Mapa Minga Nacional de Educación Superior de los Pueblos Indígenas.*

The two parts of this zigzag in the Minga's map correspond visually to the low Guajira (below), a region colonized by the Spaniards, and the high Guajira (above), a region that the Spanish empire was unable to dominate, and were the Wayuunaiki, the Wayuu language, is still prevalent (see fig. 18).

Figure 19 is another kind of zigzag comprised of two spiraled rectangles containing several firey triangles on a yellow background. The particularities of its iconography (polychromatic, multiplicity) may refer to the previously mentioned ancestral serpent, water in the broadest sense, or the great diversity of languages and communities in the Amazonian region when compared to the preeminence of the Wayuu in Guajira's monochromatic and uniform representation (see fig. 18). The topmost rectangle in Figure 19's zigzag corresponds to a jungle zone within the Amazon, while the bottom rectangle would represent the outermost limits of the Amazonian region where it connects to the Amazon River, and so is a zone of contact and exchange where three national borders (Colombia, Brasil, Perú) come together.

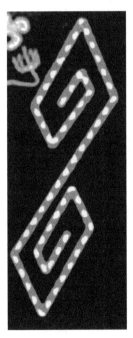

Figure 19. Zigzag representing the Department of Amazonas region. Detail. Juan Carlos Jamioy. *Mapa Minga Nacional de Educación Superior de los Pueblos Indígenas.*

Within this order of images and ideas, the dry and desert-like Guajira represented on top (see fig. 18) is contrasted with the humid, jungly Amazon below (see fig. 19). However, the two zigzags complement each other visually insofar as they are the two extremes of the national whole. In effect, the zigzag icon is reproduced at the map's extreme edges, while the textile motif of the double "E" repeats conspicuously at the map's center, almost like a chumbe girding the national body (see fig. 20).

The repetitions formed by the two "E"'s diverging from the central band, and the two "E"'s facing left in the East, are less evident than those of the zigzags (see fig. 20).

Figure 20. Repetition of the two "E"s. Details. Juan Carlos Jamioy. *Mapa Minga Nacional de Educación Superior de los Pueblos Indígenas.*

The geometric stairs are another repetition represented on the map by the stepped crosses (left) that are known as *chakanas* in the Andes, as well as by the *wiphala* (right), another of the Andean world's principal symbols (see fig. 21).

Figure 21. Geometrically staggered designs. Details. Juan Carlos Jamioy. *Mapa Minga Nacional de Educación Superior de los Pueblos Indígenas.*

A number of figures also repeat, such as triangular and/or diamond designs (see fig. 22), divergent spirals (see fig. 23), human figures with serpentine appendages (see fig. 5). There are also webbed groupings whose chromatic assortment symbolizes multiplicity and relatedness through the different patterns they have in common (see fig. 24), particularly as they represent different areas and civilizations that comprise Colombia's linguistic and cultural fabric (see fig. 25).

Figure 22. Radiant diamonds and triangles. Details. Juan Carlos Jamioy. *Mapa Minga Nacional de Educación Superior de los Pueblos Indígenas.*

Figure 23. Divergent spirals. Detail. Juan Carlos Jamioy. *Mapa Minga Nacional de Educación Superior de los Pueblos Indígenas.*

Figure 24. Net-shaped groupings. Details. Juan Carlos Jamioy. *Mapa Minga Nacional de Educación Superior de los Pueblos Indígenas.*

Figure 25. Civilization nodes (Andes, Caribbean, Pacific, Amazon, Orinoquia). Details. Juan Carlos Jamioy. *Mapa Minga Nacional de Educación Superior de los Pueblos Indígenas.*

In effect, these reiterations, chromatic variations, correspon-
dences, conjugations, and visual contrasts give the map's meta-alpha-
betic, cartographic writing a rhythmic quality, while at the same time
overturning the conventional imagining of Colombia by providing
the country with a mirror image of itself, its roots, its present, and its
undeniable millenarian plurality.

Given the recognizable international value that comes with conventional maps, Colombia's official map was designed according to
patterns of representation that reaffirm the country's borders, representing the codes of nationhood via the recurrence of alphabetic
writing, colors, and other conventional signs (points or lines, for example). Even in early colonial maps attributed to Diego de Torres y
Moyachoque, a Muisca cacique from Turmequé, alphabetic writing
is already a prominent compliment to a kind of pictorial representation that falls outside of pre-Hispanic Muisca graphic traditions
(see fig. 26). These are represented through drawings of Indigenous
parishes, a canoe with Indigenous rowers on a newly baptized Magdalena River, and a Spanish language gloss.

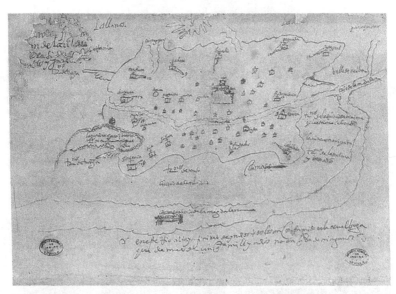

Figure 26. Map attributed to the Cacique de Turmequé. Carl Henrik Langebaek
Rueda. *Los herederos del pasado. Indígenas y pensamiento criollo en Colombia
y Venezuela,* p. 67.

Although it is uncertain if he was really the person who drew
them, scholars attribute two maps to the Turmequé cacique: a map

of the province of Santa Fe (see fig. 26), from around 1578, and another map of the province of Tunja. We can understand the different letters, lists of grievances, and maps that are attributed to Torres y Moyachoque to be some of the earliest elaborations of an Indigenous epistolary literature of denunciation and resistance. In the lower part of the map you can read, "Canoe on the Magdalena River. Along this river there was an infinite number of Indians, all of them having been destroyed because the Spanish force them to row incessantly on the river. From the over fifty thousand Indians that there once were, none remain" [Canoa del río Magdalena. En este río había infinidad de indios, todos los han consumido en el cruel boga que más de cincuenta mil indios no han quedado ningunos] (Langebaek, 67). Despite the undeniable personal interests of the nascent Indigenous elite and their desires to build new subjects and colonial powers capable of preserving their privileges over the so-called "natives," cartographic visions like Torres y Moyachoque's exercised a kind of collective Indigenous self-representation from the colony.

We can thus assert that the Educational Minga's map is the first map to be designed completely from multiple traditional and contemporary Indigenous forms of writing. Unfortunately, the map has not been re-used publically since its release in 2010, and to the best of my knowledge no one has written any critical commentary about it. Even the map's designer, Juan Carlos Jamioy, seemed surprised that I was asking about it when we spoke over the phone. Jamioy recognized that the map was incredibly significant and that its design provoked conversations with a number of his Indigenous colleagues who identified with different aspects of the map's symbolic textures.

You can now find a copy of the map in the ONIC's Office of Education, perhaps as a symbol of an intercultural challenge that it was not prepared for at the end of the millennium's first decade. In a sense, this chapter is not only an exercise in interpretation, but also a response to the pedagogical challenge issued by the Minga, insofar as it is geared towards stimulating readings, conversations, and new avenues for the dissemination of and collaboration on oralitegraphic textualities.

As a polyphonic, multimedia image of Colombia rooted in different pictographic forms of writing (basketry, textiles, rock art), the Educational Minga of Colombia's Indigenous Peoples' poster-map holds a number of symbolic and political challenges. On the one hand, the map is clearly based upon Colombia's traditional outline, and in this regard it does not negate the national cartographic framework. On the other hand, by recurring, differing, and relating to multiple visual logics, the map's polyvalent lines-textures, defy and transcend the lines that conventionally mark the republic's borders. In fact, the wide range of connections that exist among these textualities and other systems of Indigenous writing throughout the continent open up a space in which we can rethink the country through transIndigenous and transnational connections. For example, as we saw in Chikangana's poetry, the *wiphala* (see fig. 10) is a Panandean symbol used throughout the region that, through the oraliture project promoted by Elicura Chihuailaf can be also be understood as representing an ancestral Panandeanism that radiates from other centers like the Wallmapu in Chile.

Symbolic and territorial sovereignty are central themes in contemporary Indigenous literature and oraliture; I agree with Kichwa intellectual Armando Muyolema when he says that "Indigenous literatures from Abya Yala represent a political positioning and particular locus of enunciation from which the Indigenous subject articulates its languages and politics" [las literaturas indígenas de Abya Yala representan un posicionamiento político y un lugar de enunciación particular desde el cual el sujeto indígena articula sus lenguajes y sus políticas] (qtd. in Arias, Cárcamo-Huechante, and Del Valle Escalante 9). With regard to the Educational Minga's map, at first glance it seems as though the map repeats the framework of the Nation-State, a framework that was neither approved by nor done in consultation with the country's Indigenous communities. Nonetheless, its textual proposal symbolically transcends that this same conventional framework. Official maps of Colombia that have been approved by the Instituto Geográfico Agustín Codazzi (IGAC; Agustin Codazzi Geographic Institute) are dominated by alphabetic writing and internationally recognizable graphic conventions, such as the use of words written in Latin script in order to denote cities, as well as different shades of green and blue to represent land and water.[13] As we have seen before when referring to the areas and settlements that preceded the present-day border, the Minga's map possesses a similar international character through its connections to regional graphic conventions whose histories transcend those of Latin America's contemporary national borders.

The petroglyphs from the Caquetá River are a concrete example of this transregionalism (see fig. 5), as we can relate the raised

---

[13] IGAC-approved maps can be found at http://igac.gov.co

extremities of their anthropomorphic figures to some of the figures found in the ancient murals in the Chiribiquete mountain range that lies within the Amazonian Department of Guaviare in Colombia, among other pictographic traditions (see fig. 27).

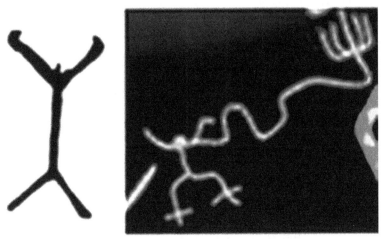

Figure 27. Comparison of anthropomorphic representations. Left: Pictograph from Chiribiquete. Carlos Castaño-Uribe. "Tradición cultural Chiribiquete." Right: Detail. Juan Carlos Jamioy. *Mapa Minga Nacional de Educación Superior de los Pueblos Indígenas.*

Carlos Castaño-Uribe calls the designs in Figure 28 "filiform," or threadlike. According to him, these designs correspond to some of the earliest figures drawn by the Chiribiquete culture, whose drawings, "leave no doubt as to the presence of man and his pictographic activity between 1500 and 500 BCE" [no dejan duda de la presencia del hombre y actividades pictográficas en el intervalo entre por lo menos 1500 y 500 años AP] (Castaño-Uribe). Chiribiquete filiform figures tend to be in groups that have noticeable visual sympathies with textile and basketry designs represented in the Educational Minga's map (see fig. 28). The anthropo-serpentine forms in the jungly southeast make more sense through their graphic connections with other Amazonian pictorial languages (see fig. 5). My argument here, however, is not that these cultures are directly related or that they influenced each other. Rather, through the notion of oralitegraphies whose intersections can be understood as transgressing the frame of any given nationality, culture, or graphic system, I expand how we can creatively read across such texts.

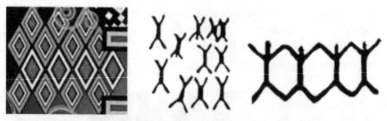

Figure 28. Comparison between threadlike figures and designs in the Minga's
map. Left: Detail. Juan Carlos Jamioy. *Mapa Minga Nacional de Educación
Superior de los Pueblos Indígenas*. Center and Right: Picto-ideograms from
Chiribiquete. Carlos Castaño-Uribe. "Tradición cultural Chiribiquete."

For example, we can take another look at the zigzag designs that
open and close the extreme top-bottom and north-south on the map
(see figs. 18 and 19). These designs can be found in a number of
the country's Indigenous pictographic systems, although its polyvalent character means that it does not have a single, unified meaning
across all Indigenous cultures. In the Putumayo, the Quechua-speaking Inga call this zigzag design *kutey* (to give back). According to
Benjamin Jacanamijoy, the *kutey* or a repeating double zigzag on
an Inga chumbe, "symbolizes a cycle" given that, "you move from
one extreme to the other, always returning" [simboliza un ciclo …
te trasladas de un extremo a otro para siempre devolverte]. When
we consider this idea in the context of oralitegraphic writing, we
can assert that this kind of symbolic cartography implies the graphic
materialization of a cycle of interactions. Within these cycles diverse
regimes of representation interact as a way of affirming multiple
worlds (a pluriverse), diverse origins, and the pluri-territoriality and
convergence of centers in the context of a "Colombia" that precedes
the stories and images of the nation-state, while at the same time
speaking to a united Colombia that imagines new horizons beyond
colonial, national, and indigenist homogeneity, and the superficial
tolerance of discursive multiculturalism.

A holistic perspective on this map lets us appreciate the necessary coexistence of multiple systems of communication and representation, which, as can be seen in the complete poster, include pho-
netic-alphabetic writing (see fig. 29).

In sum, the map produces both a mirrored vision and a series of
oralitegraphies. The map is a mirrored vision insofar as it disrupts,
stirs up, and gives back (*kutey*) different images of territory and
knowledge, while doing so through the frame of the country as it ap-

Figure 29. Poster from the National Minga on Higher Education. Juan Carlos Jamioy. *Mapa Minga Nacional de Educación Superior de los Pueblos Indígenas.*

pears and is conventionally accepted nationally and internationally. The map also presents us with a series of oralitegraphic textualities insofar as takes shape in the dynamic confluence of diverse systems of pictoideographic or ideo-symbolic-literary communication, systems whose symbols transcend—but do not negate—the nation's conventional shape, thereby inscribing themselves as a particular kind of international cartography. When we remember that the map's visual extremes are reiterated by the zigzag ideograms, however, we can also incorporate the textile concept of *kutey*, in whose cycle, "you move from one extreme to the other, but always return" [te trasladas de un extremo a otro para siempre devolverte] (Jacanamijoy, *Chumbe*). We can also assert that there is no top and no bottom, nor a North nor a South, but a constant writing and rewriting that takes place, moving from one extreme to the other, as if we were describing a textile on a loom whose textual punctuation marks enclose, but do not limit, the pluriterritorial map's possible readings and status as a palimpsest. In short, the zigzag's symbolic resonance can be expanded via the Inga-Quechua symbol of *kutey*, given that this lets us understand how the map also operates as *pachakutey* (*pachakuti*), that is, as a spatio-temporal movement, as a questioning of the national territory's conventional image of, and above all else as a returning of dominant culture's gaze, given that this symbolic cartography opens up new possibilities, precedents, and future visions of the nation and it narratives.

From this perspective, the Educational Minga's map does not deny Colombia's existence, indigenize the country either, or ignore the presence of the non-Indigenous peoples. As is the case with Manibinigdiginya, the map interpelates the country through pedagogies that arise from Indigenous communities. As in Fredy Chikangana/ Wiñay Mallki's work, the map gives it an acestral memory as if from the depths of daydreams. The map "re-alphabetizes" the country with beautiful writing and symbols of life, and problematizes it in the way that Apüshana does by giving Colombia a number of different names. It sings the country back, rhythmically, and in different languages, like Anastasia Candre, and unwinds the country like one of Jacanamijoy's chumbes. Finally, the map manages to de-subordinate the country by giving it other readings, other colors, other perspectives, and other textures.

CONCLUSION

To paraphrase the Camëntsá oralitor Hugo Jamioy, the Educational Minga's map educates us to ameliorate our "Indigenous analphabetism." Its cartographic mirrored visions and oralitegraphies enable the country to be connected to, questioned from, rooted in, and read from a number of different intertextual ways of understanding writing, orality, senses, and cosmovisions. We should remember that this cartographic proposal comes from a country in which numerous Indigenous peoples feel that they are not only not represented, but that they are forcibly included or excluded at the whims of the state's multiculturalist tendencies. Within the reading I have proposed here, the designs that make up the map are pieces of other perspectives on a Colombia that is not only pluriethnic and multicultural but also plurinational and multiterritorial, a country in which the demands and projects of Indigenous peoples are not simply spoken about. These plurinational and multicultural dimensions—which are not mentioned in the 1991 Constitution—remain vague despite the "recognition" of "ethnic minorities" who find themselves under the paternalist care of the government and other institutions, as well as within the context of the limited unity of Colombia's multicultur- alist, tolerant nation-state. Regarding the intercultural educational experience of neighboring Ecuador, Ruth Moya states that:

> As compared to the past where only the elite argued for their abil- ity to represent the entire nation, we must recognize that Indige- nous movements now seek to represent themselves, even if this is from the perspective of an "inclusive" nation that socially elimi- nates all forms of exclusion, segregation, racism, oppression, etc., and economically develops all conditions necessary to improve the quality of life materially and spiritually

> [A diferencia del pasado donde solo las élites podían argüir a favor de su capacidad de representación de la nación en su conjunto, lo que me parece fundamental es que los movimientos indígenas también buscan, ahora mismo, representar esos mismos intereses, aunque desde la perspectiva de la nación «incluyente» que, por lo mismo, en lo social elimine toda forma de exclusión, segregación, racismo, opresión, etc., y en lo económico desarrolle todas las condiciones para mejorar la calidad material y espiritual de la vida.] (170)

While self-representation is undoubtedly important for Indige- nous nations, this quote does not give us a precise definition of what constitutes an "inclusive" nation, nor does it explain what it means by "all conditions necessary to improve quality of life materially and spiritually." This lack of clarity is all the more pressing when we con- sider the global dynamics of progress and government extractivism. The search for and proposals on Indigenous self-representation in plurinational countries like Colombia and Ecuador would mean the challenge of developing collective proposals in which neither radi- cally particular nor universal criteria prevail, and which would also promote constructive self-criticism, as frequently happens when some Indigenous authors discuss their own communities. Along those lines, we should note that the map does not directly represent the presence of a "mestizo" or "non-Indigenous" society—if we can call it that for lack of more precise terminology—, given that the map itself was designed as part of an intercultural pedagogical gather- ing to develop a feeling of commonality among Indigenous Peoples, whose movements are more dispersed and scattered by the day. In sum, the map's reconfiguration of the country's borders can also be seen as its recognition of non-Indigenous peoples.

The map's symbolic and political challenges are primarily a call for Indigenous intercultural student movements themselves, as the map's pluralist cartographic value resides in its projection of policommunicative, multimodal map that is not dominated by a single cultural tradition. Moreover, the map avoids using alphabetic writing, although letters of the alphabet on the poster do fulfill a complementary intertextual role insofar as it represents the intercultural communication of "Indigenous Peoples" through a "foreign" language, Spanish, that has been appropriated and indigenized for Indigenous ends.

The map's design also promises the possibility of iconographically reappropiating the letters of the Greco-Phoenician alphabet through the double "E" figure within the central band. This kind of exercise in visual appropriating the alphabet or other audiovisual media commonly takes place in the graphic communication of transborder communities like the Gunadule in Colombia and Panamá, whose weavers incorporate and play with alphabetic letters in their molas, using them as though they were icons more so than phonemes. As a recurring mirrored vision, reverse literacy can be found in both Indigenous modalities of writing and in the oral-visual, alphabetic-literary appropriations found in some oralitegraphic proposals. In this way, the pages of a book can become a tree again, the book becomes a branch, and written words return to orality, to the mouth, to the elders, to communities, to the roots and the placentas of Mother Earth. They sit down and talk:

That's why the in these pages I am opening the book of my mother's chest, I feel, I am speaking, my voice is being born now, my words converse in this earth now with the names of the land. That is my work.	[Por eso en estas hojas estoy abriendo el libro que es el pecho de mi madre, me siento, estoy hablando, ya mi voz está naciendo, mi palabra ya dialoga en este suelo con los nombres de la tierra. Es mi trabajo.] (Muruy Andoque 25, 27)

2

ORALITURE AND TRADITIONAL LITERARY GENRES: THE ORALITERARY PROJECTS OF ELICURA CHIHUAILAF AND FREDY CHIKANGANA

IN THE FOLLOWING two chapters I propose a series of readings of contemporary Indigenous literatures that highlight the interactions among multiple graphic, oral, and literary systems. Here I expand upon several theoretical and literary proposals by Fredy Chikangana/Wiñay Mallki, an author who began participating in the oraliture movement led by the Mapuche writer Elicura Chihuailaf in the 1990s.

The previous chapter introduced the notion of oralitegraphies, defining these as textual intersections among diverse systems of oral, literary, and graphic communication. I used this notion to analyze the symbolism of picto-ideograms found in the Educational Minga's map, as well as in several contemporary Indigenous literary texts. The oralitegraphic readings in the next two chapters home in on the oraliture's concepts and practices, demonstrating how the practice of oraliture incorporates and evokes liminal genres from oral verbal art. In doing so, we will better understand how many oralitors integrate, reference, suggest, and/or evoke a number of different verbal genres through their oralitegraphic projects, such as the *taki* "song" and *haylli* "hymn" in Fredy Chikangana's Quechua work, and the *botamán biyá* "beautiful word" and the *jajuayenán* "a word sown like a seed in one's heart" in the work of the Camëntsá poet Hugo Jamioy. These authors' emphasis on the relationship between writing and verbal oral art arises in part from the concept of oraliture that was originally proposed by the African historian Yoro Fall in the early 1990s, and shows up independently in Elicura Chihuailaf's work several years later. Keeping these precedents in mind, here I propose an oralitegraphic reading of Chikangana's work that echoes Chihuailaf's initial design. These relational readings are possible given that oralitegraphies and oraliterary projects tend to be articulated from within networks of interaction such that a particular text can be understood as the expression of a collective interweaving. As I develop this analysis, I seek to examine other instances that are akin, but different to oralitures, such as communitism, oral literature, storytelling, and ethnotext.

I propose to study different textual aspects of Indigenous literary production in which the self-described oralitors emphasize both verbal genres from their communities and visual languages that are drawn from traditional Indigenous forms of writing.

ORALITURE: CHIHUAILAF'S LETTER TO ORALITORS

In his *Recado confidencial a los chilenos* [Message to the Chileans], Mapuche poet Elicura Chihuailaf explores oraliture as an intercultural project, putting forward a number of ideas that are in turn picked up by Fredy Chikangana/Wiñay Mallki in *Samay pisccok mushcoypa* [A Bird's Spirit within the Depths of a Daydream] and Hugo Jamioy in *Bínÿbe oboyejuayëng* [Wind Dancers]. Looking at Chihuailaf's *Recado confidencial*, in conjunction with Chikangana's essay "Oralitura indígena como un viaje a la memoria" [Indigenous Oraliture as a Voyage of Remembrance], and the visual proposals in Jamioy's poetic work, help us expand in the following sections possible readings of the concept of oraliture stemming out of the notion of oralitegraphies.

As both a concept and a practice, oraliture unifies a diverse set of contemporary aesthetic scripts proposed and/or taken up by writers from communities that privilege oral communication alongside their own forms of graphic, visual, and embodied communication. The Ugandan literary critic Pio Zuruma in the early 1970s coined the neologism "orature" as a way of getting around the internal contradictions of the calling oral texts "oral literature." The African historian Yoro Fall later suggested the term "oraliture." Fall states that "the term 'oraliture'—'orature' in French—is obviously an African neologism and simultaneously derived from the word literature. As a neologism, 'oraliture' is a new concept that is opposed to literature, and has its own principles and specific modes of communication" [la palabra "oralitura" —"orature" en francés— es evidentemente un neologismo africano y, al mismo tiempo, un calco de la palabra litera-tura. El objetivo de este neologismo es buscar un nuevo concepto que pueda oponerse al de literatura, y que tenga los fundamentos y la forma específica de la comunicación] (21). The Colombian literary critic Hugo Niño states that "for Fall, oraliture constitutes an aes-thetic that is similar to but ultimately richer than the literary" [para Fall, la oralitura constituye una estética igual a la literatura, pero con mayor riqueza] (36). This richness is derived in part from oraliture's open relationship with the performatic, visceral forces of oral com-munication, as well as from its evocation and rearticulation of verbal genres found in Indigenous languages.

Colombian anthropologists such as Nina S. de Friedemann were already writing about "Indigenous oraliture and Afrocolombian lit-erature" [oralitura aborigen y de literatura afrocolombiana] in the 1990s (qtd. in Mora Curriao 41–42). Oraliture has been publicly associated in the country with the literary production of Indige-nous and Afro-descended authors through calls to participate and institutions like the Ministry of Culture since the 2000s. By 1995 the Chilean Mapuche writer and activist Elicura Chihuailaf was already referring to his own work as oraliture. Speaking about this early oraliterary work, Chihuailaf recalls that, "I came to the contingent conclusion that I was already an 'oralitor,' because it seemed to me that my writing crossed over into the orality of my people, of my elders (with regard to the respect I pay them and their wisdom), and not simply in the mere artifice of the word" [llegué a la transitoria conclusión de que yo era un "oralitor", porque me parecía que mi escritura transcurría al lado de la oralidad de mi gente, de mis mayo-res (en el respeto hacia ellos, hacia ellas: a su pensamiento), no en el mero artificio de la palabra] ("La oralitura").

In 1997 Chihuailaf coordinated the Taller Suramérica de Escri-tores en Lenguas Indígenas [South American Workshop for Writ-ers in Indigenous Languages] in Chile's Araucanía region, which is called the Wallmapu by the Mapuche. The fundamental principles of oraliture were one of the workshop's primary topics of debate. Hailing from the Yanakuna community in Cauca and Huila, Co-lombia, Fredy Chikangana was among the workshop's participants. Upon returning to Colombia, Chikangana published the article, "La oralitura" [Oraliture], in Bogotá's *El Espectador* newspaper. In that article he describes the experiences of Indigenous writers from dif-ferent parts of the continent who were assembled in Chile (Kowii, Huinao, Chihuailaf, Lienlaf, Hernández Xocoyotzin), and publishes brief excerpts of their poetic work. First and foremost, Chikangana announces the oraliture project to the Colombian public, explaining that oraliture originates from an Indigenous perspective with Chihuailaf "at the head" [a la cabeza]. In the article, Chikangana recalls the words of a Chilean woman who spoke to the poets and oralitors who found themselves in one of their hemisphere's first continental gatherings: "you are called to conquer with words what others conquered with weapons" [están ustedes llamados a conquistar con la palabra, lo que otros conquistaron con las armas] (Chikangana, "La oralitura" 11). Both a chronicle and a mini-anthology, Chikangana's newspaper article was in fact one of the first things he did as co-ordinator of Colombia's Indigenous writers, a position he assumed during the workshop in Chile. Within less than a decade the author's earlier fragmented, alienated, Spanish-language work from the 1980s and 1990s would be transformed into the long-awaited voice of a continental oralitor who also wrote in Quechua, as seen in 2010's *Samay pisccok pponccopi mushcoypa*. In the year 2000, Chihuailaf's *Recado confidencial a los chilenos* received the award for best essay from the National Council for Books and Reading [Consejo Nacional de Libro y la Lectura]. Despite this award, we cannot simply understand *Recado* as an essay, given that it is first and foremost a work of oraliture that arises from the confluence of traditional genres of Mapuche verbal art, like the *nvtram* [conversation] and the *epew* [account], and genres that are more properly Chilean and "Western," like the chronicle, travel literature, the essay, and poetry. In short, for Chihuailaf the oralitor is capable of managing both written and oral "texts." The gestures people use when they speak are also forms of writing, such that people are not only speakers but also gesturers. And the *Recado* is, before anything else, an intercultural *nvtram*, which the oralitor defines as being as much "a conversation as it is an art" [conversación como arte] (*Recado* 103).

The *Recado*'s ideal readers are gathered around the hearth, the traditional Mapuche space in which words are shared. Through this connection with orality and the oralitor's childhood, the hearth becomes oraliture's *axis mundi*: "Beside the hearth, I heard my Aunt Jacinta sing and listened to my people's riddles and stories" [A orillas del fogón escuché cantar a mi tía Jacinta y escuché los relatos y adivinanzas de mi gente] (24). The hearth, "is the symbol that burns in the middle of this soliloquy, compilation, or whatever you want to call it. Maybe it is a private message" [es el símbolo que arde en medio de este soliloquio, compilación, o como desee usted llamarlo.

Tal vez, recado confidencial] (28). The oralitor addresses the reader in a conversational tone and through the medium of the written word invites her into an Indigenous world that is represented by an Indigenous person. Moreover, the reader soon discovers that he can listen, or have his own thoughts and ideas, but cannot speak. Everyone has been brought together to listen to both the oralitor speak with his people (living and "dead" [muerta]), and to the written and oral expression of those nearby: "I'm speaking with you beside the thoughts of my ancestors, of my people; and from the reflections, letters, and books of my Indigenous and non-Indigenous friends. Like I've told you, I've asked them to speak in these pages. I've asked you to hear them" [esta conversación con usted la realizo al lado de los pensamientos de mis antepasados, de mi gente; y de las reflexiones, las cartas y los libros de mis amigas y de mis amigos indígenas y no indígenas. Como le he dicho, a ellos-a ellas los he convocado a hablar en estas páginas. A usted le convoco a oírlas, a oírlos] (39).

In this way, the reader is restricted by the dynamics of a Mapuche verbal genre (the *nvtram*), the reading of which implies the reader's acceptance of the rules the author-mediator imposes. Readers are thus left to participate from a temporarily passive position as if they were school children again. This time, however, and as will be explained further later on, the oralitor hopes they become allies of the Mapuche people. The oralitor makes his case through a voice that is authorized by both Mapuche interculturality and the interculturality of their Indigenous and *winkas* [non-Indigenous] allies. Articulated from inside the Mapuche oral and symbolic universe, the *Recado*'s argument takes shape via the oralitor's strategic literary adoption of the structure of the *nvtram*, a conversational genre traditionally characteristic of the *lonkos* [heads] or Mapuche community leaders. Seated by the hearth, the oralitor is no longer the boy of his childhood memories but a *lonko* between cultures. He writes, "if we look at it from the Western space we also inhabit, the structure of the *Nvtram*, conversation as art, implies a variety or combination of "literary genres" (that would appear to have no equivalent in Chilean literature): presentation, greeting, the message as such, and 'documentation'" [la estructura del Nvtram, conversación como arte, si la observamos desde el lado occidental que también nos habita, implicaba una variedad o suma de "géneros literarios" (al parecer sin paralelo en la cultura chilena): presentación, saludo, mensaje propiamente tal, y "documentación"] (103).

The *Recado*'s conversational aspects also present Chihuailaf as an oralitor (9). For example, the article includes a greeting and bilingual homage to elders that begins with the evocation of his own childhood (16–21); a greeting-presentation of his name to his Chilean readership (23); intercultural messages that are developed throughout the text; written (letters, books) and oral (personal and communal accounts) documentation that he uses to sustain the argument of this confidential, intimate message. The gestural writing traced by his poetic texts and conversational evocations within the *Recado* are the kind of mental, graphic evocations that tend to be found in illustrated editions of Chihuailaf's *Sueño azul* [Blue Dream], which in the author's words is "the backbone of my oraliture" [la columna vertebral de toda mi oralitura] (8). An autobiographical story found in both the *Recado* and in illustrated children's editions of the "blue dream", the color blue (which symbolizes sovereignty and dreams), the word, and the hearth occupy an oralitegraphically privileged position as seen in Chihuailaf's book, *Relato de mi sueño azul* [An Account of My Blue Dream] (see fig. 30).

Figure 30. Illustration by Tite Calvo for *Relato de mi sueño azul*. Elicura Chihuailaf. *Relato de mi sueño azul*, p. 23.

Nevertheless, the *Recado*'s documentary interweaving, emphasis on orality, and the lack of images mean that we cannot refer to it as oralitegraphic text per se. The absence of graphic representations in the *Recado* likely arises from its emphasis on oral or conversational communication, as well as from the additional costs associated with publishing images. Notably, the latter impacts them in any number of texts, such as the 2010 edition of Jamioy's *Bínÿbe oboyejuayëng*, which was published without the illustrations that are found in the 2005 edition.

Conceived of as a *nvtram* or intercultural conversation, the kind of oraliture found in the *Recado* seeks to move readers to become intermediaries for the causes of Mapuche resistance in particular, and Indigenous resistance in general: "We have said that you can be our brother/sister because you have woken up and are beginning to illuminate the darkened mirror of your identity. And so it seems to us that you can be a true 'mediator,' in the most profound sense expressed by your society. This is also the Dream, the reason why I'm sending you this message, this letter" [Usted, hemos dicho, puede ser nuestra hermana-hermano porque ha despertado y empieza a alumbrar el espejo obnubilado de su identidad. Y nos parece entonces que usted puede ser el verdadero "mediador", la verdadera "mediadora", en el sentido de lo más profundo en su sociedad. Este es también el Sueño por el que le comunico este mensaje, este recado] (206).

The reader that the oralitor addresses is a common citizen without a specific identity, a literate citizen who can purchase or otherwise has access to books, a reader to whom the oralitor whispers collective messages. The oralitor slowly creates an identity for the reader that aligns him with Mapuche, other Indigenous peoples, and their struggles, while limiting the reader to only listening, at least temporarily. As with the aforementioned mirrored vision of reverse illiteracy that Jamioy put forward while on a panel with me and Chihuailaf in Chile in 2008, to a certain extent the oralitor invites the reader to be re-educated.

In the *Recado*, oraliture is a kind of interpellation, an intimate, conciliatory call: "I'm asking for us to talk" [Conversemos, les pido] (14). Part of this private letter interpellates the *winkas*, understood here as being "usurpers" or "non-Mapuche" "invaders", and considers the encounter as being with a reader who is a potential ally and specifically *kamollfvñche*: "a non-Mapuche person—like you, who may or may not be one of our friends" [gente no mapuche —como usted— que puede ser o no amiga nuestra] (72). Within the *Recado*'s logic, the oralitor has a certain amount of empathy with some *kamollfvñche*, while at the same time affirming his Mapuche roots. With this being the case, why wouldn't the average Chilean also recognize his Mapuche side?

Recado confidencial a los chilenos was published in 1999, only 10 years from when Chile had begun transitioning to democracy after the dictatorship of Augusto Pinochet. Mapuche land reclamation movements had been gaining momentum throughout the 1990s, a time when multinationals like Chile's Empresa Nacional de Electricidad S.A. (Endesa) were intensifying extractivist activities that had a profound impact on the collective territories of the Wallmapu, particularly those around the Bío Bío River. However, popular opinion since then has evolved to view the Mapuche unfavorably, associating them with "terrorist" activities, poverty, and "backwardness." Of course, all of this cannot be separated from the military occupation or "pacification" of the Araucanía that the Chilean military, encouraged by their recent "victories" over Perú and Bolivia in the War of the Pacific, carried out in 1883. In effect, the *Recado* appeals to a heroic pre-Chilean epoch when the Mapuche, previously known as Araucanos, kept the Spanish Empire at bay and were subjects of their own epic heroic poem, *La araucana*, which was written by the Spaniard Alonso de Ercilla, and originally published in three phases in 1569, 1578, and 1589. After the war against the Araucanos or the "pacification" of the Araucania in the nineteenth century, "the heroic Araucano became the barbarous and blood-thirsty Indian of the South" [el heroico araucano pasó a ser el bárbaro y sanguinario indio del sur] (Chihuailaf, *Recado* 74). Here, Chihuailaf is cognizant of the Mapuches being stereotyped as blood-thirsty "savages" opposed to their being "civilized," as in the well-known formulation of the Argentinian writer Domingo Faustino Sarmiento and his work *Facundo*. Such images have served to assuage Chileans' collective conscience over the years as they impinged upon Mapuche territorial sovereignty and subsequently "civilized" them by force.

Chihuailaf's interrogation of Chilean history lets us better understand how oraliture is much more than a traditional conversation. The oralitor interpellates both a "Chilean" and a "Latin American" reader, attempting to bring them out of their own colonized minds: "Chile's problem is that you sit down in front of the TV and the only people you see on the screen are blonde, svelte, tall women, and men who are tall, white, and athletic" [el problema en Chile es que te pones frente al televisor y ves esos tipos humanos únicos de la pantalla en que la mujer es alta, rubia, esbelta, como el hombre es blanco, alto y atlético] (88).

The oralitor asks Chile to look at its own identity in a mirror, and to recognize its similarities with the Mapuche. By doing so, Chihuailaf reframes a collective "we" that Chile and the Mapuche share, seeking to overcome their collective exclusion and victimization. However, oraliture's restrictions (interpellating some to speak and some to listen) seem to be extended into barely hinted at, actual conflicts. The oralitor's doubly-authorized voice—intra and interculturally—proposes necessary alliances with those who are marginalized or excluded, arguing that the Mapuche are not anti-Chilean while complementing his address with a petition for Mapuche sovereignty: "we want to be able to design and control the fabric of our own lives" [queremos ser nosotros los que diseñemos y controlemos nuestros proyectos de vida] (170). In fact, sovereignty is one of the social commitments that comprises the oralitor's project: "And, with an increasing insistence, our people's BLUE flag—moon, sun, and stars—begins to question the Chilean world's thoughts and speech" [Y, con vigor creciente, la bandera AZUL —luna, sol y estrellas— de nuestro Pueblo mapuche empieza a interpelar el pensamiento y el hablar mundo chileno] (210).

To understand the importance of Chihuailaf's declaration here, we should first explore how the *Recado* as an oraliterary project evolved in the mid-1990s. As a concept, oraliture was developed in part as a well-argued, even seductive political positioning, given that it included contemporary Mapuche voices from a number of different communities. As explained in the *Recado* itself, for the most part these Mapuche voices, letters, and testimonies denounce the neocolonialist pressures that the Chilean State exercises through the projects of multinational corporations across the country.

As a traveler and chronicler of this world, the oralitor moves through territories in a state of armed conflict, listening to stories of abuses committed by the military. He sees the logging companies and immediately compares his people's situation to that of Chiapas (154), where on January 1, 1994, a group comprised of Maya revolutionaries calling itself the EZLN (the Zapatista Army for National Liberation) rose up to confront injustices in Mexico. The oralitor assumes a more introspective tone as he moves further inland: "It's raining while we go through the roads of our communities. We look at them out of the corners of our eyes, observing the great pine forests through the pickup truck's foggy windows" [Llueve mientras vamos por los caminos de nuestras comunidades mirándonos de reojo, mirando los extensos bosques de pinos a través de los empañados vidrios de la camioneta] (155).

After a collective guillatún ceremony, the oralitor sits reflecting "beside the hearth" [a orilla del fogón] while he listens to "the Bío Bío shining in the words of our lamgen, our Sister, Nicolasa Quintremán Kalpán" [brilla entonces el Bío Bío en las palabras de nuestra lamgen, nuestra Hermana, Nicolasa Quintremán Kalpán]

(142).[1] Later on, the same communal female voices state, "That's why I speak: my people must know, Chileans must know, that the *winka* will not remove me from my place. I belong here, my Chaw Genechén brought me here. I will die here" [Por eso digo: Que sepa mi gente, que sepan los chilenos, que los winka no me van a sacar de mi lugar. Aquí pertenezco, aquí me trajo mi Chaw Genechén. Aquí voy a morir] (143).

The voices of the elders are presented through oral and written documents that justify the *Recado*'s central claim; as a document-story of oraliture that has been edited to create the effect of a present-tense voice—"that's how they are talking" [así están hablando] —for the *machi* [traditional doctors], for the *che* [people], and the *mapu* [earth]. As we will see in Jamioy and Chikangana, oralitors frequently poeticize these kinds of oral voices both structurally and symbolically. In the *Recado*, "our Machi, the Canelo, and the Bío Bío river (Its Spirit Owner of the Water Eyes/Sources), are speaking thus" [Así están hablando nuestras Machi, el Canelo y el río Bío (su Espíritu Dueño de los Ojos del Agua)] (147).

Oraliture thus takes shape in "The Word sustained by Memory, moved by Memory, from speech that comes out of the spring that flows from our communities" [la Palabra sostenida en la Memoria, movida por ella, desde el hablar de la fuente que fluye en las comunidades] (62). This is a word, "that flows from nature, our Nature" [que surge de la naturaleza, nuestra Naturaleza] (94). The oralitor's questioning appears to come from the earth, as if the earth itself was doing the questioning, interpelating the "ideal" reader:

> We contemplate the infinite Blue from within the silence of its gesture. Have you heard the trees' crying, or the hillsides' sobbing? Do you know how to recognize the scent of the opening flower, the growing seed, the song of the stars? What can you say with words that walk alongside the sun, that speak with the moon, that embrace the universe because from their tenderness our people's customs were whispered to the Az Mapu? Because the Pewma, the dreams so integral to our beloved people, came from its heavy breathing.
>
> [En el silencio de su gestualidad contemplamos el Azul infinito. ¿Ha oído usted el llanto de los árboles y de las vertientes?

---

[1] This Mapuche Pehuenche leader and machi (traditional doctor) fought for her people's self-determination, and in particular against the construction of a hydroelectric dam on the Bío Bío river. She was found dead, presumably from an accident, in the dam's waters in December 2013.

¿Sabe reconocer el aroma de la flor que se abre, la semilla que
crece, el canto de las estrellas? ¿Qué decir entonces con palabras
que caminan junto al sol, que hablan con la luna, que abrazan al
universo porque desde su ternura fueron susurradas para el Az
Mapu las costumbres de nuestro Pueblo? Porque desde su resollar
vinieron los Pewma los sueños de la naturaleza de la que es parte
amada nuestra gente.] (205)

Here the Mapuche, or "the people of the earth" in a direct English
translation, appear to be "translators" for the earth. The oralitor's
word in part explains Chihuailaf's decision to have non-Indigenous
readers be limited to simply listening, as the poetic voice asks, "Have
you heard the trees crying, or the hillsides' sobbing? Do you know
how to recognize the scent of the opening flower, the growing seed,
the song of the stars?" These questions suggest that readers should
recognize their own ignorance or their lack of awareness, that they
are being "educated," and that they are being "awakened," "questioned." Morever, these questions do not seem to refer to non-Indigenous people who also participate in similar intercultural or decolonial projects. We should remember that the idea of the "Indian" as a
guardian of nature, or a storehouse of natural knowledge, is common
stereotype from colonial Eurocentric thought, that non-Indigenous
writers frequently deploy in order to critique the society in which
they live. Rousseau produced the eighteenth-century idea of the "no-
ble savage" as a response to the rationalism of the Enlightenment, an
idea that that can be found recycled in the image of the ecological
native that appears in many recent enviromental discourses. Rather
than in a supposedly idyllic relationship with the earth, the problem
here lies with the absorption, acceptance, and outright identification
of different persons, and even groups of people, with a devastating,
homogenizing, extractivist modernity .

The oralitor in the *Recado* seeks to create a world in which all signs
of Indigeneity, including stereotypes of an idyllic Indigenous relationship with nature, are positive. Published on the eve of the twenty-first
century, its language takes on a Pan-Indigenous, messianic-prophetic
tone: "The buried city of Tenochtitlán has begun to wake up, and
slowly but surely, to rise ... México City is slowly opening up, its cathedral, falling" [La enterrada ciudad de Tenochtitlán ha empezado a
despertar, y, poco a poco, se levanta ... Ciudad de México se abre len-
tamente, la catedral declina] (210). These images of re-Indigenization
and de-catholization—in as much as an icon of the Indigenous city is

revived at a moment when its principal Catholic church is sinking—indirectly compare this poetic appeal to the apocalyptic hurricanes that have rocked both Central America and the US. These are all visions of political reconfiguration and change in the order of things.

The *Recado* was written on the doorstep of the new millenium. Its millenarian tone is politicized through its association with the blue flag of Mapuche sovereignty, and it closes with a conversation between the living and the dead. Ultimately, it gives us a bilingual declaration in Mapudungun and Spanish, "Pu mapuche mogeleyiñ, we are now saying that we, the Mapuche, are alive. Because the Spirit of the Earth in which we were born is alive" [Pu mapuche mogeleyiñ, los mapuche estamos vivos, decimos ahora. Porque está vivo el Espíritu de la Tierra en que nacimos] (212). Elicura Chihuailaf thus closes this oraliterary poetic project with the territorialization of a blue, sovereign oraliture.

ORALITURE, COMMUNITISM, ORAL LITERATURE, STORYTELLING, AND ETHNOTEXT

Elicura Chihuailaf's *Recado* transforms oraliture—a kind of writing that is practically and symbolically "beside orality"—into an "intercultural conversation" that validates the Mapuche's demands for sovereignty through the confluence of multiple voices and genres. Insofar as it gives priority to contemporary political and communal matters, oraliture is comparable to the concept and practice of communitism articulated by the US-based Cherokee literary critic Jace Weaver in his book, *That the People Might Live: Native American Literatures and Native American Community*. Writing during the same period as when Chihuailaf developed his oraliture project, Weaver defines communitism as a combination of community and activism (xiii). For Weaver, North American Native literature is a form of communitism "to the extent that it has a proactive commitment to Native community" (xiii). In effect, both oraliture and communitism are practical concepts that emerge from and point towards localized communal contexts, while prioritizing self-representation as well as political, historical, and cultural demands. Weaver formulates communitism out of literary criticism while Chihuailaf, Chikangana, and Jamioy do so primarily as oralitors, and only later on as "critics" or, as we shall see later on, more precisely as people who "work" or "promote" the word.

Communitism and oraliture both dialogue with concepts put forward by other US-based Native American intellectuals, such as

Osage critic Robert Warrior's notion of intellectual sovereignty. In *Tribal Secrets: Recovering Native American Intellectual Traditions*, Warrior analyzes non-fiction through the lens of sovereignty, "a process of continual self-determination" (qtd. in Teuton, "Theorizing" 207). According to Chihuailaf, the *Recado* as oraliture leads us "to formulate a new definition of the country. And from this perspective, the country's new definition will have to include the recognition and guarantee of our collective rights as a distinct People and Nation" [formular una nueva definición de país. Y la redefinición de este país tendrá que incluir, desde esta perspectiva, el reconocimiento y la garantía de nuestros derechos colectivos como Pueblo Nación distinto] (209). Chihuailaf's oraliture thus comes out of a Mapuche nationalist framework that can be rethought of as a kind of blue on blue similar to the concept of red on red proposed by the Cree literary critic Craig Womack. Red is the emblematic color of Indigenous sovereignty in the US, which both defies and reflects the literary and cinematographic stereotype of the "Red Skin."[2]

There are a number of similarities between Chihuailaf's *Recado* and Womack's *Red on Red, Native American Literary Separatism*. Both were published in 1999. Both works use a specific color to designate sovereignty, blue in Chihuailaf and red in Womack, and both authors appeal to intellectual sovereignty as one of their respective works' main political proposals; and both recognize literary precedents from their own national literatures. Chihuailaf takes on a conciliatory, conversational, if at times messianic tone, while Womack departs from the need for a kind of literary separatism, as in his view Native tribal literatures should not be nor can they be included in the canon. On the contrary, they are the canon, the great ancestral tree of the continent's oldest literatures. Womack defiantly states, "We are the canon" (7) as a response to those who bestow more legitimacy on "official" US literature, or on that produced by Shakespeare and Milton. Womack is a narrator, playwright, and literary critic, who includes fiction in his theoretical work insofar as it recognizes the importance of storytelling, the act of telling and retelling in which arguments can be put forth in a larger creative context.

---

[2] The term "red skin" is a homogenizing, racist stereotype imposed upon Indigenous peoples in the US, where they are better known as "Native Americans." It is a generalization that has been particularly fruitful in film, and the Western genre in particular, which is typically narrated from the distorted perspective of a battle between "cowboys" and "Indians." See, for instance, the documentary *Reel Injun*, directed by Neil Diamond.

Chihuailaf writes as an oralitor as opposed to a literary critic, and goes about building his text from a space of intercultural dialogue in which scriptural and oral genres flow together like the space between moving legs. Womack's text asserts, "the idea that Native America literary aesthetics must be politicized and that autonomy, self-determination, and sovereignty serve as useful literary concepts" (11). In this sense, Chihuailaf and Womack, in their own languages, agree on the importance of putting literary works in the service of their respective nation's intellectual sovereignty.

Along these same lines, Cherokee critic Christopher Teuton posits that the relationship between Native literatures and Native communities is contemporary literary criticism's most important issue ("Theorizing" 208). In effect, as the approaches of critics like Weaver, Warrior, and Womack are centered in their communities, the work of oralitors such as Chihuailaf, Chikangana, and Jamioy, is focused on the words of the elders and communitarian verbal art.

Storytelling—perhaps the term most widely used to refer to an act of narration in a Native American context in the US—can be found in the works of writers and intellectuals such as Greg Sarris (Miwok-Pomo-Philipino) and Leslie Marmon Silko (Laguna Pueblo). As Sarris states in a rather open, conversational tone, by doing so: "I am not privileging the Indian's point of view regarding the texts and topics considered. I am not interested in pitting Indians again non-Indians, insiders against outsiders, or in showing that any group of people is necessarily privileged or better or worse than another. Instead, these essays [in the volume in question] try to show that all of us can and should talk to one another, that each group can inform and be informed by the other" (7).

By comparison, Marmon Silko's *Storyteller* is an experimental, hybrid work whose author directly engages with topics like the restitution of land and the broadening of Native sovereignty, understanding these as primary issues for Indigenous peoples throughout the continent. Any given story is the beginning of other stories and so on in and endless chain that has neither cultural nor temporal boundaries. Silko believes in the wise word of the elders in the same way that writers like Okaina-Uitoto/Murui Anastasia Candre and cinematographers like Embera Keratuma Mileydi Orozco Domicó do, insofar as the works of these Indigenous Colombian creators are similarly nurtured by the oral histories and verbal genres of their respective communities. Following Silko, the most important advice that the elders give through storytelling can be summed up as, "if you can remember the stories, you will be alright. Just remember the stories" (*Storyteller* 58). Given that oraliture's chief thinkers, Chihuailaf and Chikangana, see oraliture as an act of memory, storytelling and oraliture agree on this point. Re-elaborated conceptually and narratively in works like those of the Uruguayan Néstor Ganduglia, ideas and practices concerned with revindicating oral literature in the Western hemisphere speak to the role that memory plays in so-called magical stories, despite "the every-dayness of running after eternal urgencies, which is the modern form of forgetting" [la carrera cotidiana tras las eternas urgencias, que es la forma moderna de olvidar] (13). In a conversational, intimate tone similar to that of the oralitors, Ganduglia directly interpellates the reader of *Historias mágicas de Montevideo* [Magical Stories of Montevideo] when he writes/says, "remember that writing has only recently appeared in the history of humanity. By comparison, the human community's oral history has undergone several millennia of slow evolution" [piense usted que en la historia de la humanidad, la escritura ha llegado apenas en último instante. La memoria oral de las comunidades humanas, en cambio, tiene decenas de milenios de lenta evolución] (25).

However, while the practice and processes of oral literature, storytelling, and oraliture are similar, they are also notably different. Following the critic Hugo Niño—as well as Yoro Fall and Nina de Friedemann, precursors in the use of the concept of oraliture in African and Afro-Colombian contexts, respectively—, I agree that "speaking of an oral literature is an apparent contradiction" [hablar de literatura oral encierra un contrasentido] (81), given that it would imply an amalgamation of the oral and the written. By comparison, oraliture and ethnotext propose convergence. Further, I agree with Niño when he speaks of ethnotexts as,

> new, alternative signifiers that denote a kind of text whose genealogy is generally oral, whose place of origin and circulation is primarily that of low culture as far as the canon is concerned, and whose languages of expression are not those of universal literature. It also alludes to a kind of text in which one finds nonverbal interventions, which is another reason why these texts are not strictly literary in the prescriptive sense of the word.

> [nuevos significantes alternativos para denominar un tipo de texto cuya filiación es generalmente oral, cuyos territorios de origen y circulación primaria corresponden a la baja cultura según el canon, cuyas lenguas de expresión no son las de la literatura universal. Alude también a un tipo de texto en cuya realización se reco-

nocen intervenciones extraverbales, por lo que no son productos
estrictamente literarios en ese sentido preceptivo.] (40)

As suggested by our readings of literary texts in conjunction with
the Minga's map in the previous chapter, oralitegraphies are similarly
not "strictly literary texts" given that, they also contain any number
of "nonverbal interventions." As such, the notion of oralitegraphy
and the concept of ethnotext both "transcend the limits of the verbal,
which is impossible within the realm of letters and script, and gesture
towards visual and ritualistic communication" [trascender los límites
de la verbalidad, lo que es una imposibilidad alfabetizante y escritural,
para extenderse hacia la comunicación visual y ritualística] (Niño
24).

In *El etnotexto: las voces del asombro* [The Ethnotext: Voices
of Astonishment], which won the 2008 Casa de las Américas Prize,
Hugo Niño frames a new way of perceiving texts. Echoing a debate
also found in the works by James Clifford and other anthropologists
who write on the role of narration in ethnographic writing, which
is decidedly authoritative and supposedly objective (Clifford and
Marcus), Niño questions the boundaries between history and fiction
(103–5). Niño agrees with Teuton when he writes that, "there is a
process of conceptual elaboration in narrative" [en las narraciones
hay un proceso de elaboración conceptual] (104). Such a shift in
the perception of the literary text contradicts Ong's idea of a primary orality that lacks the capacity to conceptualize abstraction,
something he only attributes to writing. In fact, Niño proposes the
concept of ethnotext in direct opposition to the "canonical concept
of literature as a verbal art that is by definition tied to writing, to
European languages, and to the parameters of a clearly Eurocentric
'universal literature'" [concepto canónico de literatura como un arte
verbal ligado necesariamente a la escritura, a las lenguas europeas y
a los parámetros de la "literatura universal" de signo claramente eu-
rocentrista] (Niño 113). According to Niño, the ethnotext is a "text
of ancestral bonds" [texto de vínculos ancestrales] (30). With regard
to the Yoro Fall and Nina de Friedemann's respective theories of
oraliture, the Colombian scholar thinks that "Indo-American oral
literature," which he also refers to an ethnotext, is "a textuality that
is produced, disseminated, transformed, and authorized in ancestral
societies that has not been absorbed into Western culture" [literatura
oral indoamericana ... una textualidad que se produce, se difunde,
se transforma y se autoriza en sociedades ancestrales no absorbidas

aún por la cultura occidental] (10). As such, he conceives of the ethnotext as an "axiological alternative" (12). For him, ethnotexts are, "texts arising from a mythological orality" [textos procedentes de la oralidad mitológica] (30). His proposal that the text originates from orality partially coincides with the work of oralitors that evokes and re-elaborates the words of the elders and the ancestors. Nonetheless, Niño's ethnotext differs from how Chihuailaf, Jamioy, and Chikangana understand oraliture insofar as, for them, oraliture also expresses personal and contemporary urban experiences that do not necessarily come from communal traditions of myth and ritual.

If oralitegraphies are, in part, the result of intercultural projects that are produced, transformed, and disseminated outside of contexts that are authorized by Indigenous communities, Indigenous authors nonetheless frequently appeal to their roles in and make appeals on the behalf of their communities of origin, which reflects Weaver's communitism. Oraliture partially overlaps with the typology of ethnotexts that Niño proposes insofar as it "transcends ideas concerning national literature" [desborda las ideas de literaturas nacionales] (37), "derives authority from its community" [su autoridad depende de la comunidad] (37), and is ultimately, "a highly intertextual and negotiated text" [un producto altamente intertextualizado y negociado] (36). Niño posits that the ethnotext seeks to move away from the "Western idea of literature" [la idea occidental de literatura] (36), something that is also expressed in the oralitor's need to define his own literary project. Oraliture also partially depends on a "Western" register as it appeals to a literate reader, is written and/or translated into Spanish and other dominant languages, and refers to genres like poetry. As compared to the ethnotext, however, oraliture is not always, "a didactic text with a practical function" [un texto útil y de función pragmática], as seen in oralitors' intimate texts as poems on love and other personal feelings. In addition, they are not "above all, an account" [ante todo, un relato] (36) as many oraliterary poetic works by Jamioy and Chikangana are poetic renderings of proverbs that use brief phrases and few images.

From its symbolic ties to oral communication, oraliture approximates Niño's ideas on production and performance insofar as, "ethnotext implies a high degree of ritualization, both with regard to its transmission-reception, and in its interpretation" [en tanto el etnotexto implica un alto grado de ritualización, tanto en el plano de su adquisición-transmisión, como en el de la interpretación] (36). Additionally, I feel that the transmission-reception of alphabetic writing, as well as its contact with other verbal and written traditions, also can be said to play an extra-traditional role.

Oralitor's intercultural roles cannot be reduced to their texts and, as with ethnotexts, "their performances are heterogeneous" [sus performancias son heterogéneas] (37). Moreover, and as one can see on the Internet, oralitors interact with different audiences in a number of different spaces through the oral telling or reading of their texts. We should also note that in most of his literary criticism, Hugo Niño recognizes that some ethnotexts include different kinds of "Indigenous genres" such as the *anent* (ritual song of the Shuar in Ecuador), and the *rafue* (the strong word of the Uitoto in Colombia and Perú). Niño also draws attention to "a variety of performance styles used in particular circumstances" [una variedad de estilos de performancia circunstancial] (80), which happen, "according to the conditions of reception and according to the functions that a particular text can have" [según las condiciones de la recepción y según las funciones que un mismo texto pueda tener] (80). We should also add that these variable conditions also apply to contexts outside of the community itself.

Hugo Niño goes on to say that the ethnotext is expressed as both "a vision from the side of Indigeneity and Indigenous languages" and as "a vision of Indigeneity seen from the lettered side" in processes of "remembrance," "intertextualization, and dialogue"; as an "intercultural vision, between two borders"; and also as a "vision of a 'we' that has assimilated the narrative properties of orality" (38). While Niño's classification here is broad and rigorous, it also reveals one of the limitations of the concept of ethnotext—although it is true that the idea of Indigenous creators does appear—, as all of these perspectives do not account for projects and ideas that have been elaborated by the country's contemporary Indigenous writers. Finally, another difference between ethnotext and oralitegraphies is that the notions of oralitegraphies and mirrored perspectives, while being limited in other ways, are continuations of critical personal conversations with thinkers and storytellers, in Colombia and beyond, who have chosen to call themselves oralitors or authors with Indigenous roots.

The Continental Group of Oralitors

Sarris, Silko, Weaver, Womack, and Warrior all pertain to a generation of Native American intellectuals in the US that initiated a profound critical turn towards the relationship between Native literature, whether oral or written, and the central issues facing their communities and nations in the last decades of the twentieth century. In this sense they are contemporaries with Indigenous writers from México, Chile, Colombia, and other Spanish-speaking regions of the continent who also began to gather and rethink things in conjunction with their respective communities and nations. Oraliture and the small group that formed around Elicura Chihuailaf in the late 1990s are similarly the result of this drive to achieve intellectual autonomy by exploring forms of expression that are deeply rooted within genres, epistemologies and verbal practices of Indigenous Peoples.

Following the Mapuche literary critic Maribel Mora Curriao (45–46), oraliture is one of three scriptural tendencies that can be observed in the poetic works of Mapuche writers who have been publishing since the 1990s. The other two tendencies have to do with works that move from the traditional to the poetic in connection with song (Leonel Lienlaf, Adriana Paredes Pinda, Lorenzo Aillapán) and poetry that is more "modern" and urban (Jaime Huenún, David Añiñir).

Indigenous literary works tend to participate in larger networks that transcend and/or question the paradigms of the States in which many nations and tribes are uncomfortably included. As such, the works of Indigenous authors frequently transcend the conventional boundaries of States and national canons. For example, the aesthetics associated with the oraliture project continue to radiate from Colombia's Andean southwest, with Elicura Chihuailaf and Fredy Chikangana having comprised the project's nucleus since 1997.

The movement began expanding in the early 2000s, coming to include oralitors such as Hugo Jamioy Juajibioy, the Camënstá writer and plastic artist from Colombia's Sibundoy Valley. As will be explained in detail in Chapter 3, Jamioy first published *Bínÿbe oboyejuagyëng* [Wind Dancers], a poetry collection subtitled "Indigenous Camënstá Oraliture," in 2005. To the best of my knowledge, *Bínÿbe oboyejuayëng* is the first published book by an Indigenous author outside of Chile to refer to itself as a work of "oraliture." In the book, Jamioy promotes contemporary Indigenous literature in Colombia and initiates the publishing project Juabna de América: Ediciones Indígenas [Indigenous Editions]. Jamioy mentions this project on the book's back cover when he says that the Community of 100 Friends of America's Indigenous Literature [Comunidad de los Cien Amigos de Literatura Indígena de América] could be funded through bilingual publications that could be distributed to bilingual educational institutions in Indigenous territories.

Keeping Jamioy's project in mind, we should remember that oraliture was initially proposed in Colombia as a pedagogical-creative project aimed at the country's Indigenous communities. As such, Jamioy and Chikangana frequently coordinated workshops and readings to disseminate oraliture in their respective communities and in urban areas, broadening the project's reach. Chikangana, for example, created workshops and presentations like "Oraliture in Colombia's Indigenous Cultures," and "Oraliture and Resistance from the Indigenous Communities from the Cauca." He was also co-creator of the Yachay Wasi, "House of Knowledge and the Word" in San Agustín (Uyumbe), the celebrated archeological site in the Andean southwest, and has directed oraliture workshops at public libraries in Bogotá.

For his part, Jamioy introduced oraliture to the Ministry of Culture's Renata literary workshop program, and in 2007 pushed for the creation of nationally-competitive scholarships from the Ministry of Culture that would be dedicated to the creation of oraliture. Chikangana and Jamioy have also teamed up with the Wayuu poet Miguelángel López/Vito Apüshana to participate in projects sponsored by the Ministry of Education, and in 2014 went on a national tour called Poetry from Abya Yala, during which they visited various institutions and high schools (see fig. 31). Indeed, as "inheritors of the circular song," Jamioy, Chikangana, and López have formed their own group, collaborating on a number of different projects that they have carried out under the auspices of the Norwegian Royal Embassy, such as the publication of their book/CD anthology, *Voces de Abya Yala* [Abya Yala's Voices] in 2014.

Collaborations among the Andean nucleus of oralitors (Chihuailaf-Chikangana-Jamioy) were well established during the first decade of the twenty-first century. Even so, some of the theoretical reflections written by oralitors from the Colombian southwest, and those by Chikangana in particular, gained a wider circulation with the 2014 publication in México of Chikangana's essay "Oralitura indígena como viaje a la memoria" [Oraliture as a Journey of Memory]. Up until that point their thoughts about oraliture were only accessible in person at readings and round tables, or in videos posted to the Internet. For example, one video shows Jamioy speaking about the term *jajuayenán* [sowing the word in one's heart], and how it ties in with his idea that oraliture comes from the wisdom of Camëntsá elders.[3] By comparison, Chihuailaf has continued to publish in print and virtually since the initial publication of *Recado*. In 2008 he published "Mis hermanos oralitores de Colombia" [My Brothers, the Colombian Oralitors] in the *El Periodista* online magazine. In it he talks about meeting Chikangana and Jamioy at Bogotá's International Book Fair in 2007, and recognizing their work as oraliture. Chihuailaf states that his *kallfv* [blue] presentation at the Book Fair was preceded by the "introductory, affectionate words" spoken by Chikangana and Jamioy, his "brother poets." He adds, "In addition, they have taken up the oraliterary proposal and given oraliture workshops" ("Mis hermanos").

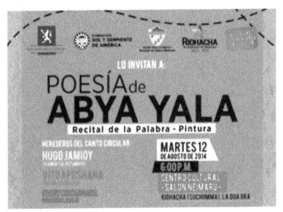

Figure 31. Promotional flyer for the Poetry of Abya Yala tour. Author's personal collection

What follows is a series of readings that highlight oraliterary practices and methodologies in works by Chihuailaf's "brother oralitors." In addition, I will present other readings of oraliture works in conversation with the notion of oralitegraphic textualities.

Two Poegrams and Oraliterary Ideas in Chikangana

In 2014 Fredy Chikangana/Wiñay Mallki wrote and published the aforementioned "Oraliture as a Journey of Memory," at the invitation of the Mexican literary critic Luz María Lepe Lira, who had already done research in the Colombian Southwest. The article was

---

[3] See the video *Sembrar la palabra en el corazón* on YouTube.

written as a poetic and/or literary manifesto and published alongside criticism of contemporary Mexican Indigenous literatures in the anthology *Palabras de vuelta, oralidad y escritura, experiencias desde la literatura mexicana* [Words of Return, Orality, and Writing, Experiences from Mexican Literature]. Edited by Lepe Lira, the volume brings together the voices of a number of different Indigenous Mexican writers, such as the Zapotecs Javier Castellanos and Irma Pineda, the Mazateco Juan Gregorio Regino, and the Yucatec Maya Feliciano Sánchez Chan and Isaac Esaú Carrillo. We can thus think of Chikangana's article as continuing the intercultural conversations among Indigenous writers that had begun in the late 1990s. In fact, the Yanakuna oralitor inserts the voices and experiences of his Mexican counterparts in his text when he names the three authors whom he considers to be the "pioneers of oraliture" ("Oralitura indigena" 84): Miguelángel López/Vito Apüshana, Jorge Cocom Pech, and Elicura Chihuailaf.

As mentioned previously, Jamioy, Chikangana, and López/ Apüshana have taken a number of trips together, published together, and collaborated on numerous national and international projects. With regard to Chikangana and Cocom Pech—a Yucatec Maya writer whose critical and literary work has generated a lot of interest among Indigenous writers in Colombia—, we must recognize the fact that both of them have participated in defining Chihuailaf's oraliture project since the 1990s. However, we should also clarify that Chikangana is the only one who compares himself directly to the Mapuche poet in his writing. Citing Chihuailaf, "I write, because I feel at peace with myself" [escribo, porque me siento tranquilo conmigo mismo] in an important declaration about his own orientation towards poetry and oraliture, he responds by saying, "I don't write, someone within me sings" [no escribo, alguien canta en mí] ("Oralitura indígena" 94). In line with this point of view, Chikangana's poetic work comes—as in verbal oral art—from intergenerational transmission. In effect, the poet does not necessarily take pride in himself, and he feels that the "true" oralitor does not seek recognition. In his experience, the wise elders of Indigenous communities are the true poets and singers (81)—a truth also shared by the educator poet Manibinigdiginya—, given that these elders are the ones who maintain the "original source" [fuente primaria], which he refers to as the "original word" [palabra original] that they use to "name, question, and advise" [nombrar, interrogar, aconsejar] (82). Poems like "El durazno en tía Julia" [The Peach Inside Aunt Julia], show how the elders are the most immediate personification of the ancestors, and storehouses of memory. In this particular poem the Yanakuna oralitor alludes to the nuances of ancestral memory, which are opposed to the miseries of official national history.

And one day
Aunt Julia's voice climbed the peach tree
in my memory of red geraniums and
         waunana parrots;
it gently caressed the wind and
clapped me on the back. It turned the
         corner of
my distant footprints and went to sleep in
         the middle of time.
They pile up in my memory, my aunt Julia's
little ants.

[Y un día en mi memoria
de rojos geranios y loros waunanas
la voz de tía Julia se trepó al durazno;
acarició suavemente al viento y
palmoteó mi espalda. Dobló la esquina de
mi remota huella y se quedó dormida en la
         mitad del tiempo.
Desde mi recuerdo, se agolpan entonces,
         las pequeñas hormigas
de la tía Julia.]
("El Durazno")

Chikangana states that what he calls the primary source of creation "lies in each Indigenous collective's orality" [que está en lo oral de cada colectivo indígena] ("Oralitura indígena" 75). Within his view, then, orality is collective. Moreover, oral communication is something that can be shared even more so than "memory," which can be lost and eventually recuperated. He goes on to state that, for him, "the art of creation and the beauty of the word are acts that can only be understood from a collective standpoint" [la creación en el arte y la belleza de la palabra es un acto que solo puede entenderse desde lo colectivo] ("Oralitura indígena" 79).

The idea that the Indigenous writer and oralitor is an artesan of the word, a kind of metalsmith, and in some senses a carver or sculptor, is a recurring image in Chikangana's poetic and literary self-reflections. Indeed, one of the foremost techniques that he associates with being a poet is being able "to shine the word so that it transmits gestures, images, music, and the sonority of an Indigenous language and the poetry that it encapsulates in a particular moment" [lograr pulir palabra para transmitir esos gestos, imágenes, la música, la sonoridad de una lengua indígena y la poesía que se encierra en el momento] (78). This work "is what we can call Indigenous oraliture" [es lo que se podría llamar como oralitura indígena] (78). This vocational self-identification is not casual, as here Chikangana describes his own work, and that of oralitors in general, as a continuation of the social and manual labor that generations of men and women have undertaken in Indigenous communities. If the raw material of the metalsmith is gold, and those of the sculptor stone and wood, Chikangana's is the word.

Processes of colonial erasure and cultural assimilation are certainly evident among the Yanakuna or Yanacona from the Cauca,
a People generally identified as "Catholics," Spanish speakers, and
considered as "farmers" before the 1990s. That said, Chikangana
and his family have participated in both the colective reappropria-
tion of the Quechua language,[4] and in the reconstruction of a historical memory that connects them with the ancient Inca of Perú, and
the pre-Hispanic metalsmiths and sculptors of San Agustín (Uyumbe), where the Yanakuna still possess some collective landholdings.
Yanakuna efforts to appropriate the historical memory sculpted in
the archeological site's stones were fully evident in their 2013 opposition to some of the site's monoliths being taken to Bogotá, when
they were scheduled to be included in an exhibition at Colombia's
National Museum.

San Agustín, Huila, and their surroundings are precisely where
the Caucan oralitor has held several of his oraliture workshops,
thereby participating in the Yachay Wasi, "the house of knowledge
and the word." Yachay Wasi is one of the intercultural educational
spaces where Chikangana collaborates in the promotion of collective values and practices of the word (in Quechua and Spanish), as
well as in projects on the exploration and recreation of memory that
are characteristic of oraliture's pedagogical and aesthetic proposals.
Chikangana thinks "reading what you wrote to the community" [leer
lo escrito a la comunidad] ("Oralitura indígena" 94) is key in order to
inspire, to be corrected, and to seek mutual support at the so-called
primary source. His understanding of poetry and the poetic act in
terms of their implying participatory, dynamic creation is represented oralitegraphically in "Takina" [Poem], which was published in
Samay pisccok pponccopi mushcoypa (see fig. 32).

An oralitegraphic text like "Takina" can be said to have at least
three dimensions. First, as a poem named "song" or "taki," it invokes an oral-collective source and invites readers to read the text
aloud instead of silently to themselves. Second, as a staircase of
words that descends-ascends to the left in each version, the poem
evokes both weaving (*kaytashuk* [a thread], *siranashuk* [a needle])

---

[4] Chikangana's Quechua-language publications are another example of his efforts to recover an indigenous language. Of these, *Kentipay llattantutamanta* [Hum-
mingbird of the Naked Night] and *Samay pisccok pponccopi mushcoypa* [A Bird's
Spirit within the Depths of a Daydream] are the most well known. As will be ad-
dressed later in this chapter, the latter of these is the most complete expression of
Chikangana's oraliture project to date.

and the weaver *makishuk* [a hand], *huarmishuk* [a woman]). Third, we can also read the text as a graphic abstraction, given that if we combine the version in Quechua with the version in Spanish they become a textilogram in the form of a stepped diamond or a squared cross, a *chakana* (see fig. 33).

Figure 32. Textilogram. Fredy Chikangana. *Samay pisccok pponccopi mushcoypa/ Espíritu de pájaro en pozos del ensueño,* pp. 60–61.

Figure 33. Graphic interpretation of the ideogram from "Takina," "Poem." Fredy Chikangana. *Samay pisccok pponccopi mushcoypa/Espíritu de pájaro en pozos del ensueño,* pp. 60–61.

As seen in Chapter 1 in our discussion of Chikangana's text "Yuyay yakuk" and its connection with the *wiphala* (the rainbow flag) found on the Educational Minga's map, the *chakana* is a Pan-Andean and Pan-Quechua Cosmological symbol that the Yanakuna oralitor evokes throughout his poetics. Known as *shinÿe* or sun among the Camëntsá, this stepped diamond figure was also part of a number of pre-Incan and Incan textile codes (see fig. 7). In fact, the *tocapus*

(quadrangular ideograms prominent in Inca textiles) can be found in
drawings from Guamán Poma de Ayala's early seventeenth century
Nueva Corónica y buen gobierno [New Chronicle and Good Gov-
ernment], that represent the Inca Wiracocha, whose clothing bears
tocapus (see fig. 34).

Figure 34. The Inca Wiracocha in Guamán Poma de Ayala. Copenhague Royal
Library. Web Archive.

Fredy Chikangana/Wiñay Mallki's "Takina" can be read as syn-
thesizing different aspects of the cosmos: the verbal staircase on
the left evokes the textuality of female textile work (thread, needle,
hand, woman), while the one on the right expresses a combination
of the sky (*waira* or wind, *inti* or sun), physiology (*ucjuqan* or "your
body") and flora (*sisashuk* or rose). All of these dimensions are wo-

ven together in a pluriversal notion of Pacha Mama, whose name possesses an earthly-feminine character in Quechua. In short, "Takina" or "Poem" holds a number of possible readings and combinations of word-images that unite the reader-singer, the oralitor-intermediary, and the play of multiple graphic-literary languages from verbal and textile traditions, in co-creating the poem's meaning. This kind of oral, literary, and graphic complementarity across the poems in Quechua and Spanish versions offers a much more complex vision of the poem that goes well beyond a focus on orality.[5]

Oralitors' approach to the earth can also be understood through their articulating the oralitor as a sower of words. Similar to the concept of the *jajuayenán* [sowing words in the heart] that is found in Jamioy, Chikangana believes that a true word exists, and that "that word that comes from the heart, that is watered and sown, that its sprouts to help build or to name the harmony that Mother Nature's spirit teaches us" [aquella que sale del corazón, que se riega y se siembra, que brota para ayudar a construir o para nombrar la armonía que nos enseña el espíritu de la madre naturaleza] ("Oralitura indígena" 86).

For Chikangana, the oralitor's texts are harvested through a voyage of remembrance. Before the Yanakuna writer had begun participating in the oraliture movement, his efforts to recuperate the Quechua language in Perú, and his community-based projects in Huila, Chikangana's poetic voice during the 1980s and early 1990s was more acculturated, alienated, and neither rhythmic nor playful. However, as seen in the poegram "Chhusak" "Del vacío" [From the Abyss], a poem that was originally written and published in Spanish in 1990 and later re-published in Quechua (Runa Simi) in 2010, the oralitor's creative, visual poetics already anticipates his later work like "Takina."

Contrasting with forms of writing like Chinese—which is based on ideograms—, and Hebrew and Arabic—where visual shapes also have a semantic content—, contemporary alphabetic writing is characterized by an abstract phoneticism in which letters—unless there is some sort of artistic intervention—do not signify anything on their own. As the historian of writing George Jean states, "everything occurs as if Western forms of writing, sure of themselves, and as is especially the case with Latin letters, accepted that they should

---

[5]   As will be seen later on in my analysis of the poem "Shimi machupay" "Palabra de abuelo" [Grandfather's Word], Chikangana's emphasis on the oral in his oraliterary work also implies a profound engagement with body language and other forms of visual communication.

not risk any of the benefits that abstraction offers" [todo sucede por tanto como si las escrituras occidentales, seguras de sí mismas, y en especial las latinas, se atuvieran al principio de no arriesgar los beneficios que comporta la abstracción] (162). In poetry, however, there are notable exceptions such as the calligram, a kind of visual poetry popular with the literary vangard at the beginning of the twentieth century, and promoted by poets like the French Guillaume Apollinaire and the Chilean Vicente Huidobro.

Unlike the calligram, the poegram is not derived from calligraphic experimentation, or the typographic possibilities offered by concrete poetry. Its primary motive is not necessarily formal experimentation or playful creationism, but the need to find and holistically transmit the particular poetics of the languages of collective, visual cultures. Moreover, the poegram cannot be thought of as an aesthetic particular to Indigenous authors, even as it takes on a special significance in the recent work of Indigenous writers. In effect, the ongoing search for autochthonous forms of literary expression has led many Indigenous writers to use Spanish in conjunction with their native languages and to seek out alternative forms of expression via their communities' graphic forms of communication. Calling these expressions poegrams reflects the need to have a basic terminology that we can use to describe certain contemporary poetic creations, given that writers such as Chikangana, Jamioy, and Candre do not, in the strictest sense, have a calligraphic tradition that precedes them. Instead, these authors are the heirs to visual languages that are expressed on painted and molded ceramics, metalwork, textiles, basketry, and multiple kinds of painting media such as rocks and the human body. Departing from the basic notion of a poegram, we can create more complex notions like the textile-gram as a way of referring to poetic works inspired by textiles—as in the case of Chikangana's "Takina" or "Poem"—and notions of visual poetry inspired by or in collaboration with other visual poetic projects that are based on or related to graphic, audiovisual, multimedia, or other systems of communication.

As a poegram, "Del vacío" or "Chhusak" is related symbolically and structurally to personal and community dismemberment (see fig. 35).[6] In the text, Chikangana graphically represents the abyss

---

[6] Both "Del vacío" and "Chhusak"'s graphic proposal and devastated sentiment communicate the kind of symbolic dismemberment characteristic of the mirrored visions that will be analyzed in detail in the second half of this book.

created by having to write in an imposed language, the alienation of a body that is cognizant of the fact it has been colonized and presents the x-ray of a culture that is disintegrating, one that is stained, torn, or *wekufiada*, that is, according to Adriana Paredes Pinda, a culture that arises from something that has fallen apart.[7] Here community memory is not perceived as being pristine or harmonious, but as a trail of rocks, letters, and stains. The claim that, "nothing will be like it was," speaks, above all else, to a sense of loss. The poem's negative space expresses this disfiguring and disfigured void in which the poetic voice clings to doubt: "(quizá)" [maybe].

Ya nada será como antes

solo
u
n

v
a
c
í
o

sobre nuestros cuerpos
como un desolado vaivén
como olas adoloridas, rabiosas,
como volcanes dormidos
(quizá)
como piedras o como manchas
en un interminable
r e g u e r o d e h u e s o s

Figure 35. Image of the poem "Chhusak," "Del vacío." Fredy Chikangana. *Samay pisccok pponccopi mushcoypa/Espíritu de pájaro en pozos del ensueño,* p. 65.

---

[7] The idea of a *wekufiada* culture came up in a personal conversation that I had with the Mapuche Williche Adriana Paredes Pinda, who is a machi (traditional doctor), literary critic, and poet. Paredes Pinda holds an MA in Contemporary Latin American Literature and a PhD in Human Sciences from the Universidad Austral in Chile. She has published two collections of poetry, *Üi* and *Parias Zugun*.

The dismemberment, nostalgia, and loneliness associated with urban migration in many of Chikangana's other poems also play a symbolic role here, where the land appears through the image of the Cauca's "sleeping volcanoes." The anger, the pain, the "ravaged wandering," the abyss over the bodies, and the "reguero de huesos" [trail of bones] represent an anguished consciousness that has experienced the same kind of dismembering shock that we will analyze in Yenny Muruy Andoque/Yíche's work in Chapter 5.

The hardships of living in the city alone generate a process of "retrospection about [the Indigenous immigrant's] surroundings and what they represent" [retrospección sobre su propio entorno y lo que representa] and he takes up the word as "a means of escaping and a refuge in singing" [vehículo de escape y refugio para cantar] (Chikangana, "Oralitura indígena" 81). The oralitor from the Cauca contrasts the emptiness produced by being away from one's community with the feeling of being culturally whole "that one has inherited" [que se tiene por herencia] (81). In his experience, the renewed self-reflection that Indigenous writers carry out can happen in any language in which they choose to express themselves and takes place between the fullness of being whole and being empty (75). In fact, in the thesis that he submitted to complete his degree in Anthropology, Chikangana states that what he refers to as the "Yanacona I" has two contradictory and complementary dimensions: "the world that has been denied and the one that had been imposed. Two worlds that have left their marks on one's memory and whose space we must carefully examine in order to revitalize what is ours. We must also take up and adapt things from other cultures that can be useful to us in order to create future generations that are critical of both their own world and the world of others" [el mundo negado y el mundo impuesto. Dos mundos que han dejado huellas en la memoria y cuyo espacio debemos examinar con cuidado para poder revitalizar lo que es muy propio, así como retomar y condicionar lo que pueda ser útil de otras culturas para la formación de futuras generaciones críticas de su propio mundo y de otros mundos] (*Yo Yanacona* 57).

Here the oralitor contrasts what has been denigrated from his culture with what is plentiful, or full, experiencing the impositions of dominant culture's values as a shocking emptiness from which the energy to create nonetheless surges forth. The oralitor himself sings from an "individual nostalgia" [nostalgia individual] as his urban loneliness not only generates waves of pain but also helps him wake up and remember his life to this point with a greater awareness of "the land, the house, the hearth, the food, the family, nature" [la tierra, la casa, el fogón, la comida, la familia, la naturaleza] (Chikangana, "Oralitura indígena" 81). As first put forward by Chihuailaf, oraliture is a sign of being at peace with oneself. In Chikangana this peace is also a journey during which one comes and goes between the worlds of one's origin and that of life in the contemporary world. For Chikangana, then, the crisis produced by the experience of urban migration is a decisive factor in the creation of oraliture. Even so, his vision here differs a good deal from the poetic subject of the Quechua migrant in Perú who, according to the literary critic Julio Noriega, "is neither Indigenous nor pretends to be. He is an ambiguous mestizo, contradictory: an acculturated Indian or a Quechua-ized white person. He is always represented as alienated culturally and physically from the Andean world. Because of the knowledge he has acquired from his Western-style education, he is distanced from what is Andean; because he is Quechua speaking, racially mixed, and provincial, he is likewise marginalized from the West" [En la poesía quechua escrita actual el sujeto poético no es un indígena ni pretende serlo. Es un mestizo ambiguo, contradictorio: un indio aculturado o un blanco quechuizado. Se presenta siempre enajenado cultural y físicamente del universo andino. Por sus conocimientos adquiridos a través de la educación occidental se aparta del andino; por ser quechua-hablante, mestizo y provinciano queda fuera del occidental] (131).

These poems ultimately leave us with the idea of an Andean identity that is alienated and contradictory because it is not necessarily tied to tradition or to the land, and they would appear to suggest that an Indigenous person who leaves the "Andean World" ceases to be authentic and by definition becomes a self-contradicting mestizo. They also presuppose the assimilation of the Indigenous migrant, a position that is highly questionable from the perspective of oraliture. In her work on the Andean writer Manuel Quintín Lame, scholar Betty Osorio does not talk about acculturation but of double-consciousness, a concept that was first theorized by the African American sociologist W. E. B. Du Bois. For her, double-consciousness in Quintín Lame is expressed through the, "contradictory positions of an individual who tries to give meaning to his own private and public experiences in a racist and discriminatory environment." Osorio concludes in his work that Quintín Lame "responds to a plurality of spaces: lettered, Christian, and judicial, but [his work] is fundamentally the work of a Nasa intellectual" (95). Her position thus contrasts with Noriega's analysis of Quechua poetry in Perú as she argues that participating in non-Indigenous spaces does not entail the migratory poetic subject's acculturation.

While acknowledging the difficulties of urban migration, Chikangana also proposes that the Indigenous oralitor is "someone who has found his people's word" [aquel que ha encontrado la palabra de su gente] ("Oralitura indígena" 80). As we have seen, finding this word is not easy or something that happens all at once, but rather the result of a constant back-and-forth to and from memory, a memory that is understood in part as the basket or receptacle-body where wisdom and collective experiences are stored, an important motif in the Amazonian traditions expressed by wise people and singers-poets-painters like Anastasia Candre. As the inspiration for its creation comes from both intracultural sources and intercultural journeys, oraliture here is understood as a both a centripetal and a centrifugal force (Chikangana, "Oralitura indígena" 80). The oralitor as traveler or *ch'aski*, the messenger between worlds since the idealized time of the Incas, plays an important role in Chikangana's work, as this figure who furthers the image of the oralitor as a traveler through memory. Oraliture can also generate connections and support solidarity between Indigenous groups within the framework of what some refer to as "our America" or "mestiza America," that is, the space of encounters and missed connections within a dominant society whose homogenizing dynamics Indigenous peoples strategically resist, and because of which they frequently need to form networks of cooperation (92). In short, in Chikangana oralitors have the double mission of fortifying their own culture and being bridges with dominant society.

In doing so, the oraliture movement's intercultural character openly manifests pedagogical and political intentions. Through his recuperation of Indigenous language and thought, the oralitors seeks to occupy a dignified political place in the multicultural society that he has been promised—as in, for example, Colombia's 1991 Constitution—while participating in the larger project of Latin American integration (93). Even so, this interculturality does not exclude unrepentantly Indigenous projects like that of Abya Yala, the name which Chikangana, Jamioy, and Apüshana gave to their last book in 2014. Pedagogically, here the Yanakuna oralitor emphasizes his participation in the re-elaboration of a kind of word of council for children and for new generations of Indigenous people, people in whom he hopes "to create an awareness of their identity within mestizo society" [crear una conciencia de identidad en la sociedad mestiza] (Chikangana, "Oralitura indígena" 96).

The oralitor thus aspires to fortify this Indigenous subject's sense of identity within dominant society, and giving it tools to recuperate and maintain its sense of identity via concrete practices like oraliture, textiles, collective work, as well as the recuperation of communication in Indigenous languages and other audiovisual means. Beyond these political positions, oraliture's social function here should not be surprising, even more so when we account for the fact that much of what dominant society designates as literature, or mythology, continues to operate within indigenous communities through practices like ritual, collective labor, and other contexts in which "words of advice" are shared. In this sense, the notion of oralitegraphies contributes to our comprehension of sociocultural contexts that would seem to be non-literary to the Western gaze, as when "poetry is composed in everyday settings while working the land, in the weaving of a textile, sung in a song used to pay nature back, or found in the advice one gives to a child" [se hace poesía en la cotidianidad, en el trabajo en la tierra, en la elaboración de un tejido, en un canto de pago a la naturaleza, en los consejos que se dan a un hijo] ("Oralitura indígena" 82).

Chikangana also understands oraliture as a way of "looking at one's community of origin from a different angle" [mirada desde otro ángulo a la comunidad de origen] (80), and includes examining material culture and oral expressions, what is ancestral and what is appropriated, the strengths and weaknesses of languages, and the songs that the elders continue to sing. He goes on to ask, "which of these songs and cultural expressions can we elevate to the place that it should have?" [cuáles de esos cantos o cuáles de las expresiones culturales podemos elevar al grado digno que les corresponde] (80). To some extent, the Yanakuna Quechua oralitor thus takes up José María Arguedas's Indoamerican project from the 1930s, in which the Quechua Peruvian writer argued for the inherent value of mestizo and Indigenous artistic expression in his *Canto kechwa, con un ensayo sobre la capacidad de creación artística del pueblo indio y mestizo* [The Quechua Song, with an Essay on the Creative Abilities of Indian and Mestizo Peoples]. Arguedas believed that is was necessary to "show that the Indian knows how to express his feelings through the use of poetic language; to show his creative, artistic abilities, and visibilize the fact that what the people create to express themselves, is an essential form of art" [demostrar que el indio sabe expresar sus sentimientos en lenguaje poético; demostrar su capacidad de creación artística y hacer ver que lo que el pueblo crea para su propia expresión, es arte esencial] (21). Similarly, Wiñay Mallki/Chikangana argues that mere transcription is disrespectful and unethical for both "Indigenous cultures" and "the interlocutor" in situations of intercultural contact ("Oralitura indígena" 80). These dynamics can be overcome through the creation of oraliture as a kind of text that respects and heeds "the wise words of the elders" (80), while at the same time being a textual production that, from its inception, recognizes that it will go out to "other interlocutors, including Indigenous ones" (80). For Chikangana, then, oraliture is ultimately an ethical form in its approach to Indigenous communities and in its re-articulation of Indigenous verbal arts, the principal practitioners of which would be a community's elders.

In a sense, it is no exaggeration to say that Chikangana generally sees ethnographic and ethnolinguistic writing as unethical. He reserves a privileged place for oralitors, who, following Chikangana, meet with their communities and so are able to follow and transmit the words of their communities and elders in alphabetic and other forms of writing. Unfortunately, he makes no mention of the potential ethical implications of Indigenous and non-Indigenous people approaching Indigenous communities and other forms of verbal art. That is, the question of who can and who cannot be an oralitor remains open.

In sum, Chikangana conceives of oraliture as the interaction between the verbal experience of collective commemoration, individual creation stimulated by a symbolic displacement to an isolated urban environment outside of that community's boundaries, and the exercise of a persistent interculturality that manages to create bridges and aid in the construction of a "multicultural society" (91). In Chikangana's view, a "true Indigenous oralitor" is one who "sings from his people," "to animate the collective voice" (80), and who, through his song, "touches the hearts of future generations" (91). From its critique of urban experience to its re-creation of community, the oralitegraphies found in the two poems analyzed here visually capture this process. The symbolic trajectory of moving between the city and the community can be found in the asymmetry of crisis in "Del vacío" or "Chhusak," to the earthen-female symmetry of "Takina" or "Poema," outlining a textual field that orally, literarily, and graphically complements the concepts and practice of oraliture.

Oraliture, *taki*, and *haylli* en Wiñay Mallki/Chikangana

Samay pisccok pponccopi mushcoypa [A Bird's Spirit within the Depths of a Daydream] (2010), is authored by Wiñay Mallki, the name that Fredy Chikangana gave himself while he was strengthening his writing in Quechua during the first decade of the twenty-first century. Chikangana's status as the collection's author appears within parenthesis. Since the work was first published, readers have had to understand it within the context of Andean dualism, expressed in both the title and in the work's bilingualism, and the author's heterogeneous identity, as in the case of the two names on the cover. In the 1990s Antonio Cornejo Polar asked "why is it so difficult for us to assume the hybridity, the 'motleyness,' the heterogeneity of the subject as it is configured in our space?" [por qué nos resulta tan difícil asumir la hibridez, el "abigarramiento", la heterogeneidad del sujeto tal como se configura en nuestro espacio] (21). The Peruvian literary critic asserts that we have assumed the image "of the modern subject, blended in the background of the Romantic I ... upon discovering that we lack a clearly defined, distinct identity" [sujeto moderno, en el fondo del yo romántico ... al descubrir que carecemos de una identidad clara y distinta] (21).

As both a name and a project, Wiñay Mallki represents the author's search for a "clearly defined, distinct identity": the Yanakuna Mitmak included within the Quechua. At the same time, both the quest for and creation of this positive Indigenous identity, including the oraliterary project, are heterogeneous expressions that do not capitulate to the idea of hybridity. As the Caucan author recounts from his own experience, the Indigenous oralitor emerges from the crisis, shock, and loneliness produced by his experience of migrating to the city. His works achieve an ever more complex, high degree of heterogeneity as he moves between re-creations and evocations of the Incan, the rural, the urban, contemporary Quechua, and Yanakuna farmers in the Colombian massif.

Chikangana translates the name Wiñay Mallki as "root that endures over time." In Quechua *mallki* refers to both the tree and the root and could symbolize the foundations of a person's identity. *Pponccopi mushcoypa* [the wells of a daydream] is a poetic expression of the originary well in which the author-bird-singer symbolically submerges himself to rest, reconnect, and be revitalized. At the same time, *samay* is the breath of life, the spirit, and refers to rest and breathing. On the other hand, the oralitor's role as a bridge and messenger between worlds can also be expressed through the liminal figure of the *pisccok* [bird], a being that connotes poetry in many cultures around the world, and *taki* [poem, song] in the author's own poetics. The oralitor-bird's immersion in the depths of a daydream, the collective roots from which they arise in the text, happens at a trying time of renovation implied by the word *wiñay*.

Indeed, Chikangana's most recent poetic project is oriented towards a transcendent dimension that seeks to integrate conceptions of time *wiñay* [permanence in time] and space *mallki* [root, tree]. In his book *Escritura quechua en el Perú*, Julio Noriega points out Quechua poet Andrés Alencastre's (Kilku Warak'a) definition of the word *mallki* as being "a special symbol of the the the Inca" [símbolo especial del inca] (124). Noriega goes on to say that *mallki* also refers to the "mediator between this world and the one above, the world of the gods, or the one below, the world of the ancestors" [mediador entre este mundo y el de arriba, el de los dioses, o el de abajo, el de los antepasados] (124), a role that coincides with that of the oralitor in Wiñay Mallki's oraliture project. *Samay pisccok* is also a bilingual book in Quechua and Spanish that collects the author's new and previously published work. Its pages tellingly represent the oraliture project as incorporating everything from political resistance, short poetry, the voices of the elders, intimacy, bilingualism, coca leaves, the heart, body language, visual forms inspired by the *chumbe* and the *chakana*, and diverse Quechua verbal genres like the *taki* [song] and the *haylli* (a hymn with agricultural, political and religious overtones). As stated by Elicura Chihuailaf, who wrote the prologue at Wiñay Mallki's request, the text is a fully realized work of oraliture. His support for the project is notable insofar as he directly states that "Fredy is an oralitor" given that he "writes from the borderlands of his people's orality" [Fredy es sin duda un oralitor ... escribe a orillas de la oralidad de su gente] (*Samay* 14). According to the Mapuche poet invested with the authority of the movement's collective voice, the Yanakuna oralitor "sustains his personal voice from and through the knowledge of his elders and ancestors" [desde y en el conocimiento de sus antepasados y de sus mayores sostiene su voz personal] (14). I would even argue that Chihuailaf positions his voice in the prologue as being authorized by the elders' and ancestors' collective "we," stating, "we are present because we are the past and only through this are we the future; time cannot be split, because it is a circle, ... they are telling us" [somos presente porque somos pasado y solo por ello somos futuro; no es posible escindir el tiempo, que es un círculo … nos están diciendo] (14). These self-referential images of permanence within time (*wiñay*), roots (*mallkikuna*), and the visual shapes of the mouth and the word (*shimi*) subtly substantiate the Mapuche prologuist's claim that *Samay pisccok* is a work of oraliture: "Forgetfulness is not possible. That is why the grandmothers' and grandfathers' conversations are present in his oraliture" [No es posible el olvido. Por eso en su oralitura está la conversación de las abuelas y los abuelos] (14). For example, "Shimi machupay" [The grandparents' word] is one of the poems from *Samay pisccok* that best represents this oraliterary aesthetic, as it transcends the mere transcription of verbal art through the re-elaboration and poetic evocation of a "conversation" with the elders and nature.

The grandfather's word:
"Do not follow that grey bird
it is a spirit and leads to a cliff,"
—it is a bird of death.
The grandmother's word: "Do not
                    play with fire
it will make you wet the bed,"
—it is cold inside your body.
The taita's word: "Pay attention to your
                    grandfather"
—you must pay to hunt.
The little mother's word: "Pay attention
                    to your grandmother,"
—you must pay to play with fire.
The grey bird's word: "Grandfather of
                    the bad omen,"
—he is a distrustful man.
The fire's word: "Grandmother of
                    the ill portent,"
—she is an insidious woman.
The word of my heart: "Welcome to
                    the mystery,"
—be the breath of this song.

[Palabra de abuelo:
«No sigas a ese pájaro gris
que es espíritu y lleva al despeñadero»,
—es pájaro de muerte.
Palabra de abuela: «No juegues con
                    fuego
que hace orinar en cama»,
—es frío dentro de cuerpo.
Palabra de taita: «Haz caso al
                    abuelo»
—hay que pagar pa'cazar.
Palabra de mamita: «Haz caso a la
                    abuela»,
—hay que pagar para jugar con el fuego.
Palabra de pájaro gris: «Abuelo de mal
                    agüero»,
—es hombre desconfiado.
Palabra de fuego: «Abuela de mal
                    presagio»,
—es mujer maliciosa.
Palabra de mi corazón: «Bienvenido el
                    misterio»,
—alienta este canto.]
(*Samay* 51)

"Shimi machupay" can also be translated as the old or ancient word. *Shimi* or *simi* is literally language or word in the broad sense. Graphically and gesturally, *shimi* also evokes the coca leaf, coca being a medicinal plant that accompanies the practice of wise and ritual conversations in the Amazon and the Andes, and occupies a special place in Fredy Chikangana/Wiñay Mallki's oraliterary and political projects.

"Shimi machupay" articulates the voices and words of the elders, the bird, the fire, and the poetic voice's own heart (*sonqo*) as proverbs that evoke the typical formulae of oral literature. Oral communication in the text is simple, formulaic, and in some sense "mysterious" and unsettling if we take the penultimate verse seriously. The words (*shimikuna*) are represented by the grandparents' body language, a language that the readers must read in order to imagine the mysterious bird's flight ("Do not follow that grey bird / it is a spirit and leads to a cliff"). The fire's movement suggests other images ("Grandmother of the ill portent," / —she is an insidious woman"), and the recurrence of fire (*nina*) becomes a proverb of warning ("Do not play with fire / it will make you wet the bed"). As seen in the oraliterary poetics of Chihuailaf's *Recado*, the oralitor has brought us to the hearth to hear these messages.

In the poem-song (*taki*) "Ñokanchi tutajuna hakpachary" or "Nosotros, la noche y el cielo infininto" [We, the infinite night and sky], the oralitor's childhood unfolds beside the hearth or *tullpa* the traditional space for conversations:

Seated around the *tullpa*,
my years encompassed the fire and the
        crackling of half-burned logs
while the smoke scattered its arms
gathering, scattering the black moths in
        a wick's light.

[*Tiyarina muyu tullpak
huatay happipacuy ninapay cjatata payta
        chintamanta
chaykama kcosñipay cheqquechiy ricrapaypa
shukpi riy hamuyri pillpintuyanamanta
        jahuapi achicuna
hucmecchamanta.*]
(*Samay* 40–41)

The presence of Chihuailaf's aunt Julia next to the hearth in *Recado* is similar to this scene from Chikangana's childhood and includes the voice of a father or taita, as elsewhere in the same poem he says, "'Yachachiy' ñiy taitay 'ima ñuqa caruta-riy causay'" ["Learn," my taita told us, "I won't be around forever"] (41).

And so today I sing to keep flowering and
        weeding
on this unfinished road
that we humans inhabit,
we children of the night
people of daydreams, the mystery and the
        smile
in times when the dawns are difficult.

[*Inallatak ñokataki cunan sisaypak
        ccorayriñancaypi mana tucussca
ima causana nuqawan runakuna
churikuna tutamanta
runakuna musccoyk misteriopay
        asirinacunari
pachapi anak pacarimanta.*]
(*Samay* 43)

The oralitor presents his song, his *taki*, as opening a path through the woods, through the night, through time, through the mystery and the smile. The song thus becomes a medium through which the oralitor examines those places in communal memory, one's roots (*mallki*) and the wells of daydreams (*pponccopi mushcoypa*), that are expressed as mysteries of space-time (*pacha*). In doing so, Chikangana's oraliture captures the return to ancestral memory that he states is one of the oralitor's characteristics. In this sense oraliture requires a re-encounter with the past, and childhood in particular:

the wind whipped the doors to my heart
and visitors came to inhabit the house:
the *wuandos* [jugs], resting against the
    gumtrees [*Sapium glandulosum*]
waiting for me to come out for water;
the birds that had been chased around
    during the day
transformed into giant white men
settling accounts, laughing what I had
    laughed;
the drowned, the people who'd fallen
from cliffs, those who'd been carried off
    by the earth and the rain
the wandering dead who had forgotten
    the *mambi* in the garrets
the Indians who died from so much living
    and returned to watch their fields.

[el viento azotaba las puertas de mi corazón
y venían visitantes a poblar la casa:
los *wuandos*, recostados en verdes lecheros
esperando mi salida por agua;
los pájaros correteados durante el día
transformados en hombres blancos y
    enormes
pidiendo cuentas, riendo lo que había
    reído;
los ahogados, los despeñados, los que se
    llevaba la lluvia y la tierra
los muertos errantes que olvidaban el *mambi*
    en los soberados
los indios que se morían de tanto vivir y
    regresaban a mirar sus chagras.]
(*Samay* 41–42)

The image of the birds, the spirits, and the forces of nature, give clarity to the world nararrated by the traveler in the wells of a daydream, crossing the "doors to my heart." Here oraliture is symbolically like a time capsule and a magnifying glass which with one closely and carefully examines memory's warp and weft "in times when the dawns are difficult" (43).

"Times when the dawns are difficult" in *Samay pisccok* are similar to allusions elsewhere in which hurricanes howl, Tenochtitlán arises, and the blue flag of the Mapuche unfurls in Chihuailaf's *Recado*. As expressed in the Quechua image of *pachakuti* or the upending of space-time, a concept that animates much of Chikangana's work, these are times of crisis that coincide with the prophesized resurgence of Indigenous sovereignty. Oraliture becomes the voice and thought of the earth itself as it announces the coming of new ages, and expresses itself through some of the book's central images, like in "Samay pisccok" or "Spirit of the Bird":

These are the songs of Mother Earth in a
    major key
as she announces the new age,
here we are, weaving the yellow butterfly's circle,
in sum, we are the spirit of the bird in the
    wells of a daydream.

[*Takicay pachamamak jatun rimaypi
hullilla kcayapacha
caypi muyupi pillpintumantak quellu
tukurita nunacay pisccomanta pponccopi
mushcoypa.*]
(*Samay* 18, 19)

Kcayapacha, the new age, resonates with the idea of *pacha* [time, space, land] and *kutiy* [movement] insofar as such movement is a kind of sociocultural reconfiguration. Remember that, beyond expressing the complex idea of time and space in a state of transformation, at its most basic *pachakuti* is connected with agricultural labor: turning the earth to make a furrow in a field. Within Chikangana's view of oraliture, *pacha-kuti* not only symbolizes the political dawn or resurgence of Indigenous sovereignty, but also the harvest of the word of generations of Indigenous and Mestizos subjects who have been discriminated against and partially silenced as a result of colonization. As a "sower" of the word, the oralitor offers his songs (*taki*) to *pachamama* and his ancestors. In the first line of "Samay pisscok," the idea of a "major key" is related to the recollection of the elders' living words: the ancestors-roots (*mallki*).

Beyond emphasizing these similarities with Chihuailaf's definition of oraliture, I should also to point that Fredy Chikangana/ Wiñay Mallki's work elaborates its own approach and makes its own contributions to the oraliture movement. One of the notable differences between the two projects lies in that they root themselves in distinct verbal genres and languages while recognizing how these have mutually influenced one another since well before the arrival of the Spanish. Indeed, despite the advent of Spanish colonization in the sixteenth century, the Quechua and the Mapuche, as well as their languages, never stopped interacting, as seen in the affinities of the oraliture movement that Chihuailaf and Chikangana led from the two extremes of the Andes in Abya Yala.

Fredy Chikangana/Wiñay Mallki, says, "Nuqa taki" "Soy Cantor" [I am a singer], and his songs (*taki*) seek to be inscribed formally and ideally within the Quechua verbal art of Incaic tradition. The *haylli* or celebratory hymn is one of the most recurrent verbal genres in *Samay pisccok*. The poem (*takicuna*) "Takimanta pacha-cuna" "Versos de la tierra" [Earth's verses] expresses Chikangana's project of sowing and reaping the word:

My verses are made out of corn	[De maíz son mis versos
and of water my essence.	y de agua mi esencia.
Today I sing like they sang	Canto hoy como antes cantaron
like a strong seed that dodges death.	como fuerte semilla que esquiva la muerte.
Like a drop feeds the fountain.	Así como gota que alimenta la fuente.
My verses are made out of corn	De maíz son mis versos
and of water my essence.	y de agua mi esencia.
Today I live from yesterday's planting,	Vivo hoy con la siembra de ayer,
with the sweet perseverance that keeps death	con la dulce insistencia que detiene la
at bay.	muerte]

(*Samay* 55)

As oraliture, the poem expresses intergenerational permanence ("Today I sing like they sang" and "Today I live from yesterday's planting"). Furthermore, this poetic practice is justified by an apparently agricultural materiality: "My verses are made out of corn / and of water my essence." The oralitor positions himself simply and plainly as one who works the word, a "planter" like many of his Yanakuna brethren in the Colombian massif. As seen in our previous discussion of his dissertation, Chikangana uses these forms of vernacular expression to reconcile the apparent contradictions between the spade and the pen.

On a similar symbolic note, Chikangana's "Nukanchis kan causay pachacaypi" "Aún tenemos vida en esta tierra" [We are still here, alive on this earth] explicitly situates itself within a Quecha verbal genre of the *haylli*. In essence, the poem is an agricultural poem-*haylli*, written in the style of Incan poetry that has been preserved in the oral and written traditions of the central Andes:

While they grind yellow corn on the stone
we sing with flutes and deer-skin drums
we laugh and slowly get drunk
bidding farewell to the sun as it flees among
             the mountains.
We laugh and we dance with flutes in our
             hands
we enter slowly deep inside the earth,
through that warm navel that drags us,
             carries us
to memory,
to that space where our dead live,
where they joyfully receive us:
"Let's drink," says taita Manuel, "long live
             corn."
"Let's drink," says mama Rosario, "long live
             the earth that warms us."
And while we dance in the furrows,
we laugh and sing with our dead,
we chase away our worries with the flutes
we sweeten our nights with chicha.[8]
"Let's drink without worrying," they shout,
"We are still here, alive on this earth."

[Mientras ellas muelen el maíz amarillo
             sobre la piedra
nosotros cantamos con flautas y tambores
             de venado
reímos y nos embriagamos sin prisa
despedimos al sol que huye entre las
             montañas.
Reímos y danzamos con flautas entre
             las manos
nos vamos metiendo hacia el fondo de
             la tierra,
por ese ombligo tibio que arrastra y nos lleva
a la memoria
a ese espacio donde habitan nuestros
             muertos,
que nos reciben con alegría:
«¡Bebamos!», dice taita Manuel, «y que viva
             el maíz».
«¡Bebamos!», dice mama Rosario, «y que
             viva la tierrita que nos calienta».
Y mientras danzamos sobre los surcos,
reímos y cantamos con nuestros muertos,
con flautas ahuyentamos las penas
y con chicha endulzamos las noches.
«¡Bebamos sin pena!», gritan,
«que aún tenemos vida en esta tierra».
(*Samay* 57)

---

[8] Chicha is a drink of fermented corn common throughout the Andes. *Translator's note.*

In this *haylli* the oralitor affirms the continuity of Andean ritual and iconographic traditions. For example, one finds similar images on several pre-Hispanic Moche vases in which the dead play musical instruments and on a number of *k'eros* (painted wooden vessels) that bear images of Incan agricultural rites.

Figure 36. Pictoral abstraction from a wooden Inca *k'ero*. Morayma Montibeller Ardiles. *Tarpui llahuayra haylli, la canción de la siembra en la iconografía de los q'eros*, p. 7.

Many of the recurring scenes on Incan *k'eros*, or at least those that refer to the Incas and continued to be painted during the colonial period, represent groups of men and women in mingas of the word. These scenes are typically represented along with the *k'ero*'s circular edges and, as can be seen in Figure 36, the agricultural labor and ritual drinking they represent have more than a casual visual relationship to the poem "Nukanchis kan causay pachacaypi."

The work that men and women perform is differentiated in both their visual representation on the *k'ero*'s and in the poem: the women grind corn and the men play music. Dance and the ritual sharing of a corn drink like chicha accompany the celebration of people's re-connecting with each other, their ancestors, and the earth. From the perspective of an oraligraphie, "Nukanchis kan causay pachacaypi" can be read as a poem in which contemporary Yanakuna Mitmak are brought into an empathetic connection with Incan and pre-Incan pictographic expressions like those found on central Andean *k'ero*s.

Indeed, the poem-*haylli* is a celebration of the survival of Yanaconas'/Yanakunas' Quechua roots. As the oralitor states through the elders' collective voice, "we are still alive." Mama Rosario and Taita Manuel express the complementary duality that invites a total sense of cultural continuity through a call to life: "let's drink" and "long live." Moreover, the entry into the earth's navel—the inside or *ucku pacha* in Quechua: "we slowly enter, deep inside the earth"— expresses another kind of access to the wells of a daydream in which one finds the dead and the root (*mallki*) that has endured over time (*wiñay*). In other words, here we contemplate an image of the re-encounter with the warm, collective "placenta," the symbolic center, the warm navel, the place from which life comes and to which it returns, as Chikangana describes and celebrates the journey of collective return to memory: "this space where our dead live."

In "Yurak yaku" "Memoria de agua" [The water's memory], the poetic presence of the mallki allows for a more intimate song. In a sense it is closer to the *harawi* or *yaraví*, a genre from Inca oral and contemporary central Andean popular tradition, that is related to absence, loss, and in the text presented here, with the dead:

The voices	[Por estas tierras
of our dead Yanakunas wander through these lands.	deambulan las voces de nuestros muertos yanakunas.
They walk, their bodies a river and their memory water,	Andan con cuerpo de río y memoria de agua,
shaking like a tree amidst the wind.	vibrando como árbol al viento.
That's why I sing	Por eso canto
so the flowers and the roads sing,	para que canten las flores y los caminos,
the mountains and the lakes;	los cerros y las lagunas;
so that the moon will know I am Yanakuna	para que sepa la luna que soy yanakuna
a man of the water and the rainbow.	hombre del agua y el arco iris.]
	(*Samay* 82–83)

The text can be divided into two parts, the first four verses (the collective voices of the ancestors as they walk the earth) and the final five verses (the more personal voice of the author). The verse, "I sing so that they sing," underscores oraliture as a collective project. In the Quechua version Chikangana says, "Ima yaraví / ñampi ttica maythu qiunquinam yaraví" (82) [That's why I sing / so the flowers and the roads sing] (83). We should note that here the oralitor uses the term *yaraví* instead of *taki* to refer to "song," and that the contemporary yaraví is a musical genre derived from traditions among both the Inca singers and the Spanish troubadours.

Further, this notion of being in dialogue with the dead, which can also be found towards the end of Chihuailaf's *Recado*, gathers a good deal of force in Chikangana's poetics, as in the poem, "Rimarichiy huañushcacunahuan" "Hablando con los muertos" 'Speaking with the Dead":

Sometimes I speak with the dead.
On starry nights
they light the zigzagging roads.
They will ask me how life is going.
And I'll tell them, "I'm just here, witnessing
                               so much death."

[A veces hablo con los muertos.
En noches estrelladas
ellos iluminan los caminos zigzagueantes.
Cómo va la vida, me preguntan.
Y yo les digo: «Aquí, mirando tanta
                               muerte».]

(*Samay* 92–93)

This is one of the few texts by Chikangana or any other of Colombia's Indigenous authors that can be read as alluding to the Colombian armed conflict and the impact of its death toll in departments like the Cauca and Huila. The spokespeople for many Indigenous Peoples firmly state that, despite the fact that the country's Indigenous population was heavily impacted by the war, the conflict had nothing to do with them, and this position perhaps explains why there are so few references to the armed conflict in works by Indigenous authors. However, it is no less certain that as the armed conflict escalated over the last two decades, denouncing those responsible opened the door to possible retaliation (kidnapping, murder, persecution). By comparison, participation in collective artistic projects like documentary film can diminish the chances that an individual artist will stand out and thus be targeted, although several Indigenous cinematographers have also been threatened. As Angélica Mateus Mora convincingly demonstrates in her *El indígena en el cine y el audiovisual colombiano* [Indigenous people in Colombian Film and Video] (2013), testimonios about the violence and Indigenous struggles to regain their land have been central themes in Indigenous peoples' audiovisual projects starting to develop in the 1980s.[9]

In "Rimarichiy huañushcacunahuan" "Hablando con los muertos" [Speaking with the Dead] the oralitor suggests that the living are perhaps more surrounded by death than the dead themselves. While Chikangana's literary work does not explore the armed conflict with

---

[9] To get a better idea of the full panorama of these audiovisual productions, the social contexts in which they have been created, and the injustices they frequently denounce, see specifically the chapters, "Representaciones de los conflictos" [Representations of the conflicts] and "Violencia y los pueblos indígenas" [Violence and Indigenous Communities] (129–73).

any considerable depth, his work as an activist and defender of the coca leaf have led him to participate in documentaries like *Mama Koka! Krieger für das Kokain* (2013), a German film directed by Suzan Seker-ci, in which the oralitor introduces himself as Wiñay Mallki, alongside his daughter and other members of theYanakuna Mitmak community involved in linguistic and cultural revitalization in San Agustín, Huila.

In one of the scenes from the film, the oralitor and another member of the community are speaking at night beside the hearth, orali-ture's traditional space according to Chikangana. Elsewhere Chikan-gana demonstrates some of the coca leaf's ritual uses, explains the industrial production of tea made from the coca leaf, walks through the city of Bogotá and, finally, leads the annual sun ceremony, car-ried out on the summer solstice in June, to remind his people that at that very moment other Indigenous Peoples are also celebrating. This reminder evokes Pan-Indigenous projects such as oraliture, as well as the collective struggle against the criminalization of the coca leaf. His denouncements of the situation of Indigenous Peoples who are caught in the middle of the armed conflict and of the apparent, collective ignorance non-Indigenous People have about the coca leaf are represented in the film's documentary space. However, we should also note that at no point in the film does Wiñay Mallki refer to his role as a writer and/or poet. In fact, none of his work is read or even cited in the German documentary. Nonethless, his presence in it helps us understand that even as Indigenous authors tend not to refer to the armed conflict in their literary work, they still provide critical commentary on the war in Colombia through their partic-ipation in other spaces and media. In *Mama Koka! Krieger für das Kokain*, Fredy Chikangana/Wiñay Mallki's role is that of a spiritual guide (*amauta*), an oralitor (even though he does not call himself that in the film), an intercultural educator, and a leader in the movement to recuperate the Yanakuna Mitmak's Quechua legacy.

Given that Fredy Chikangana/Wiñay Mallki aligns his oraliture with Quechua cultural and poetic traditions, to what extent can we also find in his work the romantic, sad tones of lamentations that are typical of contemporary Quechua huaynos? There are several possible answers. However, it is important to remember that Fredy Chikanga-na learned Quechua as a means of literary revindication as an adult, at a moment when his community was basically Spanish-speaking. The *haylli* and the *taki* (song and dance) are considered courtly Inca genres, while a popular musical genre like the Peruvian huayno is a hybrid genre, both mestizo and Indigenous. That said, the huayno played an important role in José María Argueda's introduction to the Quechua literary world when he was a child, as recounted in his *Canto Quechua* [Quechua Song] (1938), a work in which Arguedas writes and adapts the songs that had so influenced his childhood. As seen in his *haylli* to the jet airplane, "Jetman," and to the Cuban Revolution, "Cubapaq," even a genre like the *haylli* acquires a notably more modern tone in the influential Peruvian writer's work.

Chikangana's Quechua oraliture, and in particular *Samay pisccok*, represents part of a project of immersion in and the continuation of pre-Hispanic traditions like those of the Inca. In his more recent poems the elegiac tone of the *haylli* is a recurrent mode while the popular lament of the contemporary huayno is more tangential. Without necessarily claiming the huayno as a direct influence, we should keep in mind that the romantic lamentation so characteristic of the huayno was present in the poems Chikangana wrote throughout the 1980s and 1990s before he became an oralitor. During that time, he wrote some of his most well-known poems, such as "En verbo ajeno" [In another's language], "Del vacío" [From the abyss], and "Todo está dicho" [Everything is said]. Indeed, these poems' translation into Quechua and their inclusion in *Samay pisccok* lets us better understand the collection's melancholy tone.

The poem "Mushgoy" "Sueños" [Dreams] speaks to that fact that he began working in the tone of the *haylli* after he had become a Quechua oralitor:

Happy the night	[Dichosa la noche
and the grass's naked dream.	y el sueño desnudo de la hierba.
Happy the grass, growing	Dichosa la hierba, crece
and sweet word before death.	y ante la muerte palabra dulce.
Happy the grandfather	Dichoso el abuelo
who had time to die and to sing	que tuvo tiempo de morir y cantar
in the middle of the war.	en medio de la guerra.
Happy the dreams	Dichosos los sueños
of the people of the blue earth	de la gente de tierra azul
because they are from the drum, from the	porque son de tambor, de río,
river, from the woman	de mujer
from the stubborn root	de terca raíz
that defies death.	que esquiva la muerte.]
	(*Samay* 87)

In this passage the happiness (*samiyoq*) of the *haylli*-hymn prevails, as opposed to the lament found in a poem like "Llapa ñisccay" "Todo está dicho" [Everything has been said]:

those distant moons who weep with the rain
must carry a hint of bitterness in their
                          memories,
the trees, the fish,
the last revered rainbow
must have something to lament;
I,
son of sufferings and hopes,
have nothing to say.
Everything has been said.

[aquellas lunas que lloran con la lluvia
algo tendrán en sus recuerdos de amargura,
los árboles, los peces,
el último arco iris venerado
tendrán algo entre sus quejas;
yo,
hijo de dolores y esperanzas,
nada tengo que decir.
Todo está dicho.]
(*Samay* 91)

In "Mushgoy" "Sueños" [Dreams] the color blue—so characteristic of Chihuailaf's poetry—, is one of wiñay's colors, becoming a symbol of enduring over time beyond its identification with the people of the blue earth who have resisted their disappearance. Death remains the same horrifying shadow that we saw in "Del vacío," where it culminates with the poemgraphic image of a trail composed of bones, stains, and letters.

As we have already seen, Fredy Chikangana's oraliture is partially written from the perspective of a collective Quechua "we" that incorporates and amplifies Yanakuna being. This conceptualization of what is Quechua is derived from a sense of pan-Andean identity strongly tied to the Inca and to Tawantinsuyu. Other images from Chikangana's work are connected to personal and/or collective references from the pre-Hispanic middle Andes such as the prayer to the god Wiracocha, attributed to the civilizing hero Manco Capac, which was anthologized by Edmundo Bendezú in 1980. This prayer alludes to the Andean divinity as being as large as the lake of the sky. The lake (*cocha*)—Titiqaqa in particular—is one of the main *pacarinas* (places of origin) recognized by Andean peoples. In the following verses, these antecedents are connected with the search for words that are formed, "mysteriously," by a kind of "inner" lake or *cocha* that passes through the oralitor's singing, in turn suggesting a possible symbolic reconnection with the placenta as a symbolic center:

I am a singer on this earth
looking for words in this lake traversing me.

[*Nuqa taki caypi pacha
mascayri shimi paipa ccocha chacaynuqapi.*]
(*Samay* 106, 107)

Two subtle aspects of this oraliture proposal have to do with how Spanish is used in certain poems, along with implicit references to body language. On the one hand, the stilted spoken Spanish found in "Canto a la koka" [Song to koka] and the intentional use of a

Spanish that is overly literal and the byproduct of oral songs, reveal an attempt to give more literary emphasis to the Quechua. In addition, it subordinates the version in the dominant language to the version in Quechua:

Koka leaf drinks the morning dew,
the grandfather's gaze is happy.
Blue bird sings in the mature lemon grove,
the rainbow's colors fade.
I chew koka, I watch the grandfather,
I hear the blue bird
I smell the lemon's aroma
and I leave for the mountain
having the rainbow's colors.

[Hoja de koka bebe rocío de la mañana,
mirada del abuelo es alegre.
Pájaro azul canta en limonar maduro,
colores de arco iris se desvanecen.
Mastico koka, al abuelo observe,
oigo al pájaro azul
huelo el aroma de limón
y me voy a la montaña
con colores de arco iris.]
(*Samay* 52)

On the other hand, in Chihuailaf's work the perception and transmission of the speaker's—or gesturers, as Chihuailaf says in the *Recado*—body language is of particular importance. Body language is captured as vividly as possible in his literary works and once again emphasizes the importance of oral communication. A clear example of this would be Chikangana's "Ppatmay" "Partir" [Leaving]:

silence inhabits the body
the hands go
the eyes come
the lips part
the teeth come.

[*upalacuy pay causak cuerpo pay
aptay pay hatinacuy
hamuy ñahui pay
puririy huirppay
hamuy quiru pay.*]
(*Samay* 81)

Along the same lines, "Ninamanta" "Del fuego" [From the fire] is one of the collection's most suggestive works:

It is night and in the mountains
the doors are illuminated and tremble
in the fire's gleaming;
the cracks and the windows are those lines
crossing the darkness to warm our hearts.
The Yanakuna, men and women,
are people who help each other in dark times,
they talk, cry, and laugh in a river of thick
                              smoke.
A clay pot is on the fire, and in the black
                              clay pot
koka leaves spin in circles like time itself.
The elder roasts the leaves and stokes the
                              fire,
then brings three leaves to his mouth and
chews them, gazing into the ashes;

[Es de noche y en las montañas
las puertas se iluminan y tiemblan
con el resplandor del fuego;
las rendijas y las ventanas son esas líneas
que cruzan la oscuridad para calentar
                              nuestro corazón.
Los hombres y mujeres yanakunas,
que son gente que se asiste en tiempos de
                              oscuridad,
hablan, lloran y ríen en un río de humo espeso.
En el fuego está el tiesto de barro y en el
                              tiesto de barro negro
la hojita de koka que gira en círculos como
                              gira el tiempo.
El abuelo tuesta la hoja y atiza el fuego,
luego se lleva tres hojas a la boca y

he offers the fire three tender leaves,
passing them over his head.
"You must share," he says,
"they also want to chew coca,"
a thread of smoke sprouts from the fire
     and turns about the kitchen
on its journey skyward.
The grandmother's heart asks,
"And what did the fire say?"
There is a silence, broken
by the dry firewood's cracking.

mambea mirando hacia las cenizas;
ofrenda tres hojas tiernas al fuego,
pasándolas por encima de su cabeza.
«Hay que compartir», dice,
«ellos también quieren mambear»,
brota del fuego un hilo de humo y da
     vueltas sobre la cocina
mientras toma su camino al cielo.
Pregunta el corazón de la abuela:
«¿Qué será lo que dijo el fuego?».
Hay un silencio que se rompe
con el crujir de la leña seca.]
(*Samay* 69)

"Ninamanta" [From the fire] rounds out several aspects of Fredy Chikangana/Wiñay Mallki's literary project: the vital presence of the elders' words as well as that of the elders themselves (who advise and ask questions); the plants that accompany Quechua verbal art (here the coca leaf, although in others texts these also include *chicha* made out of corn and even ayawasca); the kitchen and the hearth (*tullpa*) as a symbolic center and the "ideal" space for the intergenerational transmission of knowledge; the evocation of childhood; the Yanaku-na collectivity; complementarity between the masculine and the feminine (men and women, grandfather and grandmother); daydreams and mysteries (doors that are illuminated and tremble, gleaming and smoke; shadows and the night; conversations; circular time in the image of a face-to-face dialogue with the voice of the fire). As with the speaking coca leaf in other Andean ritual contexts, the fire in the poem speaks, giving shape to ritual forms whose codes, according to the oralitor, are held by the elders, those who know, those who gather around the hearth.

In a powerful remembrance of "the other writing," the oralitor evokes the world of childhood, the bodily relationship with one's mother and with Mother Earth:

With the *callu* and the *chumbe* around her waist and her long hair
my mother watched me play in the corn-fields, chasing fine-colored
butterflies
and leaving footprints stuck to Mother Earth.

[Con *callu* y *chumbe* sobre la cintura y
     cabello largo
mi madre me vio jugar entre maizales,
     persiguiendo mariposas de
finos colores
y dejando huellas adheridas a la tierra
     madre.]
(*Samay* 41)

As argued previously, Chikangana's oraliture can also be read from the notion of oralitegraphies, and not only from the author's self-described positioning as an oralitor. Indeed, some of his poetic proposals evoke chromatic spectra like the wiphala's rainbow or the Andean flag. These gestures recall community forms of ideographic writing in textiles like woven belts ("*chumbe* around her waist") and visually reconfigure words through oralitegraphies like "Takina" "Poema" [Poem], "Del vacío" "Chhusak" [From the abyss], and "Wiñay" "Raíces" [Roots] (see fig. 37).

K'apay muñamanta urkupikuna	Aroma de poleo en la montaña
Sincca	Nariz
Taita cunay ninapaypi	Consejo de taitas en el fuego
Shimi	Boca
Caballu manñaman sarak	Caballos a la orilla del maizal
Ñawi	Ojos
Sipsicay ancha-tutapicuna	Susurros en la noche oscura
Rinri	Oídos
Shimi sayrimanta kokari	Palabras de tabaco y koka
Yuyal	Pensamiento
Yupijahuapiyupi sachapimanta	Huellas sobre huellas en el bosque
Caru-caru llaktayok	Extraños
Nima runapa huarmiri	Silencio de los hombres y mujeres
Huañushca	Muerte
Yahuar pachapura	Sangre entre la tierra
Wiñay	Raíces
Ucju	Cuerpo
Wiñay	Raíces

Figure 37. Oralitegaphy as a corporal form. Fredy Chikangana. *Samay pisccok pponccopi mushcoypa/Espíritu de pájaro en pozos del ensueño,* p. 65.[10]

In this final *taki*-poem, both memory's senses and the body language of oral communication are literally re-elaborated through a graphic composition that evokes the human body as a kind of plant with roots. The senses are positioned in the upper part of the oralitegraphic work: nose, mouth, eyes, and ears. The sense of smell

[10] Translation: "Smell of pennyroyal [*Minthostachys mollis*] in the countryside / Nose / The taitas's [elders] wisdom in the fire / Mouth / Horses at the edge of the cornfield / Eyes / Whispers in the dark night / Ears / Words of tobacco and coca / Thought / Footprints layered on footprints in the woods / Strangers / Silence of men and women / Death / Blood within the earth / Roots / Body / Roots."

brings the "The aroma of pennyroyal in the mountains." The mouth carries the spoken word, the "Advice of the taitas in the fire." Sight outlines a vision of, "Horses at the edge of the cornfield." The ears let one hear, "Whispers in the dark night." The words' placement on the page creates synesthetic sensations in the minds of both the oralitor and the reader. We can imagine the "mouths" of the horses in the cornfield. We can broaden our imaginations to see through the dark night and discover where the whispers are coming from. The stripe in the middle of the text that corresponds where a woman would wear a chumbe states, "The words of tobacco and coca" and "Thought". From there down, the words and verses correspond to a world that is more intimate (footprints, silence, death, blood, roots) and earthier (forest, land, body).

The first eight lines correspond to a dimension known in Quechua as *hanan pacha*, an upper world that gives expression to the blue celestial memory of what has gone away, and above all to the past that is at the forefront of this type of cosmovision. In contrast, the eight lower verses are representative of the *ucku pacha*, an inner dimension that is both human and earthly: the place of death, the seed, and the placenta. According to Quechua cosmovision in this dimension you can divine the future, what is at your back, what we cannot see but nonetheless are moving towards. We can argue that the verses on the central stripe, "Shimi sayrimanta kokari / Yuyal" in Quechua, represent the *kay pacha*, the plane of our earthly existence, with the here and now of our thought that mediates between *hanan* and *ucku* via the ritual words of tobacco and coca, that is, the great words, the true words from the primordial soure (the wells of a daydream) that the oralitor seeks to attain in his journey to and from memory. In sum, we can say that "Wiñay" "Raíces" [Roots] proposes an oralitegraphic textuality whose oral antecedents, graphic expression, and literary articulation enrich and complement oraliture's initial project insofar as it represents "our word already being written, but alongside orality" [nuestra Palabra ya escribiéndose, pero al lado de la oralidad] (Chihuailaf, *Recado* 62).

3
ORALITURE IN HUGO JAMIOY JUAJIBIOY: AN
ORALITEGRAPHIC READING OF *BÍNÝBE OBOYEJUAYËNG/*
DANZANTES DEL VIENTO [WIND DANCERS]

In this chapter I use the notion of oralitegraphies to analyze Hugo Jamioy's *Bínÿbe oboyejuayëng/Danzantes del viento* [Wind Dancers], which was first published in 2005.[1] More so than any other work of Indigenous Colombian oraliture, *Bínÿbe oboyejuayëng* is the fullest expression of a creative will focused on the textual intersection of different graphic systems, oral communication, and bilingual literary texts.

Oralitors like Chihuailaf, Jamioy, and Chikangana usually privilege the presence of oral voices through the use of community-based verbal genres in the works. Further, we can use the notion of oralitegraphies to approach works by Jamioy and Chikangana as these two oralitors bring oral and alphabetic-literary expressions into dialogue, juxtaposing them with traditional graphic-visual forms of representa-

---

[1] Jamioy was born in 1971 in Sibundoy, Putumayo. His father is a traditional doctor and his mother an expert weaver, midwife, and traditional doctor. Alberto Kuajibioy Chindoy, one of Colombia's pioneering Indigenous writers, was a distant cousin of his mother's, and Jamioy called him his "tío abuelo" [uncle-grandfather] as a sign of respect. His wife, Ati, is from the Iku People (Arhuaca/Bintukua). Although they live in the Sierra Nevada of Santa Marta, the oralitor frequently visits the Sibundoy Valley, his ancestral home that he calls bengbe tabanóc [our sacred place of origin]. Jamioy studied Agronomy at the University of Caldas. His first book of poetry was *Mi fuego y mi humo, mi tierra y mi sol* [My Fire and My Smoke, My Land and My Sun] (1999). In 2006 he won a national scholarship for literary research from the Ministry of Culture for his project *Oralitura indígena de Colombia* [Indigenous oraliture in Colombia]. In 2009 his *Hablando, junto al fogón* [Speaking next to the hearth] won the Ministry of Culture's National Scholarship for the Creation of Oraliture.

tion that come from a number of different media, such as the *chumbe* or ideographic woven belt, reading coca leaves next to the hearth, or ideosymbolic baskets, among others.

BÍNŸBE OBOYEJUAYËNG/DANZANTES DEL VIENTO [WIND DANCERS]

First published in 1995, *Bínÿbe oboyejuayëng* is a work of poetic oraliture that draws upon the oralitegraphic traditions of Jamioy's family. Colombia's Ministry of Culture published an expanded edition in 2010 as part of its Biblioteca Básica de los Pueblos Indígenas de Colombia [Basic Library of Colombia's Indigenous Peoples]. Although the re-edition contains 24 additional poems, the editorial criteria guiding the publication of the Indigenous Library's eight tomes meant sacrificing a number of the earlier version's graphic and structural qualities. The 2010 edition of *Bínÿbe* is richer in terms of its content, but formally far plainer insofar as it lacks the very elements of traditional Camëntsá writing whose co-presence is central to Jamioy's poetics. Although the re-edited work was widely distributed, in reality invisibilized the original's oralitegraphic textuality. While a painting done by the author's brother, Juan Andrés Jamioy, was used for the 2010 edition's cover, the original work's visual language, all but disappeared. As such, when considering the work's visual effects my analysis of oralitegraphies in *Bínÿbe oboyejuayëng* focuses on the original edition. When dealing with the work's oralitegraphic project, I cite texts as they appear in the revised and updated 2010 edition.

If the *Bínÿbe oboyejuayëng*'s free 2010 edition has been more widely disseminated and more widely read than the one from 2005, this previous edition nonetheless represents one of the most important and original works published by an Indigenous author from Colombia. The work declared itself to be a book of oraliture from the moment it was published, an important step that confirmed the concept's viability in contemporary writing. As Chihuailaf had laid out a decade earlier, a number of the texts in *Bínÿbe oboyejuayëng* are presented as though they come from the taitas or elders and represent the voices of Jamioy's People. However, the collection also portrays the confrontational and nostalgic voice of an Indigenous immigrant. As with Chikangana, here this voice becomes a point of departure for the oralitor's scriptural journey. *Bínÿbe* elaborates both the great potential and the great "loss" of contemporary urban experience, seeing it as a "directionless river" that is nonetheless subject to the elders' guiding, mythic explications of the world, as well as their and wise words. The oralitor in *Bínÿbe oboyejuayëng* thus becomes a messenger and a bridge between cultures, with many of his texts becoming calls to and clarifications for the non-Camëntsá world.

That said, Jamioy seldom self-identifies as a poet, and he has never felt completely comfortable with the word "literature." In fact, we could say that part of his being seen as a poet, as opposed to an oralitor, arises from the institutional problem of needing to present him and his work on the public stage. However, he does sometimes refer to his people's poetry while describing himself as a practitioner of *botamán biyá*, the "beautiful word." Beautiful word is a way of referring to Camëntsá verbal art, and a concept that has also been used by the K'iche' Maya writer Humberto Ak'abal, whose literary influence on Jamioy we will discuss in a moment. These are the great words, the words of wisdom, the words that are expressed in beautiful, formal language, and frequently with a specific goal in mind.[2] In an interview Jamioy says that "poetry has always existed in our languages, it has always been there for us, we the people who speak our language" [la poesía siempre ha existido en nuestras lenguas, que ha estado guardada allí para nosotros, los que hablamos la lengua] ("Hugo Jamioy"). The oralitor establishes himself from a vision-practice of poetry and the poetic that originates from Camëntsá language and its verbal genres. In this sense, part of Jamioy's work's collective linguistic origins can be understood through its emphasis on narratives of intergenerational orality, visions obtained through drinking *yajé* (a medicinal beverage that produces healing visions), brief wise proverbs, the interpretation of dreams, and the *botamán biyá* and the *jajuayenán*, among other genres and practices that structured the poet's creative background.

We can also note the intersection of Indigenous poetic texts from different parts of the continent in *Bínÿbe oboyejuayëng/Danzantes del viento*. For example, one notes the influence of the previously mentioned Humberto Ak'abal, the Maya K'iche' writer from Guatemala whose work is characterized by brief poetic texts derived from K'iche' orality. One finds that *Muk'ult'an in Nool/Secretos del abuelo* [My Grandfather's Secrets], by the Yucatec Maya writer Jorge Miguel Cocom Pech, also resonates in Jamioy's work, particularly in

---

[2] *Botamán biyá* are used, for example, when asking someone to be the godparent of one's child.

poems like "Bominÿ" "Los ojos" [The Eyes], which seems inspired
by how Cocom's text captures the dialogue between a young boy
and an older person. Last but not least, we should also note Jamioy's
open support for the Mapuche writer Elicura Chihuailaf's oraliture
project, a project that Jamioy emphasizes through the evocation of
the placenta, the community, and orality around the hearth, among
other features.

One of the literary aspects that makes the 2005 edition of *Bínÿbe
oboyejuayëng* [Wind Dancers] stand out from other works of Indigenous literature published up until that point is Jamioy's literary
proposal in which oral verbal art, alphabetic writing, and Camëntsá
ideosymbolic writing are brought together to complement each
other.

As will be analyzed throughout the rest of chapter, *Bínÿbe oboyejuayëng*'s bilingual texts—written in Camëntsá and in Spanish—occupy the top part of each page and dialogue with each other, while
the lower part of the volume's pages contains different ideograms
or *uigsas* that typically appear on chumbes or woven belts. In addition, each of the book's sections not only begins with an ideogram,
but also incorporates masks with prominent features that have been
passed down from generation to generation as a kind of gestural
memory carved in wood.[3]

Thus, the 2005 edition brings together two languages and different forms of writing as part of a multimodal literary project. As
I will explain, structurally the book's general design is based on the
chumbe. Further, I argue that *Bínÿbe oboyejuayëng* aspires to be read
the way one reads a woven belt, a visual reading based upon the Andean concept of complementary pairs, top and bottom. At the same
time, *Bínÿbe oboyejuayëng* takes up complementary dimensions of
the pictorial and the abstract which are typical of Andean weaving
and classic forms of sculpted or carved objects like the *k'eros* of the
Incas, which are painted vases that express different collective ideas
through conventional graphic representation (see fig. 36).

Accompanied by the letters that build the poems' literary versions, ideographic designs typically found on chumbes unfold
across *Bínÿbe oboyejuayëng*'s pages. The book thus takes shape as
an oralitegraphic object, becoming the physical manifestation of the
theoretical idea of an intertextual field in which readers encounter a

---

[3] The Ingas call these masks *suj ñauikuna kauachuj* [one who shows other faces]
(Jacanamijoy, "El chumbe" 133).

kind of bound chumbe, or in others words, a woven book. Traditional chumbes are girdles woven by Camëntsá and Inga weavers. Containing a number of ideograms that allude to the community and its environment, a chumbe protects the womb of the woman who wears it, identifies her, and preserves ideosymbolic memories. Talking about his mother, mamá Pastora Juajibioy, Hugo Jamioy says, "She insisted that we learn to weave, saying that by doing so we would not suffer as long as we lived; that if we forgot how to weave we would never understand what it means to live in community, because each thread represents a Camëntsá man, and every design symbolizes life itself..." [Ella insistía: aprendan a tejer, de esta manera nunca van a sufrir en la vida; si olvidan el tejido nunca van a entender lo que es vivir en comunidad, porque cada hilo representa un hombre Kamëntsá, y cada dibujo simboliza la vida...] ("Pensando, hilando" 150).

To understand these weavings' symbolic value one must recognize that chumbes are also used in other parts of the Andes, such as in the calendrical girdles of the Quechuas who live in the island of Taquile, on the Peruvian side of Lake Titiqaqa. In that part of the continent, the chumbe is used to keep chaos at bay, and to guard the maternal womb, and constitutes a measured expression of time. Basically a circle when completely unwound, the chumbe is in a sense an image of the center in space-time: the umbilical cord, placenta, womb, hearth, woman, memory, community, belonging (see fig. 38). It follows then, that the chumbe is also a book, a kind of media, and a textual field of communication. Like an umbilical cord connected to the symbolic center of the placenta and the hearth, the chumbe is a flexible, spiraling circle that communicates a graphic idea from Andean verbal communication, in the way that oraliture both departs from and takes up communitarian orality. In this sense, the chumbe iterates the idea of its own rhythm: of time linked to the origin, the mother, the family, the community. These textiles are not static museum pieces or simple intercultural expressions as, within the notion of oralitegraphic textualities, chumbes contribute to the dynamics of a "system of transmitting knowledge to future generations, through the art of weaving life and telling stories," that is, "a way of circulating intercultural events via the threads of tradition" [sistema de transmitir conocimientos a los nuevas generaciones, mediante el arte de tejer la vida y contar las historias ... una forma de hacer transitar a través del hilo de la tradición, los nuevos acontecimientos de la interculturalidad] (Jacanamijoy, "El chumbe" 133).

Figure 38. Ideograms on a chumbe woven by mamá Pastora Juajibioy. Author's
personal archive.

The texts in *Bínÿbe oboyejuayëng* "unroll" like a chumbe,
oralitegraphically, as its readings are simultaneously generated orally, graphically, and poetic-literarily. The collection's orality comes
from communal stories, the elders' words of advice, conversations
between father and son, among others. Masks, chumbes, beadwork,
the placement of texts, painting, the combination of the book's editorial design, and even its family photographs, manifest its visual
field. The literary is present via the volume's poetic form of creating,
and editing, and through Jamioy's use of bilingual phonetic script to
capture an oraliterary project that constantly evokes the hearth or
shinyak, the space of the kitchen, the house, the community, or any
of the other spaces where different generations communicate and
the oralitor's voice is expressed.

We should highlight the fact that the book also draws upon Jamioy's family, and that this is a unique quality of his oraliterary project. Juan Andrés Jamioy, the author's brother, painted the two works
that appear on the covers of both the 2005 and the 2010 editions.
The taita Camilo Jamioy, another of the oralitor's brothers, helped
translate the texts from Spanish into Camëntsá. Jamioy also dedicates several poems to his children. In turn, his children intervene
in the poems, asking their father wise questions. Indeed, many of
Jamioy's oraliterary texts emphasize questions and answers between
parents and children, a genre of learned dialogues that evoke both
the power of family histories—a topic that was described in the context of Leslie Marmon Silko's work in the previous chapter—and
the elders' words of advice. An example of this can be found in the
following fragment from "Bominÿ" "Los ojos" [Our eyes]:

Taita,   [Taita,
what are our eyes?   ¿qué son los ojos?
Son, our eyes   Hijo, los ojos
are flowers that spring   son las flores que brotan
from the soul's garden.   del jardín del alma.]
                                     (*Bínÿbe* [2010] 41)

In visual terms, the work's textual-woven composition—its textuality—is summarized in a matrix of ideograms that appears at the

beginning of the work. All of these designs are unrolled-shown in the following pages, integrated as individual motifs that complement each of the poetic texts (see fig. 39).

Figure 39. Matrix of Ideograms. Hugo Jamioy Juajibioy. *Bínÿbe oboyejuayëng/ Danzantes del viento* [2005], p. 1.

Jamioy dedicates *Bínÿbe oboyejuayëng* to the Creator (*Bëngbe Bëtsá*), to Mother Earth (*Tsëbatsana Mamá*), to the community, to the taitas or doctors who use yajé, and finally, to the University of Caldas, where he studied. In the oralitor's opinion, all of these participate in what he calls a "literary minga" or exchange with a single purpose in mind. The wind dancers are the Camëntsá themselves, as well as their ancestor, who participates physically and spiritually in the annual gathering of re-encounter in the Sibundoy Valley. However, if we think of the book graphically like a chumbe, ritually-speaking the book is also an offering to the Camëntsá people. Here, and as with Jamioy's previous book, *Mi fuego y mi humo, mi tierra y mi sol* [My Fire and My Smoke, My Land and My Sun] (1999), the central motif is once again the *bëtscanaté* or great day of re-encounter, which is also known as the carnival of forgiveness. Its pages are designed to call to mind words and things, the past and the present, the expression of the collective and individual, languages, scripts, verbal genres, oralities, and the beautiful word (*botamán biyá*). In the context of the celebration-*bétscanaté*, the dances evoked by the title include the words and the bodies of the dancers, the presence of those who return and those who have always been here. In *Bínÿbe*'s poetics the dancers are messengers who come and go, and, "poetry / is the leavening of each epoch's lifeblood" [la poesía / es el fermento de la savia para cada época] (*Bínÿbe* [2010] 65).

The book's ritual and collective character is also articulated through photographs of the author, his family, and the Camëntsá people. In fact, most of these images were taken during the celebration of the *bëtscanaté*, like the photo where the author and his wife appear carrying their children, accompanied by their family and other members of the Camëntsá nation (see fig. 40).

Figure 40. Family photo taken during the celebration of *bëtscanaté*. Hugo Jamioy Juajibioy. *Bínÿbe oboyejuayëng/Danzantes del viento* [2005], p. 19.

Jamioy's oraliterary texts seek to dialogue with and directly question dominant society, principally from the perspectives of Camëntsá and Iku culture, the latter being the Chibcha nation to which his wife pertains. His oraliture exists in permanent dialogue with his family and friends, people from his community, and even the people who visit his community. In short, *Bínÿbe oboyejuayëng* is a celebration of the physical and symbolic return to the community-nation ancestral lands, to the *bëtscanaté*, to the elders' beautiful word, and to the autochthonous or beautiful writing of the Camëntsá within the broader context of Andean textualities.

"THAT BEAUTIFUL WRITING THEY FORCED US TO FORGET"

Bínÿbe oboyejuayëng is structured in six parts, each of which is named according to the Inga-Quechua cultural matrix of the greater Andean region, with each of the *suyus* [quadrant-regions] of this printed chumbe demarcated by carved masks and *uigsas* or ideographic symbols. The *uigsa* ideogram is basically a diamond or rhombus, pictographically the female womb and ideographically a series of concepts and symbols that, while based on the human body, represent the cosmos, nature, and society. According to the Inga artist Benjamín Jacanamijoy Tisoy, who has done a good deal of research on the chumbe, the *uigsa* (diamond and womb-stomach) is the "primary symbol of life from which all concepts and shapes are derived" [símbolo principal de vida de donde parten todos los conceptos y todas las formas] (*Chumbe*).

Inga and Camëntsá ideographic textile writing is likely derived from Inca or even Pre-Incaic weaving. It also has visual similarities to the *tocapus*, small square textile designs frequently found on decorations. Considered to be a kind of visual communication, their ideographic codes seem to have been known and worn by certain elites in Tawantinsuyu and in other pre-Hispanic cultures in the central Andes. For example, in 1613 the chronicler Martín de Murúa confirms that this kind of writing had been "invented" by the Inca Wiracocha, who used it to communicate with his "ministers." After the Inca Wiracocha's death they fell into disuse (72). In her ethnohistoric research, Margarita Gentile, a scholar from the Museo de la Plata in Argentina states that:

> tocapu was a quality of cloth, not a drawing; we do not know what these figures nor the media they appeared on actually looked like. However, in contemporary scientific literature tocapu is used to refer to little square-shaped, multicolored drawings that form rows and columns on Inca *queros*, *llautos*, *chumpi*, and *uncu* de *cumbi*.[4] That said, they also appear in llautos done by the Moche and the Paracas, Tiwanaku hats and Chancay clothing, among other Andean garments. Their direct connection with the Inca is something that happened in the twentieth century.

---

[4] Traditional and Andean and Incan ways of writing on painted wooden vessels (queros) or different kinds of textiles.

[tocapu fue una calidad de tejido, no un dibujo; y no sabemos cómo eran aquellas figuras ni sus soportes. Pero, en la literatura científica moderna se llama así a unos pequeños dibujos cuadrados, multicolores, que forman hileras y columnas en *quero*, *llauto*, *chumpi* y *uncu* de *cumbi* incaicos. Aunque también los hay en algunos llauto Moche y Paracas, gorros Tiwanaku y ropa Chancay, entre otras prendas andinas, la relación directa con lo incaico tuvo lugar en el siglo XX.] (Gentile)

Gentile goes on to call the *tocapu* the "meaning unit in Andean graphic language" [unidad de sentido en el lenguaje gráfico andino]. We also find a rhomboidal graphic unit with a similar meaning in the textile writing of the Inga. Although the Inga consider themselves to be inheritors of the legacy of the Inca, the Spanish used runashimi or Kichwa as a lingua franca during evangelization, which would call into question Ingas' status of having a direct linguistic inheritance from the Inca. However, we can still hypothesize the possibility of there being a direct Inga influence upon the textile art of their neighbors in the Sibundoy Valley, the Camëntsá. In the anthology *Antes el amanecer* [Before, The Dawn], whose first chapter contains texts from Inga and Camëntsá verbal art, I claim that:

The Inga are a Quechua-speaking group that lives in the more northern parts of the Andes mountains. Perhaps out of a sense of prestige, many young Inga claim to be descendants of the Incas, while a number of elders from San Andrés talk about migrating from the San Miguel de Sucumbíos River, through the Putumayo or Balsayacu River. That migration would connect them with Indigenous groups from the Ecuadorian Amazon, many of whom were indoctrinated in Quechua (or Quichua), which the Spanish used as a lingua franca for purposes of evangelization. In any case, we should recognize that the Inca expanded their territory northward, even reaching as far as the southern part of today's Department of Nariño. Inca expansionism facilitated the displacement and exchange of populations from one region to another (mitimaes), as a form of tightening sociopolitical control. In addition, we should also note that the Spanish advanced from Perú and Ecuador with a large number of Quechua-speakers Indigenous People in their service (Yanacona or Yanacuna).

[Los ingas son considerados como el grupo quechua hablante que vive más al norte en la cordillera de los Andes. Muchos in-

gas jóvenes se autodesignan descendientes de los incas —quizás
por un asunto de prestigio—, mientras que algunos mayores de
San Andrés cuentan sobre migraciones desde el río San Miguel
de Sucumbíos, a través del río Putumayo o Balsayacu, lo que
los vincularía con grupos indígenas de la Amazonia ecuatoriana,
muchos de los cuales fueron adoctrinados por medio del quechua
(o quichua), una vez se implantó como lengua franca para la evan-
gelización. En todo caso, debe considerarse que los incas expan-
dieron sus dominios hacia el norte, alcanzando incluso el extremo
sur del actual Departamento de Nariño. El expansionismo inca
fomentaba el desplazamiento e intercambio de poblaciones de una
región a otra (mitimaes), como una forma de estabilizar el control
sociopolítico. Además, es un hecho que los españoles avanzaron
desde Perú y Ecuador con un gran número de indígenas que-
chua-hablantes a su servicio (yanaconas o yanacunas)] (Rocha Vivas, *Antes del amanecer* 48–49).

Given this history, we can speculate that at some unknown date
after the fifteenth century the Camëntsá, probably drawing upon the
Inga, appropriated and resignified the scripture legacy of the Inca
and southern Andean textiles in general, in much the same way that,
beginning in the fourth century, the Japanese took up and remade
the strokes of Chinese writing for their own ends. At the same time,
the Camëntsá also incorporated older cultural matrices from other
media like pottery and metalworking, such as those found in Paracas, Nasca, Moche, and Wari-tiwanaku iconography. The meanings, contexts, codes, and roles associated with these modes of visual
communication have varied over the years through processes of cultural reinvention. That said, we cannot reduce these to being mere
inscriptions, as suggested by Cummins and Rappaport when they
refer to communication via textiles in the Northern Andes (248).
As we have seen with regard to Chikangana's oraliture project, the
idea of claiming continuity with the past's verbal and scriptural lega-
cies similarly characterizes a good deal of contemporary Indigenous
literature. Regardless of the theoretical controversy surrounding
whether or not such autochthonous writing systems in the Andes
even exist, *Bínÿbe oboyejuayëng* is an oralitegraphic project in which
Jamioy legitimates and uses Camëntsá ideographic communication
("that beautiful writing"), while incorporating the *uigsa*'s ideographs
into his alphabetic oraliture. In my view, within the intersectional
field of what we refer to as textualities, these ideographs are visually
connected to *tocapu* and the fine weaving of the *cumbi*. If we follow

Gentile's theoretical proposal, *uigsa* and *tocapu* transmit a certain unity of feeling in an Andean graphic language. However, the format and context of the ideograms traditionally woven into chumbes change when "migrating" onto the oraliterary page where they form part of a complex oralitegraphic argument. Still, the kind of multimedia communication that Jamioy designs and transfers to the page with the help of his family is neither novel nor an isolated gesture. For example, María Jacanamijioy Tisoy, the Inga granddaughter of the celebrate chumbe weaver Concepción Tisoy, facilitated a project to "transfer chumbe designs onto woven bags" (Jacanamijoy, "El chumbe" 133). Importantly, the transfer of designs across media and the mutual influence that graphic and verbal arts have exercised on each other have been part of the Andes's cultural dynamic since well before the European invasion of the continent, and they are not necessarily the product of colonial pressures.

When we look at the table of *tocapus* proposed by Victoria de la Jara in 1972 and later reproduced by Gentile, we note the significant overlap that exists between the Inga-Camëntsá *uigsa* and the Inca *tocapu* that is given the name *mama* (it is the third design on the second row, moving from right to left) (see fig. 41). The *uigsa* and the *mama* are represented with a diamond, and both allude to the mother. The *tocapu mamacuna* (mamas) is represented with two diamonds.

The diamond is a starting point or key symbol (Jacanamijoy) in Inga-Camëntsá textile writing. However, the *uigsa* is basically inscribed in a kind of square and/or rectangle similar to the one that characterizes the central-Andean *tocapu*. A basic Inga design is the *uigsa uichca* (see fig. 42), which literally signifies a closed stomach and "simultaneously symbolizes the place where life begins (the female womb-belly) and the *suyu* [place] where people live together (the world with its four cardinal directions)" [simboliza a la vez el lugar donde se inicia la vida (vientre-estómago de mujer), y *suyu* (lugar) de convivencia de los hombres (el mundo con sus cuatro puntos cardinales)] (Jacanamijoy, *Chumbe*)

We can gain a more nuanced understanding of the design in Figure 42 when we compare it with the *uigsa pasca* design, literally "open stomach" in Quechua-Inga, that holds a profound symbolism as "the terms *Uichca* [closed], *Pasca* [open], refer to *Tuta* [night] and *Puncha* [day]" [los términos *Uichca* (cerrado), *Pasca* (abierto), hacen referencia a *Tuta* (la noche) y *Puncha* (el día)] (*Chumbe*). These cosmic and human dimensions thus represent a kind of textile writing that is closer to the ideographs of the Chinese or to Egyptian script,

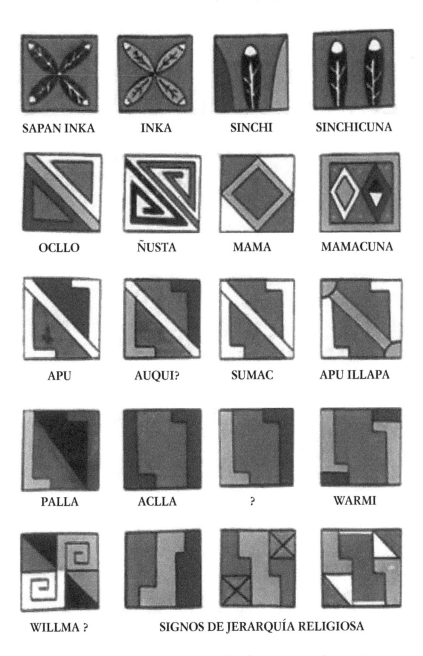

Figure 41. Fragment of the explicative table of tocapus according to Victoria de la Jara. Margarita Gentile. "Tocapu: unidad de sentido en el lenguaje gráfico andino."

than to the abstract or phonetic system developed from the Greco-Phoenician precedents.

Figure 42. *Uigsa uichca*. Benjamín Jacanamijoy. *Chumbe: arte inga.*

For example, in the ancient Chinese script that was derived from pictographic characters, the representation of the heaven, *tian*, is partially composed of the image of a human body whose head has been replaced by a line representing the horizon: what is above, the sphere that goes beyond us and which contains us.

According to Benjamín Jacanmijoy, the *uigsa* is based on the human body, beginning with a diamond for the belly. Following this, the *uigsa* expresses the macro-dimensions of the sun and the moon, as well the micro-dimensions as in the example of the frog ideogram, which above all else is associated with water (see fig. 43).

Figure 43. A frog design based on the *uigsa-pasca*. Benjamín Jacanamijoy. *Chumbe: arte inga.*

These tendencies of exchange, crossing, and complementarity in the graphic representation of relational dimensions (cosmic-human-natural), offer us an epistemological foundation from which we can understand oralitegraphic textualities and the oraliture movement. Again, these cannot necessarily be explained as the mere result of colonial processes. Oralitegraphies are the contemporary expression and realization of ancient cultural matrices that endure through their continual reinvention. Through their intercultural projects these textualities also unite multiple dimensions of the spoken, the written, and the visual, transcending traditional classifications and colonial cooptation both politically and creatively. As seen previously, *Bínÿbe oboyejuayëng* is a liminal project. The work's textualities express the continual reinvention of Andean graphic language and explicitly give voice to intergenerational dialogues through oral genres (the *botamán biyá* and the *jabueyenán*) by putting them into an alphabetic, bilingual format. The work embodies Jamioy's previously cited denouncement of how the beautiful writing was changed for him when he went through the colonizing experience of learning alphabetic literacy at school, contesting the effects of that colonizing experience and turning that experience on its head through his work's oralitegraphic structure.

Relational textualities possess specific creative structures that imply particular ways of reading derived from their multiple communicative contexts. The *uigsas* or ideograms that demarcate *Bínÿbe*'s six *suyus* [sections] grammatically and symbolically are represented in figures 44 to 49. The first two *uigsas* are equivalent to the Inga ideograms for a closed womb-diamond (*uigsa uichca*) and an open womb-diamond (*uigsa pasca*): night-*tuta*-darkness (see fig. 44) and day-*puncha*-sun (see fig. 45). In a Camëntsá context they also suggest an equivalence between the moon-sun and father-mother. The ideograms mama (*juaschón*) and taita (*shinÿe*) symbolize the book's tutelary ancestors-guides, as well as the old words that ideally articulate oraliterary aesthetics. The beautiful, old, and living words are expressed in two carved, wooden masks (see fig. 50). The one on the left gestures through a smile, beautiful in the sense of *botamán biyá*—in addition to evoking the taita's famed sense of humor—, while the one on the right expresses a gesture of shock or possibly verbal communication.

Figure 44. *Mama Juaschón*: that which turns us around, or mother. Detail.
Hugo Jamioy Juajibioy. *Bínÿbe oboyejuayëng/Danzantes del viento* [2005],
p. 23.

Figure 45. *Taita Shinÿe*: father who gives us light in time, or the son. Detail.
Hugo Jamioy Juajibioy. *Bínÿbe oboyejuayëng/Danzantes del viento* [2005],
p. 43.

Figure 46. *Flautëfi Gëhuaya*: flautist. Detail. Hugo Jamioy Juajibioy. *Bínÿbe
oboyejuayëng/Danzantes del viento* [2005], p. 59.

Figure 47. *Taita Buacuandërëch*: taita of the right arms, or the bear. Detail. Hugo Jamioy Juajibioy. *Bínÿbe oboyejuayëng/Danzantes del viento* [2005], p. 85.

Figure 48. *Bëjay*: water. Detail. Hugo Jamioy Juajibioy. *Bínÿbe oboyejuayëng/ Danzantes del viento* [2005], p. 109.

Figure 49. *Oshmëmnayshá*: nest or a basket with eggs. Detail. Hugo Jamioy Juajibioy. *Bínÿbe oboyejuayëng/Danzantes del viento* [2005], p. 135.

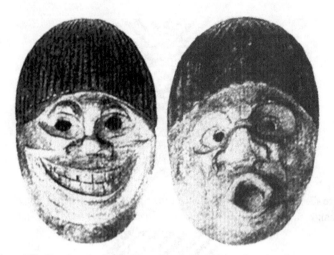

Figure 50. Camëntsá masks. Hugo Jamioy Juajibioy. *Bínÿbe oboyejuayëng/ Danzantes del viento* [2005], p. 45.

The ideogram *juashcón* suggests a circular, spiral vision of time associated with lunar agricultural cycles (that which turns us around) and gestation (mama), while the ideogram *shinÿe* communicates the daily solar cycle associated with the masculine (taita). Among other potential symbolic resonances, they are also connected to the *bétscanaté*; not just a celebration of forgiveness, but also a Camëntsá ritual festivity that celebrates the abundance of the harvest when the agricultural lunar new year begins in February, as in the Chinese calendar. Given that the *bëtscanaté* marks the beginning of the agricultural lunar new year, we should note that by beginning with *juashcón*, the moon, the book aligns itself with the most important celebration of Camëntsá socio-political belonging.

On the other hand, Shinÿe is also the name of one of Jamioy's sons. He dedicates the poem "Shinÿe Gunney" to him, in which the child is represented as coming from the blood of his father, the oral-itor. Several lines from *Bínÿbe* speak directly about the relationship between dreams and small children as sprouts, as plant roots' fruits:

Dreams are life's children
they sprout while walking
and in your steps
blood sprouts new dreams;
that's where your face remains, your soul,
the fruit of your roots…

[Los sueños son los hijos de la vida,
caminando brotan
y en tus pasos
la sangre retoña nuevos sueños;
ahí va quedando tu rostro, tu alma,
el fruto de tus raíces…]
(Jamioy, *Bínÿbe* [2010] 29)

Texts in the first *suyu* or section fall under the aegis of the ideo-gram *juashcón* and most of them allude to children as sprouts, fruit, and twigs. In short, children are the hope for the community's future and for intergenerational communication, both of which are import-ant expressions of the oraliture project.

In *Bínÿe*'s 2005 edition, in the second *suyu* under the *shinÿe* ideo-gram, the oralitor cites his literary predecessor, the taita Alberto Jua-jibioy, and turns one of his anthropological texts into an oraliterary poem.[5] In the 2010 version, Jamioy removes the poem "Jenojuaboy-an" "Evocación" [Evocation], and instead opens the *suyu* with "Es-pej ca inÿna yomn ndegombr soy" "Plateada es la realidad" [Reality is Silver-Plated], a poem in which he describes an encounter between the poetic voice and the moon. The following poems in *suyu shinÿe* deal with death and the spirits. For example, in "Chë obaná" "La muerte" [Death], the oralitor states that "the Camëntsá do not have time" [los camëntsá no tienen tiempo], while simultaneously affirm-ing that words hold an evocative, concrete power. Giving advice, the oralitor says, "If we talk about her / we are calling her. / She might take us" [Si hablamos de ella / la estamos llamando. / Pueda que nos lleve] (53).

All of the poems in the 2005 edition are accompanied by an ideo-gram on the lower part of the page. At first glance it would appear that there is no relationship between the ideograms and the poems in terms of their respective content. For example, in the Spanish ver-

---

[5]   Alberto Juajibioy Chindoy (1920–2007) was a Camëntsá researcher from the Sibundoy Valley. Among other things, his work represents the passage from the fig-ure of the native informant to that of the bilingual Indigenous writer. The traditional stories that Juajibioy collected, rewrote, and studied, are notable for how they bring together the author's linguistic and ethnoliterary interests, particularly since the latter originates from an auto-ethnographic perspective. As an informant, Juajibioy par-ticipated in several works written by the friar Marcelino de Castellví, a Capuchin scholar, as well as in others carried out by the renowned polyglot Manuel José Casas Manrique. He was also a co-researcher with the controversial Summer Institute of Linguistics (SIL) on the manuscript *El bosquejo ethnolingüístico del grupo kamsá de Sibundoy* [The Ethnolinguistic Outline of the Kamsá of Sibundoy]. Among his nu-merous academic achievements, we should mention that he received his licenciatura in Philosophy and Social Sciences from the Universidad de Antioquia in 1950, a prestigious Guggenheim Fellowship to spend 1975–1976 at the University of Texas, and in 2009 he was posthumously awarded the Michael Jiménez award from the Latin American Studies Association (LASA) in recognition of his life's work, and in particular his book, *Lenguaje ceremonial y narraciones tradicionales de la cultura Kamëntsá* [Ceremonial Language and Traditional Stories of the Camëntsá culture] (2008). The final chapter in Juajibioy Chindoy's scientific-literary work was marked by his 1978 return to his community in Sibundoy, wherein 1980 he served as gover-nor of the Camëntsá people.

sion of "Chë obaná" [Death] we can see an ideogram that is visually similar to a stylized pen: a succession of open triangles with a horizontal shaft on the left. If we connect *Bínÿe*'s oraliterary project with the pictorial structural format of the *k'eros* (wooden Inca vessels), we find another kind of tripartite structure operating here: 1) a scene with narrative-pictographic context in the upper part; 2) geometric or ideographic motifs in the middle; 3) naturalist, plant-like motifs in the lower portion. We can add the stylized, sculpted heads on some *k'eros*, which are characteristic of other pre-Inca sculptures like the wari, to this sequence. The three iconographic zones-*suyus* of the *k'ero* thus sympathize visually with the tripartite layout of the book's pages: 1) the bilingual poetic-narrative content of the page's upper region; and 2) the geometric ideographs of the middle. Although there are no plant-like motifs in the third section of *Bínÿe*'s pages, we do find a square that combines an ideogram with a number on the lower part of every page.

Under the ideogram of *flautëfj* gëhuaya (see fig. 46), the third *suyu* is accompanied by a mask (see fig. 51) whose exaggerated facial expression alludes to singing, screaming, ritual vomiting, or even playing a wind instrument. Most of this section's eleven bilingual texts re-elaborate the visions and words of advice that, in the oralitor's experience, come from the communal education one receives seated beside the hearth as well as through the medicinal consumption of yajé.[6]

The expression on the carved mask's mouth corresponds to a line in the text that operates as a kind of poetics in the book. In the poem "Binÿbe oboyejuayeng mondmën" "Somos danzantes del viento" [We are wind dancers], the oralitor writes, "Poetry / is the wind that speaks / following ancient footsteps" [La poesía / es el viento que habla / al paso de las huellas antiguas] ([2010] 61). The poetic word, the song and/or the sound of the breath/wind, even through a wind instrument like the flute, coincides materially with the air emitted by the human mouth.

---

[6] Yajé or yagé (*Banisteriopsis caapi*) is a native plant from the northeastern Amazon, which is prepared together with other plants like *chagropango* or *chacruna* (*Diplopterys cabrerana*) and taken as a traditional medicine among many Indigenous peoples in the Amazon and the Andes. During the ritual consumption of yajé, one typically vomits (as a purgatory action) and has intimate, collective visions associated with one's life, and the environment where the yajé is taken. These kinds of plants are popularly and poorly understood as being hallucinogens. Indigenous peoples themselves prefer to speak of these as plants of knowledge, power, and wisdom. To them yajé or ayawasca is a taita, that is an elder, a wise being.

Figure 51. Camëntsá mask with a vocal expression. Hugo Jamioy Juajibioy. *Bínÿbe oboyejuayëng/Danzantes del viento* [2005], p. 61.

The mask's exaggerated expression can also suggest the force with which the word is transmitted across generations. The oralitor explicitly evokes orality in this context in the 2005 edition, parenthetically confessing at the beginning of the section that "I go, remembering / my taita's words / with every step I take" [voy recordando / las palabras de mi taita / en cada paso que doy] ([2005] 63). This verse and its visual compliment were both removed, from the 2010 edition. Although the mouth's exaggerated expression visually sympathizes with the horrifying body language of the subject in Edvard Munch's celebrated "The Scream," we should remember that here it is a typical expression of someone who has imbibed the bitter, purgative yajé. The mask evokes this person being capable of contemplating that which is fascinating/ terrible... and throw up what is sick. The poem "Yagé 1" captures the reverential fear of people who ingest this medicinal purgative:

the dream thought
the hallucination, the passage
the voyage to the other world
where all truth lies,
the world where nothing
can be hidden
where nothing can be denied,
the world where everything
can be known.

[el sueño pensado
la alucinación, el tránsito
el viaje al otro mundo
donde reposan todas las verdades,
el mundo donde nada
se puede esconder
donde nada se puede negar,
el mundo donde todo
se puede saber.]
([2010] 71)

We can also posit that some of the geometric figures that accompany this edition, as well as certain allusions in this section's three poems about yajé, also evoke the drawings and geometric visions that someone who has taken yagé experiences. Elsewhere in the poem cited above, the oralitor writes, "The drunken geometry / has drawn the perfect shapes" [La geometría borracha / ha mostrado las figuras perfectas] ([2010] 71).

Under the taita ideogram *buacuandërëch* (taita with his arms straight or the bear) (see fig. 47) in the fourth *suyu*, there appears a textile figure similar to a reclining "Z" (see fig. 18), which can be found in numerous Andean graphic languages, including the Inca *tocapus*. In fact, it is the Quechua *uigsa kutey* that we analyzed in the context of the Educational Minga's map in Chapter 1. "[I]n addition to complementing others, [this textile design] is a symbol that separates the great signs-symbols (like a punctuation mark)" [además de complementarse con otros, es el símbolo separador de diseños-símbolos mayores (como una especie de signo de puntuación)] (Jacanamijoy, *Chumbe*). The eight poems in this section bring together the words of counsel with texts that portray the author's own, more personal voice appears, speaking about time and, above all, love and sexual "temptation."[7]

In Andean stories, the bear is associated with superhuman strength and the sexual abduction of young women.[8] This unlimited sexual energy and brutal strength can be expressed in the frightening expression of rage and power in the carved mask in this section (see fig. 52).

The fifth *suyu* opens with the ideogram for *bëjay* [water] (see fig. 48). Expanded in a blue rectangle with blue threads to represent water, in Inga weaving this ideogram is known as *hatun yaco* [large

----

[7] In the 2005 edition has ten, counting the poems "Ausencia" [Absence] and "Tentaciones para mis ojos" [Temptations for my eyes].

[8] "Achichuy" is a Camëntsá story in which the bear is tricked by a rabbit (Rocha Vivas, *Antes del amanecer* 74–79). The Inga also have a number of stories in which a girl is kidnapped by a bear. "Osomanda parlo" is an interesting version, as it suggests that the woven chumbe is characteristic of humans and also protects the women who wear it, as opposed to the girdles that were worn previously. This version begins, "Then there was a bear who started looking for women in the freshly sown fields. He eventually got to one where he saw a woman. Back then the women did not wear woven belts, but ones that are like the ones we use to tie up sacks, that we call 'triangular belts.' The bear took one of those, tied up the woman's hands and legs, and carried her off on his back" [Entonces un oso empezó a buscar mujeres en las sementeras. Al llegar a cierta sementera, vio a una mujer. En aquel tiempo las mujeres no se ponían las fajas tejidas, sino una faja tal como se usa para atar los costales; se llamaba "faja triángula". Con una de estas el oso le amarró las manos y las piernas a la mujer y se fue llevándosela en la espalda] (120–24).

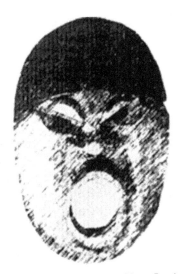

Figure 52. Camëntsá mask expressing rage. Hugo Jamioy Juajibioy. *Bínÿbe oboyejuayëng/Danzantes del viento* [2005], p. 87.

water, river]. The undulating lines and spirals recall water's movement. The oralitor originally included eleven poems in this section, but in the 2010 edition he removed the poem "Sueño en una nueva luz" [I dream in a new light]. The words of the ancestors, evocations of grandparents, the father and the mother, and a consciousness of shock and loss when dealing with the outside world, are the section's recurrent themes. The last of these is something of a borrowed history, a dream-like journey, in which the oralitor's conscience tells him: "ese no soy yo" [that is not me] ([2010] 119). We have already read important texts from this section in previous chapters, as in our oralitegraphic analysis of "Acbe bichtajac mtobopromá" "Vístete con tu lengua" [Wear your tongue/language], a text in which the oralitor elaborates upon aspects of orality (the song's murmuring) and textile designs (wearing one's language) that the ancestors can recognize and so read their people at the *viajiy* or yajé feast. In fact, according to mamá Pastora Juajibioy, the chumbe is the "writing of the ancestors," and the oralitor evokes the profound polychromatic significance of textile writing in several of the section's poems that are dedicated to his mother:[9]

---

[9] This and other observations by mamá Pastora Juajibioy are from a personal conversation.

Those tight colors on the bag
carry my mother's inspiration
... So I think:
as my mother walks, she carries
the universe in her eyes.
And I can barely distinguish
its colors.

[Esos colores apretados en la mochila
cargan con la inspiración de mi madre
... Pienso entonces:
mi madre anda llevando
el universo en sus ojos.
Yo apenas distingo
los colores.]
([2010] 109)

A mask carved with an expression of fear or shock accompanies these texts (see fig. 53). Later on we will analyze the themes of re-articulation/disarticulation through other texts from this section like "Atsbe pueblbe juabn" "La historia de mi pueblo" [My people's history], "Jtenonÿenam" "Buscándome" [Searching for myself], and "Shecuatsëng betsasoc" "Los pies en la cabeza" [The feet in your head]. They will also play an important role when discussing mirrored visions in the second half of the book, where, for example, the symbolism of having feet in one's head in "Shecuatsëng betsascoc," and the image of writing with one's feet in "Atsbe pueblbe juabn," will be analyzed as visual and symbolic inversions that defy the conventional idea of alphabetic writing.

Figure 53. Camëntsá mask expressing fear or shock. Hugo Jamioy Juajibioy. *Bínÿbe oboyejuayëng/Danzantes del viento* [2005], p. 111.

The final *suyu* or section of the 2005 edition contains five texts with a romantic theme but it was expanded to include an additional twenty-four new texts in the 2010 edition. The first edition opens with the ideogram *oshmëmnayshá* [nest, or basket containing eggs] (see fig. 49), a design executed with the characteristic refinement and precision of mamá Pastora Juajibioy's textile work. A key aspect of both Chikangana and Jamioy's oraliterary work is their perception of the earth, the maternal, and agriculture, and one of the most important philosophical concepts within the Camëntsá oralitor's work is *jajuayenán* [sowing the word in one's heart]. In his article "Pensando" [Thinking], Jamioy explains that, "in the Camëntsá language the word *ajená* means living; *aienán* means heart; *jajenán* means to be born, and *jabuaienan*, to orient oneself, would collectively mean that *jabuajenán* means to sow in someone's heart; it means sowing the word in others so that it can be born and reproduce" [en la lengua kamëntsá el término *ajená* representa vivo; *aienán* significa corazón; *jajenán* es nacer y *jabuaienan*, orientar, lo que indica que *jabuajenán* es sembrar en el corazón de alguien; es sembrarle la palabra para que ella nazca y se reproduzca] ("Sembrar la palabra" 149).

The wise character of the poetic word is derived from what the Camëntsá call *tsabe juabna* [the great thought] and implies life practices from the idealized space of the *shinyak* [hearth], from which a child's life unfolds, as expressed through the fact that children's placentas are buried there, and where the elders tell stories, educate, guide, and, in sum, sow these things in the *ainan* [heart] of future generations. The word that they sow is expressed through the cultural metaphor of the basket whose belly stores these words, or in the cup or vessel from which one drinks beverages like chicha or the curative, visionary yajé. As with corn, the words sprout, the words grow, the words become detached, the words are gathered, the words are ground, the words are fermented, and the words are consumed.

The ideogram *oshmëmnayshá* presents twenty-eight crosses in a stepped design, which in Jamioy's interpretation of Camëntsá weaving are described as eggs in a basket (see fig. 49). Coincidentally, although significantly, in the book's 2010 edition this section has twenty-nine poems as if each individual poem corresponded to an ideogram in the geometric form of a stepped cross or the figurative image of an egg. The representation of these eggs is not gratuitous, as eggs are one of the traditional foods that one generously shares during the *bëtscanaté* celebration. The image of the basket in which words are gathered, a motif of embodied wisdom that recurs in Amazonian verbal art among tribal nations like the Uitoto/Murui, occupies a central role in the poem, "Bid jashbiamoc" "En la frontera de la vida" [On the border of life]:

And I treasure your words	[Y en aquel canasto
in the basket	donde me enseñaste
where you taught me	a recoger la cosecha de maíz
to gather harvested corn.	voy atesorando tus palabras.
I'll grind them, I'll ferment them,	Las moleré, las fermentaré
and in your daily absence	y todos los días de tu ausencia
in your name, I'll raise	en tu nombre,
a little cup, a little cup, a little cup.	una copita, una copita, una copita.]
	([2010] 139)

These cryptic allusions to the basket and the cup can be read oralitegraphically given that, from an Indigenous perspective, both are physical and graphic media of memory and oral transmission. As a woven art, for many Indigenous people, and particularly for those following Amazonian traditions, with which the Camëntsá have had contact with, basketry is similar to weaving. That is, basketry is also a space for the practice of ideosymbolic expression. The oralitor symbolically gathers wise words in his basket, words of advice that nurture those who hear them, like corn. By comparison, the little cup can be related back to the wooden vessels or engraved or varnished gourds, that have been and are spaces of graphic expression throughout the Andean region. Through remembering, that is, by pouring into his heart's receptacle the elder's word, the oralitor is nurtured by these wise words that have been transubstantiated into a symbolic ritual drink. In the poem these words undergo a process not unlike the one that corn undergoes in the production of chicha. As one of the most important critics of contemporary Indigenous literature, Juan Guillermo Sánchez, explains, "through Jamioy the taita returns to speak his deep words to us. The poetic game conjures the voice of the person who is absent. The reader is a child who appears to be listening there, beside the field. It's a common paraphrase within contemporary Indigenous literature: the sweet interruption of memory (orality) in writing (the poem)" [a través de Jamioy, el taita regresa y vuelve a pronunciar frente a nosotros sus hondas palabras. En el juego poético se conjura la voz ausente. El lector es hijo y parece escuchar ahí, junto a la chagra. Paráfrasis común a la poesía indígena contemporánea: dulce intromisión del recuerdo (oralidad) en la escritura (el poema)] (qtd. in Jamioy, *Bínÿbe* [2010] 20). In sum, we can state that the relationship of the word to visual media is expressed in the visual languages of a number of different traditions in which the graphic impulse and the oral impulse complement each other within what Christoper Teuton calls the textual continuum (*Deep Waters* xviii).

However, if Chihuailaf's *Recado* is written as though it were a conversation around the hearth, *Bínÿbe* is graphically and ideo-sy-bolically written as though it were a woven *tsombiach*-chumbe in the ritual calendrical context of the *bëtscanaté* or great day, the yajé festival, the festival of forgiveness and dialogue between those who are present and those who are returning. In short, the book creates an intergenerational, textual continuum.

In Jamioy's oraliture the mother's chumbe is complemented by the grandfather's basket. A third complementary medium is the cup from which one reaffirms ancestral memory by drinking and ritual repetition ("a little cup, a little cup, a little cup"), repeatedly partaking of the cup's contents (whether the chicha here or the yajé of other poems). The space of memory in *Bínÿbe* becomes the moment to which the oralitor turns for advice, time and again.

Expressed through verbal formulas characteristic of oral tradition, words of advice are a particularly important, recurrent theme in Jamioy's oralitegraphic project. Although it does not pertain to the work's sixth section, the poem "Botamán cochjenojuabó" "Bonito debes pensar" [You should think beautifully] is a clear example of *botamán biyá* and the word of advice. The text is easy to memorize given its reiterative, proverbial rhythm:

> *Botamán cochjenojuabó*
> *chor, botamán cochjoibuambá*
> *mor bëtsco.*
> *botamán mabojatá.*
> (Jamioy, [2010] 59)

As stated above, *botamán biyá* is comparable to the ceremonial word that is used on special occasions like visits, requests, and rituals. Within the analysis I am proposing here, *botamán biyá* specifically alludes to a polished poetic language. As we have seen previously with regard to the *nvtram* and the *epew* in Chihuailaf, and the *haylli* and the *taki* in Chikangana, *botamán biyá* is central to Hugo Jamioy's work as both a theme and a motif.

Wearing a haircut typical of the one introduced to the Camëntsá by Capuchin missionaries, the carved mask that in this section's oralitegraphic proposal has a mysterious facial expression that we can perhaps be related to confusion or sadness (see fig. 54). Jamioy clarifies that:

Figure 54. Camëntsá mask with a confused look. Hugo Jamioy Juajibioy.
Bínÿbe oboyejuayëng/Danzantes del viento [2005], p. 137.

since ancient times masters of woodcarving have been able to carve
faces that manifest the spirit of life. They pay a lot of attention
to the expressions of every human being and imagine the faces of
supernatural beings; joy, sadness, loneliness, rage, the cries of man,
the rainbow, the flautist, San Juan, the mëtëtsén, among others, can
all be expressed through the features of a carefully carved mask.

[los maestros de la talla en madera, desde tiempos antiguos crearon
rostros en los que el espíritu de la vida se manifiesta. Contemplaron
con mucha atención las expresiones de cada ser humano e imaginaron
la cara de seres sobrenaturales; así, la alegría, la tristeza, la soledad,
la rabia, el llanto del hombre, del arco iris, del flautero, del san
Juan, del mëtëtsén, entre otros, se manifiestan en una máscara cuyas
facciones son talladas cuidadosamente.] ("Pensando, hilando" 149)

As seen in both Chihuailaf and Chikangana, here Jamioy implies
both a revision of urban life and a symbolic-literary return to the
earth, the mother, the community, orality, the chumbe, coca leaves,
yajé, corn. These oraliterary returns partially occur through the so-
called beautiful words that are sown in one's heart. The words of the
jajuayenán are also re-encountered around the hearth in the following
poem, which will be further analyzed in the second half of this book:

Son, the hearth from which your name	[Hijo, abandonado está el fogón de donde
stems out is abandoned	desprendiste tu nombre
while you, cold, try to warm yourself with	mientras con frío buscas abrigo fuera de
something other than your own energy.	tu propia energía.
Come back,	Regresa,
sit in the circle where your grandfather's	siéntate en el círculo donde las palabras

words spin.
Ask the three stones, they silently guard
the echoes
of ancient songs.
Dig through the ashes, and you will find
the warm placenta
your mother wrapped you in.

del abuelo giran.
Pregúntale a las tres piedras, ellas guardan
silenciosas el eco de
antiguos cantos.
Escarba en las cenizas, calientita encontrarás
la placenta con que
te arropó tu madre.]
(*Bínÿbe* [2010] 135)

If we look at the more recent edition of *Bínÿbe*, we note that this final section or *suyu* includes new texts that move beyond the short lines of the poems in the 2005 edition. Although they also address themes like the earth, the elders, love, yajé, wise proverbs, the collective spirit, mythic histories, urban experience, the return to the community, the re-encounter with the *shinyak* (the hearth or *tullpa*), a number of these newer poems assume a more ironic, questioning tone. Poems such as "Urrábe ngmenan" "Desencanto de Urrá" [Urra's disillusionment] or "Quen luar" "Esta geografía" [This geography], directly question the state, the president, and even Colombia's geographic borders, from what I refer to as mirrored visions.

Along these lines, Jamioy's oraliterary poetics directs several conversational, questioning poems to non-Indigenous readers. For example, the oralitor uses the verbal formula, "no es que" [it's not that] in "Bocoy" "Chicha" to compare how his community views the world with how *squená* or "non-Indigenous people" see it:

It's not that we want to see
each and every visitor get drunk;
chicha is a greeting of welcome.
If you accept it,
we accept you.
If you reject it
we'll never toast you again,
ever.

[No es que a cada visitante
se lo quiera ver borracho;
la chicha es un saludo de bienvenida.
Si la aceptas
te aceptamos.
Si la rechazas
nunca más te brindamos
nada.]
(*Bínÿbe* [2010] 161)

Oraliture that questions the mores of dominant society typically makes use of irony, as in the poem, "Corente uajuendayan endmën juatsbuañ" "La sed abunda en lo alto" [Thirst is abundant up high]: "It never rains upward. / Thirst is abundant up high / What damnation to go to heaven" [Jamás llueve para arriba / La sed abunda en lo alto / Qué condena ir al cielo] (41). In its criticism of the Christian cosmovision, heaven is conceived of as a place of damnation and not redemption. This ironic tone is also evident in the oralitor's criticism of people who are not sensitive to the metaphoric language of nature, as in "Che tëjañ y chë jant setëshëng" "Las montañas y las nubes" [The mountains and the clouds]:

The mountains and the clouds	[Las montañas y las nubes
love each other a lot.	se quieren mucho.
This time of year	Durante todo el día,
they spend all day	por esta época,
caressing each other.	se la pasan acariciándose.
And some people say:	Otros dicen:
"Oh,	¡Ah!
what a bad winter."	Qué invierno tan feo.]
	(ibid. 175)

Finally, we can also say that the previously mentioned inclusion of black-and-white and color photographs in the 2005 edition, as well as the participation of the author's brother Juan Andrés Jamioy in the form of his painted work on the respective covers of both editions, speaks to a kind of oralitegraphic proposal that cannot be reduced to the conventions of Camëntsá visual traditions, but rather seeks to revitalize those traditions through all available media and languages.

We can compare and contrast *Bínÿbe oboyejuayëng* two covers insofar as the cover of the 2005 edition (see fig. 55) uses a figurative language similar to an ethnic portrait, while the cover of the 2010 edition uses an abstract language similar to the complex combinations of matrices, colors, and multiple forms characteristic of painters like the Inga Carlos Jacanamijoy (see fig. 57).

Figure 55. Painting by Juan Andrés Jamioy. Detail. Hugo Jamioy Juajibioy. *Bínÿbe oboyejuayëng/Danzantes del viento* [2005], cover page.

Figure 56. A person portraying Mëtëtsén in the celebration of *bëtscanaté*.
Author's personal archive.

The cover of the 2005 edition shows the personage popularly known as matachín, who leads the procession during the *bëtscanaté* or carnival of forgiveness, that we discussed earlier (see fig. 56). This festival is also celebrated at the same time by the Inga, who call it *hatun puncha* [the great day] or *kalusturinda*.

The Camëntsá procession begins in one of the chapels on the outskirts of Sibundoy, and from there moves towards the central plaza where large carved wooden figures contrast with the cathedral into which the serpentine multitude flows.

"Matachín" is literally a wind dancer, a masked messenger who calls the community to the celebration with a bell, a horn, and his words. In this painting he holds a number of different emblems of power and memory like tusks, antlers, a crown of feathers, *capisayo* [blanket], beaded necklaces, a staff, a belt, and vertical textiles with iconographic designs (see fig. 55). It is significant that the wind dancer on the cover of the 2005 edition is an old man that guides both the community and the book itself, with the book being symbolically inspired by the celebration of the *bëtscanaté*. The old man is drawn with a look of wise serenity that the oralitor evokes throughout the book when he refers to the father or grandfather: "Just once more,

I would like to see myself in your eyes, grandfather" [Solo quisiera mirarme una vez más en tus ojos abuelo] (*Bínÿbe* [2010] 105). The fact that the old man in the painting and the matachín in the photo both wear a carved wooden mask just above their faces speaks to how they realize the presence of the ancestors. Indeed, the profile of a strange face that indicates the presence of the supernatural, and perhaps that of the taita bear, is visible in the painting's upper left. The matachín of the popular carnival becomes the external or complementary manifestation of *mëtëtsén*, of whom Jamioy writes:

When the Mëtëtsén (a mythic person) came down from on high, Shinÿë (the Sun) lent him his rays and Suftcuacuatjo (the Rainbow) lent him his beautiful colors to adorn his crown. Vinÿia (the Wind) lent him his whistle, and Tsëbatsana Mamá (Responsible Mother/ Mother Earth) gave him a tunda (a cane to make a flute) so he could play music and dance the rhythms that still live among the Camëntsá people in the Bëtscanaté today. The Mëtëtsén came down from on high and like the eyes of Shinÿe, his face is a mystery, it cannot be seen; he came down with a crown of beautiful colors, dressed in white, adorned with a Këfsaiyá (sayo or ruana) and covered his face with a red, wooden mask; in his hands he held a rattle (today a bell is used) to call people to the gathering, and a horn to lift the Camëntsá peoples' spirits. This is how Mëtëtsén came down and how he taught the Camëntsá people his music, his dances, his words, so that everyone, men and women, elders and small children, could sing, dance, and sing together during the Bëtscanaté.

[Cuando el Mëtëtsén (personaje mítico) bajó de lo alto, Shinÿë (el Sol) le prestó sus rayos y Suftcuacuatjo (el Arco Iris) le prestó sus bellos colores para adornar su corona; Vinÿia (el Viento) le prestó el silbido y Tsëbatsana Mamá (Madre Responsable/Madre Tierra) le regaló una tunda (caña para flauta) para que hiciera música y danzara ritmos que hoy el pueblo Kamëntsá aún vive en el Bëtscanaté. El Mëtëtsén bajó de lo alto y al igual que los ojos de Shinÿë, su rostro es un misterio, no se lo puede ver; bajó con corona de bellos colores, vestido de blanco, adornado con un Këfsaiyá (sayo o ruana) y cubierto su rostro con una máscara de madera roja; en sus manos un cascabel (hoy una campana) que llama al encuentro y un cuerno que despierta el ánimo del Kamëntsá. Así bajó el Mëtëtsén y al pueblo kamëntsá le enseñó su música, su danza, su verso, para que todos juntos, hombres y mujeres, ancianos y niños, cantaran, danzaran y versaran juntos en la fiesta del Bëtscanaté.] ("Pensando, hilando" 149)

The diamond that rounds off the white flag on the cover of the 2005 edition suggests the traditional writing that is part of the *uigsa*-womb-diamond. The circle represents the bell, and in turn expresses the inclusion of some aspects of European carnival celebrations that, following the Catholic calendar, have merged with the *bëtscanaté* or *clestrinye*. Another example would be the presence of hybridized characters like the spokesperson the Matachín and the San Juan, whose tongue traditionally hangs out of one side of the mask. The San Juan can be also represented by a rooster that is publicly decapitated in the *bëtscanaté*. Ritual aspects like San Juan's ritual decapitation, or throwing "flowers of forgiveness" on the heads of the bishop and the priests (who officiate the mass on the ritual festival's most important day), communicate a subliminal Camëntsá (in)version of dominant history during the *bëtscanaté*. In fact, we can understand these communal symbolic gestures as being antecedents to the kinds of mirrored visions that the Camëntsá oralitor uses to question dominant society. In fact, the Matachín becomes *mëtëtsén*, "a symbol of spiritual strength" [símbolo de la fuerza espiritual] (Jamioy, "Pensando, hilando" 149), initiating both the procession and the oralitegraphic dances in the book. The book, of course, is named *Wind Dancers* because the act of dancing means moving in unison with the entire community. Given that the *Mëtëtsén* (re)taught his music, his dances, and his poetic verses to the Camëntsá, he is the painting-ideogram and the cultural hero-message from which the book itself originates. Finally, I would argue that the oralitor himself aspires to be transfigured through this role and the figure of the *mëtëtsén*, becoming a dancer and messenger between cultures.

The illustration on the cover of the 2010 edition is called *Tiempo amanecer* [Dawn Time] and forms part of a series of paintings that adorns the jackets of the eight books in the Ministry of Culture's Indigenous Library (see fig. 57). The figures in each of these covers emerge from a background of polychromatic hues. While barely noticeable at first glance, the figure of a young man or boy, looking up and with his arms extended, stands in the middle of *Tiempo amanecer*. He seems to be drinking something or communicating with someone. Around him we can note the presence of fish, gourds [totumas], and geometric figures that recall the celebrated visions associated with yajé. These are similar to the watercolors that Juan Andrés Jamioy used to illustrate the cover of the book *Ajkem Tzi/ Tejedor de Palabras* [Weaver of Words] by the Maya-K'iche' poet Humberto Ak'abal (see fig. 58).

Figure 57. Painting by Juan Andrés Jamioy. Detail. Hugo Jamioy Juajibioy. *Bínÿbe oboyejuayëng/Danzantes del viento* [2010], cover page.

Figure 58. Watercolor by Juan Andrés Jamioy. Detail. Humberto Ak'abal. *Ajkem tzij/Tejedor de palabras*, cover page.

Both the brevity and the content of Humberto Ak'abal's work have had a profound influence on Jamioy's poetics. Here, the name

"Ak'abal" communicates the idea of the dawn in much the same way as the painting on the cover of the 2010 edition of *Bínÿbe*. In fact, this book's oralitegraphic conception owes a good deal to the design of *Ajkem Tzi* [Weaver of Words], in whose pages include images of textiles, numbers and logograms from Maya writing, and bilingual versions of its poems. Ak'abal's book also begins with a Maya calendrical inscription.

Juan Andrés Jamioy's watercolor occupies the center of the *Ajken Tzij*'s cover, surrounded by a number of different ideographic designs. Once again, this composition underscores the fact that the Indigenous oraliterary and literary movements that gained visibility throughout the continent beginning in the 1990s saw themselves as contributing to the revindication of verbal oral arts, native languages, and in some cases, autochthonous writing systems. That is, these movements explicitly promote Indigenous intellectual sovereignty. Thus, concepts such as *pachakuti* (the overturning of space-time) and the symbolic idea of the dawn allude to the textualities they created insofar as these are ways to envision a "new age," that of a new word.

However, we should clarify that Hugo Jamioy's oralitegraphies are not simply the personal reflection of a Camëntsá poet. Rather, his broader project forms part of a chain of intercultural reinvention and exercises in constructive dialogue with other societies. For example, the 1993 publication of Benjamín Jacanamijoy Tisoy's *Chumbe, arte inga*, was the first published book to be structured like a chumbe, containing fixed sections in which ideograms-*uigsas* are combined with alphabetic writing. Similarly, Humberto Ak'abal's 2001 *Ajken Tzij* is a bilingual poetry collection in which brief texts are combined with iconographic designs and an Indigenous numbering system. It is likely that Jamioy was familiar with both of these when he wrote *Bínÿbe oboyejuayëng*, and that both of them served as a basis for his oralitegraphic project, even as he channeled the ideas about oraliture developed by Elicura Chihuailaf and Fredy Chikangana, the latter of which has been a friend of Jamioy's since their time together as university students.

On the other hand, as compared to the Wayuu writer Miguelángel López, Jamioy does not make use of onomatopoeia, one of the poetic devices most associated with Ak'abal's work. Of these, "Xalolilo, lelele'" is one of Ak'abal's most original compositions. As in his other onomato-poems, the oral performance and vocal interpretation of this poem-song surpass the importance and even the possibilities of the written version. Even so, the rhythmic power of written version effectively conveys a pure sound that evokes the songs of the birds:

Xalolilo, xalolilo,	*Xalolilo, xalolilo*
lelele' lelele' lelele' lelele'	*lelele' lelele' lelele' lelele'*
lelele' lelele' lelele' lelele'.	*lelele' lelele' lelele' lelele'.*
La k'el, la k'el, la k'el	*Xaaa.*
xaaa xaaa xaaa…	(Ak'abal 419)
¡La k'el!	

By comparison, Jamioy incorporates the image of the bird in the poem "Binÿbe oboyejuayeng mondmën" "Somos danzantes del viento" [We are Wind Dancers], presenting us with images of what he understands poetry to be:

Poetry	[La poesía
is the wind that speaks	es el viento que habla
in the path of ancient footprints.	al paso de las huellas antiguas.
Poetry	La poesía
is budding flowers made word;	es un capullo de flores hecho palabra;
from its colors sprouts the aroma	de su colorido brota el aroma
that holds the dancers in the air.	que atrapa a los danzantes del aire.
In its entrails it keeps	En sus entrañas guarda
the nectar that intoxicates the hummingbird	el néctar que embriaga al colibrí
when it comes to make love.	cuando llega a hacer el amor.
Poetry	La poesía
is the orchids' magic.	es la magia de las orquídeas.
Its beautiful verses turned colors	Sus bellos versos hechos colores
are nurtured by the former lives of old firewood.	se nutren de la vida pasada de los leños viejos.
Poetry	La poesía
is the ferment of each epoch's vital energy;	es el fermento de la savia para cada época;
the messengers arrive,	los mensajeros llegan,
they get drunk and they leave	se embriagan y se van
dancing with the wind.	danzando con el viento.]
	(*Binÿbe* [2010] 61)

The image of the hummingbird suggests the oralitor's self-representation as an intercultural *mëtëtsén* or poetic dancer between worlds. Hummingbirds are symbolically pollinating messengers, and here the poem alludes to them as "dancers in the air," another way of saying, "wind dancers." The Camëntsá's neighbors the Inga, use the ideogram of the *kindi* or hummingbird on their chumbes, which "can be said to be made of pieces of *Indi-Llajtu* (sun-feathers) that mean God, power, or authority" [el diseño podría decirse que está conformado por pedazos de *Indi-Llajtu* (sol-plumaje) que significa Dios, poder o autoridad] (Jacanamijoy, *Chumbe*). Inga elders say that dreaming about a hummingbird entering your house means that a wise person (*yacha runa*) "will visit your house very soon" [visitará tu casa muy pronto] (*Chumbe*). In sum, for the Inga the hummingbird is a symbol of wisdom and divine power. In Jamioy's text this visitor, dancer, or messenger, is also an expression of love, communication, and poetry, with poetry here being the word and oral communication ("it is the wind that speaks"). But this poetry speaks, "in the path of ancient footprints," which suggests the roots of Camëntsá wisdom and its connection with autochthonous systems of writing (ancient footprints) found in beadwork and the ideograms on chumbes. At the same time, the relationship that the word has to the earth acquires tones that are less agricultural, as expressed in the philosophical concept of *jajuayenán* "sow the word in one's heart," and more flowery. For example, flowers metamorphosize into words: "Poetry / is a budding flower made word"; poetry attracts ("from its colors sprouts the aroma / that holds the dancers in the air"); enthralls ("the nectar that intoxicates the hummingbird"), and achieves transcendence in an affectionate spirituality ("In its entrails it keeps / when it comes to make love").

The poem achieves the kind of polychromatic expression found in textiles and bead of orchids." However, the line "Now colors, its beautiful verses / are nurtured by the former lives of old firewood" is an allusion to the classic image of the oralitor around the hearth, and in a broader sense to past generations that have transmitted the *botamán biyá* from the context of that idealized and ideal verbal space. The word "beauty" is expressed through the flowers' beauty, the colors of the *bëtscanaté*, the drunken movement of the hummingbirds who make love to the flowers, drinking their nectar with their beaks. As with the "old firewood," the beautiful word also implies the beauty of the ancestors' forms of expression, even more so as wood is used to carve the masks that materialize the traditional expressions of the Camëntsá world.

Here, poetry is the realization of the word or, as Jamioy says: a new word derived from the old word. This happens insofar as poetry, "is the ferment of each epoch's vital energy." The poet/oralitor and the hummingbird are messengers that, "arrive, get drunk, and leave / dancing with the wind." In sum, this poetic oraliture is a communicative proposal articulated across intersecting fields whose oralitegraphic relationships tend to express a textual continuum.

CONCLUSION

One of the foremost academic authorities on orality and literacy, Walter Ong, argues that what he calls archaic cultures lack, or do not achieve, the level of abstraction, introspection, and analytic prowess of cultures "capable" of writing. Much earlier, the Greek philosopher Plato excluded poets from his ideal Republic, saying that they pertain to a world of oral communication whose poetics require mnemonic forms, common expressions and cliches, in short: poets need formulae to facilitate memorization across generations (Ong 32). The poetic projects of the group of oralitors examined here (Chihuailaf-Chikangana-Jamioy) demonstrate that, to the contrary, the use of formulae, images and oral genres, enriches, amplifies, questions, and deepens the art of verbal composition known canonically and Eurocentrically as literature. Confluence, simultaneity, and continuity among oralities and literacies, as well as among "traditions" and "modernities," also generate alternatives within regimes of representation, whether we are referring to those of Indigenous nations or to those societies with which these nations are in tense, permanent, and creative contact. Cultural producers who frequently call themselves "Indigenous" sow these alternatives through the production of oralitegraphies, and the generation of mirrored visions about the non-Indigenous societies, practices, and people. These producers not only generate a multiplicity of intertextual proposals but, as will be seen in the second half of this book, articulate perspectives that open up new ways to question dominant imaginaries, cross representational gazes, create pedagogical projects, contribute to the rearticulation of their nations/communities, and revitalize Indigenous languages, sovereignties, and cultures.

PART II

MIRRORED VISIONS

4
WITH YOUR HEAD IN YOUR FEET: DISARTICULATION AND REARTICULATION IN CONTEMPORARY INDIGENOUS WRITING

IN THIS CHAPTER I contextualize the notion of mirrored visions by analyzing what the head, symbolic dismemberment, and decapitation symbolize in Indigenous literatures. These theoretical considerations dialogue with the demands of contemporary Indigenous Peoples, particularly with regard to how they see themselves, educate themselves, exist and, in many cases, how they question and engage with dominant societies. In looking at what the head symbolizes in Indigenous oraliterary and literary texts from Colombia, we will also examine the connections among Indigenous people that transcend Colombia's national borders, as in the case of the Gunadule in Panamá and the Quechua in Perú. This theoretical discussion of mirrored visions will then serve as the basis for the book's final two chapters.

SYMBOLIC DECAPITATION

Numerous oral narratives or stories from Indigenous literature contain images of symbolic decapitation (the loss of, or a changing of one's head) that represent cultural de-centering or dismemberment. While these images operate on several levels, let us consider how they are used to describe conventional education. In a testimonio recorded by the Panamanian-Colombian poet Manibinigdiginya, the *sagla* or wise Guna leader Manuel Santacruz states that, "The official education system has taken away our children's Guna eyes, ears, their Guna sense of smell, their tongues, their heads, and replaces them with Spanish eyes, ears, sense of smell, tongues, and heads" [La educación oficial le ha quitado a nuestros hijos e hijas el ojo, el oído, el olfato, la lengua y la cabeza dule y los reemplazó con el ojo, el oído, el olfato, la lengua y la cabeza española] (qtd. in Manibinigdiginya, *Anmal* 160). Here, the systematic, strategic, and forced transformation of Indigenous cultural forms of seeing, hearing, smelling, speaking, and feeling-thinking are precisely those that are described via symbolic decapitation. Santacruz's statement is convincing given that it conjures up many of the images and ideas that recur in contemporary Indigenous imaginaries, like those of controlled bodies and alienated minds. While the Spanish began strategically schooling the children of Indigenous elites early on in the colony,

> Systematically schooling Indigenous commoners was never considered, and even the teaching of Indigenous caciques and leaders to read and write was not automatic. Outside of the particular areas where the assimilation of Indigenous elites was undertaken (the Valley of México, the K'iche'-Kaqchikel area in Guatemala, Quito, Cuzco, the missionary reductions of the Tupí-Guaraní area), by the end of the sixteenth century few members of the Indigenous aristocracy had even acquired the rudiments of written culture. Without a doubt the famous Colegio de Santa Cruz in Tlatelolco and, more generally, the intense, high-quality educational activities that the Franciscans developed in the Valley of Mexico, was an exception, and certainly one that was very important for alternative written literature.

> [Si nunca se pensó en escolarizar sistemáticamente a los indios comunes, el acceso de los caciques y principales a la cultura gráfica no fue tampoco automático. Fuera de las zonas privilegiadas para la asimilación de las élites indígenas (valle de México, área quiché-cakchiquel en Guatemala, Quito, Cusco, reducciones misioneras del área tupí-guaraní), pocos miembros de las aristocracias indígenas habían llegado a poseer, a fines del siglo XVI, siquiera los rudimentos de la cultura escrita. El famoso colegio de Santa Cruz de Tlatelolco, y más generalmente, la intensa actividad docente de alto nivel que los franciscanos desarrollaron en el valle de México, constituye sin duda una excepción —por cierto muy importante para la literatura escrita alternativa.] (Lienhard 102–3)

Schooling, evangelization, and teaching literacy to the so-called caciques (a word of Taíno origin) furthered and complemented the physical decapitation of the cabecillas, or leaders of Indigenous movements. The most famous of these leaders is perhaps Tupac Amaru II, who was decapitated and quartered by the Spanish military in Cuzco after the rebellion he led in 1780 was defeated: "Once Indigenous aristocracies were decapitated and dismembered, they were reorganized to serve colonial power" [una vez descabezadas y desarticuladas las aristocracias autóctonas, se las reorganizaba en función de la dominación colonial] (Lienhard 100). In the Republican context at the beginning of the twentieth century, the Peruvian José María Arguedas underwent a similar and inverse "changing" of his head as a young man. Sent by his uncaring stepmother to live on her hacienda during the long absences of his father, who worked as a traveling attorney, Arguedas was partially educated by the Quechua peasants who took care of him there. Understood today as a precursor, promoter, and representative of contemporary Quechua poetry despite the fact that he was not Indigenous by birth, Arguedas left us with a number of revealing lines about symbolic decapitation in his poem "Huk doctorkunaman qayay" "Llamando a algunos doctores" [Calling some doctors], which was published posthumously in *Katatay*. Speaking from the Quechua exclusive we, in one of his lines he states: "They say we do not know anything, that we are backwardness, they say they will change our heads for better ones" [Dicen que ya no sabemos nada, que somos el atraso, que nos han de cambiar la cabeza por otra mejor] (*Katatay* 253). Elsewhere he addresses the doctors with a more individual voice: "Will I work for centuries of years and months for someone who does not know me and who I do not know can cut off my head with a little machine?" [¿Trabajaré siglos de años y meses para que alguien que no me conoce y a quien no conozco me corte la cabeza con una máquina pequeña?] (255).

These images of cutting off or changing one's head are direct denouncements of colonialism, represented here by educational policies that, in the case of "Huk doctorkunamam qayay," is seen as a kind of academicism. Certainly, there are a number of academics who criticized Arguedas's literary work, and in particular, his 1964 novel *Todas las sangres* [All the blood], and we can assert that when Arguedas shot himself in the head in 1969, he appears to have done so as one final, defiant gesture against the dominant postcolonial establishment, and above all else, as a form of sacrifice, protest, or self-immolation, that can be understood in relation to Quechua ritual combat or *tinku* of ritual warriors. In a global context, his suicide also parallels the *harikiri* or *seppuku* "suicide or ritual decapitation" of the Japanese writer Yukio Mishima,[1] and even the supposedly "self-inflicted wound" of Van Gogh, who cut off part of his ear.[2] According to the 1947 work by Antonin Artaud, the poet and French dramatist who also felt oppressed by his epoch's homogenizing culture, Van Gogh was "suicided by society" (Artaud, *Van Gogh*).[3] Further, Alberto Moreiras argues that Arguedas's suicide can be read as resistance to modernity and to transculturation. Moreiras understands modernity here as, "a quintessentially Western and hegemonic transculturizing machine" [máquina transculturante quintaesencialmente occidental y hegemónica] (224). In addition, he says that, "transculturation is a weapon of war that feeds on cultural difference, and whose principal function is to reduce the possibilities for radical heterogeneity" [la transculturación es una máquina de guerra, que se alimenta de la diferencia cultural, cuya principal función es la reducción de la posibilidad de heterogeneidad radical] (218). As such, Moreiras interprets Arguedas's suicide as being the rejection of cultural reconciliation, as according to him, "there can be no conciliation without forced subordination" [no puede haber conciliación sin subordinación forzosa] (219).

As compared to Arguedas, the works of Manibinigdiginya, Fredy Chikangana, and Berichá, who we will address in the following sections, resist the "cutting off" or "controlling" of one's head, as well as various other forms of colonialism, through educational and oraliterary proposals that evoke life, the resurgence of their communities, and their self-recognition as Peoples and members of specific collectivities.

REVIVING OUR MOTHER'S BONES: EDUCATION ACCORDING TO MANI-BINIGDIGINYA

Convened in 2010 by student organizations and a commission composed of representatives from various Indigenous organizations,

---

[1] José María Arguedas and Yukio Mishima never met and, as far as I know, did not influence each other. However, on the November 25, 1970, a year after Arguedas's suicide, the Japanese writer committed "ritual suicide" with the help of several of his friends, with whom he had taken over a military base in Tokyo in the hopes of initiating a coup d'etat and restoring the emperor to power.

[2] To date no one has been able establish if the gunshot to the chest that killed Van Gogh in 1890 at the age of 37 was an accident, murder, or suicide, resulting from the painter's well-known "depression".

[3] In 1936 Artaud decided to break away from everything and undertake a journey to "de-westernize" and "de-europeanize" himself, going to the isolated world of the Rarámuri (Tarahumara) of the Western Sierra Madre in Mexico (Artaud, *Mexico*).

the National Minga on Indigenous Peoples in Higher Education is one of numerous intercultural encounters that have been organized in Colombia and throughout the region with the goals of advancing projects focused on educational sovereignty, and interrogating dominant society from the diverse perspectives and pedagogical foundations of Indigenous peoples. The call for participation was distributed via email, and was directed towards both Indigenous Peoples and Colombian popular opinion. In the introduction, the Indigenous Peoples' National Commission for Labor and Collective Agreement on Education (CONTCEPI) stated that:

> what we have today is an education that does not recognize the ancestral wisdom of Abya Yala's originary peoples; wisdom that would help a Country which today finds itself debating between peace and violence, between democracy and the hegemony of power concentrated in a few hands, while the great majority of its people finds themselves below the poverty line if not living in extreme poverty. To build a more inclusive, diverse, culturally-sensitive country, processes of higher education should pause along their current trajectory and reflect on Mother Earth.

> [lo que tenemos hoy es una educación que desconoce los saberes ancestrales de los pueblos originarios de Abya Yala; saberes que aportarían al País que hoy debate entre la paz y la violencia, entre la democracia y la hegemonía del poder en manos de unos pocos, mientras la gran mayoría se encuentra bajo la línea de la indigencia y la pobreza extrema. Para construir un país incluyente, diverso y cultural, el proceso de formación en Educación Superior, debe hacer un alto en el camino, para reflexionar sobre el respeto a la Madre Naturaleza.] (Palacio Paz, "Re: Convocatoria").[4]

As such, the Educational Minga sought to clarify the need to reform university education in Colombia, which was then still dominated by Neoliberal economic power throughout most of the country. The idea that ancestral wisdom was ignored in "higher" education can also be symbolically connected with the generalized "illiteracy" concerning Indigenous forms of writing, an idea put forward by the

---

[4] This Contcepi e-mail call for the National Minga, and particularly its opening lines, are based in part on the work of the Gunadule writer Manibinigdiginya (Abadio Green Stócel), who was president of the Organización Nacional Indígena de Colombia [Colombian National Indigenous Organization].

Camëntsá oralitor Hugo Jamioy. It also follows that attending the Educational Minga was not so much a question of militancy, but of adding one's voice to the collective criticism that recognized the reality of this lack of knowledge, this inverse "illiteracy," and, as a result, advocated for the construction of collective processes of intercultural education for society as a whole.

The binational project Nangalaburba Oduloged Igala/Volver a Revivir los Huesos de Nuestra Madre [Reviving Again Our Mother's Bones] was a previous project of Manibinigdiginya's that was similar to the Educational Minga. Nangalaburba not only sought to fortify the use of Indigenous languages in general but also to lay the foundations for the recuperation of Gunadule culture. Although today Gunadule culture is mostly located in the Guna Yala region of Panamá, its origins can be found in Colombia in Antioquia, Chocó, and along the Atrato River. The Primer Congreso de Educación Bilingüe e Intercultural [First Congress on Bilingual Intercultural Education] was organized under the umbrella of the Nangalaburba project; it included members of the Gunadule Peoples from both Colombia and Panamá, and was lead by Indigenous writers like Manibinigdiginya/ Abadio Green from the Universidad de Antioquia. The inclusion of both countries is important insofar as the Gunadule live distinct socio-political relations in each. According to Ruth Moya, in Colombia "one of the foremost difficulties for ethno-education is the fact that questions of ethnicity are neither sufficiently understood nor assimilated into the consciousness of most Colombians" [una de las dificultades de la etnoeducación es que el problema étnico no es suficientemente asimilado ni comprendido por la gran mayoría de los colombianos] (142). By comparison, in Panamá,

> one of the country's most important achievements is the existence of a legal basis that allows for the institutionalization of Intercultural Bilingual Education (EIB). Panamá also has an advantage in that its citizens have been sensitized to the Indigenous question for more than 20 years, and Panamá's Indigenous population itself is interested in promoting its own educational system. The country's Indigenous Peoples have also had several other formative experiences, and possess the political will to promote this educational model.

> [entre los principales avances está la existencia de una base legal que permite la institucionalización de la Educación Intercultural Bilingüe (EIB). También se cuenta con la ventaja de que la población panameña se está sensibilizando acerca de la cuestión in-

dígena desde hace más de veinte años, y que los propios indígenas
están interesados en impulsar su educación. También se cuenta
con algunas experiencias y existe la voluntad política de impulsar
esta modalidad educativa.] (166).

The EIB implies processes of multicultural sensitization and intracultural revitalization within each community.⁵ In this context, the
Reviving Our Mother's Bones Again project was conceived of as an
educative proposal that would "reflect on the respect owed to Mother Nature" [reflexionar sobre el respeto a la madre naturaleza], and
ultimately, advance the rearticulation of Indigenous cultures within
distinct Indigenous territories.

   We should point out that one of Manibinigdiginya's foremost contributions to the project, and in his work with other Indigenous communities, has been his outlining a theoretical-pedagogical practice
that aims for community-based cultural rearticulation. Part of this creative pedagogy is based upon the recuperation of the deep meanings
held within Indigenous languages—we could call them "meanings of
life" or "etymologies"—, as well as the organization of workshops,
the re-appropriation of autochthonous writing systems, the reincor-
poration of musical instruments, and the reflexive re-encounter with
community naratives, among other projects. His project thus parallels
that of the Cherokee scholar Chistopher Teuton who finds that his
community's creation stories and literary criticism, "enable us to create our worlds," and are therefore indispensable ("Theorizing" 194).

   Manibinigdiginya's doctoral dissertation *Anmal gaya burba: isbeyobi daglege nana nabgwana bendaggegala* or *Significados de la vida:
espejo de nuestra memoria en defense de la madre tierra* [Meanings
of Life: A Reflection of Our Collective Memory in the Defense of
Mother Earth] (2011) offers several conceptual perspectives that
emerge from collective oral histories. Indeed, one of the mythic tales
serves as the basis for both his book and the binational project, the
story of the pregnant mother of the eight mythic siblings who is de-
voured by fish-men.⁶ The grandmother frogs preserve the mother's
Nana Gabayay [placenta]. Saved from being torn apart, the siblings
are thus able to grow up, and the birds (the welwel or toucan, the

---

   ⁵ EIB is different from Bilingual Intercultural Education, in that the latter primarily focuses on the use of Indigenous languages and incorporating them into the
"national" educative project.
   ⁶ Specifically, she is the mother of Olowagli, the sister, and her seven brothers.

saligagga-diostedés, and the sigli or Great curassow (*Crax rubra*), eventually tell them where they are from. They then rescue their mother's bones and unsuccessfully try to revive her.[7] Paradoxically, Gunadule binational bilingual intercultural education proposes to achieve what these cultural heroes could not: revive the mother from her bones, that is, to form themselves, develop themselves, educate themselves as a people (*dule*) based on the cultural matrices, contributions, and guidelines expressed in the *Babigala* or *Pab Igala* (a cycle of stories and tales sung by the *sailas*-leaders and the *argal*-performers),[8] in certain molas (pictographic writing on textiles that form the upper part of a woman's shirt), and in cyclical communal gatherings or meetings in the *onmaggednega* (great council houses). Writing about these rearticulations of Gunadule culture, Manibinigdiginya says that, "reviving her bones also means the liberation of Mother Earth" [revivir sus huesos, significaba también la liberación de la Madre Tierra] (*Anmal,* 154).[9]

By striving to revive his mother, the Indigenous scholar Manibinigdiginya becomes the personification, continuation, and actualization of one of the mythic brothers. He even assumes the role of an intercultural *argal*, that is, an interpreter or translator for the *saila* (*sagla*), the wise leaders of the community:

> After the song, the Argal (spokesperson) translates the complex metaphors of the Sagla's song into simple words so that those members of the community who are present in the great onmaggednega common house can understand it. This is why the Argal uses a language suffused with concrete examples and makes direct comparisons between life as it was and the present moment. For example, when the Sagla sings the story of the seven brothers and their sister Olowagli, they refer to the frog mothers who hid the true story of the eight siblings' mother, who was devoured by the frogs' children. As such, the frogs became the eight siblings' true

---

[7] There are several versions of this story among the continent's different Indigenous peoples. For example, the twins of Mbyá Guaraní *Ayvú Rapytá*, the twins of the Maya-K'iche' *Popol wuj*, or the those in the *Watunna* of the Makiritare or So'to.

[8] A written version of the *Pab Igala* was transcribed, translated, and edited by the poet and linguist Aiban Wagua.

[9] At different moments both Aiban Wagua, in his role as a Catholic priest, and Manibinigdiginya/Abadio Green, who spent time as a seminarian, have been part of Central and South America's Liberation Theology movement. You can also note the clear pedagogical influence of the Brazilian educator Paulo Freire in both of their works.

mothers. The eight siblings never learned this story directly from the mouths of their tutelary grandmothers, but rather found it out from the songs of the toucan and the Great curassow. Through his oratory the Argal interprets this story into the context of the community's reality, referring to envy and lies.

[Después del canto, el Argal (el vocero) traduce con las palabras sencillas el complejo metafórico canto del Sagla para que la comunidad presente en el recinto de la casa grande onmaggednega, pueda comprenderlo, por eso el Argal utiliza un lenguaje con muchos ejemplos, haciendo comparaciones de la vida pasada con la actual. Por ejemplo, cuando el Sagla canta sobre la historia de los siete hermanos y su hermana Olowagli, hacen referencia a las madres ranas que ocultaron la verdadera historia de la madre de los ocho hermanos, que fue devorada por los hijos de las ranas; y ellas pasaron a ser como las verdaderas madres de los ocho hermanos [sic]. Los ocho hermanos no conocieron esa historia en la boca de sus abuelas tutoras, sino que supieron la verdad de la historia por medio de los cantos de los pájaros: el tucán, diostedé y del pavón. El Argal con su oratoria transforma este relato en la realidad de nuestras comunidades, refiriendo a las envidias y las mentiras.] (*Anmal* 53).

Following Hayden White, "it is not so much the study of the past itself that assures against its repetition as how it is how one studies it, to what aim, interest, or purpose" (82). One of Manibinigdiginya's central aims in putting this pedagogical approach forward is translating "this story into the context of the community's reality" [relato en la realidad de nuestras comunidades] (*Anmal* 53). He seeks to tailor it to the new pedagogical needs (reviving the mother) from a methodological and symbolic matrix (the pedagogy of Mother Earth) that actualizes and contextualizes his people's sovereignty through their re-encounter with oral stories, the revindication of their autochthonous forms of writing, and a knowledge of their language and its meanings of life. In effect, these kinds of narratives of the origin play a central role in processes of re-articulation within a community, as well as in intercultural interaction. According to Manibinigdiginya, "discovering words' true meaning carries us to the histories of our ancestors, the very people who give meaning to our identity and pride in being Gunadule. That is, they are the foundation of our being and our society" [descubrir la verdadera significación de las palabras nos lleva a las historias de nuestros ancestros que son las que nos dan el sentido de nuestra identidad y el orgullo de ser Gunadule, es decir, son la base de nuestro ser y de nuestra sociedad] (*Anmal* 12). With the help of poetic writing, communal research, and other tools, in a sense Manibinigdiginya attempts to re-articulate and create from what he refers to as "the mother's bones," that is, the ideosymbolic foundations of the Gunadule collective.

For Linda Tuhiwai Smith, however, confronting colonialist fragmentation implies delicate processes of healing, recentering Indigenous identities on a broad scale, and "strategically repositioning them around international alliances" (104). The Maori intellectual understands this dynamic within a global Indigenous context, and in fact in three of her projects—writing, naming, connecting—coincides with ideas expressed by Manibinigdiginya. For example, when Tuhiwai refers to the project of connecting, she says, "many indigenous creation stories link people through genealogy to the land" (148), a connection that is implicit in the Gunadule image of the Earth Mother as an originary genealogical link. In a sense, the Gunadule educational project seeks to contribute to a trans-border, community-based pedagogical connection and re-articulation of the Gunadule in Colombia and Panamá, while also including the participation of those who have forcibly or voluntarily migrated outside the confines of their "traditional" territory.

With respect to notions of tradition and territory, when I visited Guna Yala I had the opportunity to meet a female Gunadule elder who participated in the General Cultural Congress in June 2014. Having lived for more than a decade in Panamá City, she was called upon by authorities to share her experiences using theater to fortify Gunadule culture among young people, as well as her words of advice for the women who attended the meeting. The case of Abadio Green/Manibinigdiginya is similar in that he is a cultural promotor who was born in Panamá but resides in Medellín, Colombia. He is also a nationally and internationally acclaimed promoter of the pedagogies of Mother Earth, an intercultural educational project from the OIA: Organización Indígena de Antioquia [Antioquia Indigenous Organization], that operates in part through the support of the Universidad de Antioquia's Diverser group. Today this degree program enrolls students from throughout Colombia, including Zenú, Emberá, and Gunadule students.

The pedagogy of Mother Earth revindicates communication in Indigenous languages and promotes the appropriate use of autochthonous forms of graphic writing. Manibinigdiginya feels that it is not enough to write alphabetically, or to simply recuperate stories and expressions found in orality. In fact, he states that it is essential to acknowledge, "the diversity of writing that exist in our communities as an important part of reaffirming the identity and pride in pertaining to an ancestral people, and valuing to these forms of writing since we use them at all times" [la diversidad de escrituras que existen en nuestras comunidades, como parte importante en la reafirmación de la iden tidad y el orgullo de pertenecer a un pueblo ancestral, y darle valor a estas escrituras [pues] todo el tiempo las utilizamos] (*Anmal* 203).

According to Manibinigdiginya, Indigenous peoples' forms of writing, writing which is not exclusively picto-ideographic, are complementary with orality:

> Any kind of writing is impossible without orality, given that orality is the older of the two and that many of the planet's Indigenous peoples continue to endure with their own forms of writing, transmitting their knowledge without the linguistic tools offered us by the contemporary world. That is, orality continues to sustain the recreation of the ancestors' wisdom because the songs continue the prolonged healing of their communities, the dances continue imitating the tapir's call, the movements of the Great curassow, the white-faced monkey's shouts and joy. The chicha ceremony continues to connect us with ancient history and manifests our ancestors' presence. That is, chicha makes us remember the birth of our grandmother Olowagli and her seven brothers, all of whom were born from the large clay jars.

> [Cualquier propuesta de escritura no sería posible sin la oralidad, ya que la oralidad es la más antigua y muchos pueblos de la tierra siguen perviviendo con sus propias escrituras, transmitiendo su sabiduría sin las herramientas lingüísticas que hoy nos ofrece el mundo contemporáneo. Es decir que la oralidad continúa dando aportes en la recreación de la sabiduría de los ancestros porque los cantos siguen prolongando la curación de sus comunidades, las danzas continúan imitando el silbido de una danta, el baile del pavón, el grito y las alegrías de los monos cariblancos. La ceremonia de la chicha nos sigue conectando con las historias antiguas y que hacen posible la presencia de los espíritus de los antepasados, es decir la chicha nos hace recordar el nacimiento de nuestra abuela Olowagli y sus siete hermanos cuando estaban naciendo desde las tinajas.] (*Anmal*, 210)

In light of this interconnection between orality and writing, the idea here is neither that orality is a unique attribute of Indigenous communities, nor even something that is exclusive to them. Orality is a mode of communication shared by all cultures, although it is certainly underestimated in many cases. According to Walter Ong, the ascension of phonetic writing in ancient Greece was a fundamental step towards abstraction and conceptualization, things which "elemental oral cultures" [culturas orales primarias] cannot achieve (138). Taking a contrary perspective, in his doctoral thesis Manibinigdiginya states that orality implies processes of conceptualization, and above all, of profound signification, as its intergenerational transmission sustains and recreates collective knowledge, facilitates recalling stories that transmit it, reinforces the knowledge concerning the meanings of one's language, and is an essential part of interpreting ceremonies. In this sense, many of Manibinigdiginya's poems can be understood as pedagogical texts insofar as they provide images and his interpretations of a large range of Gunadule feelings and cultural interactions.

This is clearly the case in the poem "Tinaja" [Large Clay Jar], a poem that affirms oral history, and interprets the myth about, "our grandmother Olowagli and her seven brothers who were born from the large clay jars" [nuestra abuela Olowagli y sus siete hermanos cuando estaban naciendo desde las tinajas] mentioned above:

My grandparents say	[Cuentan mis abuelos
that the clay jar holds life	que la tinaja tiene vida,
that the clay jar represents	que la tinaja representa
our peoples' resistance.	la resistencia de nuestro pueblo.
Clay Jar and Ipelele	Tinaja e Ipelele
are from the same blood;	son de la misma sangre;
that's why the Tule drink	por eso el tule bebe
fermented cane juice until they are full,	esa caña fermentada hasta la saciedad,
because drinking is remembering the road	porque beber es recordar el camino de
of our elders	los mayores
it means getting drunk on our own history.	es embriagarnos con nuestra historia.]
	(qtd. in Rocha Vivas, *El sol* 564)

To understand why the writer claims that "Clay Jar and Ipelele / are from the same blood," let's look at the *Pab Igala* (*Babigala*) story about the mother's bones, as well as other stories in which Ipelele is the main character.

According to the stories, *Ipelele, Ibelele, Ibelel,* or *Tad Ibe* (Dad Ibe), all of whom are the same cultural hero as he plays a number of different roles, rides a boat around the Sun, watching the actions of the Gunadule. He is the one who lets Ped Tuumat (Papa or the creator-organizer of the universe in other stories) know what is going on. Ipelele is one of the twelve nelegan that Pad Tuumat successively sends to create the world,[10] give people advice, and maintain equilibrium within the community and across the planet.

Ipelele directs the cutting down of the *palu'wala* (the great tree from which the animals, plants, salt, and water, all come), humanizes the person-animals, differentiates these new peoples among themselves, and teaches them to hunt, plant, use tools, live in community with each other, and gather together to listen to the *neles* and the *sailas* (*saglas*). Ipelele symbolically cuts the prehensile tails off of these first humans, an act that transforms them into *olotule*, true tule (dule) people of gold (Rocha Vivas, *El sol* 441).

Details from the story in tellings by other Gunadule narrators give us a better cultural understanding of the idea of "the people of gold." The mother of Ipelele and his mythic siblings is torn to pieces and eaten by iguana-people, peccary-people (peccary; *Tayassu tajacu*), tapir-people, and fish-people, while in Manibinigdiginya's written version only the fish-people actually devour her. These beings are the grandchildren of a toad woman who rescues the mother's intestines or placenta and starts to cook them in a clay jar, which breaks. The toad woman then puts the intestines on to cook in another jar, and so on, until a total of seven jars are eventually broken. The final jar, which is made of gold, does not break. This sequence symbolizes the births of the eight siblings (seven brothers and one sister). Other stories allude to a gold plate or platter instead of a golden jar, or even to a flying saucer in contemporary more mytho-poetic versions as in, for example, the one by the Nicaraguan poet Ernesto Cardenal, *Los Ovnis de oro* [The Gold Flying Saucers]. In *Shamanism: Archaic Techniques of Ecstasy*, Mircea Eliade finds that certain kinds of mythological heroes are cooked-formed in cooking pots, a motif and shamanic trial par excellence. In the case of the Gunadule, the heroic siblings are born in plates-jars that symbolize their divine origin, their mother's body, and their function as mediators between levels of the cosmos. The broken jars are related to sacrifice and to their mother's dismembered body. The siblings are reared in the family of their mother's murderers, another classic mythological motif in many Indigenous narratives. Another version of the Gunadule story says that once the siblings discover their true origin, Ipelele, the eldest,

---

[10] Nelegan is the plural of nele: doctor, leader, interpreter, "religious, political, and social guide" (Wagua, *En defensa* 327).

leads them in a search for their mother's bones, which they find and place in a hammock. Already having the full knowledge of a *nele*, Ipelele ceremonially sings to the bones for eight days and their mother comes back to life. In the end these rites are for naught, as the mother's reanimated body becomes animal-like and ends up falling apart. The siblings then bury her bones (Rocha Vivas, *El sol* 456).

Here, the "Clay Jar" evokes the mother, and specifically her uterus, as well as the womb-plates where the fetuses of the siblings are formed and literally baked and incubated. This is how we can understand that, in the poem, Ipelele and the mother "share the same blood," as chicha, fermented and "incubated" in the clay jar's womb, is, in this sense, a drink comprised of ritual "blood" that links the Gunadule with the mother, and in more general terms with the elders and their ancestors. The clay jar (a graphic mnemonic device) and its related mythic tales create a textual continuum that is taken up in Manibinigdiginya's poetic interpretation.

The name of the Colombian Department of Chocó, which is near the Gunadule's place of origin in the Darien Binational Region, seems to be derived from large jars or jugs that evoke and manifest the presence of the ancestors. Luis Guillermo Vasco, a scholar of vessels made by the Emberá, one of the communities whose territory borders the Gunadule in both Panamá and Colombia, states that, the famous Chocó jars are distinguished by their anthropomorphic "little bellies." Vasco maintains that the jugs represent primary beings. Chicha is fermented for community festivals in them and, as he explains, corn chicha is what generates Emberá being. The anthropologist states that during the rite of passage from a being a girl to a woman, the girl who is being initiated is isolated in a place where she will spend several days adorning her chocó, the jar that will accompany her the rest of her life (Rocha Vivas, *El sol* 580).

Manibinigdiginya explains that, in a Gunadule context, the word for the clay jar, *medde*, has the following etymology:

> *me*, "light," "shine," "open"; *d(e)* which indicates that something moves in a centrifugal direction; it means "illuminates from the center," this is emphasized given that it is repeated twice. *Med(e) de* tells us then that the shining and the light comes from the clay jar from which the seven brothers and their sister *Olowagli* were born; that is, the light is our memory, and that those who would be born from a clay jar will be the caretakers, the light for future generations who are in Mother Nature's care. This is why this story be-

came the heart of Gunadule tradition; today the ancestral authorities continue to sing this tale at various traditional Dule events; and each time they carry out a festival centered on girls they remember this story, given that the fermentation of chicha still takes place in clay jars, jars that also represent life, because we come from one of them, and because the clay jar represents a woman's placenta.

[me, «luz», «brillo», «abierto»; d(e) indica que algo sale en dirección centrífuga [sic]; «la iluminación sale del centro», enfatizado pues se repite dos veces. Med(e)de nos indica entonces que el brillo y la luz viene de la tinaja de la cual nacieron los siete hermanos y su hermana Olowagli; es decir, que la luz es nuestra memoria, ya que quienes nacerían de una tinaja serían los cuidadores, la luz para las futuras generaciones en el cuidado de la Madre Naturaleza. Por eso esta historia se convirtió en el corazón de la tradición Gunadule; las autoridades ancestrales hoy siguen cantando esta historia en distintos eventos de la tradición dule; y cada vez que se realizan las fiestas alrededor de las niñas se recuerda esta historia, ya que la fermentación de la chicha se sigue realizando en tinajas, que a su vez representan la vida, porque venimos de una de ellas, porque la tinaja representa la placenta de una mujer.] (*Anmal* 123)

In Manibinigdiginya's poem the image of the ritual consumption of chicha generates the oralitegraphic rearticulation of the continuum word-memory-blood and ancestors-clay jar, while it is realized through the pedagogical-poetic writing that the Gunadule writer uses to preserve, care for, and articulate his own history.

RECOVERING YOUR HEAD

We now turn to the Quechua poet Fredy Chikangana/Wiñay Mallki's poetic project of revindication in Colombia's Andean Southwest. One of his most important poems regarding such processes of communal rearticulation is "Umakuna" [The head]:

And a head spoke from
        Mother Earth,
saying, "We have not died.
We are in the stars' silence
Among the blue skies and
        the reddish clouds
The night's silence
The feather that speaks over
                the water

[*Mantari pachamamakuna rimay umashuk*
Mana nukanchi huañushca rimay
Nukanchicay paypinima
        kuyllurmantakuna
Paypi nima tutak
Paypi hananpacha ankas puyupucaricuna
Paypi phuru imarimay yaku jahuapi
Paypi pauchin rumi pujuyaku
Nukanchicay ccayna-punchau:

The waterfall pounding the
          rock
We are like yesterday:
In the eternal struggle.

Maccancuy: manatucukpi.]
(*Samay* 105)[11]

Uma "the head" speaks from *pachamama* "earth-time" to commemorate the *inkarri* or "Inka king" in Andean and Quechua cultural memory, whose decapitated head, according to certain messianic Indigenous narratives, seeks to be reunited with its body (Ossio Acuña). Speaking from the perspective of the *nukanchi* or Quechua inclusive we, the poetic voice denies that the ancestors' memory has disappeared. Their collective presence is expressed in the silence of the stars (*kuyllurkuna*), in the colors of the sky (*hananpacha*), in clouds (*puyu*), in feathers (*phuru*), in the water (*yaku*), in waterfalls (*pujuyaku*), in stones (*rumi*), and in the incessant struggles of cultural resistance and/or physical survival. The poem's initial images (*kuyllurkuna, puyu, phuru*) correspond to the upper/outside, cold world of Quechua and, in this case, Yanakuna, cosmovision. The second group of images (*yaku, pujuyaku, rumi*) correspond to the lower/inner warm world (*ucku pacha*). The "we are" of the penultimate verse refers to the people, the runas, the children of the sun (*punchau*) who are invigorated by the "eternal struggle," a common expression within many sociopolitical resistance movements. The collective we (*nukanchi*) claims continuity with yesterday (*ccayna-punchau*), that is, a past that in Quechua socio-linguistic cosmology is in front of a person instead of behind them. The figure of the *uma* or "the head" in the poem evokes the representations of heads that are found in central Andean pre-Hispanic textiles, sculpture, and ceramics, and which were associated with ritual war, measurements of time (Tiwanaku), and ceremonies to foster good harvest (Nasca-Paracas).

As seen in Chapter 3, transAndean and PanQuechua connections in Chikangana's poetics center on a common foundation both spiritually and physically: *pachamama* (Mother Earth, territory). In the poem "Umakuna," the head seems to be the personification and/or an extension of *pachamama*: "And a head spoke from Mother Earth." The relationship here between Chikangana's Quechua-language work and the Central Andes is not coincidental, and the oralitor himself recognizes how his experiences traveling through the

---

[11] This poem's original bilingual versions were published in double columns on facing pages. The present format follows the same structure to facilitate the reading of these versions in English translation.

Andes, as well as his living near Cusco while he learned to speak Quechua, were pivotal in his intellectual formation.[12]

In light of his own work as a writer and oralitor, Chikangana's Andean travels make him a kind of *ch'aski*. First and foremost, the *ch'aski* was a messenger, a means of communication between Inca settlements along the thousands of miles of roads that crisscrossed the territory of what was known as Tawantinsuyu (Inca Empire), approximately between 1400 and 1532. The word *ch'aski* is related to the Quechua word for foot, *ch'aki*. In a general sense, the *ch'aski* is associated with a figure who is walking, running, or a pilgrim, and is a common motif in Andean philosophy. For Chikangana this category is accentuated by the idea that the *ch'aski* is also the messenger or bridge between worlds, which to a certain extent seems to be how the poet sees himself. In a contemporary context, intellectuals and writers are frequently symbolized by a head (brain), but here they are represented by the figure of the *ch'aski* as a leg or foot. Here there is no all-encompassing totality (intellect), but simply a part (an extremity); there is no mouth-voice author-individual (he-*pay*) but an oral collective (inclusive we-*nukanchi*).

However, in the poem the head (*uma*) speaks (*rimay*): "Mana nukanchi huañushca rimay" [We have not died], its affirmation of resistance, endurance and agency also defining one of the capital functions of indigenous writers' and oralitors poetry. Further, insofar as Chikangana's is both a connection between and communication among different words and worlds (*ch'aski*), one of his recurrent messages is simply that: "we are alive, we continue to be." The written word materializes his presence but does not supplant it. Visibilization through literature acquires a particular kind of relevance in the case of a Yanakuna writer whose people were only recognized as an Indigenous "group" beginning in the 1990s.

Another of Chikangana's poems, "Nukanchis kan causay pachacaypi" [We are still alive here on this land], similarly expresses these themes of cultural persistence and rearticulation. As seen in Manibinigdiginya's poem "Tinaja," here the feeling of collective unity is urged through the renovation of a ritual involving collective "drunkenness": "Let's drink without shame," they shout, / "we are still alive here on this land" [¡Bebamos sin pena! … que aún tenemos vida en esta tierra] (*Samay* 57). In both poems ritual drunkenness is also

---

[12] This commentary on Chikangana's travels is based on a personal conversation.

a practice through which the communal body is rearticulated. The drunkenness referred to by the Yanakuna oralitor summons a space of memory where individuals collectively communicate through festive ritual genres like the *haylli*, or sung elegiac hymn. This kind of drunkenness can be contrasted with and differentiated from the alcoholism that tears communities apart, and which was introduced to Indigenous communities via the colonialist market. For example, upon visiting an Ikʉ (Arhuac) community in the Sierra Nevada of Santa Marta, the nineteenth-century Romantic novelist Jorge Isaacs reported that the Kankuamos and the Arhuaco (Ikʉ) asked him to ask the national government to regulate the importation of alcohol into their communities. In a letter written in Riohacha on April 12, 1882, one of Isaacs's Indigenous informants states: "Aguardiente (liquor) kills: this nation was great without aguardiente, and it is being destroyed! Bonache (a Spaniard) gets Indians drunk and cheats the Indian. Will you tell the government in Bogotá to prohibit aguardiente?" [Aguardiente mata: nación fue grande sin aguardiente, ¡y ya se acaba! Bonache (español) emborracha indio y engaña indio. ¿Dirás al Gobierno de Bogotá que prohíba aguardiente?] (Isaacs 243).

Delineating the boundary between drunkenness and alcoholism is complex, even more so when in some cases the excessive consumption of alcohol in Indigenous communities or among urban Indigenous immigrants seems to defy how Indigenous individuals' morality and labor are controlled by dominant society. That said, some of the most heartbreaking tales of symbolic decapitation occur in an urban environment.[13] For example, compiled by the anthropologists Ricardo Valderrama and Carmen Escalante, the celebrated testimony *Gregorio Condori Mamani* (1982) tells the life of an urban Quechua laborer who, "saw himself as being without eyes and without a mouth" [se considera a sí mismo sin ojos y sin boca] (Cornejo Polar 229). Losing the ability to see and to speak for himself has traumatic antecedents in the Andean popular imaginary, such as the deaths of Indigenous leaders like Tupac Amaru II.

Considering his voyage through the Andes and the Yunakuna's fight for recognition, we can read Chikangana/Wiñay Mallki's wor(l)d

---

[13] This does not mean that the urban experience is ipso facto "decapitating," as evidenced by a number of Indigenous movements in Colombia's large cities. For example, the ONIC was created in 1982 in Bosa (an area in Bogotá's vast urban expanse) and has its headquarters in Bogotá.

as related to the symbolic recovery of one's head and leg/feet, insofar as his literary projects call for collective, community rearticulation based upon Mother Earth.[14] Whereas Chikangana speaks of the collective's head, in the previous section Manibinigdiginya talks of reuniting and resuscitating its bones. Both the head and bones are corporeal images of Indigenous knowledge that have been suppressed by centuries of colonialist and imperialist fragmentation. As Linda Tuhiwai Smith states, "imperialism frames indigenous experience" (19).

I HAVE THE FEET ON MY HEAD, ARTICULATION AND DISARTICULATION IN BERICHÁ

Tengo los pies en la cabeza [I Have the Feet on My Head] is a partially autobiographical text written by Berichá, the traditional name of an U'wa woman from Colombia's eastern Andes who is known in Spanish as Esperanza Aguablanca. Although she published the book in 1992, Berichá says that the she began to edit the manuscript in the 1980s when she worked with health care workers, and as a teacher. Because of its thematically self-referential style, the book attained a certain degree of regional and national acclaim in the years that directly followed its publication.[15]

Tengo los pies en la cabeza is comparable to *Me llamo Rigoberta Menchú y así me nació la conciencia*, published in English as *I, Rigoberta Menchú*, the controversial testimonial work in which the eventual winner of the Nobel Prize told Elizabeth Burgos personal and collective stories about the destructive violence perpetrated against Mayas in Guatemala. According to Luis Fernando Restrepo, "unlike other testimonios and their rhetoric of urgency, and although it contains a number of descriptions and denouncements of the generalized abuses and violence associated with colonization, Berichá's

---

[14] Chikangana and Manibinigdiginya both say that Mother Earth, as either Pachamama or Magiryai, is the spiritual and physical space where the community's survival and rearticulation gestate.

[15] During the early 1990s Berichá became one of the best known U'wa and Indigenous women in the entire country, despite the fact that her written work was neither widely read nor widely disseminated on a scale suggested by the number of awards she received. For example, Berichá received the Honor al Mérito Cultural de la Alcaldía Mayor de Santa Fe de Bogotá prize, while the Gobernación de Norte de Santander awarded her the José Eusebio Caro Award for Woman of the Year. In addition, in 1993 she was given the Cafam award for Woman of the Year.

text does not resort to ... detailed accounts of torture and suffering" [el texto de Berichá, aunque sí tiene algunas descripciones y
reclamos por abusos generales y por la violencia de la colonización,
no apela a ... detalladas historias de torturas y sufrimiento, como lo
hacen otros testimonios con su retórica de urgencia] (156). Menchú
and Berichá's testimonies were written in the first half of the 1980s.
However, Berichá claims she eventually destroyed her original manuscript: "when I left for Aguablanca in 1985, I burned what I had
written; I was afraid of the searches the Army did in the school"
[cuando partí para Aguablanca en el año 1985, quemé los papeles
que tenía escritos; tenía miedo a las requisas que hacía el Ejército en
la escuela] (44). Both her decision to move and her destroying the
work's original manuscript are the results of an anonymous threat
towards her and people close to her who had supported an U'wa
organization for the defense and recuperation of their land (40–43).

As outlined in her testimonio, Berichá was born without feet, and
therefore was rejected by and exiled from her community from the
time she was born. Indeed, according to U'wa tradition her physical
condition would have meant her being sacrificed (11). Her parents,
however, opted to leave the community, and so "when I was born I
did not have the same fate as other children who are born with physical defects, as they are usually abandoned or have their throats cut"
[cuando nací no tuve la misma suerte que corren los niños que na-
cen con defectos físicos, que es ser abandonados o degollados] (18).
Her mother carried her around on her back until missionaries took
them in after the death of her father (12). Although she worked and
learned to read in the mission, her relationship with both the church
and the missionaries became strained when Berichá publicly criticized the historical excesses of the Church and the Colony during an
event in the town.

In her book, Berichá says that when she took part in the welcome
ceremony for the governor Napoleón Peralta in Cubará, Boyacá, she
seized the opportunity to denounce colonizers and missionaries in
the presence of the municipality's civil, military, and religious authorities. She also took advantage of the occasion to mention how in
the past several U'wa caciques were tied up and hung upside down
by their feet, while others had been prohibited from celebrating traditional festivals and songs, speaking their native language, or cur-
ing their family members (39). According to Berichá, these are key
moments in the community's dislocation and dismemberment, and
display the full impact of "civilization."

In *Tengo los pies en la cabeza,* the ceaseless U'wa struggle for the recognition of their collective territory and the continuity of their cosmovision are inscribed within the testimony of Berichá's own personal struggle. Fabio Gómez Cardona says that Berichá suffered from being triply marginalized, "as a woman, as an Indigenous person, and as a person who was born with a physical handicap" [condición de ser mujer, de ser indígena y de haber nacido con una discapacidad física] (62). Paradoxically, we learn U'wa history within the sensitive and intimate space of Berichá's own history. Indeed, the fact that the text's personal tone is firmly rooted within an identifiable feminine voice that affirms its own authority to speak, has probably been another factor in the author's being rejected by a society that is more accustomed to privileging masculine ritual orality through activities such as the retelling of myths in song and intercultural mediation.

If Berichá demonstrates her support for the U'wa movement and shares stories that are aimed at getting readers to understand her and her community, *Tengo los pies en la cabeza* was nonetheless eventually discredited and mostly forgotten. This disapproval can be explained in part as stemming from the accusations of some U'wa leaders who felt Berichá had betrayed them by publishing the text with the support of the Asociación Cravo Norte, which was comprised of Ecopetrol, Occidental de Colombia (Oxy), and Shell, all of them companies that exploited oil reserves found in U'wa territory. Indeed, the author closes her acknowledgements by thanking Asociación Cravo Norte for their help in publishing the book and uses both of her names (Berichá and Esperanza) (8).

However, criticism of Berichá's text did not end there. Other U'wa leaders also accused Berichá of trying to get members of the U'wa community to sign petitions against their own interests, and of leading a group that supported petroleum extraction, "which they claimed would be of great benefit to the community" [sosteniendo que los beneficios que le reportaría a la comunidad serían grandes] (Mateus Mora 181). Berichá denied these allegations until the end of her life. According to her, the publication of *Tengo los pies en la cabeza,*

> generated some controversies, as there were some people who liked the text and those who disliked it, the U'wa communities and missionaries among them. It was also popular and considered an outstanding work, but since it was published thanks to financial support from the Oxy Petroleum Company, they accused me of

being in business with them and of defending Oxy. That controversy made it hard for me to get work and made my head a target
of the guerrilla, but thanks to God there were those who advocated on my behalf and my situation was cleared up.

[generó algunas controversias, hubo quienes estuvieron a favor y
en contra, entre ellos las comunidades u'wa y misioneros. Igual-
mente trajo popularidad y fue considerado un trabajo espectacular,
y como el libro se dio gracias al financiamiento por la Oxy Petroleum Company, me acusaron de estar negociando el petróleo y de-
fendiendo a la Oxy; este hecho polémico hizo que se me cerraran
las puertas laborales y que mi cabeza fuera entregada a la guerrilla;
pero gracias a la mano de Dios hubo quien abogara por mí y fuese
esclarecida mi situación] (qtd. in Rocha Vivas, *Pütchi* 2: 82).

As Berichá states, one of the U'wa community's more traditional
sectors denounced her after the work's publication and, according
to her version, "made [her] head a target of the guerrilla,"[16] that is,
once again put her at risk of being put to death or forcing her into
exile. As such, Berichá immigrated to Bogotá, where she received a
grant from the University of the Andes to get a Masters Degree in
the Ethnolinguistics of Aboriginal Languages. During this time, she
was a student of Jon Landaburu, an expert in Colombian Indigenous
languages. She graduated in 1995 and returned to the municipality
of Cubará. Prohibited from working as a teacher in U'wa communities, she took up residence in the city and continued her studies.
Enrolling in low-residency courses, she graduated with a degree in
the Philology and Languages from the Universidad Libre de Cúcuta
in 1998. In 2000 Berichá began working at a school in the small rural
village of Villa Rica in the Department of Arauca, until she retired in
2001. According to her, she was under constant pressure to quit as a
result of the publication of her book.[17]

While the book ironically became another obstacle in its author's life, from the beginning of her literary career part of Berichá's
larger project was creating her feet in her head through writing, that
is, restoring her ability to move, think, and ultimately survive. For

---

[16] In the context of the armed conflict in Colombia, any information, whether
true or not, that was given to the guerrilla, paramilitary groups, or to the State about
a person's collaboration with the opposing side could have a grave impact on the life
of the accused, regardless of that person's possible neutrality.
[17] These comments are from my communication with Berichá in 2010.

Berichá writing the book implied a process of deep learning about the U'wa world, as well as reflecting upon her experiences within and beyond her own community. In fact, we can note that she initially intended to use the book to reshape her life and her participation within her community, and as an Indigenous methodology to recover the body, territory, memory, and identification with U'wa wisdom that, to her, were all being lost. In addition, Berichá recounts that her uncle, a *uejea* or "shaman," encouraged her to write the book so that outsiders could learn about the U'wa.

In her book the author recounts the following mythic tale of horror about Konara, a being that takes the form of a little blonde girl and can paralyze people. Their parents having gone out, two U'wa boys run and play around the house, tossing a gourd at the roof. Konara comes to play with them and decapitates one while the other is distracted. Konara then replaces his head with the gourd and continues to play with the other boy, eventually starting to kick and toss around the dead child's head. The boy finally realizes that he is playing with his little brother's head instead of a gourd. When their parents get home, the mother knocks over the dead child. Konara then paralyzes the family for several days. Kasoa, a *uejea*, shaman, or traditional wiseperson, comes in to help the family, punishes Konara, and burns her to death: "Little by little Konara was consumed in the flames; her skin turned red, the color of blood. Konara slowly shrank until she was very small, remaining the same color; then you could only see her head; then only her hair until finally, when you least expected it, Konara disappeared" [Konara se iba consumiendo poco a poco entre las llamas; el color de su piel se tornó rojo, igual al color de la sangre. El tamaño de Konara iba disminuyendo con lentitud hasta llegar a verse pequeñita, conservando su color; luego ya se veía solamente la cabeza; luego solo el cabello hasta que en el momento menos pensado Konara desapareció] (105). Berichá says that the *uejea* told the family that this had happened as a lesson to future generations that it was not good to play around the house or throw gourds at the ceiling (106). Beyond the story's deep shamanic symbolism, the story thus plays a pedagogical function in the U'wa world and is the kind of story that elders would tell to get children to pay attention. However, the *uejea* affirms that Konara's punishment and death is a "permanent" exile (106). We can understand the arc of Berichá's life in a similar way, given that it is a tale of transgression that discomforts the traditional structure of the U'wa house and results in her banishment. In other words, Konara's actions, like Berichá's book and her very body, are in-and-of-themselves transgressive. Young Berichá, disobedient before authority, without feet, with her feet in her head or even with a head instead of feet, is rejected and exiled in the way that Konara is. They are both judged to be negative spirits that paralyze and contaminate the community.

This interpretation is based in another U'wa tale recorded by Berichá, in which Karasa, an U'wa deity, builds the world the same way that one builds a house (49–52). The story says that for the U'wa, the world is a house that was shaped like a body. However, and according to Berichá, there is a progressive and practically inevitable disarticulation of this world, house, or body (57). Owing in part to the possible disappearance of the sun, in Chibcha cosmovisions—that is, among peoples like the Kogui, Wiwa, and U'wa—the cyclical transformation of the world is a feared reality that people confront through complex systems of ritual conciliation. For Berichá the transformation or end of the world is a fact. In addition, part of the book's broader project would seem to be the result of such a belief, as if on the one hand, writing is initially a search for her rearticulation with her community, while on the other, writing also implies that one must leave a record because the world of the community's knowledge is disappearing.

Fragmentation and adversity in Berichá's life and work are reinterpreted as an "eternal struggle." The image of a head that has been reunited with its feet is in a sense Berichá's greatest symbol of endurance and creativity. In a fragment from her personal diary, she says that, "I was born without legs, but I have feet in my head because I have been able to develop my intellect; that has helped me move forward, defend myself, and help my community" [Yo nací sin piernas, sin embargo tengo los pies en la cabeza porque he podido desarrollar mi inteligencia; eso me ha ayudado a salir adelante, a defenderme en la vida y a ayudar a mi comunidad] (9). The exercise Berichá proposes here implies recuperating one's head, walking with one's head, and producing images that connect her personal story of marginalization with that of her own marginalized people, in short, building connections and feelings of belonging.

CONCLUSION

Changing one's head (Santa Cruz), reviving a body and/or a head (Manibinigdiginya), recovering one's head (Tupac Amaru/Inkarri), destroying the head (Arguedas), listening to or letting the head speak (Chikangana), and relocating one's head (Berichá), represent the disarticulation and rearticulation of communal bodies. Indeed, under colonization countless Indigenous leaders and "heads" of communities have been decapitated symbolically and/or physically. In this sense, processes of community decolonization, reorientation, and articulation require recovering the community's "head," symbolically or otherwise, and Indigenous writers tend to see themselves as the visible heads and/or bodies of a new generation that is taking up that task. Recovering one's head frequently implies recuperating one's tongue (i.e. the ability to express oneself), recovering one's eyes (i.e. the ability to see and discern in new times), recovering one's nose (i.e. the ability to orient oneself), and recovering one's ears (i.e. the ability to hear). In short, this process entails the rearticulation of the territorial body as a symbol and concrete expression of the communal body. Mirrored visions express these abilities and these processes of rearticulation from the perspectives of Indigenous communities, their members, and Indigenous authors.

However, I should also state that these recoveries and rearticulations are not limited to so-called ancestral territories (reservations). As we shall see, Indigenous authors also express mirrored visions about their experiences migrating to the city. This should not be a surprise, given that during the last few decades many Indigenous movements have been headquartered in major urban centers like Mexico City, Bogotá, Lima, and Temuco.

A considerable number of works by contemporary Indigenous authors have been written in and published from Colombia's urban areas. Authors' urban experiences in turn generate mirrored visions on cultural differences, (in)voluntary migration and, in some cases, Indigenous displacement stemming from the armed conflict. More broadly, an early example of urban Indigenous literature that was not only written in a city but also reflects the need to articulate oneself in and from an urban space is the *hallyi-taki* (song-hymn) "Tupac Amaru camas taytanchisman" [To our father creator Tupac Amaru], in which José María Arguedas refers to Lima as the head of the false huiracochas, that is, the Spanish. The author of *Los ríos profundos* [The Deep Rivers] urges the reader to migrate to the city as a way to penetrate the inside of the head that has been imposed upon her. Here Lima is not any city, but, as the principal seat of the Imperial Spanish Viceroyalty in South America, "the city" of classic colonial inheritance.

"Tupac Amaru camaq taytanchisman" expresses the collective, elegiac voice of the Quechua *haylli* in a tone that comes as much from the genre of the military hymn as from the agricultural manifesto. The migrant's collective 'we' says that it surrounds the city, it binds the city, penetrating its heart with both love and hate. In this hymn-*haylli* the heart (*sonqo*), the center of powerful visions and emotions expressed in Quechua poetry, is seen as superior to the colonizers' cold head. The city is literally wrapped up and removed by the serpent god Tupac Amaru, with the serpent's body being formed by the thousands of Indigenous peasants who, by migrating to the city, become the creators of *pachakuti* (overturning of space-time). The head is partially redeemed by the heart, "We have to wash away the guilt that has sedimented on the rotted head of the false viracochas over centuries, using tears, smoke, or fire. Using whatever we can!" [Hemos de lavar algo las culpas por siglos sedimentadas en esta cabeza corrompida de los falsos wiraqochas, con lágrimas, humo o fuego. ¡Con lo que sea!] (Arguedas, *Katakay* 229).

As will be seen in the next chapter, these visions do not come across as reactionary if we read these oraliterary texts through the notion of mirrored visions. Sometimes they are expressed from a head that rearticulates complex and dynamic communal bodies from their particular perspectives on and senses of the world, territory, city, and memory. Mirrored visions imply seeing the supposed other from the perspective of a head that is "seated" or located on its own body. These diverse projects of autochthonous education, literary writing and rewriting, are also associated with complex symbolic communal processes, like those of reviving (Manibinigdiginya), overturning (Chikangana), or transforming (Berichá) the world. In sum, these processes are not anarchic or reactionary, but respond to the need for constant existential, political, and cultural rearticulation in the midst of neocolonial pressures.

5
MIRRORED VISIONS ON LITERACY, THE CITY, AND RETURNING HOME

THIS CHAPTER uses the notion of mirrored visions to construct comparative readings of oraliture and contemporary Indigenous literature in Colombia. The previous chapter examined the multiple symbolic meanings that are associated with the head in works by Indigenous authors. Within this context, we find that mirrored visions can be present in images, concepts, and stories generated through processes of decolonization, self-recognition, and rearticulation, and in moments when it seems as though these processes cannot be fulfilled or, as seen in Berichá's story when she is denounced and marginalized even by members of her own community, have unintended effects. While acknowledging the impossibility of fully exploring all of the authors from the book's introduction, this chapter and the one that follows it take up some of the more common mirrored visions found in their works.

These final two chapters are similar to the approaches taken by Meenakshi Sharma in *Postcolonial Indian Writing* (2003) and by Suzanne Lundquist in *Native American Literatures, an Introduction* (2004), and I do not look at each of the works examined here individually so much as examine thematically related mirrored visions in them. As seen when we looked at the complex networks of signification produced by oralitegraphic textualities (the Minga's Map, the oraliture project), this kind of approach emphasizes the fields of symbolic interaction that exist among these works as opposed to the works in and of themselves.

Sharma's study of how Indian writers represent the English in the decades before Indian independence (1947) incorporates a num-

ber of authors and cites a wide range of narrative works as the author develops her argument. Lundquist analyzes common themes in
Contemporary Native North American literature. As I do here, these
books consider these works as a group or a field, without classifying
them by genres like poetry, novel, or short story. As compared to the
Sharma's study of representations of the English, or the mirrored
visions I examine here, however, Lundquist introduces the reader to
common themes in Native North American writing, like the power
of words and storytelling, the inseparable connection between identity and a sense of place, issues surrounding the concept of blood
quantum, the perpetuation of gender identities, expressions of sexuality, and the possibility of healing through reconciliation (203).

I should also state that not all of the themes presented here
can be found in all of these works, and as such readings of certain
mirrored visions focus on certain literary and oraliterary projects.
Some of these texts have been explored in previous chapters via the
complementary notion of oralitegraphies. As such, here I will begin
by outlining three central themes regarding the need for an autochthonous education, urban visibilization, and communal territorial
rearticulation, that can be found in both Indigenous literary texts
and in the public demands expressed by Colombia's Indigenous
movements. What follows are comparative readings of mirrored visions on the topics of literacy, the city, and returning to one's community of origin.

Images and stories of literacy occupy a central place in Estercilia Simanca's most well-known story, "Manifiesta no saber firmar"
[Declares Not to Know How To Sign], which the author first published in a 2004 edition that included different citizens' ID cards. At
the same time, the notion of reverse illiteracy, which Hugo Jamioy
proposed in a talk in Chile in 2008, is one of the most recurrent
themes in the Camëntsá oralitor's work, *Bínÿbe oboyejuayëng* [Wind
Dancers]. We will also look at the Gunadule pedagogue Manibinig-
dinya's doctoral thesis, *Anmal gaya burba* [Meanings of Life], with
its continuous reflections upon writing and mirrored visions about
illiteracy.

Complementing these reflections on (il)literacy, we will look at
how these mirrored visions build upon the theme of the lettered and
lettering city, that is, the urban conglomerations from which, according to these works, structures of power associated with reading-writ-
ing, the government's bureaucracy and formal education, are promoted and concentrated. We will focus on Simanca's "Declares Not

to Know How to Sign" the Wayuu writer Vicenta Siosi's story "Esa horrible costumbre de alejarme de ti" [This awful habit of leaving you], and select passages concerning schooling and literacy found in Berichá's *I Have the Feet on My Head.*

Finally, we will examine mirrored visions on the physical/symbolic return to one's community or territory, a kind of rearticulation particularly associated with the poetry of Yiche (Yenny Muruy Andoque), an Andoke-Uitoto/Murui writer from the Amazonia, as well as the works of Berichá, Hugo Jamioy, and Fredy Chikangana/Wiñay Mallki. Although these works draw upon communal rural spaces, they do not necessarily imply the negation or rejection of urban immigration experiences, but rather a mirrored vision upon them.

Illiteracy

Theoretical Discussions

The word alphabet is actually a prolonged acronym. *Alpha* (in Greek letters) and *beta* (in Greek letters) are the first two letters of a system of writing that the Greeks literally renovated in the eight century BCE, adopting and adapting what the Phoenicians had originally disseminated throughout the Mediterranean Sea via circuits of interaction and exchange. In fact, the Greek letters *alpha* and *beta* are derived from the Phoenecian *alp* and *b t.* According to the historian of writing Andrew Robinson, although the first known alphabet, as far as we know, originated in the zone of ancient Palestine between the seventeenth and sixteenth Centuries BCE, the first Phoenician alphabetic inscriptions were done around 1000 BCE (158–59). The Greeks' genius lay in their successively adapting the system to write their own language while also inventing phonetic signs for vowels, a development that seems to have been uncommon in other Semitic languages (Jean 60). The letter "A" was born with the letter *Alpha*; "E" with the letter *Epsilon*; "O" with the letter *Omicron*; "Y" with the letter *Ipsilon.* Another historian of writing, George Jean, considers the "I" in the letter *Iota* to be rather innovative and argues that the Greeks' vocalic innovation arises from their importation of consonantic signs from the Aramaic alphabet that they used to transcribe these letters (60–62).

Walter Ong claims that epopeya like those sung in the *Illiad* were originally transmitted in formulaic oral language that was put into the written form of the new Greek alphabet between approximately 700–650 BCE. For Ong, this indicates that the intellectual oral world of the Greeks, "relied upon the formulaic constitution of thought" (23), with examples of such formulae being heroic epithets and uniform themes like advice or gathering an army. The use of formulaic verbal phrases aided the bards' or singing poets' rote memory. Alphabetic writing had been internalized during the Age of Plato in the fifth and fourth Centuries BCE, while at the same time the ancient formulae associated with orality came to be seen as commonplace and cliché (23). The notion that innovation of thought implied a philosophy that was written down alphabetically, independent of oral tradition, generated a certain iconoclasm toward oral formulae that had been repeated for generations, as well as toward mythic explanations and the recurrent themes of tradition. Following the philosopher Fernando Urbina, "if *mythos*'s originary meaning is memory, and *aletheia* was originally in opposition to forgetting, myth is not opposed to truth but reveals truth via the act of remembrance" [si *mythos* posee en su origen la significación de recuerdo y *aletheia* en principio significó oponerse al olvido, entonces el mito no se opone a la verdad sino que la realiza al recordar] ("Mito, Rito" 22). Instead of being opposed to "the true," myth, the opposite of forgetting, was set aside by logos, whose fixity was based on numeric-alphabetic writing and the synthesis that characterizes conceptual abstraction.

As stated previously, Ong classifies contemporary oral cultures as primary due to their supposed lack of abstraction and critical thought, things that, based on European Greco-centric standards, are attributes of the logos and alphabetic writing (30).[1] His claim that analytic thought originates in or is characteristic of "The West," is a prejudice based on alphabet-centrism. Referring to Ong's position, the Cherokee literary critic Christopher Teuton states that, "claiming oral cultures do not analyze their worlds portrays our oral contemporaries and ancestors as incapable of objective analysis and critical thought" ("Theorizing" 195).

Indigenous Literary critics, like Greg Sarris (Pomo/Miwok/Philipino), Craig Womack (Cree/Cherokee), and Christopher Teuton

---

[1] According to Ong, "one cannot but be struck by the resemblance between the characteristics of the early or 'bicameral' psyche as Jaynes describes it — lack of introspectivity, of analytic prowess, of concern with the will as such, of a sense of difference between past and future — and the characteristics of the psyche in oral cultures not only in the past but even today" (30).

(Cherokee) interrogate the supposed scientific nature of this kind of literary criticism, a criticism unaffected by the power of images or subjectivity, with a singular force. Sarris develops his criticism with a particularly experiential and subjective voice in 1993. Womack establishes his own theoretical revisions by bringing together political demands, "marginal" historical events, and literary projects, among other things. As outlined in the second chapter of this book, Teuton proposes that we broaden and reconnect the textual continuum interrupted by colonization insofar as what he calls the critical impulse does not explain so much as complement the graphic and oral impulses. In addition, the Cherokee critic positions himself subjectively, in a personal way in *Cherokee Stories of the Turtle Island Liar's Club*, a book written in conversation with a group of Cherokee storytellers. In its pages he sincerely confesses, "rather than attempt a false objectivity, I foreground my presence as a friend, researcher, listener, and student of the club" (9).

Literary criticism is partially heir to the Positivism and unadorned language that dominates the social sciences, and in a sense is a field that can at times seem dry and of little use to many people and communities outside of the academy. In fact, a good deal of contemporary literary criticism is based on conceptual and theoretical developments that privilege the alphabet and certain "objective" attitudes that conceived of as being "truly" analytic. At the same time this mode of critique excludes or casts doubt upon the use of "extra-literary" images and collective or subjective narratives that can complement the reading of literary texts, texts which are actually made of collectively held images and words. For example, many indexed publications have established stylistic regulations, requiring that authors craft their arguments along the lines of a scientific article. According to certain editors, what matters here is that ones crafts a well-honed argument that is hyper-authorized by citing numerous researchers in the field. By contrast, in many cases potential authors never have to consider the thoughts and opinions of the people they are theorizing and objectifying.

As Greg Sarris recounts in *Keeping Slug Woman Alive*, peer-reviewed articles tend not to leave much space for stories related to research, the extensive relationships people have with images, the affirmation of multiple Native languages, and the incorporation of oral stories, with notable exceptions being Fernando Urbina's texts of critical mythology, which have a large number of images and footnotes; theoretical reflections like Benjamín Jacanamijoy Tisoy's *Chumbe: arte inga*; or Hugo Jamioy's thoughts on Camëntsá weaving that, according to the poet, are derived from stories told by his people and his mother, who is also a weaver (Duque Duque 79).

During the inauguration of the Festival de la Palabra y la Imagen [Festival of the Word and Image] that was organized in the Centro Cultural Moravia in Medellín in October 2012, Abadio Green/Manibinigdiginya was asked, "Why is there so much theory and hypothesis in the Western Academy?" He responded, "Of course there is, because they [people in the West] have no memory. A people that loses their memory has to theorize, has to think in terms of hypotheses" [claro, porque no tiene la memoria. Pueblo que pierde la memoria, tiene que teorizar, que pensar en hipótesis].[2] In other words, an excess of theorization is a symptom of the loss of memory and the loss of the roots of one's mother tongue. According to the bilingual community-based researcher's perspective, in the case of Indigenous communities that still speak their languages, one finds concepts through which one thinks in relation to the world. However, this still depends on the kinds of theories one creates and articulates, and the perspective from which one understands these languages. According to the Gunadule writer, Spanish has its roots in a number of different languages, and for him Spanish's infinite number of roots and origins makes thinking clearly difficult. By comparison, he sees Indigenous languages as tending to be maternal languages that were neither learned nor imposed through processes of linguistic colonization. As Manibinigdiginya says later on in the same talk, "Indigenous languages are text" [las lenguas indigenas son texto] and "everything is in language" [en la lengua está todo] which is how he comes to conceive of language as a source, memory, and text. Moreover, we should add that all languages, not only Indigenous ones, have these characteristics. In this sense, textuality is neither produced through

---

[2] For Manibinigdiginya, memory, which is understood in part as the meanings of life that are passed down intergenerationally, cannot be replaced by theoretical concepts that are based on research or by the recreating sources of thought. According to him, this owes to the fact that losing one's native language as a means of the intergenerational transmission of knowledge implies the loss of collective memory. As such, his academic writing focuses on the study of linguistic etymologies, disseminating the results of his conversations with wise Gunadule elders, the collective creation of models and practices of binational bicultural education, and the diffusion of some findings in Spanish. In this way the results of his work are disseminated in Dulegaya in his community, and in Spanish and Dulegaya for academics. Following Manibinigdiginya, the objectivity required by processes of recuperating memory is founded upon the constant validation of communal knowledge, the wise elders' advice, and the deep feelings and visions expressed by the language (etymologies or meanings of life).

graphic composition nor tied to the written register. In Manibin-igdiginya's way of thinking, texts have been made from language, memory, and word-images, prior to phonetic writing and its subsequent conceptual theorization. This leads Manibinigdiginya to conclude that in Indigenous communities, or at the very least within the Gunadule community, "all of the wise people are poets, and all the historians are poets. All language is poetry, is metaphor. We do not make much effort in this regard, because our language is our original language, our maternal language" [todos los sabios son poetas, todos los historiadores son poetas. Porque la lengua es poesía, es metáfora. No hacemos tanto esfuerzo nosotros, porque nuestra lengua es original, es materna] (Manibinigdiginya, "Inauguración")

WRITING AND INSCRIBING

The attitude of cultural superiority associated with the belief that alphabetic writing is a determining feature of "great" civilizations continues to prejudice people against diverse systems of non-phonetic writing. As such, some people write while others, in this case the "Indians," are said to "inscribe." For example, in their book *Beyond the Lettered City*, Tom Cummins and Joanne Rappaport assert that "weaving was an essential medium of inscription" in Andean societies of the northern Andes in Colombia, "where alphabetic, syllabic, and pictographic literacy were unknown before the Spanish invasion" (248). Later on, they add that "the indigenous communities of the Andes did not know narrative pictorial representation or alphabetic or hieroglyphic literacy before the arrival of the Spaniards" (254). While these authors intend to move beyond the lettered city proposed by Ángel Rama in 1984, we should ask why these authors, given their conclusions, simply consider an amplified notion of literacy within the so-called colonial República de Indios (including architecture, painting, gestures, judicial documents), while at the same time ignoring the broad range of pictorial-narrative and ideographic forms of writing found in the pre-Hispanic Andes, and setting aside the central and northern Andes, whose cultural characteristics and patterns of commercial and technological exchange are well noted in the archeological record.

If Andean Indigenous communities had never seen pictorial representations of narratives prior to the arrival of the Spanish, what are the thousands of ceramic vases painted with ritual scenes found in pre-Hispanic Andean cultures like the Mochica of the central Peruvian coast? Further, these scenes would be unintelligible if we failed to account for their iconographic and sculptural antecedents among the Tumaco-La Tolita in the Colombia-Ecuadorian Pacific region, that is, in the northern Andes.[3] What are the circular painted plates from the pre-Hispanic Piartal-Tuza and Capulí traditions found in the archeological zone beneath the Andean border that Colombia and Ecuador's share?[4] What are the thousands of symbols, glyphs, and markings of cave art, most of which are undeciphered, and most of which are located in the northern Andes, a region that supposedly did not have any kind of hieroglyphic or sacred communication before the Europeans arrived? Even if textiles and goldsmithing were only methods of inscription in the Andes, how can we explain the painted fabrics of the Muisca and the Chancay, the complex pictorial figures of Paraca capes, the abstractions of Wari textiles, the minute studies of insects found in Quimbaya goldwork, the myth-narrative gold plaques of the Taironas, the impressive studies of the human body and its gestures found on the poporos, or the gold jars made by the metalsmiths of the ancient Andean West? It also seems strange to argue that the staffs of leadership used among Indigenous communities in the Colombian Andes are of European origin (Cummins and Rappaport 247), insofar as such a perspective fails to acknowledge immemorial Andean traditions tied to scepters, staffs, and lances. These symbols of power are clearly evident in the pre-Hispanic iconography of cultures like the Sechín and the Chavín in ancient Perú, as well as in the monoliths of the San Augustín culture in Colombia, the public art found in Tiwanaku culture of the Bolivian altiplano (first millennium CE), the gold-forged musical instruments from Colombia's Cundinamarca-Boyacá high plateau, and even the painted ceramics found in the Piartal-Tuza and Capulí cultures of the Tuquerres-Ipiales and Carchi altiplano in the centuries leading up to the arrival of the Europeans. For example, even if it is not possible to assert what type of objects the bearer has in his hands, at least it would be arcane to consider for the analysis images such as those found in pre-Hispanic painted ceramics of the binational Andean area of Nariño-Carchi (see fig. 59).

---

[3] Tumaco-La Tolita refers to a Pre-Colombian culture and ceramic style that was located along the Pacific border of the current countries of Colombia and Ecuador.

[4] In this context, Piartal-Tuza and Capulí are phases in ceramic styles within the broader pre-Hispanic cultural context, also referred to as Nariño.

Figure 59. Image from a pre-Hispanic Andean ceramic. José Echeverría. *El lenguaje simbólico en los Andes septentrionales*, p. 312

Is it absurd for us to consider the scriptural aspects of pictorial narratives found in multiple media and produced via a number of different communicative technologies before the arrival of the Spanish in the northern Andes? What are the thousands of sculptured ceramics made by the Tulato (Tumaco-La Tolita), whose work anteceded Mochica narrative representations and took up various dimensions of everyday (illnesses, sexuality, plants, social hierarchies) and religious (deities, mythological beings, shamanic metamorphoses) life? Given that they do not record oral speech, are these merely inscribed media?

However, I feel that Rappaport hits the mark when she states that "literate discourses merged with Andean means of encoding history in the landscape" (*Intercultural* 257), and it is somewhat surprising that she later warns us we will not be able to explore the subtleties and nuances of these discourses, "if we cling to the romantic but unrealistic and ahistorical notion of the 'indigenous voice'" (257). Certainly, one must recognize that a range of European cultural practices contributed to the construction and definition of what we today understand as "Indigenous" (258). Further, my critique of Rappaport's attitudes towards writing here does not discredit this particular book, or her previous work (2005), which I commented upon in the introduction. Both are invaluable. Rather, I would argue that studies that address diverse forms of contemporary or pre-Hispanic picto-ideographic writing should dialogue with the research of self-identified Indigenous writers and researchers (without quotation marks). The Camëntsá oralitor Hugo Jamioy and the Guna-dule pedagogue Manibinigdiginya, both of whose projects have been discussed previously, write using alphabetic script while also recognizing the existence of picto-ideographic writing with pre-Hispanic roots, and the need to generate creative and communicative continuities with the graphic-scriptural systems used by their communities. As we have seen, these writers do not reduce writing to the inscription of phonetic speech, and Jamioy in particular writes about the beautiful writing rejected by the colonizers.

SPEAKING WITH PAPER

Alonso de Nebrija published his *Gramática de la lengua castellana* [Grammar of the Castillian Language] in 1492. In it, Nebrija lays out how the Spanish language, and in particular its written form, could become a powerful linguistic tool of imperialism as it became the official language of Spanish expansion overseas. The work's edicts foreshadowed Spanish's use as a language of colonization and evangelization, while its content was used to measure and give European structures to numerous Indigenous languages through the production of their grammars, dictionaries, and vocabularies. These publications enabled sermons and eventually the *Bible* to be produced in these same languages. Two decades after Columbus's arrival, in 1512, the Laws of Burgos "established Spanish-language educational literacy for Indigenous peoples" [establecían la alfabetización de los indígenas en lengua castellana] (Gröll 43).

Throughout the Western Hemisphere, literacy has been one of the foremost political principles used to proselytize religion to Indigenous Peoples, and to control them administratively and educationally. From the moment Nebrija's grammar was published it regulated and domesticated the voice, that is, it controlled orality with imperial ends. According to the Peruvian researcher Julio Noriega, who has studied the "domestication" of the Quechua language, Nebrija's grammar "incentivized the production of the first grammars and vocabularies of Indigenous languages" [incentivó la confección de las primeras gramáticas y vocabularios en lenguas indígenas], while coining the phrase: "language was always the companion of empire" [siempre la lengua fue compañera del imperio] (32).

One of the most celebrated and commented upon (mis)encounters between a supposedly oral Indigenous culture and a supposedly literate European one, took place between the Inca Atahualpa and the Spanish priest Valverde, in Cajamarca, in present- day Perú, on

November 16, 1532. In one of the multiple versions recounted by the chroniclers of the Indies, and which Antonio Cornejo Polar has studied in detail, Atuhualpa seems to reject the *Bible*, or perhaps a prayer book, that Valverde was using because it would not speak to him. In his 1555 *Historia del descubrimiento y conquista del Perú* [History of the Discovery and Conquest of Peru], Augustín Zárate says that, "The Bishop said that the word of God had been written down in that book, and in response Atahualpa asked for the Bible or prayer book that the priest was holding; Atahualpa took it, opened it up, flipped through its pages from one end to the other, and saying that the book said nothing to him nor spoke his language, threw it on the ground" [El Obispo dijo que en aquel libro estaba escrito que era escritura de Dios y Atahualpa le pidió el breviario o Biblia que tenía en la mano; y como se lo dio, lo abrió, volviendo las hojas una cabo y otra, y dijo que aquel libro no le decía nada a él ni le hablaba palabra, y le arrojó en el campo] (qtd. in Cornejo Polar, 37).

This act unleashed the indignant fury of the Spaniards, and lead to the Inca's imprisonment and eventual murder before he could muster any armed resistance. Cornejo Polar says that we can understand this ironic scene of conflict between the voice and the letter as the ground zero of Andean heterogeneity. The literary critic also asserts that the "dialogue" in Cajamarca, "is not the origin of our literature. Indeed, our literature is much older insofar as we recognize that our history has a trajectory that well exceeds the limits of the Conquest" [no constituye el origen de nuestra literatura, que es más antiguo en cuanto nos reconocemos en una historia que viene de muy lejos y traspasa por largo el límite de la conquista] (27). Cornejo also offers up an important comment when he notes that the Spanish, beginning with those who captured the Inca, would similarly not have been able to read a book in Spanish or Latin, "and it is certain that here we are discussing two distinct illiteracies" [por cierto se trata de dos analfabetismos distintos] (40). That said, I disagree with his Ongian vision of there being a primary orality, particularly when he states that at the moment of their encounter with the Spanish the Inca were a "completely illiterate culture" [una cultura globalmente ágrafa]. Even before the creation of Tawantinsuyu, the central Andes were home to diverse systems of graphic communication. For example, texts such as the renowned Quipus (knotted, woven cords) were particularly used by expansionist States like those of the Wari and the Inca, and their origins lie partially with older civilizations like that of the Caral, along the central Peruvian coast. The coordinator of the Caral excavation team, Ruth Shady Solís, says that one set of textile remains found there is likely a Quipu from the third millennium BCE (96).

When we look at the classic studies on Andean textiles that have been published since the 1990s, and in particular at those by Silverman (1994) and by Lavalle and Lavalle de Cárdenas (1999), we realize that prior to colonial contact peoples in the Andes knew how to write.[5] Indeed, in many cases they even had specialist functionaries and political-religious elites who completely controlled certain forms of graphic communication, such as the *tocapus* "ideograhic designs" included on Inca *inkus* "blankets." Throughout the Andes the ideographs found on textiles, ceramics, metalworking, and other visual media, formed part of diverse and complex systems of communication that complemented both memory and verbal oral art. In other words, the heterogeneous scene in Cajamarca does not so much reflect the dis-encounter between a supposed Indigenous orality and supposed European literacy, but an incomprehensible collision between world systems that prioritized the voice while developing different forms of writing as the result of their different cultural contexts, their multiple needs to communicate, and the need to maintain social control. By contrast, the Spanish chroniclers painted the Inca as an idiot who was waiting for an object to simply speak by itself, affirming the supposedly pre-alphabetic, pagan literacy of Atahualpa who, as if that were not enough, personified one of the classic stereotypes of the Indigenous "leader."

Beyond this collision, the confusion, and historical distortions surrounding this moment of first contact between the Inca and the Spanish, the idea of talking papers or, more concretely, the expectation that papers can speak, is an idea that comes from communities that privilege the word over written abstraction. Within contemporary Indigenous literature the idea of "talking paper" represents an important kind of mirrored vision on (il)literacy.

TWIRLING A DIPLOMA, RETELLING THE BIBLE

In her preface to the story "Declares Not Knowing How to Sign. Born on December 31" (2006), the Wayuu writer Estercilia Simanca states:

---

[5] Here I am understanding "writing" as a communicative act that implies much more than the phonetic inscription of a language.

My grandfather was roughly 70 years old, and I was about 7, when, armed with pencil and paper, I gave him his first writing lessons. My small hands tried to carry my grandfather's large, calloused, wrinkled hands along the paths of the cursive letters, but when I saw how difficult my job would be, I thought it would be better to teach him to sign his name in "block letters." My grandfather let me carry him along, but he eventually fell asleep. This happened back when some cachacos came to give him a diploma that recognized him as being a Colombian farmer, for national farmer's day.[6] I heard that my grandfather had to sign a sheet stating that he had received his diploma. I got in front of the line under the covered walkway at my uncle Ramón's house (in Paraíso, Caicemapa Reserve, Baja Guajira). Among all the people there, I was the only person waiting for my grandfather to sign his name. Finally everyone would realize that my grandfather already knew how to sign his name, but no one gave him a pen. Instead they took his right hand, wet his index finger on an ink pad, and placed his fingerprint in the receipt. Everyone but me applauded as old Vale received his diploma. My grandfather looked at the document and acted like he was reading it without realizing he was holding it upside down. I was really young, so I quickly forgot about it. I stopped giving my grandfather classes and went to play with my cousins. A long time passed before I asked my grandfather why he hadn't signed the paper the cachacos had given him, and he told me that he was too old now to talk with the paper (write), and the paper didn't want to speak to him anyway (read).

[Tenía mi abuelo setenta años de edad aproximadamente, y yo siete años, cuando armados de papel y lápiz le di sus primeras lecciones. Mis pequeñas manos trataban de llevar las manos grandes, callosas y arrugadas de mi abuelo por el sendero de las letras cursivas, pero al ver lo tenaz que sería mi empresa, decidí mejor enseñarle a firmar en letra de "palito". Mi abuelo se dejaba llevar, pero al poco tiempo se dormía. Fue por aquella época cuando llegaron unos cachacos 110 a llevarle un diploma que lo acreditaba como un campesino colombiano, en el día nacional del campesino. Escuché que mi abuelo debía firmar un recibo que constatara que él había recibido dicho diploma. Me puse en primera fila, estábamos todos en la enramada

---

6 Today "cachaco" refers to someone from Colombia's Andean interior, and more specifically to someone from Bogotá, the capital. By looking at the novels of another Wayuu writer, Antonio López, we can deduce that the word originally designated members of the military who came to the Caribbean coast from the Andes.

de la casa de mi tío Ramón (Paraíso, Resguardo Caicemapa, Baja
Guajira). De todos yo era la única que esperaba que mi abuelo fir-
mara. Por fin todos se darían cuenta que mi abuelo ya sabía escribir su nombre, pero no le entregaron un lapicero, le tomaron
la mano derecha y humedecieron su dedo índice en un huellero y
estamparon su huella digital en el recibo. Todos aplaudieron, menos
yo, que el viejo Vale hubiese recibido un diploma. Mi abuelo mira-
ba el diploma y hacía como si lo estuviera leyendo, pero no sabía
que lo tenía al revés. Como era muy niña el suceso se me olvidó
al poco tiempo. Dejé de darle clases a mi abuelo y me fui a jugar
con mis primas. Transcurrió mucho tiempo cuando le pregunté a mi
abuelo por qué no había firmado el papel que le dieron los cachacos
y me dijo que él ya estaba muy viejo para hablar con el papel (escribir) y tampoco el papel quería hablar con él (leer).] (*Manifiesta* 3)

The preface has several characteristics of what I have referred to
as a mirrored vision: an Indigenous vision on a kind of foreigner's
(cachaco, arijuna) otherness; an institution (that intervenes) and/or
a foreign technology (writing with a pen, an inkpad, the receipt, the
diploma); the sui generis and intimate interpretation of these other
people's and technologies' standardizing, colonizing impact; and a
particular, critical perspective on socio-cultural difference that arises
from an Indigenous cosmovision. Dominant culture's perspective on
illiteracy is mirrored when the young girl begins teaching her grandfather to write. In a surprising inversion, it is the young girl, the em-
bodiment of a new generation, who guides her grandfather, and by
extension her elders, along the path to literacy. This is also found in
the image of the contrasting hands, in which the young girl's hands,
despite their inexperience, already know how to write. By comparison, her grandfather's hands are forced into the mold of conventional graphic phonetic writing, using so-called "block letters."[7]

As seen in a painting by the researcher and painter Guillermo
Ojeda Jayariyú (see fig. 60), hands have an important significance
among the Wayuu, particularly insofar as the hands in this painting
are the capable hands of a weaver interweaving colored threads to
create texts-textiles like the *susu* "bags" that the Wayuu use in their
everyday lives, and which are the object of national and internation-

---

[7] This is an ironic reference to an infantilized method for learning how to write
conventionally (block letters made out of straight lines, punctuation, margins on the
page). In the original text this is "escritura de palito" [writing made out of little
sticks].

al prestige. According to the Wayuu story, weavers learned how to weave from Wareket, the ancestral weaver-spider.

Figure 60. Painting by Guillermo Ojeda Jayariyú. Author's personal archive.

The contrasting image of the "slow" hand lead through the patterns of block letters as it learns to write becomes an ironic, denunciatory mirrored vision given that, although the grandfather learns to write his name, the functionaries who are from the lettered city nonetheless assume he is illiterate. Without even consulting him they use his fingerprint as proof that he has received his diploma, with the diploma itself representing another written form of control and the fingerprint taken by a controlling, dominating hand. From a Wayuu perspective, the cachacos in Simanca's story personify otherness, and it is soon discovered that the document they have brought is in reality one that de-indigenizes and above all epistemologically de-Wayuuizes the grandfather. Through the diploma, and vouchsafed via community's applause or acceptance, the lettered functionaries have subtly converted him into a rural farmer. The young girl is the only one who feels upset about what happens, and through her brief narrative offers us her perspective on the otherness of the "non-Wayuu" arijuna, as well as her intimate interpretation of the impact of colonialism's impulse to standardize peoples and cultures. In a typical mirrored vision, the grandfather pretends to read or tries to read the diploma as he holds it upside down: "My grandfather looked at the document and acted like he was reading it without realizing he was holding it upside down" (3). The narrator states she asked her grandfather Vale why he had not signed the paper the cachacos had given to him a long time later. His answer gives a sui generis twist to one's first impression of what had happened, saying that he was too old to speak with the paper, that is, to write, or for the paper to speak to him, that is, to read. At this point the preface's mirrored vision offers a unique insight on sociocultural differences (alphabetic writing and the category of farmer or peasant) from an Indigenous cosmovision, which is validated above all else by oral communication. The idea of communication with and through beings and non-humans like animals, plants, and even through the maracas of the *oütsu* (traditional female healer), run throughout Wayuu thought. Speaking with paper, even before speaking through paper, is the expression of a symbolic mentality being contrasted with a mechanical, bureaucratized one.

We can argue that the book is the classic Western format for alphabetic writing insofar as it is supposed to be the extension and concretion of thought. In this sense, some of the West's "classics" are books of European philosophy, constitutions and legal codes, including a large part of the Old Testament, and a series of so-called canonical books from different national literatures. That said, the contemporary validation of speech in Western phonetic writing has been in part the result of the literary articulations of the orality, as in the case with Latin American literary authors, such as Juan Rulfo, Gabriel García Márquez, and Nicolás Guillén.

Wayuu authors frequently produce mirrored visions through their Indigenous characters' interpretations of reality, giving surprising twists on events, institutions, and objects that they experience through their contact with the people they refer to as non-Indigenous or *arijunas*. For example, in the story *Ni era vaca ni era caballo* [Neither Cow nor Horse] by the Wayuu writer Miguel Ángel Jusayú, the young protagonist believes that the truck he sees while out attending his herd is a *yolujá* (a feared spirit of the dead). Similarly, in Simanca's "Jimaai en la tierra del maíz" [Jimaai in the Land of Corn], Jimaai believes that the bolívar, Venezuela's national currency, is a famous person: the "liberator." Equally, in "La fiesta patronal" [Feast of the Patron Saint] by the Venezuelan Wayuu poet Juan Pushaina, Jesus turns out to be the son of Mareiwa, a heroic Wayuu deity. The poem itself Wayuu-izes Biblical scenes and has them take place in the deserts of the Guajira:

Mary's	[José
husband	es wayuu
Joseph	y marido
is Wayuu.	de María.
They fell in love	Se enamoraron
in Uyatsira.	en Uyatsira.
They got married	Se casaron
in Sirapu'wa.	en Sirapu'wa.
Joseph	José
looked like he was from Cojoro	parece cojoreño
and Mary like she was from Jarara.	y María jararaña.
One beautiful night	Una linda noche
at Joseph's little ranch	al pie
at the foot	del cerro Aáyajuui
of the Aáyajuui mountain	en el rancho de José
among the goats and the donkey	entre chivos y burro
a child came down	al regazo
from the heavens	de María del cielo
into Mary's lap.	bajó un niño.
It was the son of Ma'leiwa.	Era el hijo de Ma'leiwa.
God our father.	Nuestro tata Dios.]
	(qtd. in Rocha Vivas, *El sol* 381)

Here Juan Pushaina turns the Biblical story on its head, as much creating a Wayuu mirrored vision on Christianity as Wayuu-izing and contextualizing a symbolic universe that has been used as a tool of colonial domination. In Linda Tuhiwai Smith's words, he looks to exercise, "the legitimacy of oppositional or alternative histories, theories, and ways of writing" (39). Drawing on Biblical or "sacred" history, Pushaina's poetic project responds precisely to the kind of connections Tuhiwai proposes. For Pushaina, connection with the land is expressed through nativization ("Joseph / looked like he was from Cojoro"), localization ("They got married / in Sirapu'wa"), and the appropriation of Biblical genealogies ("Joseph is Wayuu").

Pushaina's appropriation of Biblical writing and history parallels how Simanca and her characters appropriate "literacy" and "block letters." The grandfather's lack of knowledge about and separation from conventional writing corresponds to the inadequacy and initial foreignness of the canonical Biblical landscape prior to Pushaina's literary intervention, despite the fact that the Guajira, like many places in the New Testament, is also arid. In many cases, alphabetic writing and the Bible, the West's canonical book par excellence, are adapted and/or contested by Indigenous intellectuals who write from within their own historical-symbolic systems of reference, and towards specific ends (territorial revindication, the reaffirmation of

Indigenous practices and values, and the rewriting of history).[8] In this sense we can say that mirrored visions are also literary twists, communicative strategies that help overturn or help generate new perspectives on intercultural contact. They turn "the grandfather's diploma" right-side up, questioning and making the codes of dominant societies intelligible. They also seek to invert official histories and/or canons with irony, subtlety, or open confrontation, using the codes and tools of the colonizer (the *Bible*, alphabetic writing, imposed technologies) in a continual process that symbolically reverses those of the colony.

However, are such mirrored visions merely utopian fantasies? Following Dipesh Chakrabarty and his profound interrogations of eurocentrism, we can state that "hiperreal Europe will continually dominate the stories we tell" (39). According to Meaghan Morris, the domination found in telling such stories occurs "as a known history, something which has already happened elsewhere, and which is to be reproduced, mechanically or otherwise, with a local content" (qtd. in Chakrabarty, 39). Nonetheless, the mechanisms through which these stories are reproduced can also be subverted through "local adaptations," whether this be in terms of content or via their novel use of media. When we remember that Miguel Ángel Jusayú includes prologues dedicated to Wayuu readers, we better understand that his literary project privileges texts that, while written in the Greco-Phoenician alphabet, are in Wayuunaiki. There are also numerous references to Wayuu culture which arijuna readers likely cannot understand, as well as the large font that he uses to represents words found in Wayunaiki oral narratives.[9]

As such, we can assert that even if most works of Indigenous literature are read by and directed towards a non-Indigenous readership, Indigenous readers are nonetheless better situated to understand a considerable number of works, or at the very least specific parts of some works. While this may certainly be utopian in some cases, in many cases Indigenous readers can read the languages in which these works are written, thus being the privileged audience to whom these works are directed. At least for Jusayú, the hope is that

---

[8] See, for example, Guaman Poma in the seventeenth century, and the Maya Tz'utujil artist from Guatemala Benvenuto Chavajay in the twenty-first. I should also mention Odi Gonzáles in the book *La escuela de Cusco* [The Cusco School], which poetically reinterprets colonial Catholic paintings through the gazes of the Quechua poet, his family, and the broader Quechua community.

[9] See, for example, the narrative work *Achi'kí, relatos guajiros.*

these uniquely Indigenous narratives do not become lost, and that written language can be used as a tool to transmit them orally and across generations, now and in the future.

MIRRORED VISIONS IN THE ANDES, FROM THE ANDES

Hugo Jamioy Juajibioy is one of the Indigenous writers whose oraliterary work frequently constructs ironic dialogues that interpellate dominant society. However, being Camëntsá instead of Quechua, Jamioy does not talk about the Andean "utopia" of the *inkarri*, the belief in the return of the Inca king, and in the specific case of the Inca Atahualpa, the recovery of his decapitated head (see fig. 61).

Figure 61. The Decapitation of Atahualpa according to Guamán Poma.
Copenhague Royal Library. Web archive.

Instead, Jamioy takes up the challenge of re-educating dominant society. As outlined in the previous example from Santiago de Chile's

2008 International Book Fair, when he put forth the notion that non-Indigenous peoples were illiterate with regard to Indigenous peoples, Jamioy sees non-Indigenous peoples' lack of knowledge with regard to the diversity of Indigenous, non-alphabetic writing systems as a kind of reverse illiteracy. At its core this idea is a mirrored vision in which the author measures dominant society with the same ruler that he has been measured with, essentially using a hegemonic practice (literacy) to produce a decolonizing one (illiteracy). In short, he inverts dominant society's perspective, turning it on its head in a way that favors his literacy instead of the colonizer's, undermining the civilizing assumption that alphabetic writing is a superior form of communication. We should again recall the 2012 article in which the Camëntsá oralitor says, "I now think that beautiful writing they made me forget when I learned to write in Spanish, was more important back then than being illiterate" ("Pensando, hilando" 150). "Ndosertanëng" "Analfabetas" [Illiterates] is one of Jamioy's texts that synthesizes his mirrored visions on illiteracy (I have added numbers to the verse here to facilitate reading):

[1] Who are they calling illiterate,	[A quién llaman analfabetas,
[2] people who cannot read	¿a los que no saben leer
[3] books or nature?	los libros o la naturaleza?
[4] One or the other	Unos y otros
[5] know some or a lot.	algo y mucho saben.
[6] During the day	Durante el día
[7] they brought my grandfather	a mi abuelo le entregaron
[8] a book:	un libro:
[9] they told him he didn't know anything.	le dijeron que no sabía nada.
[10] At night	Por las noches
[11] he sat beside the hearth fire,	se sentaba junto al fogón,
[12] over his hands	en sus manos
[13] there was a a coca leaf turning	giraba una hoja de coca
[14] and his lips were saying	y sus labios iban diciendo
[15] what he saw in there.	lo que en ella miraba]
	(Jamioy, *Bínÿbe* [2010] 179)

Like other texts in which the oralitor questions non-Indigenous peoples, their institutions, and dominant practices, this poem is clearly a form of intercultural interjection. Indigenous illiteracy, not knowing how to read books in lines 2, 3–8, and 9, contrasts with non-Indigenous illiteracy, not knowing how to read nature in lines 2 and 3. In an ironic tone, Camëntsá readings of nature and, above all, their deeper understanding of the earth, are directly contrasted with the bookish learning of non-Indigenous peoples. To a certain extent, the image of the grandfather who is able to read the coca leaf (lines

10–15) is a stereotypical image of the Indigenous person who exists in close proximity to nature, "guarding" it.

Another writer and intellectual from the Andean Southwest, the Nasa leader Manuel Quintín Lame, similarly describes the idea of a nature-based Indigenous education in *Los pensamientos del indio que se educó dentro de las selvas colombianas* [The Thoughts of an Indian Educated in Colombia's Jungles] (1971). Laying out the characteristics of what he refers to as "my race," in *Los pensamientos* Lame claims that Indigenous peoples' racial-cultural "superiority" is derived from their education in the forest. Taking a more moderate tone, Jamioy affirms, "One or the other / know some or a lot" (lines 4 and 5). That said, the poem's initially ironic tones also refer to the violence inflicted by alphabetic colonization as an open wound, saying, "During the day / they brought my grandfather / a book: / they told him he didn't know anything."

After this act of alphabetic discrimination against the "illiterate" elder, in a sovereign act of survival the figure of a grandfather resisting colonization surges forth in verses 6, 7, 8, and 9. Beside the hearth at night, the grandfather turns over the coca leaf (lines 12–13), and moves his mouth and lips (line 14), implying that he is reading and speaking in his role as interpreter. Although not explicitly alluded to in the text, the reading of coca leaves in the Andes is also a divinatory practice. The person who reads coca leaves in reality interprets them. By reading coca leaves in the present, and in the context and intimacy of a visual community of symbols whose codes he has learned or which have been revealed to him, he can foresee events or reinterpret previous ones. Within this poem, the person who interprets the different figures and shapes on the coca leaves positions his wisdom as being superior to that of people who simply read paper. Through his relationship with nature the former is "clairvoyant", while we can infer that the later, as readers of books, remain at a distance from reality itself. Despite its global associations with the illicit production of cocaine and drug trafficking, in "Ndosertanëng" "Analfabeta" [Illiterate] the coca leaf emerges as a symbol of wisdom and resistance that constitutes a sui generis practice of reading and writing within the "natural" order.

The complementary relationship between orality and writing represented here is characteristic of Indigenous writing systems in which the graphic form tends not to supplant oral expression. As opposed to the daily schedule of national education, the night's ritual and pedagogical dimension take place in the collective family space of the hearth or *tullpa*, where the Camëntsá and other Indigenous people traditionally share food and the elders' words of wisdom.

The poem also emphasizes the hands which, in their proximity to the *tullpa*, turn over the coca leaf (lines 12 and 13). Their motion suggests a kind of cyclical, ritual reading that evokes the traditional Camëntsá practice of burying the placenta and umbilical cord under the hearth. Further, we can assert that the grandfather reads the coca leaf holistically, using both hands at the same time, given that his reading of the coca leaf is not the kind of linear reading from left-to-right that one does with books, nor writing with only one hand. In a sense, this practice is also a kind of gestural communication that is incomprehensible for those who do not participate in these kinds of intracultural literary spaces, given that, although the grandfather's hands and lips move, the oralitor does not tell us what his he actually says. Indeed, the grandfather's words are merely suggested by the very intimacy of this kind of reading itself. It is also significant that in the poem the oralitor facilitates an external gaze while reaffirming the limits of his cultural and familial universe. That is, a reading of "Ndosertanëng" evidences and produces an experience of reverse illiteracy, as the non-Indigenous, or non-Camëntsá, reader, while capable of seeing and imagining the grandfather's head, lips, hands, and body, remains limited by his own culture.

Literacy has been one of the most homogenizing tools of social control from the Colonial Period down to the present. Literacy rates are outlined in the same graphs that are used to describe supposed levels of (un)development, which in turn are characteristic of the so-called Third World (Escobar). In one graph published in a Camëntsá blog, the community offers exact illiteracy statistics: 516 (226 men and 288 women) ("Indicadores"). Arturo Escobar, who has extensively researched the invention of the Third World and developmental programs' regimes of representation, cites Trinh, who in turn cites the following words of Ivan Illich, that "the foreigners' perception of someone who needs help has taken on the successive forms of the barbarian, the pagan, the infidel, the savage, the 'native,' and the underdeveloped" [la percepción del extranjero como alguien que necesita ayuda ha tomado sucesivamente las formas del bárbaro, el pagano, el infiel, el salvaje, el "nativo" y el subdesarrollado] (qtd. in Escobar, 60). We could add the illiterate to this sequence, as (il)literacy tends to operate as a mode of representation that becomes a dominant part of the "colonization of reality" [colonización de realidad] (Escobar 58). In effect, the grandfathers in Jamioy's poem and in Simanca's story find that an illiterate "identity" is imposed upon by them by more "developed" outsiders whose dependence on phonetic writing rises to the level of fetishization (Lienhard 46). The system that discriminates against the illiterate grandfathers, and against illiterate people in general, is a fearful exercise in institutionalized political and symbolic violence that is part of the contemporary global world. As we have seen, in Simanca the grandfather is converted into a farmer, while in Jamioy he is initially seen as ignorant. The girl in Simanca's story resists alphabetizing violence via her grandfather's partial assimilation, as it was necessary that he could at least learn to sign his name. The strategy in Jamioy's text is different: the grandfather resists the alphabet's dominance by affirming that he reads coca leaves.

From an Andean perspective, *Atawallpap wayñuynin*, dramas on the death of the Inca Atawallpa, are an important textual antecedent here both in terms of how they represent the reading of a plant, and how they construct an Indigenous perspective on alphabetic writing on paper, which is simply another kind of culturally-processed vegetable medium. According to Arnold and Yapita, people began performing dramas about the death of Atawallpa around 1555, two decades after the Inca's death. These were "centered on the encounter in Cajamarca, but focused on a letter from the king of Spain or Pizarro to Atawallpa [instead of a Bible], that is, the position of the Crown instead of that of the church. They continue to be performed throughout Central Perú and in the Bolivian Department of Oruro" [se centran en el mismo encuentro en Cajamarca, pero en una carta del rey de España o de Pizarro a Atawallpa, es decir, la posición de la Corona y no la de la Iglesia. Se realizan todavía en los pueblos del Perú central y en el departamento de Oruro en Bolivia] (71). They go on to say that, in a contemporary version collected by Jesús Lara, the *amauta* "wise" Inca Waylla Wisa reflects on European writing via Andean notions of writing as he speaks with Sairi Tupác. He refers to the letter as *chala blanca*, a corn husk:

Wally Wisa: Who knows what this chala says.
It is possible that I'll never come to know.
Seen from this side it is a swarm of ants.
I see it from this other side and it seems like the footprints left by birds

[*Waylla Wisa:* Quién sabe qué dirá esta chala.
Es posible que nunca llegue a saberlo yo.
Vista de este costado es un hervidero de hormigas.
La miro desde este otro costado y se me antojan las huellas que dejan las patas de los pájaros

along a river's muddy banks.	en las lodosas orillas del río.
Seen like this, it looks like the tarukas	Vista así, se parece a las tarukas
turned upside down,	puestas con la cabeza abajo
with their heads down	y las patas arriba.
and their feet in the air.	Y si solo así la miramos
And if we look at it like this,	es semejante a las llamas cabizbajas...]
it is similar to a llama with its head down…	(qtd. in Arnold and Yapita, 71)

In the revealing interpretation of the British anthropologist Denisse Arnold and the Aymara poet-linguist Juan de Dios Yapita, this and other passages in the drama lead us to conclude that, "for the Incas paper, like weaving, is the earth, and the letters are marks or similar shapes that appear there" [para los inkas, el papel, al igual que el tejido, es el suelo, y los caracteres son huellas o formas familiares que aparecen en el suelo] (72). These dramas are dances that are sung and performed in the very collective territories to which, according to the prophecy of Inkarrí, the head of the Inca king will return to be reunited with his decapitated body. In the case of the Colombian Andes, both the Camëntsá metaphor of writing with one's feet (Jamioy), and the U'wa metaphor of writing-thinking with one's feet in one's head (Berichá), elaborate a vision of the world in which read-writing is done with and from Indigenous notions of territory. As demonstrated by Ann Osborn, an anthropologist from Oxford University, U'wa sung myths are also ways of retelling and strengthening collective memory in their land. As seen in Chapter 3, Hugo Jamioy's writing creates a poetic guide that helps one continue in and follow the elders' footprints. However, we should also note that, in addition to the footprints, in the version of *Atawallpap wayñuynin* cited above, the Inca describes alphabetic writing on the sheet of paper as *tarukas* [deer] "turned upside down / with their heads down and their feet in the air" [puestas con la Cabeza abajo / y las patas arriba]. This surprising and literal mirrored vision on writing suggests that Indigenous peoples have re-interpreted alphabetic writing from their own cultural borders and needs since early on in the Colonial period, and also shows how these reinterpretations reconsider their own scriptural practices. Finally, it demonstrates that the symbolism of being placed "head down" has operated in the Andes through both the relationship of collective writing with the earth and the need to question, ironize, and subvert the broad relationship between alphabetic writing and colonizing bureaucratic power (Crown-Church-State-School). This symbolic background means that writing upside down not only restores one's vision, but also one's sensibility and sanity in a world that has itself been turned upside down. Andean reinterpretations of alphabetic writing also generate reconsiderations about autochthonous Andean scriptural practices. The image of letters as inverted *tarukas*, and perhaps even the llamas with their heads down, in *Atawallpap wayñuynin* also indirectly alludes to some of the oldest visual communication in the Andes and in all of South America, such as the pictographic and ideographic depictions of hunters pursuing camelids in prehistoric cave art from Lauricocha, Toquepala, and Chaclarragra in Perú (see fig. 62).

Figure 62. Sequential image that likely depicts the hunting of camelids. Chaclarragra cave. Jean Guffroy. *El arte rupestre en el antiguo Perú*, p. 52.

The domestication of camelids in South America occurred at some point between the years 9000 and 2500 BCE. As a landmark of civilization in the Andes and Patagonia, it constitutes a major point of reference in Andean cultures and in multiple Andean graphic systems. The domestication of camelids is even culturally more relevant in South America than the development of a system of phonetic notation, given that it facilitated peoples' adaptation to and settlement in hostile environments while also dynamizing intercultural communication throughout the region via commerce and territorial expansionism characteristic of, but not limited to, the Incas. Moreover, we can assert that the invention of phonetic writing would not have been as important as the domestication of camelids, a civilizational achievement that facilitated communication, in a part of the continent characterized by adaptation to the largest mountain range on the planet, and where the Spanish were met by innumerable different languages upon their arrival.

Although we can argue that phonetic writing was not a necessity for Indigenous Peoples in the southern part of the continent, narratives such as those from the Incas and the Taironas claim that Indigenous Peoples "knew" it and "threw" it away. According to a tale recorded by Gerardo Reichel-Dolmatoff, the controversial Austrian ethnographer who lived with the Kogui, a group who are partially the heirs to the Taironas in the Sierra Nevada de Santa Marta, "Mother Kasumma made a huge book. They wrote and they read. When it dawned and there was a sun and a moon, Mother said, 'This isn't for us, but for one of our foreign little brothers.' We took writing and reading, everything to our little brother, and that's why our little brother will take care of us until the end of the world with tools" [Madre Kasumma hizo un libro grandotote. Ellos escribían y leían. Cuando amaneció y ya hubo sol y luna, Madre dijo: "Eso no luce a nosotros sino a hermanito extranjero". Entregamos escritura y leer y todo a hermanito y por eso hermanito nos cuida hasta fin del mundo, con herramientas] (qtd. in Reichel-Dolmatoff, 2: 30). According to Arnold and Yapita, Indigenous chronistas like Santa Cruz Pachacuti Yamqui and Spanish ones like Blas Varela and Montesinos claim that writing existed in the pre-Hispanic Andes. In his chronicle from 1643 Montesinos claims "that the Incas had writing—*qillqa*, parchments or tree leaves covered with figures—but they prohibited its use under penalty of death, and went so far as to burn the wise people (*amawta*) who used it, due to the problems that writing brought" [que los Inkas tenían escritura —qillqa, pergaminos u hojas de árboles cubiertas con caracteres— pero que ellos lo prohibían bajo pena de muerte, hasta quemaban a los sabios (amawta) quienes lo usaban, por los problemas que la escritura trajo] (Arnold and Yapita 70). Both of these stories reopen debates about phonetic writing in the Americas, such as how some Indigenous Peoples could assimilate and then reject Greco-Semitic phonetic writing, how we must consider the internal dynamics of cultural constructions and deconstructions of certain communities, as well as their own needs and limitations regarding communication, the impacts of graphic writing's hierarchies of power, and Indigenous communities' mythic visions on other human communities' writing and communication systems.

Post-Mortem Illiteracy

A story recorded by Manibinigdiginya/Abadio Green shows how certain areas of Gunadule tradition see the impact of alphabetic literacy even after death: "When someone dies, the dead person wakes up in the cemetery and finds a large mola on which the stories of every man and woman are written. If the person was selfish, prideful, or bad, their sight will be clouded and they will become illiterate, the same if someone used the figures of letters used to write in Spanish. They won't be able to read the writing on the mola, which uses different fabrics and different colors" [Cuando alguien se muere, el difunto al despertar en la casa del cementerio, encontrará una mola grande, donde estará escrita la historia de cada hombre y de cada mujer. Si la persona fue egoísta, orgullosa, maldadosa, la vista se nublará y se convertirá en una analfabeta, así mismo si alguien manejó las grafías de la lengua castellana, tampoco podrá leer la escritura de la mola que estarán escritas en diferentes tejidos con múltiples colores] (*Anmal* 217).

Although this story rejects the use of Spanish's alphabetic script, Nele Kantule, the leader of the 1925 Revolution in Panamá's San Blas (Guya Yala) archipelago, held a less traditionalist perspective, as he thought it necessary to maintain tradition while also recognizing the possibilities inherent in *waga* [non-Indigenous] writing. By comparison, in the more traditionalist perspective above, alphabetic writing acquires a taboo character, and those who would access it are given explicit warnings. As emphasized in mirrored visions dealing with (il)literacy, alphabetized persons are seen in relation to behaviors that are rejected by the community, such as individualism, pride, and egoism. These are associated with both other graphic forms of writing and the *waga*, non-Indigenous Peoples. Despite this apparent resistance, the image of a funerary writing through which one can decipher the life of any given person might be connected to the influence of Biblical imaginaries that have been established in Guna Yala during three decades of Protestant Evangelism. In Figure 63, a mola made by a nineteen-year-old Gunadule woman, we find a self-portrait and alphabetic script depicting the Biblical scene of "Noah's Arc." Further, the woman plays with the Spanish "Larcadneo," with the "e" and "o" inverted in the textile representation of the Biblical patriarch's name.

According to Manibinigdiginya in *Anmal gaya burba*, we can understand the mortuary house as an allusion to a *galu* [a cave], dwelling or sacred place, where ancestral knowledge is symbolically guarded in Gunadule narratives. For Perrin, *galus* are settlements of spirits located near the coasts, as well as places where animals come from (*Magnificent* 109). In a sung tale from the *Pab Igala*, mama Nagiryai, Nagegiryai or Nakekiriai, is said to be the first woman to enter the *galu* Tuipis or Dugbis, where she saw and memorized the scriptural designs of molas. This civilizing heroine then

Figure 63. Mola depicting Noah's Arc. Michel Perrin. *Magnificent Molas: The Art of the Kuna Indians*, p. 31.

returned to the human world and taught Guna women to cut, sew, and elaborate molas' secret designs. As in the passage cited above, here molas' graphic symbols are revealed in one of the underworld's galus. Compared to this mother-weaver who comes and goes from the underworld (galu), the deceased Gunadule in Manibinigdigin-ya's work has a post-mortem encounter with the molas. Depending on how they lived their lives, and whether or not they used Latin letters, the dead person is able to read and understand the great mola, a collective written history through which they can interpret their own story. The deceased is sentenced to a kind of postmortem illiteracy if they cannot read the personal and collective narratives in the multicolored woven mola. Within the logic of this particu-lar mirrored vision, the tense relationship between being illiterate in one's own script and literate in an imposed system generates a kind of double death that results in blindness, confusion, and ulti-mately, one's disappearance. However, the story also points toward a postmortem "continuity" of the Gunadules' ability to know their personal and collective history through the reading of molas, and illiteracy in Spanish becomes a path to salvation insofar as, by being illiterate, ones avoids the punishment of becoming colorblind or completely dead due to alphabetic egoism. In this sense, this mirrored vision expresses a will for collective survival, identity, and grounding, through the molas' colorful designs.

We should remember another Gunadule graphic system, the healing picto-ideographic writing of the *neles, nelegan* or traditional healers. According to Gordon Brotherston, the *neles* themselves invented writing, which in the case of the *neles* is a therapeutic epic composed of sung and written texts. The *ikala* or *igala* [road/path] is a kind of writing used to register traditional verbal art, or so-called canonical literature (Brotherson 69). As such, in Manibinigdiginya's passage we can find the shamanic qualities of writing as reflected in the deceased's readings of the great mola.

This mirrored vision presents the complementary, multi-modal relationship between song and writing, sound and image, orality and literacy, as one of Indigenous "literacy"'s primary characteristics. In the particular case of Gunadule traditions, it also alerts us to the disorienting and confusing character of the predominant phonetic writing system.

Some Final Thoughts on Illiteracy

Using mirrored visions to read these situations of reverse illiteracy, we find at least four distinct personifications of this phenomenon: the grandfather who is turned into a farmer with a diploma held upside down; the young girl who insists on teaching her grandfather to sign his name; the grandfather who defies his supposed illiteracy by reading coca leaves and nature; and the dead who, if they managed to maintain their illiteracy while living, are capable of reading their own history.

Aspiring to teach her grandfather how to write, Simanca's Wayuu child reflects an attitude in which literacy can be assimilated and turned into a mode of resistance. Jamioy's poetic voice interpellates dominant society. The poetic voice uses alphabetic writing to affirm a traditional Indigenous writing system, and creates an experience of reverse illiteracy for non-Camëntsá. Manibinigdiginya's text portrays the more traditionalist perspective of certain sectors of Gunadule society. In death, the use of alphabetic writing can impede the dead's being recognized in the underworld, making them illiterate and unable to read their own history and collective writing. By comparison, those "illiterate" in alphabetic script are "literate" in the reading of molas. Beyond the political or cosmological understandings of this more traditional position, however, the pedagogy of mother earth, Manibinigdiginya's proposal based upon a profound sense of Gunadule interculturality, recognizes that one needs to be proficient in a number of forms of writing. That is, it understands the need to navigate between the shores of what we have discussed as the binary literacy-illiteracy as, when speaking with young people from Indigenous communities, one notes their desire to know and use multiple languages and forms of communication.

Cities Within

General Thoughts

The following mirrored visions address Indigenous images and literary texts in which cities are spaces where notions like "inside" and "outside" can be questioned and resignified. We will see how dominant structures are not only imposed in these spaces of "socio-cultural conflict" (Lienhard), but also how Indigenous peoples create new processes of identity and community organization. For the most part, in the works we examine here, the city tends to be constructed as an "outside" that contrasts with the "inside" of communal and collective territories.

That said, the supposed "outside" of the city and the "inside" of Indigenous communities has become blurred since the middle of the past century, a moment in the Colombian Civil War when different political factions (liberals and conservatives) generated new waves in the disruption of rural life, disruptions which in turn increased the migration of farmers, and Indigenous and Afro-descended peoples, to the country's so-called urban core. From the mid-1990s until the present, tensions between armed guerrilla movements, paramilitary groups, and state military forces have put a tremendous amount of pressure on Indigenous areas, where some of the worst battles over natural "resources" and the ability to control goods and routes for drug trafficking have taken place (Sierra Nevada de Santa Marta, Urabá in Antioquia, Guajira, Cauca, Putumayo, Caquetá, Catatumbo, the Eastern plains, and the Amazonia).

Despite the peace agreement with the FARC and the efforts of government officials and NGOs to compile statistics about the conflict, there is no database to help us establish the number of Indigenous youth who were recruited by different armed groups.[10] Meanwhile, the coercion, disappearance, and selective assassination of Indigenous leaders are ongoing occurrences. Along these lines, we should also mention the dynamics of the drug trade based on the illegal cultivation of poppy and coca, as well as successive campaigns aimed at eradicating these, whether by hand or through the use of lethal chemicals like glyphosate. All of these activities directly impact the sovereignty, political order, health, foodways, and other social dimensions of life in collective territories. National campaigns like the one that demonized coca during the Uribe government (2002–2010), in which a little girl refers to coca as "the plant that kills" [la mata que mata], have been forcibly introduced into the collective unconscious through the broad rejection of coca, and the places where people believe that both coca and the "great" national problem of the armed conflict and drug trafficking originate. In this way, the "inside" of Indigenous cultural nations is not necessarily a symbolic reservation (Teuton, "The Cycle"), or a territory articulated by the "protectionist" policies of the Spanish crown or Simón Bolívar in his famous decree restoring Indigenous lands on May 20, 1820 (Sánchez Gutiérrez and Molina Echeverri 395). Rather, as we will explore in Chapter 6, these Indigenous territories are multifold spaces crosscrossed by an infinite number of (multi)national interests through the slow march of dams, mines, oil fields, and bullets.

Cities in Colombia today are veritable conglomerates of regional migrants in which class differences are marked by the very kind of access one has to public services, security, the architectural configurations of neighborhood zones, and one's level of access to education, public health, transportation, and food. The growing numbers of Indigenous migrants to the cities has occurred within the context of the 1991 Constitution's promise of a multicultural and pluriethnic country. As a nation-state, Colombia promised to become an almost utopian, inclusive "inside," with its large cities being pluralistic spaces. Bogotá, the country's capital, now validates the cabildos or autochthonous governmental systems of the Inga, Muisca, Ambiká-Pijao, and Kichwa, and processes are underway to similarly recognize those of the Misak-Guambiano, the Yanacona/Yanakuna, and the Nasa.

---

[10] Although limited, databases with reliable national statistics have been created by the Observatorio de Derechos Humanos de la Vicepresidencia de la República, the Agencia Colombiana para la Reintegración, the Centro de Investigación y Educación Popular (CINEP), and the Fundación para la Paz (FIP).

An article from Bogotá's daily *El Espectador* states that "in 2013, the Ministry of the Interior received 83 applications for the 'constitution of urban cabildos' in 20 of the country's states" [en 2013, el Ministerio del Interior analizó 83 solicitudes para la "constitución de cabildos urbanos" en 20 departamentos del país] (Valenzuela). Conversations with urban- and rural/community-based Indigenous leaders demonstrate the tensions generated by processes of urban organizing with respect to the traditional norms of governance from rural Indigenous territories. In effect, numerous leaders in cabildos that were formed during the colonial period distrust the increase in urban Indigenous governments, perceiving them as a challenge to or even showing contempt for the authorities and organizations in a community's ancestral territory. The realities of these urban organizations are far more nuanced, however. The cabildos of the Muisca, for example, are the expression of an identity in a process of self-re-invention after centuries of colonial erasure.[11] By comparison, urban cabildos have also been an important development for the Kichwa, who settled in Colombia and throughout the rest of the world as a result of their commercial activities, and whose ancestral territory is located in Ecuador's Imbabura province. According to Angélica Mateus Mora, "with the promulgation of the 1991 Constitution, Indigenous peoples have reoriented their mobilization within the framework of reordering their territory. They have reduced their attempts to directly recuperate lands. Acts of violence against Indigenous peoples have diminished during the first few years of the 1990s but, since 1997, the Indigenous population has more directly suffered the effects of the war among Colombia's armed groups" [con la promulgación de la nueva Constitución de 1991, los indígenas reorientan su movilización en el marco del proyecto de reordenamiento territorial. Reducen sus acciones de recuperación directa de tierras. Los actos de violencia contra los indios disminuyen durante los primeros años de la década 1990, pero, a partir de 1997, la población indígena

---

[11] Pre-Hispanic Muisca culture is archeologically located in the Cundinamarca-Boyacá plateau, in the Colombian Eastern Andes, between the eight century and the first three decades of the sixteenth century CE, when its disarticulation at the hands of European colonizers began. Beginning with the end of the twentieth century, many movements comprised of people and communities who see themselves as the descendants of the Muisca sought to revindicate Muisca culture. These neo-Muisca movements have become more and more prevalent, and have been organized in both Bogotá's interior (Soacha, Suba) and its outskirts (Cota, Sesquilé), as well as in Tunja and other towns of this high plateau region.

padece más directamente los efectos de la guerra entre los diversos actores armados] (143).[12]

As a kind of refuge from the war, the city within has also been seen as an opportunity to achieve a desired intercultural education, and in the past few years a number of universities, high schools, and even preschools have offered special programs, scholarships, and subsidies to promote intercultural learning.

The first Nasa Catholic priest from the Cauca, Álvaro Ulcué Chocué, fought for Indigenous peoples' rights and education until his assassination in 1984. Today, higher education scholarships and grants bear his name. Álvaro Ulcué scholarships are controlled by the Instituto Colombiano de Crédito Educativo y Estudios en el Exterior (Icetex) as support and incentive for young Indigenous grantees who want to attend public or private universities, many of whom have previous experience studying in rural or community high schools, and would like to continue studying. However, the online platforms through which one applies for these scholarships, which in reality function as loans, are inaccessible in the country's most isolated regions. Further, scholarships are allotted according to regional statistics that continue to follow the literacy measures of the Instituto Colombiano para el Fomento de la Educación Superior (ICFES), whose standardized state exam for bachelor's level students is one of the criteria to access the Álvaro Ulcué Chocué fund and Colombia's universities.

The politics of the virtual-electronic state tend to reward success within a homogenizing system of schooling, which stems from the national educational model of literacy; even within regions where ethnoeducation is the pedagogical norm, in many cases general educational content, which is radically decontextualized, is simply translated into Indigenous languages.[13] However, the relationship that

---

[12] Some of the data here have changed, but not drastically, as a result of the 2016 peace agreement with the FARC.

[13] Following the National Law for Education: "when speaking of the education of ethnic groups, we are referring to that which is offered to groups or communities within the national whole who possess a culture, a language, traditions, and autochthonous jurisdiction of their own" [se entiende por educación para grupos étnicos la que se ofrece a grupos o comunidades que integran la nacionalidad y que poseen una cultura, una lengua, unas tradiciones y unos fueros propios y autóctonos] (R. Moya, 140). Ruth Moya adds that "ethnoeducation is centered on three sustaining principles: autonomy, communal and intercultural participation, the last of which is understood as a socializing horizon that contributes to the recognition of rights to difference and diversity. Ethnoeducation implies that education is centered on a

ethnoeducation has with life projects implies, at least ideally, the slow contextualization of this education's contents in accordance with the cultures and territories in which it operates, most commonly with a mixed labor force of native and foreign teachers. A homogenizing vision of literacy is rewarded insofar as the national scholarship system tends to set aside those candidates who score low marks in the ICFES exam due to their low levels of literacy and Spanish language acquisition and does not consider the fact that they come from areas where Spanish is still a foreign language and numerous Indigenous languages do not have a phonetic writing system. As a result, greater opportunities are given to Indigenous students from systems where Spanish is the dominant language, or where Indigenous languages disappeared centuries ago as a result of colonial pressures from the dominant language.

In Bogotá, the report titled "District's public policy participatory formulation for the recognition, warrant, protection, and restoration of the rights of indigenous peoples" [Formulación participativa de política pública distrital para el reconocimiento, garantía, protección, y restablecimiento de derechos de los pueblos indígenas] synthesizes its diagnosis of the causes of "voluntary" migration and forced displacement to the city, by stating:

> Displacement due to violence in the 1940s and 1950s and more recently due to the country's armed conflict. ... Migrations which are due to megaprojects (dams, indiscriminate cutting of forests, mono-crop agriculture, the exploitation of hydrocarbons, mining, etc.) in ancestral territory. ... The search for better working conditions in the city of Bogotá stemming from a lack of opportunities in [Indigenous] lands, leading [Indigenous Peoples] to participate in employment activities like domestic service, security guards, informal sales, growing flowers, among others. ... The displacement caused by natural phenomena, avalanches, floods that affect the

---

project of communal life: from there that the specific project is the *Project of Life or Communal Ethnoeducational Project*, a plan "negotiated" with regional authorities from the educational sector and which holds the conservation and development of a given culture as its primary objective" [La etnoeducación se sustenta en tres principios esenciales: autonomía, participación comunitaria e interculturalidad, y esta última se visualiza como un horizonte socializador que contribuye a reconocer el derecho a las diferencias y a la diversidad. La etnoeducación implica que la educación se centra en un proyecto de vida comunitario; de ahí que el producto específico sea el *Proyecto de Vida o Proyecto Etnoeducativo Comunitario*, plan "negociado" con las autoridades regionales del sector educativo y que tiene como objetivo primordial la conservación y desarrollo de la cultura respectiva] (139).

survival of Indigenous communities in their territories. ... The expansion of haciendas which began causing migration to Colombia since the early 1940s. ... The migration of Indigenous youth who sought to continue their university studies since the 1980s upon the signing of 1986's Agreement 22, and its later amendments.

[El desplazamiento por la violencia de los años 40 a 50 y más recientemente el conflicto armado que se vive en el país. ... Las migraciones producto de los megaproyectos (represas, tala indiscriminada de bosques, monocultivos, explotación de hidrocarburos, explotación minera, etc. en los territorios ancestrales. ... La búsqueda de mejores condiciones de trabajo en la ciudad de Bogotá debido a la carencia de oportunidades en sus territorios, llevándolos a desarrollar actividades como empleadas del servicio doméstico, vigilantes, venta informal, cultivos de flores, entre otros. ... El desplazamiento por causa de los fenómenos naturales, avalanchas, terremotos, inundaciones que afectan la pervivencia de los pueblos indígenas en sus territorios. ... La expansión del régimen hacendatario que motivó desde los primeros años de la década de los 40 del siglo pasado la migración a Colombia. ... La migración de los jóvenes indígenas hacia las ciudades desde la década de los años 80, con el fin de adelantar estudios universitarios luego de la firma del Acuerdo 22 de 1986 y sus modificaciones posteriores] ("Formulacion participativa" 6).

As outlined in the report, the forced or (semi)voluntary displacement generated by the war, the latent prestige of the modern metropolis, the internal disarticulation of many communities, the search for work, cosmopolitanism, and the need to align oneself with pan-Indigenous political and cultural movements, are some of the dynamic factors that help us understand why a large number of Indigenous oraliterary and literary works have been written and published in Colombia's cities during the last twenty years. Estercilia Simanca and Vicenta Siosi (Wayuu) have written from Riohacha and published in Barranquilla;[14] Hugo Jamioy (Camëntsá) from Bogotá and Manizales; Fredy Chikangana/Wiñay Mallki (Yanakuna Mitmak) from Jamundí and Bogotá; Anastasia Candre (Okaina-Uitoto) from Leticia; Yenny Muruy Andoque (Andoke-Uitoto) and Francelina Muchavisoy (Inga) from Bogotá; Manibinigdiginya/Abadio Green

---

[14] Two of their Wayuu literary predecessors, the Wayuu writers Antonio López and Miguel Ángel Jusayú, published in the Venezuelan city of Maracaibo.

(Gunadule) from Medellín; and Vito Apüshana/Miguelángel López (Wayuu) from Riohacha, although he has also been published in Bogotá, Quito, and La Habana.

A careful reading of texts by contemporary Indigenous authors helps us understand their tendency to conceive of pages, books, and cities, as creative spaces of struggle, memory, reinvention, and rearticulation. As we will explore later on, many texts that operate like ideosymbolic mirrors favoring physical and/or spiritual return, do not necessarily imply the negation of urban experience. In Chikangana, for example, "experiences of contact with the urban, [aid him in finding] a way of expressing himself, a way of recording, via writing, his world, which is a voyage of return to his own memory" [experiencias de contacto con lo urbano ha encontrado una forma de expresarse, una manera de plasmar a través de la escritura lo que es su mundo, lo que es el viaje de regreso a su propia memoria] (qtd. in Lepe Lira 79).

Indigenous authors tend to interpellate dominant society, ironize ways of seeing the world that are imposed upon them, and advocate for their own experimental forms of Spanish hybridized with their own languages, while writing or being translated into them. The city is not simply lettered (Rama), but literate, or paraliterate when it is opened up to visual systems of representation that many writers recognize as their own forms of writing. At Expoartesanías, a yearly international fair in Bogotá that convenes creators from throughout the country, so-called "Indigenous artisans," a name bestowed them with a good bit of controversy, resolutely affirm the value of their own writing in diverse media such as weaving, basketry, beaded necklaces, and wood carvings.[15]

The term "artesanía" still connotes a certain amount of prejudice given that for many people it designates a lesser regional or exotic art, characterized as popular and in this fashion linked to folklore, folk's art, the term that was used until the 1980s for what is known today as oralitures and Indigenous literatures. A concrete example of this transition is the Camëntsá writer Alberto Juajibioy Chindoy, who collaborated with the Summer Institute of Linguistics (SIL) on several linguistic projects, such as the *Bosquejo etnolingüístico del grupo Kamsá de Sibundoy* [Ethnolinguistic outline of the Kamsá of

---

[15] A clear example of this is mamá Pastora Juajibioy, an exceptional weaver and the oralitor Hugo Jamioy's mother. Her testimony regarding the scriptural character of the beadwork and chumbe textiles appears in Chapter 3.

Sibundoy] which was published in collaboration with Álvaro Wheeler in 1974. Despite being a US-based missionary group, through an agreement signed with the administration of Alberto Lleras Camargo in 1962, the SIL effectively controlled education in a number of Colombian Indigenous communities during the last four decades of the twentieth century, and the term "folklore" was officialized via the SIL's compilations of verbal texts recorded by missionary linguists. Even after distancing himself from his role as ethnolinguistic collaborator, for a time Juajibioy continued using the term "folklore" to refer to Camëntsá texts he would later call traditional narratives and ceremonial language.[16]

As seen in our explorations of oraliture in Chapters 2 and 3, today self-described Indigenous authors defy the folklorized and institutionalized stereotyping of their identities and forms of expression through multimedia projects that unfold across collaborative intercultural networks. The fact that they self-identify as writers, in some cases of literature and in others of oraliture, is justified by their common project of overcoming the prejudice that stigmatizes their languages, ways of life, and verbal arts as things that are given, static, limited to and about their reservations, and which supposedly can only be understood in the public sphere as kinds of collective, anonymous voices found in the verbal genres they were permitted to use in the 1990s: folklore, myth, and legend.

As methods of interpellating national and international institutions, the case of numerous manifestos and communiqués written by community leaders and spokespeople is somewhat different, and many of these have been compiled in the important anthology by Enrique Sánchez Gutiérrez and Hernán Molina Echeverri, *Documentos para la historia del movimiento indígena colombiano contemporáneo* [Documents for a history of Colombia's contemporary Indigenous movement] (2010). However, a number of texts by Indigenous writers in the cities, where the urban experience facilitates the evocation or reconsideration of collective territories, tend to reverse primitivist-folkloric expectations of non-Indigenous peoples by incorporating Indigenous communities' demands, critiques, and sociopolitical interpretations. We should also note that while the diffusion of literary works and the proposals of Indigenous authors have gained vis-

---

[16] See, for example, his posthumous work, *Lenguaje ceremonial y narraciones tradicionales de la cultura kamëntsá* [Ceremonial language and traditional narratives of the Kamëntsá culture].

ibility through the proliferation of the Internet and increased access to it in cities and the countryside since the early 2000s, video and documentary film have become the most effective tools for the public expression of Indigenous communities' demands. Further, "the advent of video technology and its boom since the 1980s coincides with the development of the new Indigenous movement in Colombia and Latin America" [la aparición de la técnica del video y su auge desde la década de 1980 coincide con el desarrollo del nuevo movimiento indígena en Colombia y América Latina] (Mateus Mora 213).

According to the Colombian researcher Angélica Mateus Mora, when community leaders created the Consejo Regional Indígena del Cauca (CRIC) in 1971, Indigenous leaders were already thinking about how to broaden their use of mass media. As such, they created the newspaper *Unidad Indígena* [Indigenous Unity], which came under the editorial control of the Organización Nacional Indígena de Colombia (ONIC) in 1982. The CRIC began producing radio programming in the 1980s, at a moment when they also began collaborating with non-Indigenous audiovisual producers like Jorge Silva and Marta Rodríguez, co-creators of the documentary *Nuestra voz de tierra, memoria y futuro* [Our voice of earth, memory, and future] (1982). CRIC's communication program began to use video in the 1990s. The Asociación de Cabildos Indígenas del Norte del Cauca (ACIN), the communications arm of one of the Nasa cabildos associated with the CRIC, has produced some of the most recognized and best disseminated Indigenous documentaries of the past decade, such as *País de los pueblos sin dueños* [Country of towns without owners] (2008), which won the Ministry of Culture's national documentary prize in 2011. We should also mention audiovisual projects by the Organización Gonawindúa-Tayrona's Centro de Comunicación Zhigoneshi, which was founded in 1987 with representatives from the Iku, Kogui, Wiwa, and Kankuamo peoples from the Sierra Nevada de Santa Marta. In 2008 Zhigoneshi made a series of short documentaries entitled *Palabras mayores* [Elder words] for Telecaribe, a regional television chain. Nine of its ten installments were created by Indigenous filmmakers such as Amado Villafaña (Iku), Saúl Gil (Wiwa), Silvestre Gil (Kogui), while the tenth was done by Pablo Mora, an anthropologist and filmmaker who collaborated on the project. The collective produced the full-length film *Resistencia en la línea negra* [Resistance on the black line] in 2011. Amado Villafaña, the director, has received death threats because the film denounces the Colombia Civil War from the perspective of the Chibcha Peoples in the Sierra Nevada. The Iku documentary filmmaker won first prize in the first Colombian Film Festival in Paris and has since gained a certain amount of international acclaim (Mateus Mora 119–28). For Mateus Mora these processes imply a "collective appropriation of the image" [apropiación colectiva de la imagen] (127), a new age, "given that from now on traditions and knowledge will not be transmitted exclusively via the spoken word" [dado que en adelante las tradiciones y saberes no se transmiten únicamente por medio de la palabra] (126), as well as, "certain preconditions for creators from outside of the community" [ciertas condiciones para los realizadores externos a la comunidad] (127), and, in the words of the Zhigoneshi collective, they are a fully formed declaration of Indigenous Peoples' permanence as peoples, of their ability to communicate, and an affirmation of self-representation, "the vision of our land and our culture" [la visión de nuestro territorio y nuestra cultura] (128).

Beyond the Lettered City

"Manifiesta no saber firmar. Nacido: 31 de diciembre" [Declares Not to Know How To Sign. Born on December 31] is a story whose documentary and judicial ramifications mean that its function is similar to that of the manifestos and denunciatory letters composed by Indigenous organizations (see fig. 64). Written by Estercilia Simanca Pushaina during the first years of the new millennium, both this story and the Priscila Padilla-directed documentary based upon it, *Nacidos el 31 de diciembre* [Born on December 31], denounce the violence associated with (il)literacy, and falsified ID cards as a means of controlling the Wayuu people. In the story and its preface, the alphabetic writing on ID cards, votes, advertisements, names, and certificates arrives at the ranchería (community) through the efforts of interventionist government officials from the nearest urban center (Riohacha) or elsewhere in the interior.[17]

Using intimate, conversational language, Estercilia Simanca Pushaina denounces the state's beaurocratic graphocentrism. The story does not naively pine for orality and is cognizant of the need for writing, with the young girl in the story's prologue even aware

---

[17] Although the author does not give us any actual data, corruption and vote buying were already matters of public debate in the Guajira when the story was originally published in 2004. They continue to be.

of the need to teach her grandfather how to sign in "block letters."
As for the power of the written word, although Simanca began writing poetry, she soon opted for the more direct, critical language that
characterizes her narrative production, focusing on short stories that
can be easily disseminated and thus have a greater social impact.

"Manifiesta" begins its critique of government bureaucracy
when the narrator expresses a paradoxical attitude towards the poster portraying a political candidate and future governor. Feeling both
seduced and rejected, she says:

> that Mr. Candidate, the same one who called me "little princess"
> while he was kissing me close to my mouth and promised to marry
> me when I was older, is the same one who refused to help us when
> Toushi got sick, the same one who said, "Those Indians are such a
> pain" as he was driving away.
> I remember that kiss robbed me of my dreams for a number of
> moons. That moment kept repeating itself in my mind, again and
> again, while I was trying to sleep in my hammock. I wanted Mr.
> Candidate to come back, to kiss me again, but he never did. He
> didn't even look at me when we went to his mansion.
>
> [ese señor Candidato, el mismo que me dijo «princesita» mientras
> me daba un beso cerca de la boca y que prometió casarse conmigo
> cuando yo creciera, fue el mismo que se negó a ayudarnos cuando
> Toushi enfermó y el mismo que dijo cuando nos alejábamos de él:
> «¡Esos indios sí joden!».
> Recuerdo que ese beso me robó el sueño por muchas lunas. Ese
> momento se repetía en mi mente una y otra vez mientras trataba
> de dormir en mi chinchorro. Quería que el señor Candidato re-
> gresara y me besara nuevamente, pero no lo hizo. Ni siquiera me
> miró cuando fuimos a su casa grande.] (Simanca, *Manifiesta* 7)

Along these same lines, Simanca's text reveals the day-to-day reality of Wayuu communities in the Guajira, where state functionaries take advantage of illiterate members of the Wayuu, giving them
credentials with denigrating names, and saying that they were been
born on the liminal date (neither here nor there) of December 31, a
birthdate to which the Wayuu "legally" attest through a fingerprint
and a signature that "validates" their imposed name (see fig. 64).

As denounced with great irony and narrative acuteness by Simanca, the kind of credentialing that arrives in Wayuu communities

Figure 64. The cover of Simanca's "Declares Not to Know How to Sign."
Author's personal archive.

from urban centers does not achieve the promises of inclusion found in Colombia's 1991 constitution, a document which was coincidentally signed in the capital, Bogotá. Rather, these documents come from corrupt regional politicians' eagerness to obtain Indigenous votes through promises that they will never fulfill.

"Manifiesta"'s use of literary language, fictional characters, and the genre of the short story, formally distinguish it from the denunciatory letters (c. 1584) sent to the king of Spain by the Muisca author and cacique Don Diego de Torres y Moyachoque.[18] That said, a comparative reading of these documents suggests that the overall colonial situation they describe has not really changed, as both Diego de Torres and Estercilia Simanca denounce many of the same colonial abuses (intimidation, abduction, exploitation). Writing in 1584, the cacique states,

> every woman married to an encomendero keeps a number of other women in her house who have been removed from their towns in the encomienda. These women must spin thread, weave, work, and do other jobs that they did in their own houses. Most of them are the daughters of Indian leaders, and this is something that deeply offends these parents seeing their daughters, nieces, and family members, who are caught in such an ungrateful state of

---

[18] See examples in the book by Sánchez Gutiérrez and Molina Echeverri.

perpetual servitude, living their entire lives under lock-and-key, seeing neither the sun nor the moon, which makes their lives extremely poor and miserable.

[y es que cada mujer de encomendero de indios tiene en sus casas muchas mujeres que sacan de los pueblos que tienen en su encomienda para que les hilen hilo, tejan y labren y hagan otros servicios y granjerías que han usado tener dentro de sus casas y estas mujeres las más son hijas de indios principales, que es una cosa que los padres naturales sienten mucho, ver a sus hijas, sobrinas y deudas en un cautiverio tan perpetuo y servicio tan ingrato, que toda la vida viven debajo de llave, que no ven sol ni luna, haciéndoles padecer extrema y miserable vida.] (qtd. in Sánchez Gutiérrez and Molina Echeverri, 393)

For her part, Simanca turns the colonial custom of bringing people to urban centers and assimilating them into a mirrored vision—that is, into her own and ironic perspective on *arijuna* or non-Wayuu colonizing practices. Texts by Simanca and her fellow Wayuu writer, Vicenta Siosi, shed light on the lives of Guajiro "godchildren," little Wayuu children who are adopted as domestic servants under the guise of educating them for their own good and according to their parents' "own" will. Revealing that she was one of those children, the story's protagonist, Coleima Pushaina, articulates a mirrored vision on these relationships:

And their women, their women come looking for children to make their godchildren. Or so they say, they then have the Christian obligation to care for them and educate them. Educate them? What are they calling education when they make our children servants in their concrete houses; when they tell them that you eat with a spoon and not with your hands; when they tell them that you shouldn't walk around with bare feet like an Indian, as if that wasn't what we are; when they tell them that it's "yucca" not "ay," not "wattachón" but "tomorrow," not "arika" but "afternoon," not "aipá" but "night," that your name isn't Tarra Pushaina but Sara Ramírez. And Ramírez? Why? Because you are my goddaughter. And my lineage? Little girl, they only talk about that in the outback. And they call us *chinito* or *chinita*, which is why I didn't want to keep living with my godmother in Puerto López.[19]

---

[19] The colloquial, and racist, terms "chino, china, chinito, chinita" are used in Colombia to refer to a child in derogatory terms or as a way to mark social difference. The person named "chino" is deemed as having a lower status. *Translator's note.*

[Y sus mujeres, sus mujeres vienen buscando niños para conver-
tirlos en sus ahijados y así, según ellas, tener el deber cristiano de
cuidarlos y educarlos. ¿Educarlos? A qué le llaman ellas educación
si lo que hacen con nuestros niños es tenerles de sirvientes en sus
casas de cemento; decirles que la comida no se come con la mano,
sino con la cuchara; que uno no debe andar por ahí con los pies
descalzos como los indios, como si no lo fuéramos; que no es ay
que es yuca, que no es wattachón que es mañana, que no es arika
que es tarde, que no es aipá que es noche, que tú no te llamas
Tarra Pushaina que te llamas Sara Ramírez. ¿Ramírez? ¿Por qué?
Porque eres mi ahijada. ¿Y mi casta? ¡Ay, no niña eso solo se usa
en el monte! Y se refieren a nosotros como la chinita o el chinito,
fue por eso que no quise seguir viviendo con mi madrina en su
casa de Puerto López.] (Simanca, *Manifiesta* 5)

Here the incorporation of Indigenous People into the alphabetizing city, in this case the city of the arijuna (non-Wayuu), is carried out
through the forced hispanicization of Wayuu names, identities, and
languages. The countryside, the desert, by extension nature itself,
and in a certain sense any Indigenous traditional territory, become
places of ignorance and barbarity. Within this context, during the
first few decades of the twentieth century the Nasa leader Quintín
Lame defied these paradigms when he asserted that the jungle is the
privileged space of traditional education and thought. His mirrored
vision implies that one can understand literacy and the urban center
through the concept of jungle civilization, a topic studied by Mónica
Arango (2009).

The young characters found in works by the Wayuu writer Vicenta Siosi provide an even more detailed portrait of the collision
between urban schooling and community life. In the story "Esa horrible costumbre de alejarme de ti" [This awful habit of leaving you],
a young Wayuu girl's mother takes her to her godmother's home in
the city and forces her to grow up among the arijuna. Although she
escapes and returns to her community, her own mother returns her
to the "godmother"'s house. She becomes a young woman without
ever having gone through the Wayuu rite of passage known as "enclosure," and ends up completely rejecting rural life when she returns to the ranchería years later:[20]

---

[20] "Enclosure" is the time of isolation a young Wayuu woman undergoes when
she menstruates for the first time. During this time, she can only have contact with
certain people, like her aunt or mother, and she has a number of dietary restrictions.

With the exception of the stone-faced desert, everything has changed. The first night I could not sleep because of the mosquitos and I fell out of my hammock. I miss electric lights and TV. I get too bored and don't like to bathe in the river, I see that the water is too dirty. I only lasted for a week.

I go back for a few days every time I have a vacation, spending less time there every time I go. I hide when I see someone I know in the market so I don't have to say, "hello." I can't even explain why I dislike my own race.

[Todos han cambiado, excepto el paisaje inquebrantable del desierto. La primera noche no pude dormir por los zancudos y me caí del chinchorro. Añoro la luz eléctrica y los programas de televisión. Me aburro demasiado y no me gusta bañarme en el río, veo el agua demasiado sucia. Solo duré una semana.

En cada asueto voy unos días y cada vez demoro menos. Cuando me encuentro con algún familiar en el mercado me escondo para no saludarlo. Ni yo misma me explico este desafecto a mi raza.] (Siosi Pino, "Esa horrible" 60)

Here Siosi describes the psychological transformation of someone who winds up becoming stuck between worlds. Her Wayuu head is symbolically replaced by an arijuna one, in her own words becoming, "An unnatural, wretched Indian!" [¡India desnaturalizá y desgraciá] (61).

Like Jusayú, the young boy in the previously mentioned "Neither cow nor horse...," Siosi's character becomes an adult who does not belong anywhere (see fig. 65). In effect, these characters are migratory entities who resemble the feared and monstrous literary personifications of the mestizo in Wayuu novels such as *Los dolores de una raza* [The Sufferings of a Race] by Antonio Joaquín López Epieyú, and *Hermano mestizo* [Mestizo Brother] by Ramiro Larreal.

Writing in *Los dolores*, López Epieyú calls upon civil and religious authorities to redeem the Guajiro mestizo: "Conquer for your venerable brow the glorious halo of redemption, the redemption of a race that succumbs to the heavy pressures of pain, ignorance, and misery! Direct your compassionate gaze to the heart of the plains beating with violence towards the generous hand that would lift it to a better way of life!" [¡Conquistad para vuestra esclarecida frente

---

It is also common that during this period the young woman learns to weave and receives other bits of wisdom associated with her becoming a woman.

Figure 65: Photo of the cover of Siosi's story. Author's personal archive.

la aureola gloriosa de la redención de una raza que sucumbe bajo el peso abrumador del dolor, la ignorancia y la miseria! ¡Dirigid una compasiva mirada al corazón de la pampa que late con violencia en requerimiento de la mano generosa que la levante a un nivel más alto de superación!] (140). In the novel the topic of Wayuu children being taken to the city for an education reveals how the custom arose from abductions carried out in the name of evangelization and was also something done as a last resort in times of hunger and drought:

> The poorest families sell their skeletal children to the traffickers one-by-one, until they are gone, not because they stopped loving them, but in the hopes that they will avoid a painful death. Others migrate to the neighboring Country, leaving behind their empty homes, while the rest of the hungry mothers, unable to give their newborn children nectar from their impoverished breasts, start cutting up cacti, eating it grilled in the hopes of prolonging the martyrdom of their life. With their rags lifted above their knees, weak and dry, others look more like ghosts from another world than human beings, appearing at the doors of the Orphanage of Nazareth to beg some act of charity. They don't want bread or clothes, but for their rachitic children to be let in before they have to go up for public auction. The Reverend Missionaries tell them that there is no money to take care of their children, that the paltry

sum given to them by the Government barely covers the expenses of the children who are already there.

[Las familias más pobres, uno por uno van vendiendo al traficante los esqueléticos hijos, hasta agotarlos, no por que deje de amarlos, sino por evitarles una angustiosa muerte, en tanto que otras emigran para el País vecino dejando desiertos los hogares, mientras las demás madres hambrientas, impotentes ya para prodigar al tierno hijo el néctar vital del pezón empobrecido, también se dedican a cortar cardón y comérselos asado en el afán de prolongar unos días más el martirio de su vida; otras con los harapos reguindados arriba de la rodilla, lánguidas resecas, que más parecían espectros de otros mundos que seres humanos, se arriman a las puertas del orfanato de Nazaret a implorar un rasgo de conmiseración; no quieren pan, ni ropa, sino únicamente que se les admitan los raquíticos niños en el Internado antes que ponerlos en subasta pública. Los Reverendos Misioneros le dicen que no hay dineros con que mantenerlos, que la mísera suma destinada por el Gobierno para el instituto apenas alcanza para los niños que ya están internados.] (López Epieyú 81–82)

This passage helps us understand the relationship between evangelization, processes of communal disarticulation, and forced displacement to cities in Colombia and Venezuela, which is sometimes also caused by drought. In Colombia and throughout the rest of the continent, numerous religious communities have been agents of colonization through their educational projects, promoting the teaching of Spanish, evangelizing, and nationalizing members of Indigenous communities. To better grasp the history of evangelizing educational missions among the Wayuu in Colombia, one should first recognize that the government placed Indigenous nations under the tutelage of Catholic missionaries in 1890's Law 89. In other words, the Colombian government gave the Church the mission of civilizing and nationalizing those communities. As the Basque-French linguist Jon Landaburu states, "Indigenist politics were [subsequently] in the hands of the Catholic Church until the first half of the twentieth century" [Hasta la primera mitad del siglo XX toda política indigenista estaba en manos de la Iglesia] (qtd. in Gröll, 56). Hence the missionaries in the novel receive money from the government to run the Nazareth Orphanage.[21]

---

[21] The Capuchine religious order has been one of the religious orders charged with carrying this out in regions such as the Guajira and in the Sierra Nevada de Santa Marta, from which the Iku expelled them in 1982.

In another of Vicenta Siosi's stories, "El dulce corazón de los piel cobriza" [The Sweet Heart of the Copper Skin People], similarly addresses education but in a different historical moment. In the text, a group of urban arijuna children ventures into the rural countryside with one of their Wayuu classmates. In a series of events that verge on the real maravilloso, and following popular images of the Wayuu as savage abductors, at first it is believed that the children have been kidnapped and then rescued. The students' own version of their voluntary trip, "is not taken into account." On the contrary, prevailing prejudice against the Wayuu is further rooted through generalized loathing: "Without cause, several students beat a young Indigenous classmate, breaking two of his ribs and one tooth. The police found them *in flagrante* but did not detain them, alleging that there was no one to press charges" [Algunos estudiantes, sin motivo, maltrataron a un joven indígena, le rompieron dos costillas y un diente. La policía encontró *in fraganti* a los escolares y no los detuvieron, alegando que no había quién los demandara] (Siosi Pino, *El dulce corazón* 46).

Through this mirrored vision the Wayuu author of Italian descent literarily re-dramatizes the arijuna children's supposed abduction. As we have seen previously in passages by López Epieyú, Jusayú and Simanca, what actually occurred in the story is the exact opposite of what people believed to have happened.

Berichá is yet another writer who has both used and problematized literacy, evangelization, and urban migration, taking advantage of the so-called civilized world where she has a number of friends. The following passage represents one of her most powerful testimonial mirrored visions on urban evangelical literacy from *Tengo los pies en la cabeza* [I Have the Feet on My Head]:[22]

> Like a parrot that has no idea what it's saying, I went to school and I "learned" everything; I recited the sentences and most of the readings and lessons along with the teacher. When I was in religion class and they made us say that, "our first parents were Adam and Eve," I thought they were referring to corn because in U'wa, Eba means "corn."

> [Entré a la escuela y allí «aprendí» todas las cosas, como los loros que no saben qué dicen; repetía con la maestra las oraciones y la

---

[22] This passage is based on the Spanish-language translation from U'wa that the author obtained from Berichá for the anthology *Pütchi biyá uai*, vol. 1.

mayor parte de la lectura y las lecciones. Cuando en la clase de religión nos hacían repetir que «nuestros primeros padres fueron Adán y Eva», yo pensaba que se estaban refiriendo al maíz porque en la lengua U'wa, Eba significa maíz.

Iskuer íkar raúr rio áhkan esar sinháro ké'rasai sinir etar teũhákuakir semár, semartra ba sinharo maestraata bi'tá uákta ra ahatát im eia kesót teubeihakro. Kab ihti sir chi't imárat uakit réhkam kes sumá bí't ákan Adan y Eva uakiat as tan siũtra eb kokik ei okór teuk si'ũro, sumá úw akútra maizan ébro.] (qtd. in Rocha Vivas, *Pütchi* 1: 85)

In this mirrored vision Eva, the originary mother-womb turns into Eba, corn, a primordial source of life in the communitarian context of U'wa life in Boyacá and Arauca. Also note that Berichá puts "learned" in quotation marks, questioning the processes of colonial education.

The imposition of these colonizing names, languages, prejudices, and identities that are promoted by the civilized assumptions of alphabetizing, Spanish-speaking urban spaces are captured, and at the least symbolically inverted, through the use of ironic mirrored visions. These inversions arise from the need to create images that demonstrate how colonial processes of de-Indigenization have only been partially successful. Through the creation and diffusion of oraliterary and literary texts, among other media, Indigenous writers use the names, languages, scripts, and technologies that circumstances have imposed upon them to represent themselves and their feelings-visions, as well as those of the communities in whose stories, rhythms, and existence they see and feel themselves.

THE RETURN

GENERAL THOUGHTS

As outlined earlier, temporary and/or permanent migration to the city are frequent instances of forced displacement caused by the armed conflict, the search for "better" economic or educational conditions, and even the result of a desire to be more involved with Pan-Indigenous organizing in cities like Bogotá, Valledupar, and Medellín. Compared to delegates from urban Indigenous organizations, however, Indigenous writers tend not to be their communities' formal representatives. Although their roles as mediators frequently place them in contact with cultural institutions and government ministries, their works seek to reach a general public far beyond the nation's bureaucratic apparatus. Despite the fact that their circulation and sale of literary texts continues to be fairly limited, there are nonetheless cases in which their literary texts have made a broad impact on public opinion and on the mass media. As we will see in Chapter 6, Vicenta Siosi's 2012 letter to Colombia's president Juan Manuel Santos regarding a project to re-direct the flow of the Ranchería River,[23] and Estercilia Simanca's "Manifiesta"[24] are among the notable Indigenous texts that have achieved a national impact in their demands of state reparations.

Potential readers' first encounters with texts by self-identified Indigenous authors frequently take place in spaces such as poetry festivals, university gatherings, book fairs, presentations in educational institutions, YouTube videos, and national and international conferences. In this sense, we can argue that these authors' literary works and political-cultural activism promote dynamics of a textual *continuum* through hybrid communicative strategies rooted in their communities' orality, a key aspect of works by those who consider themselves oralitors (Jamioy) or even singers who also write (Candre and Chikangana).

Audiences are invited to read texts that are primarily disseminated via the internet, such as the works found in the Ministry of Culture's *Biblioteca básica de los pueblos indígenas* [Basic Library of Indigenous Peoples] (2010), and those of other initiatives like the Ministry of Education's call to participate in "Territorios narrados" [Narrated Territories], and the collaborative project "Libro al viento" [Book in the wind], sponsored by the Fundación Gilberto Alzate, the Secretary of Culture, and Bogotá's mayor's office. These publications are characterized by broad, digital, free distribution, as well as for reaching numerous schools in both Indigenous and non-Indigenous territories, thus serving as pedagogical materials in support of Indigenous education. Further, Indigenous organizations such as the ONIC, and governmental institutions like the Ministry of Education, the National Library, and the Ministry of Culture, have worked to ensure that their books are available in the Indigenous communities

---

[23] The letter was published on Estercilia Simanca's blog and elsewhere, such as in the *El Espectador* newspaper.

[24] See also the documentary film based upon the short story, *Nacimos el 31 de diciembre* [Born on December 31], directed by Priscila Padilla.

from which they originate. For its part, Bogotá's Luis Ángel Arango Library has included Mincultura's collection of Indigenous writing and literature in its open-access, virtual library.[25]

REARTICULATION AND RETURN IN YɨCHE AND ORALITORS

Although they originate from Aotearoa/New Zealand and North America/Turtle Island, the global project of recentering Indigenous identities analyzed by Linda Tuhiwai Smith (1999), and the return to the reservation and symbolic center articulated by Teuton (2015), are connected to the experiences of a number of Colombian Indigenous authors insofar as all of these describe projects of rearticulation. On the one hand, authors of oraliture and literature create images that facilitate others' understanding of their experiences. On the other, pertaining to, desiring to be in, or identifying with multiple possible centers, Indigenous or "originary" spaces, even within cities, characterizes a number of their mirrored visions about the physical and/or spiritual return to their collective territories. However, how can we say that certain images and narratives about this return to the community and about communal rearticulation are mirrored visions?

One potential response sees the return to the community and community rearticulation as not necessarily being definitive or permanent. Indeed, there are more complex dynamics in play here, in which return and rearticulation are not simply physical and conclusive acts, but the fluid processes of a constant coming and going. In some circumstances rearticulation can happen outside of one's territory of origin, and leaving does not always imply forced disarticulation. We should recall that, as seen in Chapter 2, Chikangana/Wiñay Mallki says that oraliture writing comes out of urban experiences, such as the evocation and creative continuation of communal knowledge. In many cases, migrants create a new consciousness of belonging that has little to do with leaving their so-called ancestral territory.

In *Indigenous Cosmopolitans, Transnational and Transcultural Indigeneity in the Twenty-First Century*, Maximilian Forte brings together a series of texts that are key to how we understand diverse

----

[25] See the complete list of the *Biblioteca básica de los pueblos indígenas de Colombia*'s free books on its Internet database.

contemporary Indigenous experiences. Central to his book is the concept of cosmopolitanism through which, "people create and use transnational networks" (5), a concept which clearly applies to how we understand the translation processes through which Indigenous oralitures and literatures are created in the Americas. To distribute their work, and intervene as activists, Indigenous authors move in transnational networks that have expanded considerably via the Internet, and international recitals or festivals like the International Poetry Festival in Medellín. In this sense, Forte argues "that indigenous cosmopolitans can be both rooted and routed ... provincial without being isolated, internationalized without being de-localized" (6). As Linda Scarangella states, "it is commonly presumed that indigenous people are the Others linked to locality that cosmopolitans engage with, not cosmopolitans themselves" (qtd. in Forte, 12).

These ideas about a cosmopolitanism that can exist without becoming unrooted better explain why spaces that are supposedly outside of communities are not always or even necessarily spaces of cultural loss, de-localization, or an acceleration of processes associated with disarticulation. In this sense we can examine why works of contemporary Indigenous literatures and oralitures tend to recount, complicate, deconstruct, and reimagine communal and/or originary spaces and compare them to similar spaces that transcend cultural frontiers, despite the fact that many of such works are written from "outside" or indeed "inside" the conventional schools found in many communities.

We find this retooling in several poems that Chikangana wrote in Nebraska, others by Allison Hedge Coke in the US, and in Miguelángel López's poetic voyages in *Encuentros en los senderos de Abya Yala* [Meeting along the Roads of Abya Yala]. If the hearth is a symbol of oraliture in Chihuailaf's *Wallmapu* in Chile, and in the Andean southwest in Jamioy and Chikangana, oraliture can also be read and told in any space where one can "plant the word," which is what oralitors in Colombia aspire to do.

The physical and/or symbolic return to one's territory also comes out of a desire, nostalgia, and need to rearticulate oneself. In many cases, this represents a single step towards participation in more complex social dynamics. For example, although Berichá was educated by missionaries and lived for a time outside of U'wa territory, she recognizes her nostalgia for her ancestral territory and, from the depths of her personal experience, her desire to recuperate and to articulate her people's memory, particularly that of the U'wa in the

Aguablanca region. Upon destroying the first version of her book, she says that she "began to write again, not just my story but the story of a group that was about to see its cultural traditions extinguished; that authentic and beautiful culture was about to be displaced by a pseudoculture; this all made me very nostalgic, but I gained nothing by it" [comencé nuevamente a escribir, no solamente mi historia sino la historia de un grupo que estaba a punto de ver extinguida su cultura tradicional; aquella cultura auténtica y hermosa estaba a punto de desaparecer para cambiarla por una seudocultura; todo esto me daba nostalgia pero yo no ganaba nada con esto] (44–45).

Berichá's case is an example of how complex these processes of rearticulation and return can be. On the one hand, she evokes the "beautiful vision" [hermosa visión] of an authentic culture from which she has been separated for a number of years. She is partially able to return to that culture via her teaching in the community. In *Tengo los pies* she reiterates the importance of the ideal physical return to one's community, saying, "My book is not only about the Aguablanca region. I was born there. After I had lived with missionaries in the 'civilized' world for 25 years I had the opportunity to return to my people, to enjoy that beautiful vision that I had abandoned for so many years" [Mi libro no solamente trata de la región de Aguablanca. Allí nací. Luego de haber convivido durante veinticinco años con los misioneros y con el mundo "civilizado" tuve la oportunidad de regresar nuevamente a mi gente, a disfrutar de esa hermosa visión que por tantos años yo había abandonado] (46).

On the other hand, although *Tengo los pies* was written at the request of one of Berichá's uncles (a *uejea* or U'wa religious authority), and partially tells the story of her mother, the book's publication and the subsequent polemic stemming from the fact that it was published with help from oil companies sent her into an exile that was much more intense than the one she had endured previously. Written outside of her ancestral homeland and in acknowledgment of the fact that Berichá would never be reunited with her people in her ancestral homeland, her final, unpublished book, *Mi vida en el exilio* [My life in exile], came out of these experiences. That said, her experience contrasts sharply with that of the female protagonist in Siosi's "Esa horrible costumbre de alejarme de ti." After her mother forces her to live among the arijuna as a young girl, when she grows up and returns to the ranchería she no longer sees herself among her people. She cannot even take a drink from the well, and finally returns to live in the city, feeling that she belongs to neither world.

However, one of the similarities between Berichá's autobiographical text and Siosi's fictional one is that both begin with the figure of the mother. Berichá says that her mother is a wise woman who educated her in U'wa culture from the time she was a young child. By comparison, perhaps bowing to either economic necessity or to social pressure, the mother of Siosi's character ardently hopes that her daughter gets an education and goes to live among the arijuna. In effect, the mother forces her daughter to live in a foreign world and thus participates in her de-Wayuuanization. This situation has long been a reality for several generations of Wayuu mothers who, feeling that Wayuu men are machistas who drink too much, tell their daughters that they need to find arijuna husbands who will treat them better. In addition, a central factor in the loss of their native language for many young Wayuu has been the fact that their parents did not want to teach Wayuunaiki to their children, feeling that their children would be discriminated against for speaking it, and that they would have "better" opportunities if they spoke Spanish.

As we saw in Chapter 2, Fredy Chikangana/Wiñay Mallki used literature for similar processes of rearticulation and return in the 1980s. His particular case even defies linguistic stereotypes as he grew up speaking Spanish and learned Quechua as an adult, later teaching it to his family and community. Following Teuton's terminology ("The Cycle"), Chikangana's time studying in Jamundí and at the National University in Bogotá took place "outside" of what we could call "symbolic city," and it is during this period that Chikangana began to craft his evocative poetic style. A chronological reading of his work reveals the different routes one can use to enact return, moving from the alienation and fragmentation expressed through his earlier poems in Spanish in the 1980s and 1990s, to his personal and collective reconfiguration through oraliture in the new millennium, both of which were conceived of as part of a process of learning to use Quechua as a poetic language. His new Quechua name, Wiñay Mallki, complements his Colombian and Caucan name: Fredy Romeiro Campo Chikangana.

Wiñay Mallki expresses the author's broader identity, which he refers to in Quechua as "*sonccoycaimi* / my heart is Quechua" (*Samay* 97). As stated previously, he translates this name as "root that endures over time." As such, Chikangana's renaming himself suggests that the rearticulation of the oralitor's identity that takes place in a transcendent dimension that integrates concepts of time (*wiñay* or permanence in time) and space (*mallki* or root, tree). In addition, the confluence of space-time in Quechua is expressed through the word *pacha*, which is usually translated as land or time, and even as universe, along with its warm name: mama. 'Pachakay' [The Earth] is the title of one of Mallki's poems on the theme of return, the root (*mallki*), rearticulation, and permanence in time (*wiñay*):

The earth	[*Pachakay*
is the origin of happiness and suffering;	*callarinasha cusicuymanta huaccayripi*
turned to black stone,	*causaypiy llaphllahuachai puka*
the red placenta dwells in her	*tukuna rumipi yana*
in her the rituals of subterranean beings	*paypicay yupaychayniok cayiniyokmanta*
tie down our blood	*uku pacha*
with the vines of time.	*huatanima nukanchi yawar*
	waskakunawan huaymapacha.
On this earth you'll find	
the toucan's plumage	*Pachachaipi*
that guards the colors of life,	*phurupay tukanta*
the free and restless water,	*ima huacaychina llimpikuna causaymanta*
the aroma and flavor of all of the plants	*yakucapay munainiyok ttukiri*
that take us to heaven, to hell,	*k'apakpay yachikpayri tucuimanta*
you'll find us, you and me,	*quihuakuna*
with the strength of our dreams.	*ima pusapayayman ananpachaman*
	ukupachaman
Sucked clean in the mouth of time,	*nukansha*
these bones will go	*callpawan mosccoykunamanta.*
into the black or yellow earth;	
then we will return to the placenta,	*Chaiman pacha quilluyana*
that source, the water that touches all bod-	*rinacay tullu*
ies;	*jaika shimikuna pachamanta chhonccasca*
we'll go singing into those plants' green	*tarinakuna*
threads,	*nuka tikramuna caimán llapllahua*
to feed all peoples' dreams.	*millma caimán, yakuman ima llancana*
	aichakuna
We'll be the tiger's tooth again,	*nukarina takiman kcaytacunapura huailla*
the night's poem, "tambor de yegua,"	*quihuachaymanta*
the sound of a flute late at night	*micjunapak mosccutucuy runakunamanta.*
deep in the high mountains.	
	nuka tukana kirushata uturunkumanta
	taqui tutakunamanta tinya uyhuamanta
	kenataquimanta tuttaypachajahuaman
	ukupachapita urkujatunmanta.]
	(*Samay* 21–22)[26]

This poem is one of the *takis* (poems or hymns) that character-ize Chikangana's spiritual poetics. The oralitor suggests that the full rearticulation with one's territory and ancestral memory only occurs

---

[26] Here we have placed the Quechua in italics to facilitate a bilingual Quechua-English reading of the poem.

at "death," that is, upon returning as an ancestor-root (*mallki*), with the promise of revitalization and permanence expressed through the word *wiñay*, which can also be translated as "eternity." "Death" is seen as a return to the earth's womb (*ucku pacha*), and a re-encounter with mother time (*pacha*) that sucks on bones (*tullu*) or licks them with her tongue (*shimi*). This earthly return implies a reintegration into the red placenta (*llaphllahuachai puka*), completing a life cycle and setting other cycles into motion: singing among the plants' green threads, feeding the dreams of humanity, being a nocturnal poem, mountain music, a protecting spirit. This final image is suggested through the tiger's tooth, which some taitas or shamans use as protection. Many people in the Andes believe that the dead can protect and advise the living, and among the Quechua there is a ritual in which one leaves coca leaves and other offerings for the spirits who guard the mountains.

The poem expresses the memory of a collective "we" via the image of our blood (*nukanchi yawar*). In this *taki* images and sensations of death are liberating: musical sounds, the toucan's plumage, the water touching bodies, the plants' green threads, the dreams, or the night.

The reencounter with the red placenta that has become a dark rock resonates with the Quechua narrative motif of litomorphosis, when things that are memorable are turned to stone, and through which the mythological ancestors are remembered as in the case of Ayar Uchu in the stories of the Ayar brothers, the mythic founders of Cuzco. As we will see further on in relation to Yiche, this reencounter with the placenta is a key symbol of return. Following Teuton,

> An Indigenous nation's Symbolic Center is both a literal place and psychic space. Literally, it is the place—the landscape or range of landscapes—which a people use to define its place of origin. In psychic terms, it is the space from which a people originate and continue to self-define through culturally specific patterns of thought. The Center is where myth is tied to place; where the patterns of cultural meaning form; where tradition as an unending link between past and present lives. ("The Cycle" 48).

The mouth of time (*pacha*) that sucks on the bones and turns them into *mallki* (ancestor and roots) is an image related to Andean agricultural cosmovision. As celebrated through the andean *hayllis* (elegiac pre-Hispanic agricultural songs that are revindicated in the oralitor's poetics) burial or returning to the earth is comparable to planting a seed.²⁷ However, in "Pachakay" the poet positions himself as a singer, an ancestor, root (*mallki*), and wiseman (*amauta*). This is expressed through images of growth and permanence (*wiñay*), such as his certainty that he will one day participate in the communal fabric and communal *taki* (song, music, poem) "in the plant's green threads" [en los hilos verdes de las hierbas] as well as in his vision of the vines (*wascas*) that ties the collective blood (*nukanchi yawar*) to the earth.

The vines, ties, or roots that communicate with the inside, *ucku pacha*, which poorly translates as "hell," where "[you'll find] the rituals of subterranean beings" [están los rituales de seres subterráneos] also connects to the community of the blood's (*nukanchi yawar*) collective "we," and the earth (*pacha*) where things are born and transfigured, since it "is the origin of happiness and suffering" [es el comienzo de la alegría y el llanto]. The text can be read across the chromatic range from the red placenta, buried beneath the *tullpa*, and the black placenta that one meets upon dying and being buried in the earth.

In Hugo Jamioy's previously cited "Jatinÿá jabajtotan" [Dig Through the Ashes] the ideas and images of return and rearticulation are expressed in a call to reconnect with one's placenta:

Son, the hearth from which you got your
        name has been abandoned
while you seek shelter from the cold in
        others' energy.

Come back,

sit in the circle where your grandfather's
        words turn.
Ask the three stones, as they silently guard
        the echoes of ancient songs.

Dig through the ashes, where you'll find
        the still warm placenta
that your mother clothed you with.

[Hijo, abandonado está el fogón de donde desprendiste tu nombre mientras con frío buscas abrigo fuera de tu propia energía.

Regresa,

siéntate en el círculo donde las palabras del abuelo giran.
Pregúntale a las tres piedras, ellas guardan silenciosas el eco de antiguos cantos.
Escarba en las cenizas, calientita encontrarás la placenta con que te arropó tu
        madre.]
(*Bínÿbe* 135)

---

²⁷ The idea of a collective return to the earth (which, as seen in the poem, is understood to be a broader dimension than the human) expresses aspects of ancient philosophies concerning the redistribution of energies in spaces where everything is connected. A good example of this is the Quechua belief of continuity between the Milky Way or *willkamayu* and certain rivers here on earth, like the Vilcanota in the sacred valley near Cusco, Perú.

As with Chikangana's text, here the three stones guard one's origins and sustain one's memory, "the echoes of ancient songs." The oralitor returns to position himself in the space where ritual, wise, intergenerational words are spoken. He receives a specific call to return to the circular, protective space of his grandfather, mother, placenta, circle, family, and community. We can assert that the return is produced by the force of a centripetal web that spins around the fire, or interior circle, with words, stories, and family members all turning and unfolding as they orbit around it. In this sense, the words evoke the umbilical cord that unwinds in a spiral from the placenta. The great word advises through commands: return, sit, ask, dig. To a certain extent, it manifests the voice of one's conscience.

Based on our analysis here, we can understand the first two lines as a mirrored vision. The person being called to return receives, first and foremost, a call to pay attention: "Son, the hearth from which you got your name has been abandoned." This abandonment comes "while you seek shelter from the cold in others' energy." This moment presents us with the previously explored idea of a communal or ancestral territory that is understood as an inside that symbolically contrasts with an "outside." The elder's word calls on the poet to recognize his loss, that he is on a misguided search, that he is out of his element, that he has spent all of his own energy, as symbolized by the words and in the echoes of the ancient songs of the hearthstones. As opposed to the warm placenta and the hearth ("from which you got your name"), the outside is cold. In the poem returning implies reconnecting with one's name, maternal language, the originary words that protect one, like the placenta and the hearth fire. The poem's critical position here does not idealize this dynamic, but simply portrays it.

The poetic call to return, to dig, to search, and to sit in the warm interior symbolized by the mother, the placenta, the community, the elders, and the word itself, is broadly developed in *Versos de sal* [Verses of Salt]. This book's bilingual texts were written collectively through the poetic ritual dialogues in a mambeadero, between the taita Óscar Román, Murui/Uitoto from the Enókay clan, and those around him:[28] the anthropologist Juan Álvaro Echeverri, Simón

---

[28] The *mambeadero* is a place where the Murui Muina (Uitoto) and other Amazonian communities share their words accompanied by the ritual use of coca and *ambil* (a thick mixture of tobacco and mountain salt). The mambeadero is usually found in the maloca or community house.

Román and Yenny Muruy Andoque/Yɨche.[29] Yɨche was only given "authorship" when they decided to submit the manuscript for a regional poetry prize in 1998.

Although *Versos* is a collective work and Yɨche is one of its authors, many of its verses reflect an intimate, personal voice, while its story is connected to a literary project about symbolic processes of loss, purification, and re-encountering one's origins. As we shall see, this process is suggested by the ten bilingual poems in Minika and Spanish. According to Yɨche, the rest of the work remains unpublished, she affirms that individual authorship is secondary in this kind of spoken poetry, saying, "My voice isn't just my own. It belongs to my people, the word which is constantly reborn, and I represent it. Although I'm young, a woman, and a mother, an ancient voice resounds in me. It is a word that does not die, verses of salt, poems that you speak" [Mi voz no es solo mía. De mi gente, la palabra que viene renaciendo, yo soy la portavoz. Aunque joven, mujer, madre, en mí resuena una voz que viene desde antiguo, palabra que no muere, versos de sal, poemas que se dicen] (23).

The first salient mirrored vision is one that explores the poetic voice's disorientation and dislocalization, and it is worth noting that Yenny Muruy/Yɨche lived part of her life in the city, where she had to work hard to survive. Describing loss and contamination, the poetic voice says,

Just with words, just with stories	[De puras palabras, de puras historias
I'm contaminated.	estoy contaminada
What did I do?	¿Qué fue lo que yo hice?
Where did I go astray?	¿En qué sitio me desvié?
What happened to me?	¿Qué me pasó?]
	(29)

---

[29] Also known as Yenny Muruy Andoque, Yɨche is Andoke-Uitoto. She was born in Puerto Santander, Amazonas, in 1970. She is a member of the Aduche Indigenous reserve on the Guacamayas river, a tributary of the Caquetá. Her parents are Abraham Muruy, from the Aménanɨ clan in the Uitoto ethnic group, and Raquel Andoque (Ninka), from the Grey Deer clan of the Andoke (pɵɵsiɵhɵ) nation. Her brother is Tonfy (Willinton Muruy Andoque), a singer and researcher of his people's cultural traditions. Yɨche knows the Minika and Nipode dialects of the Uitoto language and also speaks Andoque. She has a knowledge of traditional ceramics, basketry, and work in the chagra. She studied at the Indigenous boarding house school Fray Javier de Barcelona in Araracuara, Caquetá, and spent part of her high school years at the Inem José Eustasio Rivera, a night school in Leticia, Amazonas. The stories told during traditional gatherings in the house of her father-in-law, Óscar Román, inspired her to write. She remembers that Óscar would say, "These aren't only words, they are what you do every day" [no es solo la palabra, es lo que se hace a diario]. She now lives in Bogotá, where she is a domestic worker.

Elsewhere in *Versos*, her poetic voice invokes experiences of de-centering and of a search for one's center, which are both characteristic of mirrored visions created by oralitors and Indigenous poets. As we have seen, in "Jatinÿá jabajtotan" the wise word encourages Jamioy to return to the abandoned hearth. Chikangana recognizes this kind of alienation in one of his first poems, "En verbo ajeno," while many of his later, Quechua-language poems look to the placenta as a symbolic center (*Samay* 21–22). Yiche's "Moo Eiño" [Father, Mother] makes the desperate search for one's origins palpable:

Where are they?	[¿Dónde están?
Where are their footprints?	¿Dónde está su rastro?
I'm looking.	Estoy buscando
Where is my father?	¿Dónde está mi padre?
Although he's there	Aunque existe
I don't see him	no lo veo
he's ignoring me	me ignora
my father, my mother	mi padre, mi madre
ignoring me	me ignoran
I can't get to my father	no alcanzo hasta mi padre
I can't get to my mother.	no alcanzo hasta mi madre.
Every day	Todos los días
Father!	¡Papá!
Mother!	¡Mamá!
I'm calling	estoy llamando
I'm praying	estoy orando
When will I hear my father's voice?	¿Cuándo voy a escuchar la voz de mi papá?
When will I hear my mother's voice?	¿Cuándo voy a escuchar la voz de mi mamá?
I'm getting old	Sin escucharla
Without their voices	me estoy envejeciendo
I'll grab this snake and call it my father	Tomo esta culebra y digo que es
I'll grab this opossum and call it my mother.	mi padre
	tomo esta chucha y ya digo que es mi
	madre.]
	(Muruy Andoque 32–33)

Here disarticulation is understood as the abandonment of or alienation from the center symbolized by the parents, or more specifically by their voices. Unlike Jamioy's "Jatinÿá jabajtotan," in which the call seems to come from someone else, in "Moo Eiño" the poetic voice calls attention to itself from an undefined "outside." The desolate voice realizes that it has lost its life ("I'm getting old"), that it has become confused in the absence of these parental voices, and, in a final image of loss, replaces them with a snake and an opossum, animals that are associated with transformation (the snake sheds its skin), sexuality (in the case of the serpent), and kidnapping (the opossum "steals" domestic animals like chickens).

Similarly, in the poem "Kue jénua" [My search], the poetic voice questions why it keeps searching, asks what it is looking for, and even why it had to leave its home.

What am I searching for?	[¿Para qué busco?
My home	Para mi hogar
because I need it	porque necesito
If I had no home, if I had no children,	Si no tuviera hogar, si no tuviera hijos
I wouldn't search	yo no buscaría
but now	pero ya
I have	mis hijos
children now	ya los tengo
so no one	Para que nadie
can scold them	con un guiño del ojo
with a gesture	los reprenda
I am searching	estoy buscando
for someone else's pain	El dolor de otro
the death of a little boy	la muerte de un niño
of a little girl	de una niña
I am not searching	yo no busco
I am not searching	Yo no busco
in the faces of others	en las caras de los otros
I'm searching for the seeds of life	Yo busco la simiente de la vida
the word	la palabra
of life, that's what I'm searching for	de la vida es la que busco
Who has it?	¿Quién la tiene?
Who	¿Quién es aquel
who has	que tiene
the prayer that dispels troubles	la oración que conjura los problemas
that acts	que resuelve
that sweetens	que endulza
that gives life?	que da vida?]
	(34–37)

This poem captures the voice's living by doing odd jobs, its survival, and especially its profound questioning. The female poetic voice justifies her alienation from the center by saying that she has to feed her children. In fact, Yenny Muruy Andoque, like many other people in Colombia, migrated to the capital in search of work. Beyond this or any other biographical connection, however, the poetic voice is searching for the strong word, the word of advice, the words of conjuring, the words of life. In Murui/Uitoto cosmovision the wise grandfather is the person who has the sweet words, as well as tobacco and coca. As we will see, in *Verses* the word manifests itself through a kind of wise word that locates, purifies, transforms, and guides the desolate voice. In a fragment from another of her poems, verbal processes affirm rearticulation and return:

I sit, I'm speaking my voice is now being born, now my words dialogue with the earth with the names of this earth.	[me siento, estoy hablando ya mi voz está naciendo, mi palabra ya dialoga en este suelo con los nombres de la tierra.] (Muruy Andoque 25, 27)

The poetic voice takes solace in the center, the place of origin, the basket where wise words are kept. In *Verses* the poems themselves appear to be "seated" likewise words on little benches located on the dirt floor of a "maloca" or communal house. These are the seats from which Murui/Uitoto elders communicate strong words (*rafue*) and other genres of sage oral expression, and we should remember that these texts are poetic re-elaborations of Óscar Román's words. In addition, within the communal house the center is also associated with the hearth. Like the fire, the words of *rafue* transform. In fact, the image of the fire appears in the text "Biikɨ Iraikɨ" [Fire], transforming the poetic voice:

Like fire I burn on the floor, like a rock salt, like salt from the woods, I consume myself, to fertilize all this soil. Because many things bother me, I fix them. Everything in this soil, on this earth, in this life, I'm fixing. So now what is dirty, what is ugly, I toss into the fire. It burns there. Right away, the spines, I throw them in the fire. Right there, I take the thorny vine and throw it into the fire. They burn there, they are destroyed there. I'm fixing things. Where are the spines? Where is the brush? The road does not close, the road is open, you can see the trail. Right there, I pull out the budding	[Como candela estoy ardiendo en este suelo, como piedra de sal, como sal de monte me consumo, para fertilizar todo este suelo. Porque muchas cosas me molestan, las arreglo. Este suelo todo, esta tierra, este espacio de vida, lo estoy arreglando. Entonces ahora, lo sucio lo feo lo arrojo en la candela. Allí arde. Enseguida, a las espinas las arrojo en la candela. Allí mismo, arranco el bejuco espinoso y lo lanzo a la candela. Allá arden, allá se vienen destruyendo. Yo estoy arreglando. ¿Dónde hay espinas? ¿Dónde hay palizadas? El camino no se cierra, el camino está abierto, ya se ve el rastro. Allí mismo, la hoja espinosa que estorbaba en el camino,

spiny leaf that blocked the way,   desde el cogollo la arranco
and burn it in the fire.   y la quemo en la candela.
So now,   Entonces ahora,
that dangerous spider   a esa araña peligrosa
with its shining crown   que luce su corona
I throw it in the fire.   también la arrojo en la candela.
I burn the bullet ant in the fire.   A la hormiga conga la quemo en la candela.
I'm burning everything on this soil.   A este suelo todo lo estoy haciendo arder.
I'm fixing things,   Yo arreglo,
I've come   yo vengo
burning everything in the fire,   quemándolo todo en la candela,
all of the filth,   toda la mugre,
all of the pain,   todo el fastidio,
all of the confusion.   toda la confusión.
I'm burning the fleas,   Estoy quemando las pulgas,
I'm burning the mosquitos,   estoy quemando los zancudos,
I'm burning the ticks.   estoy quemando las garrapatas.
What don't I burn?   ¿Qué es lo que no quemo?
With this fire's heart   Con el corazón de esta candela
I'm fixing I'm burning   estoy arreglando estoy quemando
for life to be born   para que nazca la vida,
for there to be no obstacles   para que no tenga traba,
so it doesn't choke   para que no se asfixie,
so that life is good.   para que sea sabrosa.
Now, at this point   En este punto ya
I'm out of breath,   me quedo sin aliento,
I'm crushed,   estoy pulverizada,
stretched out like ash.   como ceniza estoy tendida.]
                    (Muruy Andoque, *Versos* 48–53)

The final verses thus consummate the poetic voice's symbolic in-cineration. Here, articulation is preceded by the fire's complete dis-articulation, expressed as its being "crushed." From the perspective of Murui/Uitoto culture, this passage can be interpreted as the selec-tive burning of the jungle to clear a fertile field (*chagra*) where some-one can plant. The land regenerates. The jungle will arise from the ashes. The words spoken by the poetic voice are curative visions. Its transfiguring power consumes the lost body and the voice that had lost its connection with its origins in the ritual fire. The fire in which everything is burned expresses this ritual character. The incinerating verb shines. The desolate voice is burnt and pulverized like a coca leaf, which tends to be female in many Indigenous stories (Kogui and Wiwa for example).

The poetic voice in "Biiki Iraiki" experiences a purifying ritual through its visions of loss. The fire opens the road of rearticulation and return, and it burns away everything that is negative, sickly, or sharp, in sum, the trash and anguish that the poetic voice de-scribes from the poem's outset. The poem is sacrifice, rebirth, and reconnection. Return and rearticulation are completed through the voice's resurgence from the dusty ashes. The mirrored vision consists, in part, of the idea that "Everything here, / everything here on earth, everything in existence" can be fixed. The "outside" of loss and fight for survival seem to be reconfigured, or completely burned away.

But these processes are not finished here. After this ritual death, a new collective and clear identity arises, symbolized by *monifue* [water] in the poem "Iidɨ Ni ɨaibi" [Salt of Life]. The poetic voice declares, "I am water / I am all life, / I am the liquid of life" [Yo soy agua, / soy la vida toda, / yo soy líquido de vida] (57). In the following and final poem, curiously entitled "Rayiraɨ jiyakɨ" [Beginning] the poetic voices of the "we are" effectively return to the origin, what it calls a little ball or yolk, but which could also be a little head, a cell, a drop, a zygote, the iris of one's eye—the place where, according to traditional Okaina narratives, the Lord of the Earth resides—, and the base of the maloca's central pillar, a metaphor for the collective body.

We are the humidity	[Todos somos humedad
If we were not wet	Si no fuéramos húmedos
if we were dry	si estuviéramos secos
we would not be able to live	no viviríamos
We were born	Nacimos
in the nurturing	en el agua
water	nutritiva
We are water that settles	Somos agua que se asienta
that receives	que recibe
that sustains	que sostiene
a yolk	una yema
a little ball	una bolita
rolling	que retoza
through this patio	en este patio
on this soil	en este suelo
in this womb	en este vientre
in this cradle	en esta cuna
—that rolls—	—que retoza—
it does not speak, it is voiceless	no habla, está sin voz
it has no hands	no tiene mano
I am an orphan	Soy huérfana
it says	dice
I'm barely alive	Apenas tengo vida
it says	dice
That's the base	Así es el comienzo
of the maloca's	del pilar
pillar.	de una maloca.]
	(Muruy Andoque, *Versos* 58–61)

In conclusion, the ten poems found in *Verses of Salt* symbolize the spiritual experience of rearticulation and returning to one's origin. They arise from the hollow human experience generated when we come into the world and our umbilical cord (*igai*) is cut:

for us,	[a nosotros,
we humans,	generación humana,
that cord of light,	ese cordón de luz,
cord of wisdom,	cordón de sabiduría,
they cut it	pues nos lo cortaron
and we were left empty.	y quedamos vacíos]
	(*Versos* 25)

We go through an initial stage of confusion, remembering loss, and later achieve purification and transfiguration. Our experiences culminate in the return to the iris, the point, the drop, and the center. The return to the little ball, the yolk of the egg or the originary cell, evokes the re-encounter with the red placenta that had become a black rock in Chikangana's "Pachakay." Crushed and turned to ash, the feminine presence is also connected with the ashes on the hearth, the ashes to which the masculine presence is invited to return in Jamioy's "Jatinÿá jabajtotan." In these authors' respective projects the physical and/or symbolic return to one's ancestral territory is initiated by one's following a call, or even as the result of a crisis from their having abandoned themselves, something, or someone of deep spiritual significance.[30] Rearticulation with the community is achieved by digging through the ashes, by rising from them, or by simply reintegrating oneself into the totality expressed through the connections between the mother, the fire, the water, and the land. This mirrored vision culminates visually in the circular plenitude of the central point from which everything emanates, to which everything returns, and where all contradictions are resolved.

---

[30] This does not imply ignoring an idealized return to the land, which, as seen in contemporary examples like Berichá, is frustrated and impossible.

6
MIRRORED VISIONS: FINDING AN AUTONOMOUS RHYTHM AGAINST TRAINS, MULTINATIONALS, THE STATE, AND TOURISM

TIME, RHYTHM

Every literary work has its own rhythm, it's way of breathing. Rhythm is not simply verb tenses, musicality, and pulse, but also a vision of the world, a sensation, a feeling of the pluriverse, a symbolic compendium of mind and culture that the text captures through its creative spirit. Studying the different rhythms found in contemporary Indigenous works is a great challenge, given that these works are frequently written in or translated into Spanish or other hegemonic languages, like English, French, or Portuguese. Following Emilio del Valle Escalante/Emil' Keme, we can assert that "we still lack a full understanding of these worlds that originate from their own linguistic and epistemological universes. Achieving such an understanding will be the work of the present and future generations of Indigenous and non-Indigenous critics, who upon learning to express themselves in these languages will guide us in new directions" [falta todavía conocer plenamente estos mundos desde sus propios universos lingüísticos y epistemológicos. Será esta la tarea de las actuales y venideras generaciones de críticos indígenas y no indígenas, quienes al aprender a expresarse en los idiomas originarios nos guiarán por estos nuevos rumbos] (14).

This chapter is not specifically focused on verbal rhythms and verb tenses, but on the cultural tenses and rhythms that certain literary works express as mirrored visions. Indigenous authors question, and even openly criticize, the time and rhythms of the hegemonic societies that surround them. The time and rhythms of the community, the family, and interculturality that can be found among their families in their ancestral territories are directly and indirectly compared with the accelerated forms of existence one encounters in the city or elsewhere. Migratory experiences of being in the city are not only contrasted with communal experiences, but also with idealized, nostalgic visions of life in the past, such as that expressed by Chikangana in his writing on the struggles of Quintín Lame (*Samay* 24–27), or by the narrative voice of Simanca's *El encierro de una pequeña doncella* [The Confinement of a Young Virgin] when the narrator confesses that she wishes she had gone through that female Wayuu ritual, saying, "I know that the Iiwa-Kashí confinement might seem harsh to you, but I still would have liked to have done it. Although my father is Wayuu, my mother is arijuna, that is, a non-Wayuu, and I wasn't seen as deserving of that privilege. Iiwa-Kashí is proud of being Wayuu, and going through the period of confinement makes a young woman special" [Sé que les pudo parecer riguroso el encierro de Iiwa-Kashí, pero a mí me hubiera gustado pasar por el encierro. Pese a que mi padre es wayuu, el ser hija de una alijuna—no wayuu—no me hizo merecedora de tal privilegio. El ser indígena wayuu a Iiwa-kashí la enorgullece, pero haber pasado por el encierro la hace especial] ("El encierro" 20).

Camëntsá poet Hugo Jamioy is one of the writers whose oraliture is most concerned with articulating mirrored visions about autochthonous time and rhythms, contrasting these with those imposed by Western modernity. In "Pont ora" [Punctual], he defies the temporal *status quo*, saying,

I have to walk until I'm tired
and although I'm in a hurry
I won't hurry my steps,
I have to arrive just
when I'm supposed to.
Although I've left you waiting
many times, a thousand times
although I'm late to meet people
and this place is filled with your absence
I'll just say
that I've never been on time
but I have always arrived
when I was supposed to.

[He de caminar hasta el cansancio
y aunque tengo afán
no aligeraré mis pasos,
solamente he de llegar
en el momento preciso.
Aunque te deje esperando
muchas y mil veces
aunque llegue tarde a las citas
y el lugar esté lleno con tu ausencia
solamente te digo
que nunca he cumplido
pero he llegado siempre
en el momento indicado.]
(*Bínÿbe* 93)

This text reflects on diverse intercultural experiences, and as such is directed to a non-Indigenous audience. Its temporality underlying appears to be based on personal and cultural beliefs regarding the precise moment in which things can and should happen. As in other texts by the author, this poem comes out of an oral genre of familial and communal advice. Why should one hurry if things can only happen when they are supposed to happen? This kind of mirrored vision implies defying the demanding rhythms of ordinary urban time, as the oralitor ironically supports leaving people waiting and arriving late, and strikes against the contemporary world's mechanized movement that are seen as a "lack of education." This mirrored vision affirms Jamioy's own idea of time, a time that does not necessarily lie outside of the reader's contemporary world. Instead, this is a time that defies hegemonically established time. Analyzing how the notion of the other's temporality is fundamental to the construction of the anthropological object, Johannes Fabian states that, "As I see now, the anthropologist and his interlocutors only 'know' when they meet each other in one and the same contemporality" (164).

From Colombia's southern Andes, the Pasto Cumbal writer, painter and former member of congress Efrén Tarapués has called the time that the West imposes on people "working time."[1] As with Jamioy and other Indigenous artists and intercultural figures, Tarapués has personally had to deal with the urbanized pressure of too many meetings, too many appointments, and too much bureaucracy, all of which tend to be unproductive and are frequently a waste of time. Colonial time can be seen as a kind of hegemonic time that abducts other forms of time through forced labor and the imposition of temporal frames. The voice in "Pont ora" literally demonstrates temporal sovereignty by marking its own time: "that I've never been on time / but I have always arrived / when I was supposed to." Here the consideration of one's own idea of time also affirms a particular rhythm and above all an autochthonous history. The negation of imposed histories responds to historic conditions of an imposed temporality and its objectification of supposed others, while also responding to imperialism's all-encompassing spatiality. As Fabian explains, "the expansive, aggressive, and oppressive societies which we collectively and inaccurately call the West needed Space to occupy. More profoundly and problematically, they required Time to accommodate the schemes of a one-way history: progress, development, modernity (and their negative mirror images: stagnation, underdevelopment, tradition)" (143–44).

---

[1] This and further comments by Tarapués are based on a personal conversation with him.

Hugo Jamioy Juajibioy studied in Bogotá and in Manizales, and these cities in turn appear in his reflections on urban space. In "Ats be pueblbe juabn" [My People's History] he compares the rhythms inside the community with those of the urban outside:

My people's history
has my grandfather's clean footsteps,
and walks to its own rhythm.
This other history goes in a rush
with borrowed shoes
walks writing with its feet, without its head
                                      on the side,
and they are carrying me down
in that directionless river.
Grandfather, I only want to see myself
in your eyes one more time.
To embrace your face with my eyes,
to read the lines
that time left in its passing
for my feet to write
just a period
in this story of life.

[La historia de mi pueblo
tiene los pasos limpios de mi abuelo,
va a su propio ritmo.
Esta otra historia va a la carrera,
con zapatos prestados
anda escribiendo con sus pies sin su
                                      cabeza al lado,
y en ese torrente sin rumbo
me están llevando.
Solo quisiera verme
una vez más en tus ojos, abuelo.
Abrazar con mis ojos tu rostro,
leer las líneas
que dejó a su paso el tiempo,
escribir con mis pies
solo un punto aparte
en este relato de la vida.]
(*Bínÿbe* 105)

In a global context the Maori intellectual Linda Tuhiwai Smith argues that in crafting decolonial methodologies, "[by] rewriting and rerighting our position in history ... Indigenous peoples want to tell our own stories, write our own versions, in our own ways, for our own purposes" (28). Contemporary Camëntsá history is the history of fewer than 10,000 people that nonetheless interpellates the history and rhythm of the millions of people connected to Colombian and Latin American societies. I agree with the oralitor insofar as that "other history," hegemonic history, is disarticulated ("walks writing with its feet without its head on the side"), alienated ("borrowed shoes"), under temporal pressures ("goes in a rush"), and has a rhythm that disorients and confuses ("directionless river"). As personified by the grandfather, by comparison, his own history is familiar and soothing. The grandfather has clean steps and the oralitor finds himself in his eyes, with wrinkles on his face, lines "that time left in its passing" and translate his own rhythm. This mirrored vision suggests that letting oneself be absorbed by this other history is to be upside down, to accept the decapitation of one's own history, to write with one's feet without also having one's head, that is, to walk without thinking, without being connected to community notions of space and time. Embracing the grandfather's face with one's eyes and reading time in the marks that it has left on his face, imply becoming aware and having a clear mind. These images also enact the symbolic recuperation of the visible head, one's own history, and one's own space-time. By recovering his head, the oralitor can write his period, that is, articulate his own vision and rhythm within the story of existence.

In another of Jamioy's poems, "Shecuatsëng betsasoc" [Feet in My Head], the voice of the taita or elder is portrayed as advising the listener through words that the Camëntsá refer to as *botamán biyá*, [beautiful words], saying, "My taita says / it's always good to have your feet in your head / so that your steps will never be blind" [Siempre es bueno tener los pies en la cabeza, / dice mi taita, / para que tus pasos nunca sean ciegos] (*Bínÿbe* 114–15).

In other words, for Jamioy and Berichá having your feet in your head implies seeing your path with clarity, having discernment as you move across cultures, being deeply rooted in ancestral thought, and going at a pace that is clean and one's own. In short, the image of having feet in your head is not simply a symbolic inversion, but rather the correct way to behave, a rhythm or way of walking in connection with the footsteps of the elders and one's ancestors. If we keep in mind the Andean and Quechua idea of a past before us and a future behind us, they are the ones who have gone first. As expressed in another of Jamioy's poetic proverbs, "Shecuatsëng" [Footprints], rhythms and one's own time are things that leave a mark and follow marks that others left previously.

If your footsteps do not leave a mark you are throwing your time away… Along life's wide path make sure to make your weak footsteps on water.	[*Acbe shecuatsëng ndoñ tmonjëftsinÿnanas* *Tiempo ndoñ tsabá quecatabomá* *Tëntsá bid benachiñ* *Acbe uenan anán* *Tsabá inamn bejayiñ jtëshbuajuan.*]

Si tus pasos no dejan huella
andas malgastando el tiempo…
En el camino ancho de la vida
tus pasos débiles
procura ponerlos sobre el agua.]
(*Bínÿbe* 154–55)

The first proverb makes clear the idea that wasted or lost time leaves no trace. Within Jamioy's poetics, this situation can also be connected to the notion of *jabueyenán*, or sowing the word in one's heart, which according to Jamioy, can only be done with the true word. This beautiful, ancient word is characterized by its ability to leave a mark, inviting others to follow the footprints that have been left along the road. This, in turn, applies to the field of intercultural dialogue, and the oralitor frequently uses this expression in his public talks.[2] Here ancestral territory becomes a privileged space for no other reason than it is the place where footprints have been left. As seen in our analysis of oralitors in Chapters 2 and 3, this privileging of ancestral territory arises from the fact that it is the space where the words and teachers of the elders are "harvested." However, the close relationship with water as the source of life and germinating force in agricultural societies like the Camëntsá may also suggest why the oralitor says that weak footsteps should be made "on water." Perhaps like celestial or underground water, this is the deep space, the place of origin from which all the reparative and fortifying forces on "life's wide path" originate. Another possibility is that the water cleans or washes away the weak footsteps, steps that will not leave a mark if we think in the image of water as a surface on which fixed impressions cannot be made.

As seen previously, for the U'wa writer Berichá having feet in one's head meant knowing how to move via one's thoughts. Jamioy's emphasis is different, as he presents us with with a cultural metaphor that we cannot understand completely unless we know the Camëntsá language and its particular cosmological system.[3] The image of writing with one's feet is one of the most interesting in Jamioy's poetry, given that it has a gestural relationship to both poetry and oraliture. As an action it implies leaving a trace, following other traces, being connected with the earth, connecting thoughts and actions, and, of course, retelling in order to contest colonized history. The following verses from the Wayuu poet Vito Apüshana express a similar sentiment:[4] "we grow, like trees, inside / the footprints of our ancestors" [crecemos, como árboles, en el interior / de la huella de nuestros

---

[2] See, for example, the video of his talk: "Sembrar la palabra en el corazón" [Sowing Words in the Heart], which can be found on *YouTube*.

[3] As demonstrated by John Holmes McDowell (1989), Camëntsá culture is rich in wise proverbs, many of which come from the interpretation of dreams. In turn, these interpretations reflect larger Camëntsá cosmology.

[4] Vito Apüshana/Miguelángel López Hernández is a Wayuu writer from the Guajira region. Vito Apüshana and Malohe are among his better-known pen names. He was born in 1965 in Carraípia, a town near Maicao, on the Colombian side of the peninsula. One of his grandfathers, Alcibíades López Pimienta, was in the Pushaina clan on his mother's side. His grandfather's death in a family conflict meant that Miguelángel had to move around with his family frequently from the time he was seven years old, living in Carraípia, Maicao, Riohacha, and Medellín. When Miguelángel returned to Guajira at the age of 23, he no longer spoke Wayuunaiki. He now works to recover that language through his poetry.

antepasados] (*Shiinalu'uirua* 68). However, the wise words of the *alaüla* or elder tell the young poet:

Your foot should not despair to leave a mark, because the ancestors' ancient steps are already in your new one. Don't despair about arriving, because you are already here... son of the people, son of the sweat of the rain.	[Que no desespere tu pie en hacer la huella, pues ya los viejos pasos de los ancestros están en el nuevo tuyo. No desesperes en llegar, que ya estás aquí... hijo de gente, hijo del sudor de la lluvia.] (*Shiinalu'uirua* 74)

Giving their addressee the epithets son of Juyá (the rain), and son of the Wayuu (people), Apüshana's verses reveal the communal idea of the co-presence of footsteps and intergenerational footprints. Once again, the call here is to find one's own rhythm: "Your foot should not despair to leave a mark." The poet should not seek the ancestors but instead recognize their footprints on his own. The poet thus becomes the personification and actualization of the ancestors in the present: "you are already here." According to this wise voice, one does not need to search but to reconnect, to know peacefully actualizes the presence of the ancient in the new.

Following these kinds of mirrored visions, writing with one's feet also means thinking and living with one's own head and own rhythm, and not heading the demands of the accelerated world outside, where the ancestors' footprints are replaced by concrete streets and borrowed shoes. The image of borrowed shoes in Jamioy above corresponds to the image of the borrowed verb in Chikangana:

They come and so I sing, I raise my verses in neither hate nor vengeance, without biting my lips, only looking for a corner for my sleeping song for my people's voice in these borrowed verbs.	[Vienen y entonces yo canto, levanto mis versos sin venganzas ni odios sin labios mordidos, solo buscando un rincón a mi canto dormido a la voz de mi gente desde un verbo prestado.] (qtd. in Rocha Vivas, *Antes* 296)

As a project, writing with one's feet simultaneously implies differentiating oneself from other writers, other textualities, and even from other "literatures." Jamioy, Chikangana, and Apüshana insist that, as oralitors, what separates them concretely and ideally from literary authors is that their writing is done with their feet, that is, in connection with their ancestors' footprints, articulated with their ancestral lands expressing these relationships in the present.

In Vito Apüshana's poetics the *arijuna* or non-Wayuu are opposed to calmness. They do not seem to know how to listen, and they are always restless, anxious, and fearful. As seen in the poem "Sümüshe'e alijuna" [Arijuna Fear], they also do not know how to be silent:

The arijuna will come again tomorrow
bringing us more questions about ourselves,
and they will know nothing if they don't
    listen to the silence of our dead
in each sound of our lives…
	[Mañana llegarán nuevamente los alijuna
	y traerán más preguntas acerca de nosotros,
	y nada sabrán sino escuchan el silencio de
	    nuestros muertos
	en cada sonido de nuestras vidas…]
	(*Shiinalu'uirua* 64–65)

In Apüshana's poems the *alaüla* [elder] take the word, narrate, advise, tell dreams, and establish the rhythms and time associated with being calm:

Talhua, an *alaüla* from Toolünare, has told us
that we also come from other worlds…
that we accumulate an ancient wisdom that
    created other tears,
other dreams, other footsteps…
that our smile extends to other lips
beyond this side of the sea.
As our blood there is an invisible river
that runs through all of us… where the same
    smile
and same silence travel.
Talhua, *alaüla* from Toolünare, sleep with
    your hands open.
	[Talhua, *alaüla* de Toolünare, nos ha contado
	que también provenimos de otros mundos…
	que acumulamos un saber antiguo creador
	    de otros llantos,
	de otros sueños, de otros pasos…
	que nuestra sonrisa se extiende en otros
	    labios
	más allá de esta orilla de la mar.
	Como nuestra sangre hay un río invisible
	que nos recorre a todos… donde viajan
	la misma risa y el mismo silencio.
	Talhua, alaüla de Toolünare, duerme con
	    las manos abiertas.]
	(*Shiinalu'uirua* 77)

Adriana Campos Umbarila, who has researched Apüshana's poetics and written the prologue to *Shiinalu'uirua*, says that, "the 'Blood weaving' (*isha'aluu Atulaa*), the invisible river, the transfiguration, weaving itself, and the networks of roads and paths, among others images, are metaphors [in Apüshana's poetry] that symbolize interweaving and fluctuation" [el "Tejido sangre" (isha'aluu Atulaa), el río invisible, la transfiguración, el tejido mismo, la red de caminos o de senderos, entre otras, son metáforas que simbolizan en los poemas [de Apüshana] el entrelazamiento y la fluctuación] (14). Campos Umbarila also interprets the interweaving of Apüshana's texts along three lines:

> The Remote-origin (*ii*) refers to Wayuu culture's starting point, the origin of everything from which the elements (Light, Wind, Land, Rain, Darkness, Cold…) came to form Life. This world is present in the continuous evocation of the elders on sad days, in

the closeness of death, in the tales that explain the myths, or that explain Wayuu social order. To speak of the origin of everything, of the "Ii," is to speak of Wayuu originality, of the justification for their collective being. It is the dimension of the ancestors.

The Hidden-invisible (*Pulasü*): is the dimension of what cannot be touched, the invisible, what is on the other side of everyday life, and sustains it, nurses it, regulates it. The Pülowi and their agents (ghosts) are found there, as are the voices of the dead, Dreams, Jepira…

The Natural-visible (*Aku'wa'ipa*): this is the world of daily life, the Wayuu everyday, the body's mortality… is the final product of the Remote-origin and the Hidden-invisible. It is social organization, the land, the arts, customs, language…

[Lo Remoto-origen (*ii*) se refiere al punto de partida de la cultura wayuu. El origen de todo, de donde salieron los elementos: Luz, Viento, Tierra, Lluvia, Oscuridad, Frío… a formar la Vida. Este mundo está presente en la permanente evocación de los ancianos en los días tristes, en la cercanía de la muerte, en los relatos que explican los mitos, que explican el orden social de los wayuu. Hablar del origen de todo, del «Ii», es hablar de la originalidad wayuu, de la justificación del ser colectivo. Es la dimensión de los antepasados.

Lo Oculto-invisible (*Pulasü*): es la dimensión de lo intangible, lo invisible, lo que está al otro lado de la vida cotidiana, sosteniéndola, amamantándola, regulándola. Allí están Pülowi y sus agentes (los espantos), allí están las voces de los muertos, los Sueños, Jepira…

Lo Natural-visible (*Aku'wa'ip*a): este es el mundo diario, la cotidianidad wayuu, la mortalidad del cuerpo… es el producto final de lo Remoto-origen y de lo Oculto-invisible. Es la organización social, el territorio, las artes, las costumbres, la lengua…] (14)

Each governed by its unique rhythm and time, these three dimensions flow together to create the *Aku'wa'ipa wayuu* or Wayuu cultural universe that is made up of their beliefs, land, language, and people. According to David and Linda Captain's dictionary, *akuaippa* means form, nature, manner, conduct, custom, and life (16). The *Aku'wa'ipa* dimension contains other dimensions and different rhythms that can also be expressed through *pütchi* (the word) via the narration of *lapü* (dreams), stories about encounters with *pulowi* (a female water being) or even with *arijunas*, as in Miguel Ángel Jusayú's *Ni era vaca ni era caballo* [Neither Cow nor Horse]. In the serene lines of "Miichipa'apünaa" [Ranchería-We've Arrived Home from Tending the Flock], Apüshana opens a window through which he lets us see, smell, and listen to the *Aku'wa'ipa* rhythm of Wayuu everyday life:

Someone is playing the *türompa* in the rancheria Our sisters have stopped weaving for the day Night returns Uncle Kato'u will tell us something about the animals' wisdom Our mother is already soothing us We drink smoking mazamorra.	[Hay música de *türompa* en la ranchería Nuestras hermanas han terminado el tejido del día Regresa la noche El tío Kato'u nos contará algo sobre el saber de los animales Nuestra madre ya nos alivia Tomamos mazamorra humeante.] (*Shiinalu'uirua* 32)

An instrument whose rhythmic metallic sounds accompany the shepherd on his long journeys, the *türompa* or birimbao provides the background for the uncle's voice, the mother's soothing, and the sisters' ceasing to weave. Their activity not only symbolizes the fabric of the everyday, but also the days themselves. This typical pastoral scene on a Wayuu ranchería would be incomplete without steam rising off of the mazamorra (a corn drink). Like chicha in Manibinigdiginya's "Tinaja" (*Anmal* 564), mazamorra celebrates coming together, the return, and collective identity. The steam of the mazamorra symbolizes the rhythm of Wayuu daily life in *Aku'wa'ipa*. The following poem by Anastasia Candre, a singer-painter who died young in 2014, is a similar call to celebrate the ancestors' return to the present of the living:

I wish someone would give me cahuana to drink My heart wants to be dry From the longhouse in the village downriver You hear the voice of abundance rising And it is the word of summer The old man shouts "Wife," prepare our cahuana to drink Like our ancestors did Cahuana is our life Our mother's strength and breath Like the cradle where our lives are reproduced.	[Quisiera que alguien me diera de tomar la cahuana Mi corazón ya quiere secarse De la maloca de la gente de río abajo Desde allí se escucha que viene la voz de la abundancia Que es la palabra del verano El anciano grita «mujer», prepara nuestra cahuana para tomar Así como hacían nuestros antepasados La cahuana es nuestra vida La fuerza y el aliento de nuestra madre Como la cuna donde se reproduce nuestra vida.] (qtd. in Rocha Vivas, *Pütchi* 2: 127)

In this text *cahuana* (a drink traditionally made with starch from the bitter cassava tuber [*Manihot utilissima*]) is a food for the heart, containing vitality and accompanying a ritual encounter with people from other towns downriver. The sweet cahuana in Candre, the steaming Wayuu mazamorra in Apüshana, and the fermented chicha in Manibinigdiginya, are all associated with community rhythms and sharing, intergenerational continuities, and family relationships in the context of inalienable temporalities. Sharing communal drinks simultaneously represents the contemporaneity found in the ritual word, Indigenous history, and the continuity of the wisdom that the ancestors have passed down to the elders. In short, the space-times and collective rhythms symbolized via ancient words, feet, ritual drinks, the hearth (see fig. 66), and community gatherings, are but a few of the images that contemporary Indigenous authors use in their works as a way of affirming the spatialities and temporalities of symbolic centers.

Figure 66. The Hearth of Word *Mingas*. Autor's personal archive.

TOURISM AND BORDERS

SMUGGLING IN VITO APÜSHANA'S VERSES

In "Rhumá," a poem published by Miguelángel López/Vito Apüshana in the 1990s, a contemplative walk through the land ends suddenly when it is interrupted by non-Wayuu, *arijuna* visitors:

This afternoon I was
on Rhumá hill
and I saw old Ankei from the Jusayú clan
        go by...
and I saw the family
of my friend Gouriyú, "The Traveler."
And I saw the lizard's survival
and I saw the *paraulata*'s [*Mimus gilvus*]
        hidden nests
and I saw Pulowi sidereally dressed ...
and I saw Jurachen—the *palabrero*
    [mediator, negotiator]—
walking towards new fights...
and I saw kashiwana—the serpent—hunt
a lost young goat,
the cardinal bird come out of a hollow
        cactus...
and I saw the red of the day's last sun...
and, when I was about to go, I saw a group
        of arijuna
who'd come from far away,
happy
as if they found themselves in a living
        museum.

[Esta tarde estuve
en el cerro de Rhumá
y vi pasar al anciano Ankei del clan
        Jusayú...
y vi pasar a la familia
de mi amigo «el caminante»
        Gouriyú.
Y vi la sobrevivencia del lagarto
y vi nidos ocultos de paraulata
y vi a Pulowi vestida de espacio...
y vi a Jurachen —el palabrero—
caminar hacia nuevos conflictos...
y vi a kashiwana —la culebra— cazar
a un cabrito perdido,
al ave cardenal salir de un cardón hueco...
y vi el rojo del último sol del día...
y, ya a punto de irme, vi a un grupo
        de alijuna
venidos de lejos,
felices
como si estuvieran en un museo vivo.]
(qtd. in Rocha Vivas, *El sol* 374)

    The poem's final lines offer a unique mirrored vision that upends the stereotyped gaze which tourists have of the "natives," in this case the exoticized Wayuuu, who are the "objects" of a distant gaze that turns them into a living museum. For example, on a webpage dedicated to tourism in the Guajira, "Tres días en Riohacha" [Three Days in Riohacha], an image of the colorful, flowing dresses of a Wayuu dance is equated with the striking flight of pink flamingos above a group of tourists. This stereotypical image collapses cultural and natural diversity into the same exoticized continuum while a lone tourist stares out at the sea.[5]

---

    [5] Although so-called ethnotourism has become a more widespread practice in Colombia during the past few years, we should clarify that, in general, Indigenous peoples' territories are located within or close to hotspots in Colombia's armed conflict, where groups fight for control over the cultivation of illicit substances, as well as for access to other sources of wealth, i.e. "natural" resources (gold, gas, oil, water, precious stones, etc.). This situation has meant that the self-exoticizing ethnotourism industry has not taken off in many regions, particularly when compared with places in the Peruvian Amazon like Iquitos, with its neo-shamanic businesses, or Yucatán, Mexico, where you can find the tourist complexes like Xelhá and Xcaret, the "Maya" Disneylands, whose owners are not even from the Maya communities. On the other hand, in some Colombian communities they offer ethnotourism packages such as those found in Cabo de la Vela in the Guajira, and in Leticia and its surrounding areas along the Amazon River, that are themselves not without touches of self-exoticization.

All of the beings in the poem "Rhumá" occupy a serene, vital space within the territory articulated by the poetic voice. The old man, the family, and the *palabrero* exist within the every day of the Wayuu world, which is called *aku'wa'ipa* [the visible-natural], according to Campos Umbarila (14–17). The lizard survives in desert-like conditions. The *paraulata* mockingbird hides in its nest. The serpent hunts a goat. The cardinal comes out of the cactus. The sun gets red. Pulowi, a fearful protector deity, dresses with space itself, becoming omnipresent. However, the poet's internal gaze suddenly crosses with the external gazes of the visitors. The spontaneity of daily life and its dynamism contrasts sharply with the external perspective that tends to petrify it, objectifying people in the broadest sense (the continuity between animals-people). The serene continuum of the first lines, which traces similarities between the existence of humans and animals, contrasts with the exalted objectification (living museum) of the last four lines. The poem's mirrored vision contrasts the external gaze ("come from far away") with the internal gaze ("I was," "I saw old Ankei"), as Apüshana's incorporation of this external gaze is something that, while uncomfortable, is nonetheless inevitable. His mirrored vision's intervention lies in how it captures the gazes of so-called non-Indigenous people at the very moment where they seem to exoticize the Woumain, or Wayuu territory. Following Linda Scarangella, "images of nativeness circulate globally in media and popular culture and are also constructed and performed at tourist sites internationally in response to the public's desire to gaze upon and consume Nativeness (in addition to it being an economic opportunity)" (163).

In "Woumain" [Our Land], Apüshana eschews the irony of the mirrored vision in "Rhumá" to deliver a direct, symbolic message to a visitor, who is presumably an *arijuna*:

When you come to our land	[Cuando vengas a nuestra tierra
you will rest under the shade of our respect;	descansarás bajo la sombra de nuestro respeto;
when you come to our land	cuando vengas a nuestra tierra
you will also hear our voice	escucharás nuestra voz, también,
in the sounds of the ancient open space.	en los sonidos del anciano monte.
If you arrive to our land	Si llegas a nuestra tierra
with your life exposed	con tu vida desnuda
we will be a little happier…	seremos un poco más felices…
and we will look for water	y buscaremos agua para esta sed
to quench this interminable thirst for life.	de vida, interminable.]
	(qtd. in Rocha Vivas, *El sol* 371)

Here the poet does not reject the visitors, but subtly introduces them to the idea that they need to have respect when visiting this place where the people and the land form a "continuum": the collective voice of nature and the people ("you will also hear our voice / in the sounds of the ancient open space"). The native voice does not impose its authority on this outsider, however. Rather, it informally directs itself to "you," inviting the visitor to follow the poet and to come "with your life exposed." The poem's conciliatory vision implies opening oneself up to understanding things from the depths of what unifies us all, this "interminable thirst for life," which is a common facet of the human condition. The vision of a collective search for water ("we will look for water"), an image of particular resonance to the Wayuu, given that they live in semi-desertic regions, implies the recognition of certain necessities that they share with *arijunas*. Asking the visitor to come with his "life exposed," is likely an allusion to being transparent, and to the importance of not understanding this interaction via prejudices and stereotypes about the Wayuu. In this sense, such "nakedness" and respect harmonize with the collective affirmation that: "we will be a little happier..."

In the previously cited "Sümüshe'e alijuna" [Arijuna Fear], a more recent bilingual poem written in Spanish and Wayuunaiki, Apüshana re-elaborates his mirrored visions about *arijuna* visitors. This time he indirectly addresses an undefined "them," evoking a conversation among godparents:[6]

Tomorrow the arijuna will arrive again
and bring us more questions about
          ourselves,
and they won't know anything if they don't
          listen to the silence of our dead
in every sound of our lives...
and they won't carry anything if they don't
          hang their fears inside the family's
          woven bags
and receive the dawn's shock from our
          trembling...
together with the fear of the ghosts.
	[*Anteena watta'a nachuku'wa'a na
	          alijunakanairua
	je ko'omüinjeerü natuma nasakkiijüin
	          wanain
	je nnojoleerü kasain natijaain o'u wachiki
	          müle aka nnojorüle
	naapajüin ko'utüin na waamakakanairua
	sünainwai shi'ira tü waku'wa'ipakalüirua...
	Je nnojoleerü kasain nalü'üjain müle aka
	          nnojorüle nakacherüin tü
	namüshe'ekaa sulu'u
	tü susuiakalüirua apüshii
	Je kamüinjeena, wamüshe'enainjee...
	tü ainkia aa'in maaliajatkaa süma'alee
	          sheema tü mmarülakalüirua.*

---

[6] These kinds of conversations are the basis of the novel *Los a'laulaa y compadres wayuu* [The A'laulaa and Wayuu Compadres], by the Venezuelan Wayuu author Nemesio Montiel.

Mañana llegarán nuevamente los aliijuna
y traerán más preguntas acerca de nosotros,
y nada sabrán sino escuchan el silencio de
                    nuestros muertos
en cada sonido de nuestras vidas...
y nada se llevarán sino cuelgan sus miedos
                    en el interior de las mochilas
familiares
y reciban, de nuestro temblor, el asombro
                    de la madrugada...
junto al temor de los espantos.]
(*Shiinalu'uirua* 65)

As is apparent, the poem is a bit longer when translated into Wayuunaiki. The tone of the Spanish version is a bit more "impatient" than that of other poems, given that here the visitors will bring more questions... The poem represents the tourists' exoticizing happiness as noise, mental excess, constant anxiety incapable of understanding unless it achieves a certain closeness, a certain familiarity, that not only requires setting aside one's prejudice, but also what the Wayuu call "the fears."[7] This mirrored vision suggests that the *arijuna* act the way they do out of anxiety, unease, and fear. Hanging one's fears in the family's woven bags can signify nakedness, getting rid of them when coming near, learning to listen... Being shocked by the dawn is the image of sharing in the rhythm of daily Wayuu life. This vision contains within it the shock and shudder caused by the words of dreams (*lapü*) that tend to be shared when the sun comes up or early in the day. In the poem sharing the Wayuu gaze implies being able to see ghosts, that is, the beings of the *pulasü* world (the invisible-hidden) according to Campos Umbarila (14–17). In essence, they exchange the fear of prejudice for the dread of amazement.

"Como los caminos de la mano" [Like the Roads of the Hand] is a poem that Apüshana published virtually as an audio file. After recounting bits and pieces of ancestral knowledge, the elders (*alaüla*) tell their "nephews" or their younger counterparts, "But we do not know... we do not know who will come from far away to exchange the new fruits of this life we celebrate... but with this knowledge, nephews, you will receive them" [Pero no sabemos... no sabemos quiénes vendrán de lo lejos a intercambiar los nuevos frutos de esta vida celebrada... mas con este saber, sobrinos, ustedes los recibirán] ("Como los caminos").

---

7   In Wayuunaiki *mmoluu*: "to have fear."

Receiving visitors with respect is one of the most profound aspects of Wayuu culture, as the Wayuu have been open to exchange and commerce since their first encounters with European colonizers in the sixteenth century. In Apüshana these perspectives on and ideas about receiving guests are poetically equivalent to the contemporary idea of intercultural dialogue. In some of Apüshana's mirrored visions the *arijunas* are distant, and so called upon to let go of their prejudice and respectfully visit within the framework of receiving guests. By comparison, "close *arijuna* friends" appear in many of the Wayuu writer's other texts. With them, one can establish alliances when smuggling, which has historically been one of the more original Wayuu ways of describing certain processes of resistance and intercultural exchange.

Threatened by accelerated social change in the twentieth century, illegal smuggling has been a constant of the Wayuu economy for centuries. In the sixteenth, seventeenth, eighteenth, and part of the nineteenth centuries, alliances smuggling arms and other goods with the British and the Dutch constituted a strategic defense against the Spanish (Friedemann and Arocha, 15). In the twentieth century, smuggling became one of Wayuu men's sources of labor, as they trafficked in electronics, foods, arms, gas, and every other kind of merchandise along the Colombian-Venezuelan border, which was usually closed by the authorities, or via maritime ports in the Antilles. Apüshana's first collection, *Contrabandeo sueños con aríjunas cercanos* [Smuggling Dreams with *Arijunas Nearby*] (1992) celebrates smuggling's symbolic value as Wayuu cultural resistance. In the poem "Culturas" [Cultures] which serves as a kind of early statement of the Wayuu author's poetics, the poet compares himself with the *jayeechimajachi* (a specialist in singing the *jayeechi* in Wayuunaiki).

Tarash, the jayeechimajachi from
    Wanulumana, has come
to sing to those who know him...
his language celebrates our own history,
his language sustains our way of seeing life.
By comparison, I write our voices
for those who don't know us,
for visitors seeking our respect...
I smuggle dreams with *arijuna* friends.

[Tarash, el jayechimajachi de Wanulumana,
    ha llegado
para cantar a los que lo conocen...
su lengua nos festeja nuestra propia
    historia,
su lengua sostiene nuestra manera de ver
    la vida.
Yo, en cambio, escribo nuestras voces
para aquellos que no nos conocen,
para visitantes que buscan nuestro
    respeto...
Contrabandeo sueños con alíjunas
    cercanos.]
(qtd. in Rocha Vivas, *El sol* 372)

According to Miguel Ángel Ramírez Ipuana (a Wayuu philosopher and *jayeechimajachi*), the *jayeechi* "is an oral art" [un arte de la oralidad] that "is created via the artistic and lyric function of some of the community's important people" [se realiza en la función artística y lírica de algunos importantes personajes en la comunidad] (qtd. in Rocha Vivas, *Interacciones* 110). Originally written in Spanish, the eight lines of "Culturas" are divided into two sections: the first four about the *jayeechimajachi*, and the final four, which are about the writer. The first part makes clear that this singer is also an historian ("celebrates our own history") while emphasizing that he sings in Wayuuniki ("his language"). The historian-singer has a proper name, Tarash, and is from a specific place within traditional Wayuu territory: Wanulumana. The text begins by announcing his arrival as the active and suspenseful presence of the *jayeechimajachi*. His words, his song and, in short, his language, celebrate and sustain, and are expressed via a collective "we." The singer not only expresses "our" history, but he celebrates it and actualizes it. It thus follows that his language sustains the collective's way of "seeing life," with this by its nature being an intercultural reflection. As we have seen in other texts that elaborate reflections on interculturality, such as Jamioy's 'Illiterates' and 'Dress Yourself With Your Language,' the unknown implied by the ellipses, or information that hints at but does not divulge the nature of these communal scenes, are literary strategies capable of generating an internal referent from which the non-Indigenous world can be interpellated and compared.

The second part of the text creates a mirrored vision beginning in the fifth verse, in which the "I" of the poetic voice appears, and the transition between sections begins with the I's affirmation that it writes about "our voices." With these words, the new role of the smuggler-poet is described and announced. In addition, the second half of the text clearly affirms that the poet mediates between collective voices, that he writes for people he does not know, for visitors, in short, for *arijunas*.

In fact, works by Indigenous authors are indeed mostly read by people who do not belong to an Indigenous community. However, we should note that "Culturas," which was written in the early 1990s, is a kind of poetic declaration that places Apüshana in the role of bridge or intercultural mediator. The author turns the image of alphabetic writing on its head by making a way to continue the Wayuu practice of smuggling. From this perspective, we can understand his role here as constituting a uniquely Wayuu form of resistance within the context of the textual continuum between sung oral tradition and poetic writing. The poet becomes a particular kind of smuggler who trafficks dreams, that is, images, words, and visions. In this sense, his perspective on writing, and ultimately on intercultural contact, inverts both internal and external perspectives on smuggling. Given smuggling's illegality, the writer resignifies a negative image from the Colombia-Venezuelan popular imaginary, as well as something that is controversial among many Wayuu, to provide an intercultural vision of smuggling as a tool for making oneself known ("for those who do not know us"), and making oneself respected ("for visitors who seek our respect"). However, the poetic voice seems to suggest that this smuggling can only take place with "friendly *arijuna*," that is, "those who seek our respect." In the following decades, the Wayuu poet comes to refine this idea across other poems via the act of and attitudes surrounding receiving, that he describes in the poem "Como los caminos de la mano" [Like the Roads of the Hand].

"Smuggling dreams" is a mirrored vision that has several relevant meanings. Dreams, or *lapü* for the Wayuu, are one of Wayuu spirituality's most profound elements. According to Wayuu stories, *lapü* produce encounters with the ancestors, and through them one receives guidance and omens. In addition, according to the French anthropologist Michel Perrin (*Los practicantes del sueño*), dreaming is a cultural practice among the Wayuu. As a vision and practice, then, smuggling dreams is a culturally specific way to refer to what we call Wayuu literature, and the narration of dreams of Wayuu literature and verbal art's most important genres. In this sense, smuggling dreams is a poetic, self-defined way of describing the role of the contemporary writers within Indigenous society, people for whom the dynamics of exchange are a constant of cultural survival. The writer-smuggler is someone whose visions and words are exchanged through writing and intercultural dialogue. In sum, the *jayeechima-jachi* speaks and looks inward, while the writer-smuggler speaks outward while looking inward. His goods are his own mirrored visions about a practice that is condemned for being illegal in both Colombia and Venezuela.

Apüshana's work also invites us to think of smuggling as a process that challenges the metropole's control over commerce and defies borders (Colombia, Venezuela, Aruba, Curaçao). This author creates his poetic role through this attitude towards smuggling, and his writing tends to defy the city's control while, as seen in his references to other Indigenous cultures, also managing to cross borders. First, the Wayuu poet distances himself from the city's literary canon by drawing on Wayuu verbal traditions, whether these be the oral arts of narration or the progressive presence of Wayunaiki in his work. Second, his writing cannot be considered Colombian, Venezuelan, or even exclusively Wayuu or "Indigenous." His roots in Wayuu verbal art have not prevented him from exploring other Indigenous poetic voices from throughout the continent, or from writing in diverse genres like the essay, political treatises, and journalism. In effect, having a trans-border character and a not exclusively Indigenous voice enabled Miguelángel López Hernández to situate his following book, *Encuentros en senderos de Abya Yala* [Encounters along the Paths of Abya Yala], within the symbolic and multicivilizational space of Abya Yala. The book won Cuba's Casa de las Américas Prize in 2000. In fact, its first edition as a chapbook published by the Government of Guajira in 1992, his first collection of poetry was only a point of departure whose smuggled texts continue to multiply and to be published across written and audiovisual media.

BORDERS AS POINTS OF ENCOUNTER

In the narrative poem "Quen luar" [This Geography], Hugo Jamioy crosses the social fences that are imposed on Indigenous collectivities. Fredy Chikangana similarly refers to the colonial limitations placed upon Indigenous territories in his "Hapttay pachamanta" [Handful of Earth] (*Samay* 20–21). When we remember that Jamioy's wife is Ikʉ from the Santa Marta's Sierra Nevada, we grasp how Jamioy's life itself constitutes a kind of challenge to the idea of Indigenous identities that are static and isolated, as he lives in both Colombia's North and South, and participates in multiple international forums to obtain new spaces for Indigenous communities (the US, Mexico, Chile).

The dividing lines that Jamioy critiques in "Quen luar" are not only arbitrary for Indigenous peoples, but they have also been imposed on people everywhere via the invention of national and racial borders.[8] As Jamioy states, it is *not* that Indigenous peoples do

---

[8] According to Langebaek Rueda, since the mid-nineteenth century in Colombia and only three decades after the country's independence, one already finds an ideology of mestizaje that, "did not so much refer to the mixing of blood as to the predominance [of specific traits] through the mixture of superior moral attributes"

not recognize borders or differences, but that, as seen in his poem "Quen Luar", borders should be points of encounter instead of lines that separate:

This geography is telling me	[Esta geografía me está diciendo
that the lines traced by their limits	que las líneas dibujadas por sus límites
are moving me away from my brother's house	me alejan de la casa de mi hermano
and I cannot hug him	y no puedo abrazarlo,
because he lives on the other side of the river	porque vive al otro lado de la orilla
where people wear	donde la gente se viste
the laws of a different government.	con las leyes de otro gobierno.
My taita says	El pasaporte de los antiguos,
that the ancestors' passports	cuenta mi taita,
were how they dressed	era su propia forma de vestir
their language	su propia lengua
their food:	sus propios alimentos:
that's how they recognized visitors.	así se reconocía al visitante.
Borders	Las fronteras
weren't lines that separated	no eran líneas que separan
they were gathering places.	eran puntos de encuentro.
The guardians of the ancient territories	Los guardianes de los territorios antiguos
celebrated visitors	en las entradas
in the thresholdwith a gift in their hands.	celebraban al visitante
When they were traveling,	con un regalo en sus manos.
visitors carried a passers-by gift in their woven bags.	Los visitantes,
	cuando eran pasajeros,
	llevaban en sus gigras un regalo de transeúnte.
But if their steps	
traced the dance of remaining	Pero si sus pasos
on their shoulders they carried	marcaban la danza de la estancia
the fruits of their labor turned into corn,	a sus espaldas cargaban
the symbols of life	los frutos de su trabajo hecho maíz,
drawn on a blanket	los símbolos de la vida
to warm their dreams	dibujados en una cobija
in their brothers' land.	para abrigar los sueños
The taitas	para abrigar los sueños

[no se refería tanto a la mezcla de sangres, sino al predominio mediante la mezcla de atributos morales superiores] (274). That is, "civilization would be offered by the white and the resistance to the tropical latitudes wold be in the hands of the black and the Indian" [la civilización la aportaría el blanco y la resistencia al trópico correría por cuenta del indio y del negro] (274). Since then, the idea of the creation of a mestizo nation is reinforced, one in which "the native past continued symbolizing the effort of nation building: the living Indian of the present would have to disappear, or better, be fused into the national whole, to give way to civilization" [el pasado nativo continuaba simbolizando el esfuerzo de construcción de nación: ahora el indígena vivo tendría que desaparecer, o mejor, fusionarse, a medida que se abriera paso la civilización] (275). Modern processes of Indigenous self-representation that were fortified in the 1970s questioned the popular stereotype of the supposedly degenerate Indigenous "race"—although even now calling someone an "Indian" is meant to be derogatory—while in more official discourses members of the country's Indigenous communities are referred to as, in an expression of ongoing paternalism, "our Indigenous peoples."

always knew who would visit them.	en la tierra de sus hermanos.
Long before their arrival was announced	Los taitas
they would predict who would come	ya sabían quién los visitaría.
with the Yagé dance;	Mucho antes de anunciar su llegada
so they would prepare the best food	con la danza del Yagé
the best blankets to warm their dreams	predecían quién vendría;
and harmonized their meeting	entonces preparaban los mejores alimentos
with a fraternal hug	las mejores mantas para abrigar sus sueños
and then,	y armonizaban su encuentro
fortified their gazes	con un abrazo fraterno
through the rituals of Yagé…	y luego,
	fortalecían sus miradas
	con el ritual del Yagé…]
	(*Bínÿbe* 150–53)

Jamioy poetically recreates oral stories told to him by others. Here the Camëntsá oralitor generates a new mirrored vision about the arbitrary geography of contemporary nations, the "lines traced by their limits" that separate brothers and make them subject to the laws of different governments. As we saw in our analysis of the Map from the Minga in Chapter 1, these kinds of mirrored visions tend to offer stories and images that interrogate hegemonic histories (Tuhiwai), such as a country's official national cartography or the idea that the country only has a single literary tradition that is written in Spanish, published in books, limited to a few well-known authors and precisely defined literary movements, and allocates Indigenous peoples' stories to the appendices in Anthropology books, collections of folklore, and ethnolinguistic studies.

For example, in *Historia de Colombia, el establecimiento de la dominación española* [Colombian History, the Establishment of Spanish Rule], the well-known historian Jorge Orlando Melo includes Indigenous peoples as a mere introduction to Colombia's history that, above all else, lacks any kind of relationship to the present. It is no less common for people to believe that contemporary Indigenous history better fits within the realm of Anthropology, a position that usually denies, via indifference and ignorance, Indigenous peoples' own forms of writing, their own histories, and their own struggles of self-representation. Quintín Lame's work, for example, is still being recovered from obscurity, and his *Los pensamientos del indio que se educó en las selvas de Colombia* was published in 1971, four years after his death.[9]

Breaking with these established prejudices, Juan Friede stands out among twentieth century Colombian historians. He not only

---

[9] Here I am referring to initiatives to recover Lame's full bibliography, such as the Universidad de los Andes in Bogotá's Proyecto Quintín Lame.

met Lame in the south of the Department of Tolima in 1943, he also wrote the prologue to the third edition of *Los pensamientos*, which was published in 1987 by the Organización Nacional Indígena de Colombia (ONIC). Friede also conducted historical research on contemporary Indigenous peoples that focused on land tenure and reclamation: *El indio en lucha por la tierra* [The Indian and the Fight for Land] (1944) and *Problemas sociales de los arhuacos: tierras, gobierno, misiones* [Social Problems of the Arhuacos: Land, Governance, and Missions] (1963). By comparison, Rafael Granados's *Historia general de Colombia, prehistoria, conquista, colonia, independencia, y república* [A General History of Colombia, Prehistory, Conquest, the Colony, Independence, and the Republic] (1953) takes a far different approach, with its hegemonic, even colonial voice assuming a paternalizing tone in statements such as, "Our aboriginals in the Eastern regions are numerous; even if they look well-built, they have a weak constitution and only live for a short time; their faces do not get wrinkled and their hair does not gray; they pull out their eyebrows and their eyelashes; their eyes are dark and their noses almost eagle-like" [Nuestros aborígenes de las regiones orientales son numerosos; aunque en apariencia sean fornidos, su constitución es débil y su vida corta; su faz no se arruga y sus cabellos no encanecen; se arrancan las pestañas y las cejas; sus ojos son apagados y la nariz es casi aguileña] (27). Here the "aboriginals" are possessed by a collective "we," which stands in for the State, the Church, and the country at large. Moreover, the priest-historian sees them as a "degenerate" and lacking people with customs that are capable of frightening him.

That said, many of these hegemonic historical narratives have not been directly contested by Indigenous writers. Nonetheless, the images and visions of persistence, contemporaneity, and cultural strength found in many of the Indigenous works cited here certainly respond to Colombian society in general, which recognized and formally accepted the multicultural participation of Indigenous peoples in national life in the 1991 constitution. The poetic voice in "Quen luar" begins by affirming its ability to listen to the geography, an image associated with the possibility of reading nature. This perspective upends the narrative of a national geography which is closed off and limited by the imaginary lines that delineate its borders and impede close contact among human beings.

The image of dressing oneself with the laws of another Government suggests written national constitutions, as well as the

documents that regulate peoples' particular identities. Such papers are just as arbitrary, if not more so, than international borders themselves, as they pretend to define people through numbers, photos, and official seals. Governments outline national
otherness and separate communities within the border zone, and
the mirrored vision here takes up the image of the passport, the
conventional international identification document, and inverts
it as a way of repositioning the Camëntsá's collective perspective on borders. The image of the "ancestors' passports" moves
us from the "conventional outside" to the "intracultural inside,"
constructing identity based upon the language one speaks, what
one eats, and how one wears "the symbols of life / drawn on a
blanket."

The poem presents a perspective on contact and exchange with
foreigners through the oral narration of the taitas, who are in turn
the communal voices of authority. The exchange of gifts between
the traveling visitors and those guarding the land takes place along
borders "that were gathering places." Whether or not this is an
idealized vision of the past, referencing these memories lets Jamioy
question contemporary national borders and reclaim territorial
sovereignty. Nevertheless, this right to the land is not articulated
via the typical argumentation found in the letters by Indigenous
leaders, as in Quintín Lame or Vicencio Torres.[10] Jamioy's history
articulates a way of making memory through networks of ancestral
exchange (corn, blankets, dreams), that includes a knowledge of
diverse visual graphic systems such as the symbols of life drawn on
the blanket, that is, their own way of dressing, and sharing a specific ritual, the yagé ceremony. By envisioning national borders as places of encounter, the oralitor further reveals his mirrored vision on
the border associated with the laws of contemporary governments,
given that these borders "are moving me away from my brother's
house / and I cannot hug him / because he lives on the other side
of the border." Here situating one's head would imply a more
human approach to these "lines traced by their limits" (Jamioy,
Bínÿbe 151).

---

[10] Vicencio Torres Márquez was an Ikʉ (Arhuaco) spokesperson from the Sierra
Nevada of Santa Marta, who in 1978 published a collection of his letters to the Colombian government.

The State, Multinationals, and "Development"

Taking your head to the train

"Daño emergente, lucro cesante" [Consequential Damage, Profit Loss] is a story that Estercilia Simanca published on her personal blog. Its protagonist, Rukarria Epinayú, is a woman who, like many Wayuu women, uses a donkey to carry bags of hardwood charcoal to her ranchería. This Wayuu *mujusu* (someone who is poor or from a less prestigious lineage) talks to her donkey, Mushaisa, and her testimonial voice articulates a powerless critique of the extractivist violence the multinational corporation El Cerrejón exercises via its seemingly infinite black train that carries millions of tons of coal from its mine to huge merchant ships on the coast (see fig. 67).

Figure 67. Car from El Cerrejón's train. Author's personal archive.

A character whose marginalized voice would likely not appear in any other context, Epinayú denounces the commercial train, a global symbol of colonization since the nineteenth century (whether in India or the Western US). The story's mirrored vision initially focuses on how the donkey also seems to disapprove of it:

> I remember how the poor donkey was always frightened when he heard the train coming, and when he heard the whistle he'd stop and shake his head disapprovingly. I frequently told him the train was also carrying coal, but it wasn't from wood. It was coal taken from inside of Mma—the earth—which was like opening up your own mother and taking out parts of her insides.
>
> [Recuerdo que el pobre siempre se asustaba cuando escuchaba venir el tren, cuando escuchaba el silbato se detenía y movía su cabeza en señal de desaprobación. Muchas veces yo le decía que el tren también iba cargado de carbón, pero ese carbón no era de leña, ese carbón lo sacaban de las entrañas de Mma —la tierra—, que era como abrirle las entrañas a mamá y sacarle de a pedazos las entrañas.] (Simanca, "Daño emergente")

For context, I should mention that El Cerrejón's train runs for approximately 150 kilometers, from the mine to Puerto Bolívar, where boats of over 180,000 tons capacity are docked (see fig. 67). These commercial ships have increased the ocean's temperature, and greatly impacted the region's marine flora and fauna. In addition, the train leaves coal dust in its wake, contaminating the few available sources of water, such as the *jagüeyes*, wells for gathering rainwater, or subterranean wells, from which both people and domestic animals drink. Respiratory illnesses have increased throughout the region and if that were not enough, the train cuts through the routes that shepherds traditionally use to take their flocks to pasture.

As the story makes clear, the utter disarticulation of a culture that had resisted colonization for centuries can be found in the train's profanation of Wayuu cemeteries:

> He and I never got used to the train and I think that the people on the other side of the tracks, in the town, never did either. Not the goats, the children, no one around here did. In my earliest memories it was already here, crossing the Peninsula from Uchumüin—in the South—to Wüinpumüin—in the North. They say it goes all the way to the sea and that a large boat comes and takes away the coal the train brought, and then the train goes back to look for more coal that has been scraped from inside Mma—the earth—, which holds the blood of our giving birth and the placentas of the newly born. My father says that the cemeteries of a number of families used to be there, where the train goes by, but the train didn't care, because he had to get through there, because the bones could simply be carried from one place to another and placed in a new cemetery, a prettier, whiter one than before, but the train couldn't go elsewhere, NO! The train had to go through there, and that's what happened, hmmm... and that's what happened, the train keeps going by every day, and in the morning on Mondays.

> [Él y yo nunca nos acostumbramos al tren y creo que la gente del otro lado, en el pueblo, tampoco. Ni los chivos, ni los niños ni nadie en este lugar. Desde que tengo memoria él ya estaba aquí, atravesando la Península desde Uchumüin —Sur— hasta Wüinpumüin —Norte—. Dicen que llega hasta el mar y que viene un barco grande y se lleva el carbón que el tren traía, y luego el tren se devuelve a buscar más carbón arañando las entrañas de Mma —la tierra—, la que guarda la sangre de nuestros partos y el ombligo de los recién nacidos. Mi tata dice que por donde pasa el tren,

estaban los cementerios de muchas familias, pero al tren no le importó, porque él tenía que pasar por ahí, porque los huesos simplemente se podían llevar de un lugar a otro y hacer un cementerio nuevo, más bonito y más blanco que el de antes, pero el tren no podía hacer otro camino, ¡no!, él tenía que pasar por ahí, y así se hizo, ajá... y así se hizo, el tren sigue pasando todos los días y los lunes por las mañanitas.] (Simanca, "Daño emergente")

El Cerrejón is one of the largest coal mines in the world. When this multinational project began in 1976, the Colombian government entered into an agreement with Exxon through its business Carbocol, S.A. to exploit resources in the so-called Northern area. They planned on extracting approximately 5 tons of coal every ten seconds. After more than two decades of unprecedented environmental impact, in January 1999 the Colombian government extended its agreement until 2034. However, most of the coal produced goes to support European industries. In spite of its celebrated surpluses in coal mining, the Department of Guajira has some of the highest rates of childhood malnutrition and social inequality in the whole country. Year after year government reports and national media highlight how this department is one of Colombia's most corrupt, implying that many government officials, including members of the nascent Wayuu upper class, take a large part of the "benefits" of the mine's government royalties and the multinational cooperation's surplus for themselves. While this happens, the prolonged droughts, which global warming and the constant trade winds are making longer and more frequent, are the framework for the Department's hunger, thirst, and ill health, extreme situations that kill more and more people every year in the Guajira, with the Wayuu being the group most visibly affected by these impacts of multinational extractivist industries. According to statistics published in the *El Espectador* newspaper, "between 2008 and 2013, 2969 children younger than 5 years old died in La Guajira, most of them being members of the Wayuu, Wiwa, Kogui, Arhuaco, or Kankuamo communities" [entre 2008 y 2013 han muerto 2.969 niños menores de cinco años en La Guajira, quienes en su mayoría pertenecían a comunidades indígenas como las wayuu, wiwa, kogui, arhuaco y kankuamo] ("Cerca"). Statistics from the NGO Organización Nacional Indígena de Colombia (National Indigenous Organization of Colombia), claim even more Wayuu children have died from malnutrition. In July 2014, even Bogotá's *Semana* magazine titled one of its articles, "Alert: in the Guajira there are 37,000 malnourished children" [Alarma: en la Guaji-ra hay 37.000 niños desnutridos]. Meanwhile, a number of public institutions and universities have designed interventionist programs in these situations. With astuteness, they have managed processes of so-called informed consent, standing in open opposition to the direct criticisms by Indigenous movements, which they in turn shrug off as "corrupt." Offering more statistics and less food sovereignty, these programs benefit the pockets of organizational functionaries and re-validate colonial practices like anthropometry and the study of traditional seeds at a moment when such science is dominated by corrupt multinationals like Monsanto,[11] and systematically take blood samples without weighing the possible consequences of these being coopted by the illegal international biomedical market. Refer-ring to the global corporations that map the genetic diversity of the planet's Indigenous populations, Linda Tuhiwai Smith calls the cel-ebrated Human Diversity Genetic Project (HUGO) "Project Vam-pire" (100). Further, the intervention of national health organiza-tions is similarly no guarantee of legality or oversight, as seen in cases like that of the US government, which tried to patent a person from the Hagahai people in Papua New Guinea (Tuhiwai Smith 100).

This disarticulation of Wayuu culture operates by undermining Wayuu foodways, which are devastated by large scale multinational extractivism, political corruption in which members of the commu-nity themselves are compromised, and self-enriching institutional assistance, among other things. Simanca's story portrays this devas-tating neocolonialist extractivism through the mirrored vision of the train running over the donkey (an animal symbolically connected to the Epinayuu e'iruku or clan). The Wayuu call the donkey pülüikü, a Wayuunization of the Spanish word "borrico," or ass. This accident involving an animal that fulfills symbolic and daily functions that are to a certain extent totemic and a form of collective identification, announces the inhuman, armored triumph of the train as an object associated with the Western imaginary and national progress. The mirrored vision here upends the civilizing image of the train insofar as here it becomes a dehumanizing, acculturating nightmare.

The Wayuu social worker Eliana Palacio Paz recorded oral sto-ries by Ricardo Palacio Tiller as part of her undergraduate work. In

---

[11] Monsanto is a US company that, among other things, markets its agricultural chemicals on a global scale and has virtually cornered the market for genetically modified seeds.

these stories, Palacio Tiller recalls a dream that a Wayuu man named Kaichaule Pushaina had in the 1970s. Bearing all the hallmarks of a mirrored vision, in his dream the extractivist company's train takes the form of a huge, all-devouring snake:

> in his dream, he could see an immense snake approaching from far away, something he'd never seen before. The snake was so large that by comparison he was the size of a defenseless rabbit. It was moving so fast that it destroyed everything in its path, coming so close to him so quickly that he felt it was going to run over him without even noticing. He was afraid, very afraid, so much so that he could hear his heart beating loudly, and the closer it got the more afraid he became...

> [en su sueño a lo lejos veía acercarse a una culebra inmensa, algo jamás antes visto. Era una serpiente tan grande que él ante ella era del tamaño de un indefenso conejo. Y esta culebra corría tanto que iba destruyendo todo a su paso, y se acercaba a él con tanta velocidad que él sentía que lo iba a maltratar y a pisar sin que ella pudiera notarlo. Sintió miedo mucho miedo, tanto, que podía escuchar los fuertes latidos de su corazón, entre ella más se acercaba más miedo sentía...] (Palacio Paz).

Following Palacio Paz, when the dream was first told, it could not be interpreted according to traditional Wayuu methods. However, it presaged the coming of the Cerrejón project in the 1970s. In this sense, the Wayuu oral tradition of recounting dreams also offers mirrored visions and perspectives, with the train here being an uncontrollable snake, a mechanical problem destroying the entire country.[12] As such, it encapsulates a Wayuu perspective on modern processes of neocolonial depredation. The fact that the Wayuu compares himself with a rabbit not only underscores his defenselessness, but also constitutes a strategy of resistance as the cunning rabbit, as seen in Wayuu stories about *atpanaa*, laughs at the predators, and by extension the non-Wayuu colonizers, who try to catch him.[13]

---

[12] Coincidentally, miners in El Cerrejón found in 2009 fossils from 28 specimens of the *Titanoboa cerrejonensis*, at 12 meters the largest species of prehistoric snake in the world. Dating from the Paleocene, the Titanoboa lived around 68 to 50 million years ago.

[13] See the stories about *atpanaa*, the rabbit, in *Mitos, leyendas y cuentos guajiros* (1972) by Ramón Paz Ipuana, and in *Achi'kí, relatos guajiros* (1986) by Miguel Ángel Jusayú.

The ending of Simanca's "Daño emergente, lucro cesante" becomes even more dramatic when we analyze it as also constituting a mirrored vision on illiteracy. When Rukarria Epinayú files a claim with the company for having run over her donkey, "the people from the train argued that where the accident occurred there was, there is, a huge, an enormous sign, which said, says in Wayuunaiki, the language of the Wayuu: "NNOJO PAAPÜIN PIKII SÜNAIN OUKTA SULU'U SÜPUNA TÜRENKAT " which means, "DON'T GIVE YOUR HEAD TO DEATH, BECAUSE OF THE TRAIN." But Rukarria Epinayú "Declares not to know how to sign." [los del tren argumentaron que por donde ocurrió el accidente había, hay, un letrero grande, grandote, en el que decía, dice en wayuunaiki, el idioma de los wayuu: "NNOJO PAAPÜIN PIKII SÜNAIN OUKTA SULU'U SÜPUNA TÜRENKAT". Que significa: "NO ENTREGUES TU CABEZA A LA MUERTE, POR EL TREN". Pero Rukarria Epinayú "manifiesta no saber firmar"] ("Daño emergente").

Given that Simanca Pushaina'a texts tend to be interwoven, here the narrator makes an explicit reference to the story "Manifiesta no saber firmar," which similarly develops mirrored visions on illiteracy and corruption. The protagonist of "Daño emergente, lucro cesante," Rukarria Epinayú, is also illiterate. Although she is Wayuu, she does not know how to read Wayuunaiki, whose orthography was created by Venezuelan linguists (Gröll 98), and subsequently adopted by the Wayuu in the 1970s in their efforts to organize. Despite the work of linguists such as Miguel Ángel Jusayú from the University of Zulia in Venezuela, the writing system still lacks a unified set of guidelines. Literacy in Wayuunaiki is limited to just "2% of the population, given that it was introduced via ethnoeducation in [Wayuu] schools" [un 2 % de la población, ya que su introducción se ha dado en los procesos de etnoeducación en las escuelas] (Gröll 98). In this sense, Wayuunaiki-language warnings about the train are just a joke for the multinational corporation, something that helps them comply with the parameters of grapho-centric security, while at the same time the consequences of their massive coal mining operation continue to impact the Wayuu, La Guajira's ecosystem, and the planet at large.

Simanca's story emphasizes the multinational's warning about the train, "Don't give your head to death, because of the train," which for the illiterate Wayuu becomes something quite different. Given the kind of irony operating within this mirrored vision when we invert its wording to state, "You are giving your head to death, because of the train," we find that the warning suggests a new kind of symbolic and physical decapitation. In addition, this inversion happens because Rukarria Epinayú cannot read the warning in either Wayuunaiki or Spanish, and the multinational's warnings presuppose a certain level of alphabetic literacy that simply does not exist in the zone of El Cerrejón. By making this confusion part of the story's profound irony, Simanca overturns the discourses of modernity through which the multinational corporation and the government present statistics about economic development in La Guajira and the rest of the country by showing how the people who live right next to the mine, its ports, and the train, are understood as existing in a premodern state in which they lack water and use animals like donkeys to get around. On the one hand, these images correspond to the supposed "cultural authenticity" that is found in the state's tourist brochures, while at the same time allowing outsiders to see these as "normal" characteristics of Wayuu ancestral culture.

As compared to being run over by the train (an image of "modernizing" speed) like the donkey (an image of supposedly "premodern" sloth), using one's head in other ways implies using colonization's tools (alphabetic writing, education, the law, audiovisual technology) to decolonial ends. Rukarria Epinayú tells her story despite being illiterate, and even though her illiteracy is the reason the multinational corporation appears to "wash its hands" of her, claiming their publication of the aforementioned bilingual warning signs fulfills their obligations. However, this situation is different to the story of the young protagonist in "Manifiesta no saber firmar," where knowing how to read and write in Spanish can also be an act of resistance and self-awareness. The "illiteracy" that hinders an understanding of the multinational's ironic signs seems to also be one of the factors that prevents the Wayuu—represented here by Epinayú—from being aware of dangers of the train, literally and figuratively as an all-devouring, disarticulating serpent of accelerated "development," neocolonialism, and political corruption.[14]

---

[14] "Giving your head to death, because of the train," also evokes the increasing number of Wayuu youth who literally kill themselves by letting the train run them over. The Wayuu anthropologist Johana Barros studied these suicides in her undergraduate thesis, *Matarse a sí mismo en la comunidad wayuu de la alta y media Guajira: una mirada antropológica sobre el suicidio indígena en Colombia* [Killing Oneself in the Wayuu Community of the Upper and Middle Guajira: An Anthropological Perspective in Indigenous Suicide in Colombia] (2014).

Regarding the impact of "development" led by multinationals and the state on the Wayuu, we should mention that Vicenta Siosi's approach differs from the ironic and untrusting tone found in Simanca. Siosi wrote an open letter to Colombia's president—whom she identifies as a possible "savior" (or executioner) of Wayuu communities—with the hopes of rebuffing a new attack by the Cerrejón multinational, that had plans to divert the Ranchería River. Written from the perspective of a collectivist Indigenous "we," this kind of personal missive has been a characteristic of the epistolary genre from the celebrated colonial-era letters to the king of Spain, like that written by the cacique of the Turmequé people at the close of the sixteenth century in Colombia or Guamán Poma de Ayala at the beginning of the seventeenth century in Perú, to the more recent letters that community spokespeople have written to the government directors of Indigenous affairs in Colombia in the twentieth century.[15] What is unusual here is that Siosi explicitly states that she is the spokesperson for the Pancho Ranchería, using a personal style that simultaneously positions her as an Indigenous citizen. Further, Siosi's letter is unique insofar as she also presents herself as both a writer and a spokesperson. This is how the letter came to be distributed in Colombia's foremost newspapers and TV news shows, as well as on Simanca's popular blog.

When Siosi's letter was published in the Bogotá's *El Espectador* on April 13, 2012, the columnist who ran it said that it was a communiqué from a Wayuu writer to the president, whom she was asking to stop the Cerrejón company's project to divert twenty-six miles of the Ranchería River in order to be able to mine even more coal:

> Juan Manuel Santos
> President of the Republic of Colombia
>
> Respectful greetings:
>
> I am writing to you from Pancho, a Wayuu village made of mud houses with zinc roofs, that exists on the right-hand side of the banks of the Ranchería river, the only river in the middle and high Guajira. Tens of settlements exist in Pancho because we, the Wayuu people, live throughout this dessert God gave us.

---

[15] See, for example, the previously mentioned Vicencio Torres Márquez (1978), the Iku-Arhuaco writer and spokesperson, and the letters and public reports he published in his book.

The people that inhabit this area lives from fishing. The children fish lisas [*Brycon moorei*], bagres [*Pseudopimelodus bufonis*], bocachicos [*Prochilodus reticulatus*], and shrimp as they are our sustenance.The women pick cherries, iguarayas [fruit from the *Stenocereus griseus*], mamoncillos cotoprix [fruit from the *Melicoccus bijugatus*], wild coas [fruit from the *Brosimum alicastrum*] to sell them.

The Fall, with its thunderous noise, let's us know the rain is coming, and then we prepare the fields for the beans, watermelon, pumpkins, and corn. Harvesting these is joy that can't be described.

Some Wayuu have permanent fields alongside the river. With great effort, they carry buckets filled with water to take care of the plants one by one. Others take mud and water from the river to make bricks for the construction of city housing.

Because the vegetation alongside the river is thick, a group cuts the branches of the trupillo trees [*Prosopis juliflora*] and they make charcoal out of the wood. We do not have cooking gas or electric stoves in our houses.

Some men go along the banks of the Ranchería river and hunt for blue crabs. They remove their claws to sell in the market and then they return the crabs to their caves.

We the Wayuu raise goats. The herds go to the river to drink.

The Ranchería river is the only river for the Wayuu people. The only water current that crosses this ancestral territory. To the river, we go to bathe. It is jubilant fun. There, the young fall in love and grow friendship ties. Mothers wash clothes and the little ones learn to swim.

With the soft mud from the riverbanks girls build dolls, and little cups and plates, which they dry under the sun.

In a book by Cerrejón entitled: "Summary of the expansion project for interested groups" on page 60, it is stated that global climate change (GCC) will affect us: "the climate in La Guajira could turn cooler and drier, with a reduction in pluviometry of 5 to 10%. The glaciers of the sierra Nevada Santa Marta could disappear by 2050 which would affect the availability of water springs in the region". What would life be like for the Wayuu people without the Ranchería River?

On March 28th, 2012 Cerrejón employees arrived in Pancho and informed the community that they are projecting the diversion of 26 kilometers of our river. They advised us that the river would dry up in the summer time and added that they would possibly build a reservoir on the Palomino River (Barrancas). Then, how can a dry creek provide us with water?

They announced that the 500 million tons of coal under the river would generate royalties. In 30 years of exploitation of the mineral the royalties have not helped La Guajira for anything.

Hospitals remain halted and our education occupies the last place in the country. According to research done by the Bank of the Republic, 50% of Wayuu children suffer from malnourishment. This year they informed that the Department of La Guajira has the highest level of poverty and destitution in Colombia, reaching 64%. I see that these royalties have not helped us on what is important.

Why would we trade our only river for royalties? At the end of the meeting they concluded that it would be a great piece of engineering and that everything would remain the same. To this, a young woman from the community asked:

"If all will remain the same, why do you want to compensate us? Our lives in the peninsula of La Guajira are directly related to the river, he is the grace and life here."

Please Mr. President, do not allow the foreign company Cerrejón to destroy the aquifer that sustains the Ranchería River and dry out the only source of water we possess.

If the transfer is allowed and we begin to suffer the damages there will be no turning back, the damage will be irreversible.

Please help the Wayuu people.

[Doctor Juan Manuel Santos.
Presidente de la República de Colombia.
Respetuoso saludo.
Le escribo desde Pancho, una aldea wayuu con casas de barro y techos de zinc, que se levanta en la margen derecha del río Ranchería, el único río de la Media y Alta Guajira. Decenas de rancherías circundan Pancho porque los wayuu vivimos diseminados por este desierto que Dios nos dio.

Las gentes por aquí viven de la pesca. Aún los niños capturan lizas, bagres, bocachicos y camarones que son nuestro alimento. Las mujeres recogen cerezas, iguarayas, mamoncillos cotoprix, coas silvestres para venderlas.

El otoño, con sus truenos escandalosos nos avisa de las lluvias, y se preparan las huertas para el frijol, la patilla, la auyama y el maíz. Recoger la cosecha es un gozo indescriptible.

Algunos wayuu tienen rosas permanentes junto al río. Con gran esfuerzo, cargan el agua con baldes y riegan mata por mata. Otros toman barro y agua del río para fabricar ladrillos destinados a la construcción de viviendas citadinas.

Como en la orilla del río hay espesa vegetación, un grupo corta las ramas de los árboles de trupillo y hace carbón de madera. No tenemos gas domiciliario, ni estufas eléctricas.

Algunos hombres van a la ribera del Ranchería y cazan cangrejos azules para vender sus muelas. Luego los devuelven a sus cuevas. Criamos chivos, y los rebaños van al río a tomar agua.

El Ranchería es el único río de los wayuu. La única corriente de agua que atraviesa este territorio ancestral. Al río vamos a bañarnos. Es una diversión exultante. Allí, los jóvenes se enamoran y fundan lazos de amistad. Las mamas lavan ropa y los pequeñitos aprenden a nadar.

Con el barro blando de las orillas las niñas fabrican muñecas, tacitas y platicos que secan al sol.

En un libro del Cerrejón titulado: «Resumen del proyecto de expansión para grupos de interés», en su página 60, dice que el cambio climático global (ccg) nos afectaría: «El clima en la Guajira podría tornarse más cálido y seco, con una disminución en la pluviometría de 5 a 10 %. Los glaciares de la Sierra Nevada de Santa Marta podrían desaparecer hacia el año 2050, lo que afectaría la disponibilidad de fuentes de agua en la región».

¿Cómo será la vida del wayuu sin el río Ranchería?

A Pancho llegaron el día 28 de marzo del 2012 funcionarios del Cerrejón e informaron a la comunidad que tienen proyectado desviar 26 kilómetros de nuestro río. Advirtieron que este se va a secar en verano y añadieron que posiblemente construyan un embalse en el río Palomino (Barrancas). Entonces, ¿cómo nos proveerá un arroyo seco?

Anunciaron que los 500 millones de toneladas de carbón bajo el río generarían regalías. En 30 años de explotación del mineral, las regalías del departamento le han servido para nada.

Los hospitales permanecen en paro y la educación ocupa el último lugar del país: según una investigación del Banco de la República, el 50 % de los niños wayuu padecen desnutrición. Este año informaron que la Guajira ostenta el más alto nivel de pobreza e indigencia en Colombia, con un 64 %. Veo que las regalías no han ayudado en lo fundamental.

¿Por qué cambiaríamos nuestro único río a cambio de regalías? Al final de la reunión concluyeron que sería una gran obra de ingeniería y que las cosas seguirían igual. A lo que una jovencita de la comunidad preguntó.

«Si todo permanecerá igual ¿por qué nos quieren compensar? Nuestro transcurrir en la península Guajira gira alrededor del río, él es la gracia y la vida aquí».

Señor Presidente, por favor no permita que la empresa extranjera Cerrejón destruya el acuífero que mantiene el Ranchería y seque la única fuente de agua que poseemos.
Si se licencia el traslado y empezamos a padecer los perjuicios, no podremos volver atrás, el daño es irreversible.
Por favor ayude a los wayuu.] (Siosi Pino, "La carta")

The first thing that strikes one about the letter is its openly literary tone. The poetic narrative of the first part deals with the river's kindness and precedes her argument about why this reportedly modernizing project must be stopped. In addition to her studies in Planning and Regional Development at the Universidad Jorge Tadeo Lozano, Vicenta Siosi Pino received formal training as a journalist at the Universidad de la Sabana. Beyond her work as a writer, she has also been a professor, documentary filmmaker, correspondent, and press officer with the Department of Guajira's government. Given her background, Siosi managed to publish her letter throughout the country's mass media platforms (print, Internet, TV). The letter's tone, however, contains a self-validating, collective Wayuu "we" (we are, we live, we have), which in turn roots itself in its own territory that the "divinity" has provided ("this desert that God gave us). The writer appeals to the reader's sensibilities from a "poor but dignified world," where young girls make dolls from clay and adults depend on the river for their basic survival (branches from the trupillo trees and blue crabs). In sum, one of the letter's central ideas is that life in Pancho revolves around the river, and that without it the people themselves would disappear. Here, the tranquility of communal life is interrupted by the arrival of El Cerrejón's functionaries, a situation that suggests, but does not make explicit, the deeply traumatic, subconscious image of foreign colonizers arriving in Indigenous territory. The presence of neocolonial functionaries is also found in the announcement of the "progress" a dam is supposed to bring, as well as an increase in the royalties that the state pays out to these communities. The Wayuu narrator's lyric voice then shifts to the typical statistics found in documentaries in order to continue its argument by outlining overall conditions in the region.

Along these lines, the Wayuu writer not only openly criticizes the famous multimillion-dollar royalties that El Cerrejón supposedly pays out to a region wracked by childhood malnutrition and higher than average rates of homelessness and poverty, but she also cites a document from the El Cerrejón corporation on the project's long-term environmental impacts. Speaking from Pancho, Siosi overturns the weak arguments of the multinational's functionaries, who promise to develop the region in exchange for diverting the river while also saying that nothing will actually change. At this point, she incorporates the voices of one of the young people from the community, who asks the multinational's employees, "If nothing will really change, why do you want to compensate us?" This voice evokes Rukarria Epinayú, who receives nothing from the Company when her donkey is hit by the train. As compared with Simanca's protagonist, however, Siosi's voice takes an environmentalist approach that sounds the alarm about the destruction of wrongly named natural "resources," the lack of water, and the mine's irreversible and irreparable damage. Indeed, by making the letter public, Siosi's letter addresses not only the president (as an ancient king), but also the common reader. By raising the reader's awareness of the situation, the letter in turn seeks this reader's support, a literary strategy seen previously in Elicura Chihuailaf's *Message to the Chileans.*[16]

Siosi's letter did receive a response "from the President of the Republic's Private Secretary" on April 20, 2012, announcing that the letter was "transferred to six entities or branches of the state" [se le da traslado a la carta a seis entidades u organismos del Estado] (Guerrero Barriga). Despite this answer, Siosi's letter and in particular a series of protests by Wayuu in Riohacha and Pancho managed to temporarily halt the insatiable voracity of this powerful multinational mining company that had allied itself with the state for the supposed good of the majority of Colombians. In fact, in a public communiqué dated November 8, 2012, El Cerrejón explained its reasoning concerning the project referred to as P500, and announced the temporary, though not permanent, suspension of preliminary studies on the possible diversion of the Ranchería River:

> After an internal assessment Cerrejón has decided to postpone studies on diverting the Ranchería River due to current conditions in the international carbon market. ... Cerrejón has stated that these studies concern only one of its possible avenues for expansion, beyond its current growth path. ... Cerrejón continues to be completely committed to its plan to expand production from 32 to 40 million tons of coal extracted annually in 2015. ... To reach

---

[16] Or, should it be necessary, support for national mobilization as in the case of the Minga of Resistance, led by Nasa from the Cauca in 2008.

that goal Cerrejón will invest 1.3 billion dollars and generate more than 5000 new jobs during the project's life cycle. ... As it reaches its goal of extracting more than 40 million tons of coal annually, Cerrejón will continue considering alternatives that do not involve diverting the Ranchería River.

In agreement with Cerrejón's longstanding commitment to maintaining full and timely awareness of its projects among all concerned parties in La Guajira and the country, the company had let people know that it is studying options for expansion within the zone of the concession. Specifically, one of the studies was related to the possibility of partially diverting the Ranchería River (also known as Project P500), which Cerrejón has decided to postpone owing to the current international price of coal. Over the past few years the price has tended to fall, resulting in a 35% drop in the overall price.

Studies on the partial diversion of the Ranchería River that have been undertaken to date, as well as feedback we have received from communities during this process, will be the basis for future projects when conditions permit. Until then, Cerrejón will continue studying options for growth that do not include the diversion of the Ranchería River.

[Después de una revisión interna Cerrejón decidió posponer los estudios sobre el desvío del río Ranchería debido a las condiciones actuales del mercado internacional del carbón. ... Estos estudios habían sido comunicados por Cerrejón como una de sus opciones de expansión, más allá de su actual ruta de crecimiento. ... Cerrejón sigue plenamente comprometido con su proyecto actual de crecimiento que tiene como fin elevar la producción de 32 a 40 millones de toneladas anuales para 2015. ... Para llevar a cabo este crecimiento Cerrejón realizará inversiones de US $1.300 millones y generará más de 5.000 trabajos durante todo el ciclo de vida del proyecto. ... Cerrejón continuará considerando alternativas para elevar su producción a más de 40 millones de toneladas anuales, que no involucran la desviación del río Ranchería.

En concordancia con el compromiso histórico de Cerrejón de mantener informados de manera oportuna y completa a todos los grupos de interés, a La Guajira y al país, la compañía ha comunicado que actualmente se encuentra en estudio de opciones de crecimiento dentro de los terrenos de concesión. Específicamente, uno de estos estudios era el relacionado con la opción que contemplaba la posible desviación parcial del río Ranchería (también conocido como Proyecto P500), sobre el cual Cerrejón ha decidido posponerlo debido a las condiciones del precio internacional del carbón. La tendencia de los últimos dos años ha sido a la baja, registrándose una caída en el precio del carbón del 35 %.

Los estudios realizados a la fecha con relación a la desviación parcial del río Ranchería, así como la retroalimentación y aprendizaje recibido por parte de las comunidades durante el proceso, será la base para el desarrollo de proyectos futuros cuando las condiciones lo permitan. Mientras tanto, Cerrejón seguirá estudiando opciones de crecimiento que no impliquen el desvío del río Ranchería.] ("Cerrejón pospone")

If here Cerrejón appears to be listening to "feedback" and "learning" from the dialogues it held with the Wayuu community, it is no less certain that they also provide the real reason for not moving the project forward: the fall in the price of coal. A possible future spike in the price of coal is implied by their reasoning, as are an increase in production, and the project possibly reappearing at that time. In fact, they clearly state that they need to expand within the territory they already hold, that is, in their "own country," which is regulated by tendencies in the international market and by a supposed long-term commitment to La Guajira and Colombia. They do not, however, have any kind of long-term commitment to the Wayuu, whom the company does not even directly name here.

In a partially decapitated society, many of whose visible heads/ leaders have been manipulated or bought out by interventionist agents of multinationals or the state, the death train tends to symbolize the tragedy of a "development" that runs over the living and the dead alike, especially if we consider the fact that the Cerrejón train passes near or directly on top of numerous Wayuu cemeteries. In this context, the response to an interpellation of exploitative economic projects, more than being a matter of indignation over the few earnings or material benefits that communities receive, becomes a matter of defending their particular vision of existence and sense of place.

In his studies on the representational regimes surrounding "development," Colombian Professor Arturo Escobar states that in their declarations social movements "are not only fighting for 'goods and services,' but for their very definitions of life, economics, nature, and society" [estos no solo luchan por "bienes y servicios" sino por la definición misma de la vida, la economía, la naturaleza y la sociedad] (17). In this sense, the defense of life in a broad relationship with the territory-body-head is present in both Wayuu mobilization and in these denu dnciations by Simanca and Siosi in their literary works.

DISPLACEMENT, LAND STRUGGLES, AND MINGA

The Urrá hydroelectric dam is located in the Department of Córdoba in northwest Colombia. The project dammed up the Sinú River and its tributaries, which flow out of Paramillo National Park. Despite fierce opposition from many of the communities it affected, such as the Emberá-Katío, Phase I took place from 1993 to 2009, flooding some 7412 hectares of land within the National Park and displacing, "more than 6000 people, Indigenous people and fishermen who lived along the Sinú's shore" [a más de 6000 personas entre indígenas y pescadores de la ribera del Sinú] (Ramírez Hincapié). Visibly impacted by how the project disarticulated Emberá-Katío territory and resulted in their mass migration to Colombia's urban centers, Hugo Jamioy wrote, "Urrábe ngmenan" [The Disenchantments of Urrá], a text whose poetic vision upends the notion that development and State intervention are for the benefit of dominant society. In the poem, Jamioy refers to a hydroelectric project that was forced upon the collective territories of Indigenous communities like the Zenú and Emberá-Katío with approval of the Colombian government. This textual opening allows the poet to denounce these peoples' being turned into wandering beggars and their urban "decapitation" as a result of their displacement:

[1] When the Urrá was flooded
the cities were flooded with hungry
                                    migrants.
[2] When they made light
the Emberá families became blind.
[3] When their dreams float in the dammed
                                    Urrá
bodies sleep on the city's streets.
[4] When ancestral hands are extended
the passers-by deny their roots.
[5] When Emberá children cry
in the arms of their exiled mothers
the ICBF has for them responsible parents.
[6] When they look for refuge in the city
the guardians of the nation's security
kick them off of land that isn't theirs.
[7] When the sun comes out
you see night in their eyes.

[[1] Al tiempo que se inundó Urrá
las ciudades se inundaron de transeúntes
                                    hambrientos.
[2] Al tiempo que se hizo la luz
se quedaron ciegas las familias emberá.
[3] Al tiempo que flotan los sueños en el
                                    Urrá inundado
duermen los cuerpos en las calles de una
                                    ciudad.
[4] Al tiempo que se extienden manos
                                    ancestrales
los transeúntes niegan sus raíces.
[5] Al tiempo que lloran los niños emberá
en los brazos de sus madres desterradas
el icbf les tiene padres responsables.
[6] Al tiempo que buscan refugio en la ciudad
los guardianes de la seguridad nacional
los destierran de aquella que no es su tierra.

[8] When the night falls
in this country's cities
the Emberá wrap themselves with the
mantle of their longing.

[7] Al tiempo que sale el sol
se ve la noche en sus ojos.
[8] Al tiempo que llega la noche
en las ciudades de este país
los emberá se arropan con el manto de
sus añoranzas.]
(Jamioy, *Bínÿbe* 146–47; numbering added
to facilitate the reading)

Textually, "Urrábe ngmenan" [The Disenchantments of Urrá] is comprised of 8 stanzas whose contrasting images simultaneously unfold through the use of the word "when." Each of these mirrored visions emphasizes disenchantment with modernity, as well as the dam's impact on the community.

In the first stanza ancestral territory is flooded to produce electricity, and the city is flooded with hungry, displaced immigrants. The generation of artificial energy thus also takes people away from their land, their vital energy, and they are forced to migrate to the city as a consequence. The second stanza begins with what is possibly an ironic reference to Genesis in the Western Bible, "they made light." The project creates electricity so people in the cities and towns can see, that is, light is brought to non-Indigenous and Indigenous people who live in urban centers. Meanwhile, Emberá families are "blinded," which implies their being disoriented, being in the dark. In the third stanza, the verse "dreams float in the dammed Urrá" alludes to the impossibility of carrying out communal and family-based projects in the collective territories affected by the flooding. Another possible reading of "floating dreams" relates to the shortened lives of murdered community leaders, such as the Emberá-Katío Kimy Pernía Domicó, whose body was found thrown in the Sinú River after his kidnapping and assassination at the hands of paramilitary forces in 2001. The image "bodies in the streets" refers to the displaced Emberá who, with nowhere else to go, sleep in the streets. In the fourth stanza "ancestral hands" are extended, that is, these people are begging for money. Passersby do nothing to help and are likely unaware of their indirect complicity in the situation. Further, these passersby "deny their roots," seeing the Emberá as other, a poor person, a beggar. In the fifth stanza "the Emberá children" weep in exile while their mothers carry them in their arms, an image drawn from daily life in the city where Emberá women carry their children through the streets as they ask for money. We should also note the absence of Emberá men here, as many of them have either died or left their families to search for work elsewhere. Meanwhile, the State, in the form of the Instituto Colombiano de Bienestar Familiar (ICBF; Colombian Institute for Family Wellbeing) wants to adopt the children out, and thus give them "responsible parents," a mirrored vision of the State's well-known paternalism. The Emberá seek refuge or at the very least minimal conditions for subsistence, in stanza six. The city not only becomes a refuge from a Civil War that displaced thousands, but also a kind of shelter for those suffering the abuses of modernizing projects like the Urrá dam. In turn soldiers and the police, figures who represent the government and its authorities, reject the Emberá in the city, ironically displacing them once again from what never was "their land." Alluding once again to light, this time natural light, "the sun comes out" in stanza seven. However, the image "seeing night in their eyes" suggests opposing or inverted worlds, given that for many Emberá the city is a place where they cannot even sleep with any dignity. Stanza eight, "When the night falls in this country's cities / the Emberá wrap themselves with longing," indicates their ongoing removal, and that despite their condition, the Emberá have both a sense of nostalgia for what they have lost, and a certain amount of hope for an uncertain future.

The mirrored visions that Jamioy weaves together here invert the ideals of urban immigration and national progress based on the neo-colonizing exploitation of Indigenous peoples and natural resources, resources which are usually thought of as reserves that are stored away for a better tomorrow (whether via development, tourism, or exploitation). The Camëntsá oralitor presents the reader with a vision of a society that is not only the inverse of but also opposed to the effective survival of Indigenous communities. The text demonstrates the total contradictions between light in the city and Indigenous communities' being blinded. At its core, the poem denounces the image of a State committed to "illuminating," via modernizing process, the "eyes" (dreams) of its citizens, while "blinding the souls" (extinguishing the sovereignty and dignity) of Colombia's originary Peoples, who are given their social status of minority groups in the country's official discourse, as just one more merely demographic measure of social value.

In "Nday biyañ" "En qué lengua" [In What Language], the oralitor directly questions the country's "president," who represents the visible head of government power. Interpellating the president, the text articulates a new mirrored vision of the language in which dreams are written:

I find myself in your office today,	[Hoy, que me encuentro en su oficina
pleading for the life of my people,	abogando por la vida de mi pueblo,
and I ask you, Mr. President:	le pregunto, señor presidente:
In what language	¿En qué lengua
are your dreams written in?	están escritos sus sueños?
They seem to be	Parece que están escritos
in English, they're not even in Spanish.	en inglés, ni siquiera en español.
Mine are written	Los míos están escritos
in Camëntsá.	en camëntsá.
In this way	Así
we'll never understand each other.	jamás nos entenderemos.]
	(Jamioy, *Bínÿbe* 181)

Through this ironic mirrored vision of the State, the oralitor emphasizes the government's being coopted through its alliances with the forces of international colonialism. In the same way, the poem's announcement of a failed intercultural dialogue also questions the frequently hypocritical and tolerant multiculturalist politics of a State that servilely capitulates to US interests. The Wayuu novelist Antonio López Epieyú had already taken a similar position in his *Los dolores de una raza* [The Sufferings of a Race], specifically referring to the loss and "independence" of Panamá in 1903 due to the intervention of US interests concerning the use of the interoceanic canal.[17] In "Nday biyañ," dreaming in English alludes to the power that it holds over another's head, a head that speaks in a language that is out-of-tune with the dreams of the country's people and yet associated with arbitrary behavior like its attitude toward the denouncement of the Urrá dam. By comparison, and as the oralitor makes clear in the text's Camëntsá version, he uses his own language as a kind of self-affirmation:

Mënté muents sëntsemna or
atsbe yentsangbiam sëntsoyebuambná
cbotjá muentsa utabná:
¿nday biyañ

[17] The complicated and unequal relations that Latin American countries have with the United States are a central theme of the Uruguayan intellectual Eduardo Galeano's book, *The Open Veins of Latin America* (1971). In the particular case of Colombia, one of the more recent interventionist episodes is Plan Colombia, which was agreed to in 1999 by Bill Clinton and Andrés Pastrana, who were then presidents of their two countries. Plan Colombia forwarded a gigantic, strategic military investment in Colombia focused on disrupting drug trafficking networks, eradicating the cultivation of coca and poppy using chemicals, the sharing of military intelligence, and geopolitical control over the region. The strategy reached its apogee when the creation of seven military bases in Colombia was announced in 2009, during the government of Álvaro Uribe Vélez.

chëngbe otjenayan tmojuabem?
Sontsinÿan tmojuabem
ingles biyañ, ni mo españoliñ ndoñ.
Atsbeng entsabeman
camëntsá biyañ.
Chca
chcá ndocnaté quemochatenyeonan.
(Jamioy, *Bínÿbe* 180)

The poem's most forceful verses suggest a further irony in that Colombia does not even have a head who governs in Spanish, the country's official language, but in English, the imperial language of the twenty-first century: "*Sontsinÿan tmojuabem / ingles biyañ, ni mo españoliñ ndoñ*" [(His dreams) seem to be written / in English, they're not even in Spanish] (Jamioy, *Bínÿbe* 180–81).

Far from producing an exclusivist celebration of Indigenous languages, this kind of bilingual publication opens up spaces for both Indigenous and non-Indigenous readers who can only approach the text in Spanish. This intellectual project is shared by most Indigenous writers, who seek to alphabetize their readers "in reverse." That is, through their work these writers share their political, cultural, and linguistic positions with their readers. These positions constitute alternatives to hegemonic projects in a country that is thought in its official language, Spanish, and in English, a language that is an object of desire and international prestige. Instead of being a baseless critique, this hegemonic linguistic situation can be found in Colombia Very Well, the country's recently created National English Program, that hopes to have most Colombian undergraduates speaking English between 2015 and 2025. According to an ex-functionary from the Instituto Caro y Cuervo, the project's overall budget is said to be double that of the Ministry of Culture's. Indeed, Colombia Very Well's budget is some 1.3 billion pesos, and it has been proposed that "through the National English Program 2015–2025, Colombia will increase the number of undergraduates speaking English at an intermediate level from 9000 to 186,000, train and support 12,000 English teachers and hand out 6 million basic and intermediate English education books to strenghten the spaces in which this foreign language is taught" [a través del Programa Nacional de Inglés 2015–2025, Colombia aumentará de 9000 a 186.000 los bachilleres con nivel de inglés intermedio, se formará y acompañará a 12.000 docentes de inglés y se entregarán 6 millones de libros en educación básica y media para fortalecer los ambientes de aprendizaje de esta lengua extranjera] (Programa Nacional de Inglés).

This national quest to be bilingual in Spanish and English also reflects governmental and private policies that have followed traditional formulas concerning "progress" and "competition," as well as thoughts about the appropriate "exploitation of natural resources" found in the subsoil, that is, beneath the surface of any territory occupied by a sovereign community. In many of the prescriptions and offers of "support" from institutions such as the World Bank and the International Monetary Fund, the use of land and accessible capital are mediated by the "economic interests" of national and international elites, governments and NGOs, none of which recognize multiple ways of socially existing and socially being in a territory, or the significance of such modes of living. These relationships with land and the revindication of meaning in these spaces are central themes of Fredy Chikangana's life and oraliture project. An example of the latter is his elegiac hymn or *haylli* to the Caucan leader Quintín Lame, known throughout the twentieth century for his struggle to recover Nasa lands, and for his confrontational stance towards members of the Cauca's elite and Colombia's centralizing government.[18] In "Hatun sonccopay Quintín Lame pawaymanta" [Quintín Lame's Dizzying Flight], the Yanakuna oralitor describes the Nasa leader as opening up a path by climbing "the mountains between the sun and the rain" [montañas entre el sol y la lluvia], working the land "to feel its insides" [para sentir sus entrañas], and ripping at "the subjugating clothes" [las vestiduras del sometimiento] worn by "a spirit borne of thunder" [un espíritu hijo del trueno]. Chikangana's strategic positioning emphasizes the fact that his poem-*haylli* is a declaration that people need to continue Quintín Lame's struggle:

Your fights that are our fights	[*Chaypimanta paccariok qan atipanacuy*
were born there	*ima ñukanchicay atipanacuy*
and you liberated yourself	*nanaypari piñascay qanpi pachacaqqe*
from the pain of being a hostage in	*munayniokta.*]
your own land.	(Chikangana, *Samay* 24–25)

---

[18] In addition to his activism focused on the recovery of Indigenous lands in the Colombian Southwest, Manuel Quintín Lame Chantre (1880–1967) was a prolific writer of letters and manifestos of great importance to Indigenous movements today. Originally titled *En defensa de mi raza*, his important book, *Los pensamientos del indio que se educó dentro de las selvas colombianas*, was published posthumously in 1971. It is available in Gonzalo Castillo Cárdenas's English translation, *Liberation Theology from Below, The Life and Thought of Manuel Quintín Lame*. See also Mónica Arango's *La civilización montés, la visión india y el trasegar de Manuel Quintín Lame en Colombia*.

This kind of mirrored vision affirms that the recovery of literary space is in itself an announcement of and accompaniment to the recovery of land, and above all else the recovery of autonomous epistemic spaces. In "Hatun sonccopay Quintín Lame pawaymanta," ñukanchi, the exclusive collective "we" of the Quechua, is broadened to include Quintín Lame. Chikangana weaves Lame's struggle into the Andean Quechua imaginary, which is populated with other figures like those of Indigenous central-Andean mestizo writers who participated in struggles for cultural revindication, like Titu Cusi Yupanki in the sixteenth century, Guamán Poma de Ayala at the beginning of the seventeenth century, and José María Arguedas in the twentieth century. Chikangana adds Lame to this sequence through the emancipatory declaration that, "these are our fights" [son nuestras luchas]. The Yanakuna Mitmak author exalts the Nasa leader as a "hero," while the Andean image of *yawar* (blood, continuity, sacrifice, resistance) extends through memory's collective river: "The mountains know your confident steps / and the winds know your long flights, / the Cauca river is witness / to the blood your community has spilled" [Las montañas saben de tus pasos firmes / y el viento conoce de tus largos vuelos, / el río Cauca es testigo / de la sangre vertida de tu pueblo indio] (Chikangana, *Samay* 25).

Mirrored visions about nature, like the rivers who "witness" history, are a recurrent theme in Fredy Chikangana/Wiñay Mallki's poetics, as the oralitor frequently foregrounds poetic observations about animals, the stars, and natural phenomena. His personal critique of history is expressed through nature's tense silence, a sense that it must say something, and that it does speak in its own way, although sometimes it speaks from the depths of a mysterious jungle that is stereotyped as the "natural" place of Indians, savages, primitives, in short, the other:

Sailing down a silent river	[*Sucuy jahuapi yakuk mucmikuk*
a brother said:	*Suttin-rimay huauk:*
"If the rivers could talk,	*"paylla yakucuna atipay upallalla rimay*
what stories they'd tell…"	*Hayk'a yupayuyay…"*
And from the depths of that mysterious	*Pi-maypas suttin-rimay acumanta*
jungle, someone responded,	*animasachachaymanta*
"History is so miserable	*"yuyaycuna ancha mica*
that the rivers prefer to remain silent…"	*Ima yakucuna acllay upallay…"*

Navegando sobre un río silencioso
dijo un hermano:
«Si los ríos pudieran hablar,
cuánta historia contarían...».

Y alguien habló desde lo profundo de esa
selva misteriosa:
«La historia es tan miserable
que los ríos prefieren callar...».]
(*Samay* 28, 29)

In this conversational poem, two people who are "brothers" in the general sense of two people who are related, sail down a river. After one of them asks a question, a third voice intervenes in their conversation from deep in the speaking jungle. Anima-*sacha* is a word in mixed Spanish-Quechua (spirit and sacha, or jungle), that would translate, more so than "mysterious jungle," as "jungle of the spirits," or "from which the spirits speak," and we can easily imagine the speaking spirits as the dead victims of that history (*yuyacuna*) which is so miserable (*ancha mica*). The rivers (*yakucuna*), literally "the waters," are conspicuously silent in Chikangana's poem and reinforce the Quechua image of *yawar mayu*, the river of blood. These images of inception problematize questions concerning origins, and particularly the histories of diverse Indigenous communities that have been repressed, silenced, or decapitated. The poem "Yaku-cunamanta" "De los ríos" [From the Rivers] suggests the dialogic nature of oral histories, the constant participation of ancestral memory in its creation, and the particular ways in which these stories are situated within a territory (jungle, rivers) that is positioned textually through the living witness of human actions. The relationships of collective memories and histories to rivers is a metaphor previously developed in Quechua by the Peruvian writer José María Arguedas in his novel *Los ríos profundos* [The Deep Rivers] (1958). In that novel, the young protagonist Ernesto finds himself looking for his roots. He finds them in the Inca stones of Cusco, in the calls of women selling Chicha, and in the rivers which are metaphors for the roots of an ancient world that nurtures the young man's identity. By comparison, Chikangana's world is that of an adult who invokes his childhood and interrogates the present in which nature has both witnessed colonization and been its victim. It is a nature that, despite its silence, still transmits the memory of Andean peoples and the Yanakuna Mitmak, in a process of linguistic, political, and cultural rearticulation.

"Hapttay pachamanta" "Puñado de tierra" [Handful of Earth] is another of Chikangana's poems that expresses an attitude of open struggle for the recovery of lands. The poetic voice proposes taking up his people's collective history with his own hands:

They gave me a handful of earth so I could
                live there.
They told me, "Here, earthworm."
"That's where you will plant, where you'll
                raise your children,
there you'll eat your sacred corn."
Then I took that handful of earth,
encircled it with rocks so the water
wouldn't carry it off,
I guarded it in the palm of my hand,
                I warmed it,
I caressed it, and I began to work it…
Every day I sang to that handful of earth;
then the ant came, the cricket, the nocturnal
                bird,
the snake from the brush,
and they wanted to take from that handful
                of earth.
I removed the rocks and gave each one
                their part.
I was alone again
with my empty palm;
so I closed my hand, made a fist, and
                decided to fight
for what others had stolen from us.

[Me entregaron un puñado de tierra para
que ahí viviera.
«Toma, lombriz de tierra», me dijeron,
«Ahí cultivarás, ahí criarás a tus hijos,
ahí masticarás tu bendito maíz».
Entonces tomé ese puñado de tierra,
lo cerqué de piedras para que el agua
no me lo desvaneciera,
lo guardé en el cuenco de mi mano, lo
                calenté,
lo acaricié y empecé a labrarlo…
Todos los días le cantaba a ese puñado
                de tierra;
entonces vino la hormiga, el grillo,
                el pájaro de la noche,
la serpiente de los pajonales,
y ellos quisieron servirse de ese puñado
                de tierra.
Quité el cerco y a cada uno le di su parte.
Me quedé nuevamente solo
con el cuenco de mi mano vacío;
cerré entonces la mano, la hice puño
                y decidí pelear
por aquello que otros nos arrebataron.]
(*Samay* 21)

This poem presents an Indigenous perspective on colonization in Colombia. At the beginning, it alludes to territories being marked with fences: reservations or reductions that Indigenous people were forced to live in beginning in the sixteenth century on (the "republics", towns or pueblos de indios). According to the historian Jorge Orlando Melo, one version of these, the encomienda, can be thought of as "an institution that was above all else a system for controlling labor, and secondly a mechanism for the acculturation of Indians and the military defense of Spanish holdings against Indigenous rebellions" [una institución que era en primer lugar un sistema de control y utilización de mano de obra y en segundo término un mecanismo de aculturación de los indios y de defensa militar de los establecimientos españoles contra las rebeliones indígenas] (64). This aspect of Indigenous history is summed up in the first verse, "They gave me a handful of earth so I could live there."

At the same time, the poem points out various moments and actors in the tearing down and recreation of these fences by interests as diverse as the Spanish empire, the First Republic, and the contemporary Colombian State. Here certain animals seem to represent different types of colonists, "then the ant came, the cricket, the nocturnal birds, / the snake from the brush, / and they wanted to take from that handful of earth." In this sense, these verses also allude to the continual dissolution of reservations (collective territories that were titled during the colonial period), their being parceled out, and in particular their privatization and subsequent sale: "I removed the rocks and gave each one their part. / I was alone again / with my empty palm." As the Colombian researcher Carl Langebaek explains, "one of the policies that, from the point of view of the criollos, revindicated Indigenous Peoples, was the dissolution of their reservations" [una política que desde el punto de vista de los criollos reivindicaba al nativo fue la disolución de los resguardos] (62). However, according to Simón Bolívar's May 20, 1820 Decree, which he delivered in Cúcuta in what is now Colombia, "All the land which formed part of reservations according to [colonial] titles will be returned to the natives, their legitimate owners, regardless of who alleges to be their owners at present" [Se devolverá a los naturales, como propietarios legítimos, todas las tierras que formaban los resguardos según títulos cualquiera que sea el que aleguen para poseerla los actuales tenedores] (Sánchez Gutiérrez and Molina Echeverri, 395). In the Decree of October 15, 1828, "Bolívar restored the tribute system" [Bolívar restauró el tributo] (Langebaek Rueda 262), and in that same year, in light of the fact that Indigenous people had returned to "the woods with great damage to the State" [los bosques con mucho perjuicio al Estado] as well as of the need "to instruct them in religion, morality, and in the skills necessary for life" [instruirlos en la religión, la moral y en las artes necesarias para la vida], Bolívar ordered the reestablishment of the missions (July 11, 1828 Decree) (Langebaek Rueda 262).

The fight to recover Indigenous lands continued throughout the nineteenth and twentieth centuries. In the 1970s Colombia found itself in the middle of the Frente Nacional (1958–1974), during which the country's traditional liberal and conservative political parties agreed to rotate being in power. Partially inspired by the military victory of the Cuban revolution in 1959, armed guerrilla groups appeared in the country, like the Fuerzas Armadas Revolucionarias de Colombia (FARC, Colombian Armed Revolutionary Forces, 1964), the Ejército de Liberación Nacional (ELN, National Liberation Army, 1965), and the Ejército Popular de Liberación (EPL, Popular Liberation Army, 1967). During this period of social upheaval, "in 1968 an important farmer's union, the Asociación Nacional Unida de Campesinos [ANUC, United National Farmers' Association], promoted agrarian reform on a national level, as well as the direct

recovery of farmers' lands. After several years the ANUC was weak-
ened from being the target of government oppression and of land-
owners' hostility, seeing several of its members murdered, as well
as the onset of internal divisions" [se crea en 1968 un importante
sindicato campesino, la Asociación Nacional Unida de Campesinos
(ANUC), que promueve a nivel nacional la reforma agraria y las re-
cuperaciones directas de tierras por parte de los campesinos. Al cabo
de algunos años la ANUC se debilita, víctima de la represión oficial,
de la hostilidad de los terratenientes, del asesinato de varios de sus
miembros y de divisiones internas] (Mateus Mora 141).

The cases of Indigenous communities associated with the
ANUC were different. Given that 1961's agrarian reform Law 135
had produced a new round of land privatization, the law meant that
wide swaths of land were parceled out and sold, whether they were
in collectively held territories or in haciendas, whose lands Indigenous communities had long sought to recuperate, especially in Colombia's Andean Southwest.

Contemporary struggles to recover lands runs parallel to a
greater Indigenous organizing in Colombia's Southwest, particularly
in the Cauca during the 1970s. This situation can be connected to
the verse, "so I closed my hand, made a fist, and decided to fight / for
what others had stolen from us." Indeed, the Consejo Regional Indígena del Cauca (CRIC, Regional Indigenous Council of the Cauca)
was created in 1971, "bringing together members of the 'little town
councils' that governed the reserves" [aglutinando a los miembros
de los "pequeños cabildos" que gobiernan los resguardos] (Sánchez
Gutiérrez 1781), and had a different system of organization from
that of the farmers. In fact, the CRIC then became the model for
other organizations, given that, according to Sánchez Gutiérrez, "the
CRIC's success in recuperating around 30 thousand hectares of land
that had been usurped from reservations, in the reconstruction of
previously disarticulated reservations, and in the defense of Indigenous rights, became a model for how other people could create regional organizations" [el éxito del CRIC en la recuperación de cerca
de treinta mil hectáreas que habían sido usurpadas a los resguardos,
en la reconstrucción de resguardos antiguamente extinguidos y en la
defensa de los derechos indígenas, sirvió de base para que, siguiendo
su ejemplo, otros pueblos constituyeran organizaciones regionales]
(1782).

In short, in "Hapttay pachamanta" Fredy Chikangana/Wiñay
Mallki offers personal poetic images on the collective histories of

Indigenous struggles with which he identifies, and in which he participates as the text's first-person poetic voice (they gave me, I took
this handful of earth, I encircled it with rocks, I guarded it, I caressed
it, I began to work it...I sang to it, I removed the rocks, I was alone
again, then I closed my hand, I decided to fight). In this text, the
poetic voice is transformed from the passive image of an earthworm
into an empty hand, and then into a fist with which he decides to
reclaim what has been stolen from him.

In one of the original texts from *Samay,* also published in a subsequent anthology that brought together works by Vito Apüshana,
Fredy Chikangana, Hugo Jamioy, and even a poem by Abadio Green,
the Yanakuna oralitor takes a more conciliatory and hopeful attitude
regarding both his relationship with the land and his relationship
with non-Indigenous people, whom he includes when referring to
"the people":

With a foot on Mother Earth
we are all united for all of us under the
                  wide sky
we come from the sun
but we are also beings of the night
the lightning and the thunder
we are here as though we were ears of corn
under indifference's thick smoke
hardening our bodies every day
in the grinding hours
sprouting in the minga
tying ourselves to the land and
taking flight like birds
towards the dreams of people looking
in the same fountain.
	[Con el pie sobre la madre tierra
	somos uno para todos sobre el ancho cielo
	venimos del sol
	pero también somos seres de la noche
	del relámpago y el trueno
	aquí estamos como si fuéramos racimos
	                 de maíz
	bajo el humo espeso de la indiferencia
	estamos cada día curtiendo nuestros
	                 cuerpos
	en el trajinar de las horas
	retoñamos en minga
	nos amarramos a la tierra y
	como pájaros elevamos vuelo
	hacia los sueños de la gente que indaga
	en esta misma fuente.]
	(qtd. in A. García, 19)

Similar to Apüshana's previously analyzed image of smuggling
dreams with his *arijuna* friends, here Chikangana expresses a connection to "the dreams of people looking / in the same fountain."
The fountain connecting a collectivity of bodies, the lightning-thun-
der, and the flight of the birds, among other images, seems to be the
earth itself. With one foot on the ground, the minga's collective voice
states that "we are all united for all of us under the wide sky." In
addition, the Yanakuna Mitmak being is represented as having come
from the sun and as "beings of the night," things that they share
with Inca-Quechua cosmovision. Indeed, *Yana* is a Quechua word
that alludes to the color black, to what is dark, and in the poem it

alludes to a night that is complemented by both the light of the sun and the lightning and thunder. The Yanakuna-Quechua collectivity is also represented via the image of ears of corn, "under indifference's thick smoke," an indifference that could also be in reference to their marginalized and minoritized situation according to dominant society's demographic data. Now a leader in processes of communal rearticulation in San Agustín (Uyumbe), Huila, Bogotá, and the Cauca, Chikangana is particularly sensitive to the experiences of younger Yanakuna who tend to migrate to cities and towns for any kind of work they can find. The image of bodies hardening "in the grinding hours" can be tied to the complex conditions of homogenizing, servile labor in which innumerable people find themselves. Through the collective "we" the poetic voice relates the sprouting of the minga gathering the strength: "we are all united for all of us under the wide sky." This sprouting or resurgence occurs when one is connected with the earth in the sense that the *wasca* or cord, whether natural or woven, connects one to both ancestral beings and to the rest of the people. From these strong ties to the community here on earth and in connection with the oralitor's vision, we can see the birds take flight towards the dreams of people looking "in the same fountain."[19] The wide sky and Mother Earth are thus the possible relational horizon for all of her children in the "we are all united for all of us" found in the mingas of the word.

---

[19] After reading some of their poetry in schools and cultural spaces during a group poetry tour for peace in 2014, Apüshana, Jamioy, and Chikangana held open discussions with young people and gave them copies of the anthology *Herederos del canto circular* [Heirs to the circular song], in which the poem "Minga" was published.

7
CONCLUSIONS

My taita says
it's always good
to have your feet in your head,
so your footsteps are never blind.

[Siempre es bueno
tener los pies en la cabeza,
dice mi taita,
para que tus pasos nunca sean ciegos.]
(Jamioy, *Bínÿbe* 115)

I wanted to have the poetry show the energy
that language is, the way that energy is used
and transformed into vision, and the way this vision
becomes knowledge which engenders and affirms
the substance and motion of one's life.
(Ortiz 151)

I

At a round table held in November 2008 as part of Santiago de Chile's International Book Fair, an audience member asked Hugo Jamioy and Elicura Chihuailaf why they were talking about reverse illiteracy in the context of an event like the Book Fair. Someone else even asked how we could still consider someone illiterate if they had read more than one thousand books. The answer, surprising as it seemed, was that to a certain extent yes, someone could still be illiterate despite their vast list of books read. The Camëntsá oralitor then began to read, unwinding a chumbe his mother had woven and continued speaking while he turned in his hands the woven *tutu* (bag) that his Iku wife had made. Each one of the fine, complex, and poly-chromatic ideograms of these textiles was interwoven with the orali-tor's family history and multiple communal narratives. Jamioy alluded to some of his poetic texts and recited stories from memory, while his complementary reading of the textiles responded to the interpre-tation of collective codes that could not be simply improvised. The Camëntsá poet was reading and telling through his own systems of co-mmunication that years later he would refer to as "the beautiful writ-ing that they made us forget" [esa bonita escritura que le hicieron olvi-dar] when he learned to write with Greco-Phoenician letters at school.

The moment that the ideograms on the textiles were displayed, the entire audience began a new schooling in the "letters" of tex-tualities that had been previously unknown to them, entering into conversation with languages they did not speak. Today we can re-read this important reversal, which took place at a Book Fair where more than 100,000 books were on sale, as a mirrored vision insofar as it symbolically inverted the image of alphabetic writing and the cultural attitudes that surround it. We can also understand this ex-ercise's multiple readings in reverse illiteracy through the notion of oralitegraphies, that is, through its textual confluences and intersec-tions among oral, literary, and graphic systems of communication.

II

A number of Indigenous authors in Colombia and Abya Yala use the terms oraliture and literature to refer to their writing. Through-out this work I have revealed how we should move beyond a focus on ethnicity when referring to this group of literary works, emphasizing scriptural aspects of these literatures such as orality as a communal project in oraliterary works (Chihuailaf, Chikangana, Jamioy). In this context, we have explored these texts via their singular, and frequent-ly simultaneous, ability to be created in and communicated through oralitegraphies and mirrored visions, two ways of reading these texts whose complexities can be approached in a number of other ways.

The readings and perspectives enable us to expand our reception and understanding of different creative projects from a number of Indigenous literary authors in Colombia, and in related fields, works, and movements throughout the continent. As such, we have established intertextual and thematic relationships between a number of works, with a particular emphasis on texts by Fredy Chikangana/ Wiñay Mallki (Yanakuna Mitmak), Berichá (Uwa), Vito Apüshana/ Miguelángel López (Wayuu), Y̕che/Yenny Muruy Andoque (Andoke-Uitoto/Murui), Hugo Jamioy Juajibioy (Camëntsá), Estercilia Simanca Pushaina (Wayuu), and Manibinigdiginya/Abadio Green (Gunadule).

Although they are aware of the presence of their own systems of visual writing and codes, the writers we have focused on here all write in alphabetic script. According to historians of writing like Andrew Robinson, writing with a capital "W" is recognized as representing language independently of its speakers. Following this position, other forms of graphic communication are not writing given that they do not directly represent speech. In most of the world, or at the very least throughout the western hemisphere, alphabetic writing is the current valid paradigm for communication, with the alphabet being the dominant measure, form, and system of communication. The problem here is not alphabetic writing in itself, but the prejudiced uses of this alphabet-centric and literate paradigm by certain sectors of hegemonic society. These prejudices consist of marginalizing and negating the graphic expressions and written forms of the large majority of global cultures who have not privileged the development of a phonetic system for representing speech. Even so, whether by force or of their own will, many of these cultures have adopted the alphabet for their own ends. As such, we cannot base our readings of oraliture and Indigenous literatures on the traditional binaries of orality/literacy and writing/inscription. Instead of adding to academic debates that ignore the self-reflections of Indigenous critics and their communities, I have proposed that we begin from Indigenous communities' own recognition that they exist in a pluricommunicative and multi-modal space, where these texts participate in and belong to communal life. I have also argued that we must account for how these authors' projects reference this very communicative field, especially when they write in the collective, exclusive "we" of particular communities and in languages that are unknown to most of their readers. These readers, whether they are non-Indigenous or from other Indigenous nations, will read these texts in translation. We have seen how such projects, beyond calling themselves literature or oraliture, also become manifestations of oralitegraphies that in many cases directly interpellate non-Indigenous readers through mirrored visions. By understanding that these literatures and oralitures are also oralitegraphic textualities, we have seen how even the dominant paradigm of alphabetic writing can be used to Indigenous ends, becoming a mirrored vision on reverse (il)literacy.

Throughout this work, I have insisted on a plural notion of textualities that unite oral, graphic, and alphabetic-literary expressions that creatively flow together in specific texts. These are oralitegraphies insofar as these come from the projects and perspectives that are produced, transformed, and disseminated beyond spaces of communal authority, even as these same authors continually refer to their communities of origin and to their respective roles in those communities. These gestures situate their projects as being related to Jace Weaver's concept of communitism. They are similarly related to intersecting fields comprised of oralitegraphic textualities that lie along a textual continuum of the graphic, oral, and critical impulses, a concept used by Teuton in *Deep Waters* to refer to a continuity that has been interrupted by colonialism's privileging of alphabetic writing. Oralitegraphies are also the present-day expression and actualization of cultural practices that have endured via re-invention, and oralitegraphic texts unite multiple dimensions of the spoken, the written, and the visual. These textualities are practices for the revitalization, production, realization, and communication of knowledge.

Word Mingas contributes to the study and appreciation of oraliture and Indigenous literature in Colombia while suggesting avenues for further research throughout Abya Yala and Turtle Island. Its foremost contribution to scholarship lies in its privileging the voices of self-described Indigenous authors and critics, over and above non-Indigenous societies, practices, institutions, and people. In this way, we have seen how the frequently ironized non-Indigenous people in situations of intercultural contact, like the functionaries who register names on ID cards, the excited tourists who are on a quest for the exotic, politicians looking for votes, indifferent urban pedestrians looking down on displaced Indigenous communities, religious educators, a president who dreams in English and to whom people must appeal as if he were a savior, urban godmothers, and the urban reader who is called upon to identify with Indigenous struggles. These same works also highlight the young girl who tries to teach her grandfather to write, the farmer who decides to fight for his stolen land, the wise elder who can read coca leaves, the young woman who complains to her donkey about a multinational corporation, the dirtied woman who, turned to ash, rises from the earth as a drop of water, the young migrant who aspires to gaze into his grandfather's eyes again, the figure of the traditional singer-historian in contrast with that of the smuggler-poet, the verbal power of the feminine figure who speaks with the ritual drink yajé, the autobiography of a woman without feet who rebuilds her life in exile, the child shepherd who becomes a truck driver, and the young woman who uses common sense in arguing against the neoliberal logic of an extractivist corporation's functionaries. Many of these perspectives and literary representations comment upon modernity's advantages and disadvantages and create mirrored visions that seek to spark intercultural dialogue, denounce injustice, and promote social transformation through their constant interpellation of dominant society.

Word Mingas also seeks to shift how we approach oraliture and Indigenous literatures, arguing that we begin from these texts' own pedagogical textual practices (concepts of the "book," oral verbal genres, oraliture projects, the meaning of life, the Educational Minga's cartographic project). *Mingas* also contributes to the field of literary studies through the notion of oralitegraphies by broadening our readings of works of contemporary Indigenous literatures. In suggesting that we read these works within their cultural contexts and pay attention to how they resonate with different ideosymbolic expressions and/or graphic traditions, the work argues that we must reconsider practices that are commonly considered extraliterary or preliterate according to the phono-centric criteria that dominate literatures written and published in the alphabetic format of the book or digitally on the internet. Establishing fields of thematic and textual interaction among the works of different authors and oralitors, we have seen the similarities and differences among these authors' projects and (ora)literary works. Finally, *Mingas* also insists on historicizing the context in which these projects and tendencies of the works we call contemporary Indigenous literatures take shape while paying particular attention to those works that emerged as part of the oraliture project from the mid-1990s to the present: *Bínÿbe oboyejuayëng* [Wind Dancers] (2005) and *Samay pisccok pponccopi mushcoypa* [A Bird's Spirit within the Depths of a Daydream] (2010).

Mingas leaves a number of other possibilities open for future discussion, such as whether or not we could use the notion of oralitegraphies to analyze the growing number of videos and films produced by Indigenous peoples in Colombia and throughout the continent. We could also suggest other notions such as audiolitegraphies and musilitegraphies as ways to understand not only Indigenous texts, but works by artists from around the world, as well as works by afro-descended authors like Uriel Cassianim who writes in the afrode-scendant Palenquero language that is inspired by communal, collective rhythms. Future analyses can deepen our understanding of the intermedial projects of musical groups like the Kronos Quartet, which uses the violin, viola, and violoncello to incorporate musical registers from around the world, and in some instances tells stories like that of the First World War through mise-en-scène that combines music with projections of photographs, video, and other narrative forms.

In Colombia, a country that finds itself in the middle of a drawn-out peace process and is tortured by social inequality, racism, neocolonial interventions, successive internal wars, the notions expressed in the Educational Minga's map and the works of oraliture by Indigenous authors, pose old/new possibilities for dialogue, co-creative interaction, and social construction. Oralitegraphies and mirrored visions allow us to feel and think a country that is not only multicultural, but also plurinational and multi-scriptural, a country that is beyond the grip of multinational corporations and drug trafficking networks, a millenarian country not bound by borders that are only centuries old, an ineffable country that has always been, is, and will continue to be a continental bridge between the pluriverse's languages, knowledges, feelings, visions, and perspectives.

WORKS CITED

Ak'abal, Humberto. *Ajkem tzij/Tejedor de palabras*. Cholsamaj, 2001.

"Alarma: en la Guajira hay 37000 niños desnutridos." *Revista Semana Digital*, 23 July 2014, www.semana.com/nacion/articulo/en-guajira-hay-37000-ninos-con-desnutricion/396788-3. Accessed 16 Feb. 2021.

Allen, Chadwick. *Trans-Indigenous: Methodologies for Global Native Literary Studies*. U of Minnesota P, 2012.

Apüshana, Vito (Miguel Ángel López; Miguelángel López). "Como los caminos de la mano." *Lyrikline*, 24 Feb. 2014, www.lyrikline.org/en/poems/como-los-caminos-de-la-mano-789. Accessed 22 Dec. 2020.

———. *Contrabandeo sueños con aríjunas cercanos*. Universidad de la Guajira, 1992.

———. *Encuentros en los senderos de Abya Yala*. Travesías, 2009.

———. *Shiinalu'uirua shiirua ataa/En las hondonadas maternas de la piel*. Ministerio de Cultura, 2010.

Arango, Mónica. *La civilización montés, la visión india y el trasegar de Manuel Quintín Lame en Colombia*. Universidad de los Andes, 2009.

Arguedas, José María. *Canto kechwa, con un ensayo sobre la capacidad de creación artística del pueblo indio y mestizo*. Editorial Horizonte, 1989.

———. *Katatay*. Editorial Horizonte, 1984.

———. *Los ríos profundos*. Editorial Losada, 1958.

———. *Todas las sangres*. Editorial Losada, 1964.

———. *Tupac Amaru camac taytanchisman. Haylly-taki/A nuestro padre creador. Himno-Canción*. Ediciones Salqantay, 1962.

Arias, Arturo, et al. "Literaturas de Abya Yala," *Lasaforum* (digital), vol. XLIII, no. 1, 2012, pp. 7–10, forum.lasaweb.org/files/vol43-issue1/OnTheProfession2.pdf. Accessed 5 Dec. 2013.

Arnold, Denise, and Juan de Dios Yapita. *El rincón de las cabezas: luchas textuales, educación y tierras en los Andes*. Universidad Mayor de San Andrés, Facultad de Humanidades y Ciencias de la Educación, ILCA, 2000.

Aroca Araujo, Armando. "Una propuesta metodológica en etnomatemáticas." *Revista U.D.C.A.*, vol. 11, no. 1, 2008, pp. 67–76.

Artaud, Antonin. *México y viaje al país de los Tarahumaras*. Fondo de Cultura Económica, 1984.

———. *Van Gogh: le suicidé de la société*. K Éditeur, 1947.

Ballestas Rincón, Luz Helena. *La serpiente en el diseño indígena colombiano*. Universidad Nacional, 2007.

Barros, Johana. *Matarse a sí mismo en la comunidad wayuu de la alta y media Guajira: una mirada antropológica sobre el suicidio indígena en Colombia.* 2014. Universidad Externado de Colombia, BA thesis.

Bendezú, Edmundo. *Literatura quechua.* Ayacucho, 1980.

Berichá. *Tengo los pies en la cabeza.* Los Cuatro Elementos, 1992.

Brotherson, Gordon. *La América indígena en su literatura: los libros del cuarto mundo.* Fondo de Cultura Económica, 1997.

Campo Chicangana, Fredy Romeiro. See Chikangana, Fredy.

Campos Umbarila, Adriana. "Prólogo." *Shiinalu'uirua shiirua ataa/En las hondonadas maternas de la piel,* by Vito Apüshana, Ministerio de Cultura, 2010, pp. 13–19.

Candre, Anastasia. "Jaigabi" o "La caguana." *Pütchi biyá uai, antología multilingüe de la literatura indígena contemporánea en Colombia, Precursores,* vol. 2, edited by Miguel Rocha Vivas, Fundación Gilberto Alzate Avendaño, 2010, pp. 126–27.

———. "Unao" o "El Yagé." *Pütchi biyá uai, antología multilingüe de la literatura indígena contemporánea en Colombia, Precursores,* vol. 2, edited by Miguel Rocha Vivas, Fundación Gilberto Alzate Avendaño, 2010, pp. 124–25.

Captain, David, and Linda Captain. *Diccionario básico ilustrado, wayuunaiki-español, español-wayuunaiki.* Buena Semilla, 2005.

Castaño-Uribe, Carlos. "Tradición cultural Chiribiquete." *Rupestre Web,* 2008, www.rupestreweb.info/chiribiquete2.html. Accessed 5 Jan. 2021.

Castillo Cárdenas, Gonzalo. *Liberation Theology From Below, The Life and Thought of Manuel Quintín Lame.* Orbis Books, 1987.

"Censo general 2005." Departamento Administrativo Nacional de Estadística de Colombia (DANE). www.dane.gov.co/index.php/estadisticas-por-tema/demografia-y-poblacion/censo-general-2005-1. Accessed 30 Dec. 2020.

"Cerca de 3.000 niños han muerto en La Guajira en seis años." *El Espectador Digital,* 26 Mar. 2014, www.elespectador.com/noticias/nacional/cerca-de-3000-ninos-han-muerto-en-la-guajira-en-seis-anos/. Accessed 16 Feb. 2021.

"Cerrejón pospone estudios sobre la posible desviación del río Ranchería." *Cerrejón. Minería responsable,* 8 Nov. 2012, www.cerrejon.com/index.php/cerrejon-pospone-estudios-la-posible-desviacion-del-rio-rancheria/. Accessed 16 Feb. 2021.

Chakrabarty, Dipesh. *Provincializing Europe: Postcolonial Thought and Historical Difference.* Princeton UP, 2000.

Chihuailaf, Elicura. "Mis hermanos oralitores de Colombia." *El Periodista,* 2007, www.elperiodista.cl/newtenberg/1897/article-77321. Accessed 28 Jan. 2013.

———. "La oralitura (segundo avance)." *El Periodista,* vol. 3, no. 69, 27 Aug. 2004, www.elperiodista.cl/newtenberg/1682/article-63822. Accessed 28 Jan. 2013.

———. "Prólogo." *Samay pisccok pponccopi mushcoypa/Espíritu de pájaro en pozos del ensueño,* by Fredy Chikangana, Ministerio de Cultura, 2010, pp. 13–15.

———. *Recado confidencial a los chilenos.* Editorial Lom, 1999.

———. *Relato de mi sueño azul.* Pehuén, 2011.

Chikangana, Fredy (Wiñay Mallki). "El durazno en tía Julia," *Prometeo. Revista Latinoamericana de Poesía,* no. 59–60, 2001, www.festivaldepoesiademedellin.org/es/Revista/ultimas_ediciones/59_60/chicangana.html. Accessed 22 Dec. 2020.

———. "Fredy Romeiro Campo Chicangana." *Sing, Poetry From the Indigenous Americas,* edited by Allison Adelle Hedge Coke, U of Arizona P, 2012, pp. 119–27.

———. *Kentipay llattantutamanta/El colibrí de la noche desnuda.* Ediciones Catapulta, 2008.

———. "La oralitura," *El Espectador,* 17 Aug. 1997, pp. 10–11.

———. "Oralitura indígena como un viaje a la memoria." *Palabras de vuelta, oralidad y escritura, experiencias desde la literatura indígena,* edited by Luz María Lepe Lira, PRODICI, 2014, pp. 73–97.

———. *Samay pisccok pponccopi mushcoypa/Espíritu de pájaro en pozos del ensueño.* Ministerio de Cultura, 2010.

———. *Yo Yanacona, caminos y huellas de una cultura.* 1997. Universidad Nacional de Colombia, thesis.

"Chumbe inga." Photograph. Instituto Colombiano de Antropología e Historia, coleccio-
netnograficaicanh.wordpress.com/2012/09/25/chumbe-inga-2/. Accessed 17 Feb.
2021.

Clifford, James, and George Marcus, editors. *Writing Culture, the Poetics and Politics of
Ethnography.* 1984. U of California P, 1986.

Cocom Pech, Jorge Miguel. *Muk'ult'an in Nool/Secretos del abuelo.* Universidad Nacional
Autónoma de México, 2001.

Cornejo Polar, Antonio. *Escribir en el aire: ensayo sobre la heterogeneidad socio-cultural en
las literaturas andinas.* Editorial Horizonte, 1994.

Cummins, Tom, and Joanne Rappaport. *Beyond the Lettered City: Indigenous Literacies in
the Andes.* Duke UP, 2012.

Diamond, Neil, director. *Reel Injun.* Rezolution Pictures; National Film Board of Canada,
2009

Duque Duque, Cecilia, editor. *Lenguaje creativo de las etnias indígenas de Colombia.* Suramericana, 2012.

Echeverría, José. *El lenguaje simbólico en los Andes septentrionales.* Instituto Otavaleño
de Antropología, 1988.

Eliade, Mircea. *Shamanism: Archaic Techniques of Ecstasy,* translated by Willard R. Trask,
Arkana, 1989.

Escobar, Arturo. *La invención del desarrollo.* 2nd ed., Universidad del Cauca, 2012.

Fabian, Johannes. *Time and the Other: How Anthropology Makes Its Object.* Columbia
UP, 1983.

Fall, Yoro. "Historiografía, sociedades y conciencia histórica en África," *Estudios de Asia
y África*, vol. 26, no. 3, 1991, pp. 17–37.

"Formulación participativa de la política pública distrital para el reconocimiento, garantía,
protección y restablecimiento de derechos de la población indígena en Bogotá, documento de trabajo." *Docplayer*, Feb. 2011, docplayer.es/81056668-Formulacion-par-
ticipativa-de-la-politica-publica-distrital-para-el-reconocimiento-garantia-protec-
cion-y-restablecimiento-de-derechos-de-la.html#show_full_text. Accessed 10 Feb.
2021.

Forte, Maximilian, editor. *Indigenous Cosmopolitans: Transnational and Transcultural Indigeneity in the Twenty-First Century.* Peter Lang, 2010.

Friede, Juan. *El indio en lucha por la tierra, historia de los resguardos del macizo central
colombiano.* Ediciones Espiral Colombia, 1944.

———. *Problemas sociales de los arhuacos: tierras, gobierno, misiones.* Universidad Nacional
de Colombia, 1963.

Friedemann, Nina S. de, and Jaime Arocha. *Herederos del jaguar y la anaconda.* Carlos
Valencia Editores, 1982, babel.banrepcultural.org/digital/collection/p17054coll10/
id/2806. Accessed 15 Feb. 2021.

Galeano, Eduardo. *Los hijos de los días.* Siglo XXI Editores, 2012.

———. *Las venas abiertas de América Latina.* Siglo XXI Editores, 1971.

Ganduglia, Néstor. *Historias mágicas de Montevideo.* Planeta, 2006.

García, Ángela, editor. *Herederos del canto circular.* Universidad Externado de Colombia,
2011.

Gentile, Margarita. "Tocapu: unidad de sentido en el lenguaje gráfico andino." *Espéculo,
Revista de Estudios Literarios*, vol. 45, 2010, webs.ucm.es/info/especulo/numero45/
tocapu.html. Accessed 22 Jan. 2021.

Gómez Cardona, Fabio. "Encuentros y desencuentros en los espacios de la interculturalidad. El caso de Esperanza Aguablanca-Berichá," *La Manzana de la Discordia*, vol. 7,
no. 1, 2012, pp. 61–70.

Gómez Rincón, Carlos Miguel. *Interculturality, Rationality and Dialogue.* Echter, 2012.

Gonzales, Odi. *La Escuela de Cusco*. Santo X Oficio, 2005.

Granadino, Cecilia. *La faja calendario de Taquile. Descifrando los símbolos de un arte y una ciencia*. Editorial Minka. 1997.

Granados, Rafael. *Historia de Colombia, prehistoria, conquista, colonia, independencia y república*. Editorial Bedout, 1953.

Green, Abadio. See Manibinigdiginya.

Gröll, Ilse de. "Las lenguas amerindias y criollas en Colombia, desarrollos político-lingüísticos en el marco de la constitución política de 1991." *Las lenguas autóctonas en Colombia, consideraciones alrededor de su legitimación en la constitución de 1991*, edited by Daniel Aguirre Licht, Universidad de los Andes, 2009, pp. 13–116.

Guamán Poma de Ayala, Felipe. *Nueva corónica y buen gobierno*. Biblioteca Ayacucho, 1980.

———. *Nueva corónica y buen gobierno*, Biblioteca Real de Copenhague, 2001, www5.kb.dk/permalink/2006/poma/info/en/frontpage.htm. Accessed 30 Dec. 2020.

Guerrero Barriga, Sandra. "Un clamor por el Ranchería." *El Heraldo Digital*, 16 June 2012, www.elheraldo.co/region/un-clamor-por-el-rancheria-71433. Accessed 16 Feb. 2021.

Guffroy, Jean. *El arte rupestre en el antiguo Perú*. IFEA, 1999.

Gutiérrez Aguilar, Raquel. *Rhythms of the Pachakuti: Indigenous Uprising and State Power in Bolivia*. Duke UP, 2014.

Hill Boone, Elizabeth. *Stories in Red and Black: Pictorial Histories of the Aztecs and Mixtecs*. U of Texas P, 2000.

———. "Writing and Recording Knowledge" (Introduction). *Writing Without Words, Alternative Literacies in Mesoamerica and the Andes*, edited by Elizabeth Hill and Walter Mignolo, Duke UP, 1994, pp. 3–26.

Holmes McDowell, John. *Sayings of the Ancestors: The Spiritual Life of the Sibundoy Indians*. UP of Kentucky, 1989.

"Indicadores demográficos del pueblo camentsa." *Pueblo indígena camëntsá biyá*, 18 May 2012, puebloindigenacamentsabiya.blogspot.com/2012/05/ubicacion-el-pueblo-indigena-kamsa. Accessed 5 Jan. 2021.

Isaacs, Jorge. *Estudio sobre las tribus indígenas del estado del Magdalena*. Universidad Externado de Colombia, 2011.

Jacanamijoy, Benjamín. *Chumbe: arte inga*. Ministerio de Gobierno, 1993.

———. "El chumbe, el arte de tejer la vida y contar historias." *Lenguaje creativo de las etnias indígenas de Colombia,* edited by Cecilia Duque Duque, Suramericana, 2012, pp. 124–42.

Jamioy Juajibioy, Hugo. *Bínÿbe oboyejuayëng/Danzantes del viento*. Universidad de Caldas-Juabna de América, 2005.

———. *Bínÿbe oboyejuayëng/Danzantes del viento*. Ministerio de Cultura, 2010.

———. "Hugo Jamioy, poeta kamentsa. Interview by Marcela Hernández." *YouTube*, 24 Aug. 2013, youtu.be/Oqp7Tacb8VM.

———. *Mi fuego y mi humo, mi tierra y mi sol*. Infección Editores, 1999.

———. "Pensando, hilando y tejiendo los símbolos de la vida." *Lenguaje creativo de las etnias indígenas de Colombia*, edited by Cecilia Duque Duque, Suramericana, 2012, pp. 46–168.

———. "Sembrar la palabra en el corazón." *YouTube*, 16 Aug. 2010, youtu.be/85cfRJzrV5M.

Jamioy, Juan Carlos. *Mapa Minga Nacional de Educación Superior de los Pueblos Indígenas*. Comisión Nacional de Trabajo y Concertación de Educación de los Pueblos Indígenas, 2010.

Jean, Georges. *La escritura, memoria de la humanidad*. Ediciones B, 1998.

Juajibioy Chindoy, Alberto, and Álvaro Wheeler. *Bosquejo etno-lingüístico del grupo Kamsá del Sibundoy*. Imprenta Nacional, 1974.

———. *Lenguaje ceremonial y narraciones tradicionales de la cultura kamëntsá*. Fondo de Cultura Económica, 2008.

———. *Relatos ancestrales del folclor camëntsá*. Fundación Interamericana, 1989.

Jusayú, Miguel Ángel, editor. *Achi'kí, relatos guajiros*. Universidad Católica Andrés Bello, 1986.

———. *Ni era vaca ni era caballo...* Ediciones Ekaré, 2004.

———. *Takü'jala, lo que he contado*. Universidad Católica, 1989.

Lame, Manuel Quintín. *En defensa de mi raza*. La Rosca/Editextos, 1971.

———. *Los pensamientos del indio que se educó dentro de las selvas colombianas*. Biblioteca del Gran Cauca, 2004.

Landaburu, Jon. "La diversidad de las lenguas nativas de Colombia y su situación actual," *Fiesta de las lenguas nativas*, documento de divulgación, Ministerio de Cultura, 2009, pp. 4–7, www.mincultura.gov.co/SiteAssets/documentos/poblaciones/Fiesta%20 de%20Lenguas%20Nativas%20(Internet).pdf. Accessed 30 Dec. 2020.

Langebaek Rueda, Carl Henrik. *Los herederos del pasado. Indígenas y pensamiento criollo en Colombia y Venezuela*. Universidad de los Andes-CESO, 2009, 2 vols.

Larreal, Ramiro. *Hermano mestizo*. LES-Instituto Superior Salesiano, 1983.

Lavalle, José Antonio de, and Rosario de Lavalle de Cárdenas, editors. *Tejidos milenarios del Perú*. Integra AFP, 1999.

Lepe Lira, Luz María, editor. *Palabras de vuelta, oralidad y escritura, experiencias desde la literatura indígena*. PRODICI, 2014.

"Ley 1381 de 2010." *Función Pública*. *www.funcionpublica.gov.co/eva/gestornormativo/ norma.php?i=38741*. Accessed 17 Feb. 2021.

Lienhard, Martín. *La voz y su huella, escritura y conflicto étnico-cultural en América Latina 1492–1988*. Editorial Horizonte, 1992.

López Epieyú, Joaquín. *Los dolores de una raza, novela histórica de la vida real contemporánea del indio guajiro*. La Columna, 1956.

López, Miguel Ángel. See Miguelángel López. See Apüshana, Vito.

Lundquist, Suzanne. *Native American Literatures, an Introduction*. Continuum, 2004.

Manibinigdiginya (Abadio Green). *Anmal gaya burba: isbeyobi daglege nana nabgwana bendaggegala/Significados de vida: espejo de nuestra memoria en defensa de la madre tierra*. Universidad de Antioquia, 2011.

———. "Educación superior desde la Madre Tierra." *Revista Debates*, no. 67, Jan.–Apr. 2014, pp. 20–29.

———. "Inauguración del festival. La palabra y la imagen." *Internet Archive*, uploaded by paulav, 3 Oct. 2012, archive.org/details/AbadioGreenInaguracinDelFestival.La PalabraYLaImagen.

Mateus Mora, Angélica. *El indígena en el cine y el audiovisual colombianos*. La Carreta Editores, 2013.

Melo, Jorge Orlando. *Historia de Colombia, el establecimiento de la dominación española*. La Carreta, 1977.

Mignolo, Walter. "Signs and Their Transmission: The Question of the Book in the New World." *Writing Without Words, Alternative Literacies in Mesoamerica and the Andes*, edited by Elizabeth Hill Boone and Walter Mignolo, Duke UP, 1994, pp. 220–70.

———. "Writing and Recorded Knowledge in Colonial and Postcolonial Situations" (Afterword). *Writing Without Words, Alternative Literacies in Mesoamerica and the Andes*, edited by Elizabeth Hill Boone and Walter Mignolo, Duke UP, 1994, pp. 293–313.

Montibeller Ardiles, Morayma. *Tarpui llahuayra haylli, la canción de la siembra en la iconografía de los q'eros*. Pacha Illary, 1994.

Montiel, Nemesio. *Los a'laulaa y compadres wayuu*. Universidad del Zulia, 2006.

Mora Curriao, Maribel. "Poesía mapuche: la instalación de una mismidad étnica en la literatura chilena," *A Contracorriente, una Revista de Historia Social y Literatura en América Latina*, vol. 10, no. 3, 2013, pp. 21–53.

Moreiras, Alberto. "José María Arguedas y el fin de la transculturación." *Ángel Rama y los estudios latinoamericanos*, edited by Mabel Moraña, Instituto Internacional de Literatura Iberoamericana, 1997, pp. 213–31.

Moya, Alba, and Ruth Moya. *Derivas de la interculturalidad: procesos y desafíos en América Latina*. Cafolis/Funades, 2004.

Moya, Ruth. "Reformas educativas e interculturalidad en América Latina," *Revista Iberoamericana de Educación*, vol. 17, May–Aug. 1998, pp. 105–87, doi.org/10.35362/rie1701105. Accessed 7 Jan. 2021.

Murúa, Martín de. *Historia General del Perú*. 1613. Historia 16, 1986.

Muruy Andoque, Yenny (Y che). *Versos de sal. Pütchi biyá uai, antología multilingüe de la literatura indígena contemporánea en Colombia, Puntos aparte, vol. 2*, edited by Miguel Rocha Vivas, Fundación Gilberto Alzate Avendaño, 2010, pp. 21–61.

Muyolema, Armando. "De la 'cuestión indígena' a lo 'indígena' como cuestionamiento. Hacia una crítica del latinoamericanismo, el indigenismo y el mestiz(o)aje," *Convergencia de tiempos, estudios subalternos/contextos latinoamericanos, estado, cultura, subalternidad*, edited by Ileana Rodríguez, Rodopi, 2001, pp. 327–63.

Nebrija, Antonio de. 1492. *Gramática de la lengua castellana*. Editorial Nacional, 1981.

Niño, Hugo. *El etnotexto: las voces del asombro*. Casa de las Américas, 2008.

Noriega, Julio. *Escritura quechua en el Perú*. Pakarina Ediciones, 2011.

Orán, Reuter, and Aiban Wagua. *Gayamar sabga: diccionario escolar gunagaya-español*. Equipo EBI Guna-Fondo Mixto Hispano, 2010.

Ong, Walter. *Orality and Literacy: The Technologizing of the Word*. Taylor & Francis, 1982.

Orgambide, Pedro. "El mapa dado vuelta." *Revista Todavía*, no. 4, Apr. 2003, pp. 47–49, www.revistatodavia.com.ar/. Accessed 4 Jan. 2021.

Ortiz, Simon. *Woven Stone*. U of Arizona P, 1992.

Osborn, Ann. *Las cuatro estaciones, mitología y estructura social entre los u'wa*. Banco de la República, 1995.

Osorio, Betty. "Manuel Quintín Lame Interpreted from Inside: Cognitive Practices in Discourse," *Latin American Indian Literatures Journal*, vol. 24, no.1, 2008, pp. 82–98.

Ossio Acuña, Juan. *Ideología mesiánica del mundo andino*, edited by Ignacio Prado Pastor, Gráficas Morson, 1973.

Palacio Paz, Eliana. *Na lapümajanaka/Los Wayuu, una cultura de sueños, la influencia de los Testigos de Jehová en la práctica ancestral de los sueños (Lapü) entre el pueblo indígena wayuu*. 2011. Universidad Externado de Colombia, thesis.

———. "Re: Convocatoria Contcepi Minga de Educación Superior." Received by Miguel Rocha Vivas. 4 March 2010.

Paredes Pinda, Adriana. *Parias Zugun*. Lom, 2014.

———. *Üi*. Lom, 2005.

Paz Ipuana, Ramón. *Mitos, leyendas y cuentos guajiros*. Instituto Agrario Nacional, 1972.

Perrin, Michel. *Magnificent Molas: The Art of the Kuna Indians*. Flammarion, 2004.

———. *Los practicantes del sueño: el chamanismo wayuu*. Monte Ávila Editores Latinoamericana, 1997.

Pushaina, Juan. "La fiesta patronal." *El sol babea jugo de piña: antología de las literaturas indígenas del Atlántico, el Pacífico y la Serranía del Perijá*, edited by Miguel Rocha Vivas, Ministerio de Cultura, 2010, pp. 381–88.

Rama, Ángel. *La ciudad letrada*. Ediciones del Norte, 1984.

Ramírez Hincapié, Christian Esteban. "Cuando el río suena, piedras lleva: los embera-katío y la hidroeléctrica de Urrá I." *OPCA*, no. 4, Nov. 2012, opca.uniandes.edu.co/cuando-el-rio-suena-piedras-lleva-los-embera-katio-y-la-hidroelectrica-de-urra-i/. Accessed 16 Feb. 2021.

Rappaport, Joanne. *Intercultural Utopias: Public Intellectuals, Cultural Experimentation, and Ethnic Pluralism in Colombia*. Duke UP, 2005.

Reichel-Dolmatoff, Gerardo. *Los kogi, una tribu de la Sierra Nevada de Santa Marta*. Procultura, 1985. 2 vols.

Restrepo, Luis Fernando. "Tengo los pies en la cabeza, de Berichá, los u'wa y los retos de la cultura del reconocimiento," *Cuadernos de Literatura*, vol. 11, no. 22, 2007, pp. 153–67.

Rivera Cusicanqui, Silvia. *Pachakuti: los aymara de Bolivia frente a medio milenio de colonialismo*. Ediciones Aruwiyiri, 1991.

Robinson, Andrew. *The Story of Writing*, Thames & Hudson, 2007.

Rocha Vivas, Miguel. "Oralituras y literaturas indígenas en Colombia: de la constitución de 1991 a la Ley de Lenguas de 2010." *A Contracorriente, Una Revista de Historia Social y Literatura en América Latina*, vol. 10, no. 3, 2013, pp. 74–107.

———. *Palabras mayores, palabras vivas, tradiciones mítico- literarias y escritores indígenas en Colombia*. Taurus, 2012.

———, editor. *Antes del amanecer, antología de las literaturas indígenas de los Andes y de la Sierra Nevada de Santa Marta.* Ministerio de Cultura, 2010.

———, editor. *Pütchi biyá uai, antología multilingüe de la literatura indígena contemporánea en Colombia, Precursores*. Fundación Gilberto Alzate Avendaño, 2010. 2 vols.

———, editor. *El sol babea jugo de piña: antología de las literaturas indígenas del Atlántico, el Pacífico y la Serranía del Perijá*. Ministerio de Cultura, 2010.

———, editor. *Interacciones multiculturales: los estudiantes indígenas en la Universidad*. Universidad Externado de Colombia, 2009.

Ruano, Aldemar. *Kury pugyu, coloreando y pintando la cultura pasto, Nariño*. Consejo Mayor de Educación Indígena de los Pastos.

Sánchez Gutiérrez, Enrique. "Movimientos campesinos e indígenas (1960–1982)." *Historia de Colombia, Colombia contemporánea I*, vol. 8, Editorial Salvat, 1987, pp. 1775–95.

Sánchez Gutiérrez, Enrique, and Hernán Molina Echeverri, editors. *Documentos para la historia del movimiento indígena contemporáneo*. Ministerio de Cultura, 2010.

Sarris, Greg. *Keeping the Slug Woman Alive: A Holistic Approach to American Indian Texts*. U of California P, 1993.

Scarangella, Linda. "Indigeneity in Tourism: Transnational Spaces, Pan-Indian Identity, and Cosmopolitism." *Indigenous Cosmopolitans: Transnational and Transcultural Indigeneity in the Twenty-First Century*, edited by Maximilian Forte, Peter Lang, 2010, pp. 163–88.

Sekerci, Suzan, director. *Mama Koka! Krieger für das Kokain*. Storytellers GmbH & Co. KG, Corazón international Filmproduktion, 2013.

Shady Solís, Ruth. "Caral." *Encyclopedia of Latin American History and Culture*, edited by Jay Kinsbruner and Erick D. Langer, vol. 2, Charles Scribner's Sons, pp. 95–98. 2nd. ed. 2008.

Sharma, Meenakshi. *Postcolonial Indian Writing, Between Cooption and Resistance*. Rawat Publications, 2003.

Silko, Leslie Marmon. *Storyteller*. Arcade Publishing, 1981.

———. *Yellow Woman and a Beauty of the Spirit*. Simon & Shuster Paperbacks, 1996.

Silva, Jorge, and Marta Rodríguez, directors. *Nuestra voz de tierra, memoria y futuro*. Ministerio de Cultura de Colombia, 1982.

Silverman, Gail. *El tejido andino, un libro de sabiduría*. Banco Central de Reserva del Perú, Fondo Editorial, 1994.

Simanca Pushaina, Estercilia. "Jimaai en la tierra del maíz." *El encierro de una pequeña doncella*, Lama Producciones & Representaciones, 2006, pp. 23–34.

———. "Daño emergente, lucro cesante." *Manifestanosaberfirmar*, manifiestanosaberfirmar. blogspot.ca/2011/03/dano-emergente-lucro-cesante.html. Accessed 5 Apr. 2014.

———. "El encierro de una pequeña doncella." *El encierro de una pequeña doncella*, Lama Producciones & Representaciones, 2006, pp. 9–20.

———. *Manifiesta no saber firmar. Nacido: 31 de diciembre*. Edición de la autora, 2008.

Siosi Pino, Vicenta María. "Esa horrible costumbre de alejarme de ti." *Woummainpa*, no. 1, Universidad de la Guajira, 1994, pp. 1–8.

———. *El dulce corazón de los piel cobriza*. Fondo Mixto para la Promoción de la Cultura y las Artes de la Guajira, 2002.

———. "La carta de una escritora wayuu a Santos." *El Espectador Digital*, 14 Apr. 2012, www.elespectador.com/noticias/actualidad/la-carta-de-una-escritora-wayuu-a-santos/. Accessed 16 Feb. 2021.

———. "Ranchería River Issue." *Indigenous World Forum on Water and Peace*, 26 Aug. 2012, waterandpeace.wordpress.com/2012/08/26/rancheria-river-issue-defendiendo-al-rio-rancheria/. Accessed 2 June 2020.

Teuton, Christopher. *Cherokee Stories of the Turtle Island Liar's Club*. U of North Carolina P, 2012.

———. "The Cycle of Removal and Return: A Symbolic Geography of Indigenous Literature." *Canadian Journal of Native Studies. Special Issue: What We Do, What We Are: Responsible, Ethical, and Indigenous-Centered Literary Criticisms*, vol. 29, nos.1–2, 2009, pp. 45–64.

———. *Deep Waters, the Textual Continuum in American Indian Literature*. U of Nebraska P, 2010.

———. "Theorizing American Indian Literature." *Reasoning Together*, edited by Craig Womack, et al. The Native Critics Collective, U of Oklahoma P, 2008, pp. 193–215.

Torres-García, Joaquín. "The School of the South," *El Taller Torres-García. The School of the South and Its Legacy*, edited by Mari Carmen Ramírez, curated by Cecilia Buzio de Torres and Mari Carmen Ramírez, U of Texas P, 1992, pp. 53–57.

Torres Márquez, Vicencio. *Los indígenas arhuacos "y la vida de la civilización."* América Latina, 1978.

Tuhiwai Smith, Linda. *Decolonizing Methodologies, Research and Indigenous Peoples*. U of Otago P, 1999.

Urbina Fernando. *Diïjoma. El hombre serpiente águila*. CAB, 2004.

———. "Mito, rito, y arte rupestre en la amazonia." Unpublished manuscript.

———. "Mitos y petroglifos en el río Caquetá," *Boletín Museo del Oro*, no. 30, 1991, pp. 2–41.

———, editor. *Las palabras del origen: breve compendio sobre la mitología de los uitotos*. Ministerio de Cultura, 2010.

Valle Escalante, Emilio del (Emil' Keme). "Introducción. Teorizando las literaturas indígenas contemporáneas." *A Contracorriente, Una Revista de Historia Social y Literatura en América Latina*, vol. 10, no. 3, 2013, pp. 1–20.

Vasco, Luis Guillermo. *Semejantes a los dioses*. Universidad Nacional, 1987.

Valderrama, Ricardo, and Carmen Escalante, editors. *Gregorio Condori Mamani, autobiografía*. Centro de Estudios Rurales Andinos Bartolomé de las Casas, 1982.

Valenzuela, Santiago. "Una política para los indígenas urbanos." *El Espectador Digital*, 30 Mar. 2014, www.elespectador.com/noticias/bogota/una-politica-para-los-indigenas-urbanos/. Accessed 10 Mar. 2021.

Villafaña, Amado, et al., directors. *Palabras mayores*. Centro de comunicaciones Zhigoneshi, 2009.

Villafaña, Amado, et al. *Resistencia en la línea negra*, Zhigoneshi, 2011.

Wagua, Aiban, editor. *En defensa de la vida y su armonía, elementos de la espiritualidad guna, textos del babigala, Kuna Yala*. Proyecto EBI Guna/Fondo Mixto Hispano Panameño, 2011.

———. *Kaaubi, selección de algunos poemas, 1972–1992*. Editorial Chen, 1997.

Walsh, Catherine. *Interculturalidad, estado, sociedad: luchas (de)coloniales de nuestra época*. Universidad Andina Simón Bolívar y Abya Yala, 2009.

Warrior, Robert Allen. *Tribal Secrets: Recovering American Indian Intellectual Traditions*. U of Minnesota P, 1995.

Weaver, Jace. *That the People Might Live: Native American Literatures and Native American Community*. Oxford UP, 1997.

White, Hayden. *The Content of the Form: Narrative Discourse and Historical Representation*. Johns Hopkins UP, 1987.

Womack, Craig. *Red on Red, Native American Literary Separatism*. U of Minnesota P, 1999.

———. "A Single Decade: Book-Length Native Literary Criticism between 1986 and 1997," *Reasoning Together. The Native Critics Collective*, U of Oklahoma P, 2008, pp. 3–104.

Wood, Denis, et al. *Seeing Through Maps: Many Ways to See the World.* ODT Inc, 2006.

Worley, Paul, and Rita Palacios. *Unwriting Maya Literature: Ts'íib as Recorded Knowledge.* The U of Arizona P, 2019.

Scan the QR code to see more titles from the North Carolina Studies in the Romance Languages and Literatures (NCSRLL) series.

www.ingramcontent.com/pod-product-compliance
Lightning Source LLC
Chambersburg PA
CBHW061620230125
20746CB00001B/31